AFRICAN HISTORICAL DICTIONARIES
Edited by Jon Woronoff

Historical Dictionary
of
Rwanda

by
LEARTHEN DORSEY

African Historical Dictionaries, No. 60

The Scarecrow Press, Inc.
Metuchen, N.J., & London
1994

British Library Cataloguing-in-Publication data available

Library of Congress Cataloging-in-Publication Data

Dorsey, Learthen.
    Historical dictionary of Rwanda / Dorsey, Learthen.
       p.   cm.—(African historical dictionaries : no. 60)
    ISBN 0-8108-2820-0 (alk. paper)
    1. Rwanda—History—Dictionaries. I. Title. II. Series.
DT450.115.D67   1994
967.571' 003—dc20   93-42203

For
Hattie and George, Sr.,
Jeff and Jeffrey,
Harrison and George, Jr.

CONTENTS

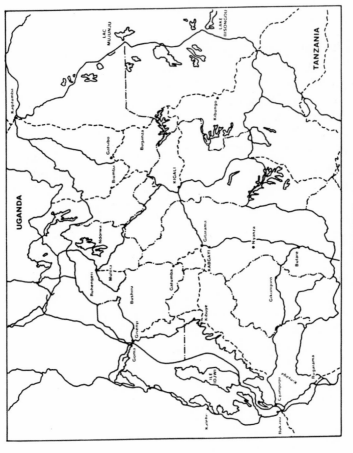

RWANDA

EDITOR'S FOREWORD

Rwanda is one of Africa's smaller countries, more so in size than population. It is relatively remote, was long quite inaccessible, and, in addition, fell under German colonial rule before becoming a Belgian mandate and then trust territory. No wonder Rwanda is also one of the least known African countries, particularly in English-speaking circles. That is why we are particularly pleased, after many years, finally to publish a Rwanda historical dictionary. It not only fills a gap in this series, it should also fill a gap in libraries and private collections.

All considerations of size, inaccessibility, and language aside, Rwanda is one of the most interesting countries on the continent, because of its ethnic diversity and rivalries, rich traditional culture and social mores, efforts at economic development and strivings for political stability, and, above all, an amazingly long and intriguing history. This can finally be fully grasped thanks to a comprehensive historical introduction and an even more extensive chronology.

It was obviously not easy to produce such an informative volume, and we are therefore indebted to Learthen Dorsey, Assistant Professor of History at the University of Nebraska-Lincoln. He has been studying Rwandan history for many years, and conducted field research in 1977 and 1978, which resulted in a dissertation, the *Rwandan Colonial Economy, 1916–1941*. Since then, he has followed events closely and keeps us abreast of their many twists and turns in this very useful book.

Jon Woronoff
Series Editor

ACKNOWLEDGMENT

I am indebted to my Rwandan assistants for helping with my research in their country. The staff at the Library of Congress, especially Beverly Gray and Joanne Zellers in the Africa Section; Onuma Ezera and Joseph Lauer at the Africana Library, and Anita Marshall, Gifts and Exchange librarian at the Michigan State University Libraries; and Gretchen Walsh, African Studies Librarian at Boston University, were helpful in locating data and biographies and compiling the bibliography. Special thanks to John Wunder, Director of the Great Plains Center, for reading portions of the manuscript and for his comments, and to Gretchen E. Holten, Central Reference Service, and to the staff at the Inter-Library Loan Department of Love Library at the University of Nebraska/Lincoln for their assistance. I am also indebted to Frank Mauldin, Office of Human Resources, Clemson University, for finding research funds that enabled me to spend the summer of 1989 in Washington, D.C., compiling the bibliography for this dictionary.

ABBREVIATIONS AND ACRONYMS

ACP	Group of Seven for European Private Sector Cooperation with Africa, the Caribbean, and the Pacific/Groupe des Sept pour la Coopération du Secteur Privé Européen avec l'Afrique, les Caribes et le Pacifique
ADB	African Development Bank
ADF	African Development Fund
AE	Archives Unit, Ministère des Affaires Etrangères
AFP	Agence France-Presse
AGCD	Administration générale de la coopération au développement
AGRI	Agriculture
AI	Amnesty International
AIDS	Acquired Immune Deficiency Syndrome
AIMO	Service des Affaires Indigènes et de la Main-d'Oeuvre
APROSOMA	Association pour la Promotion Sociale de la Masse
ARD	Alliance pour le renforcement de la démocratie/Alliance for the Reinforcement of Democracy
ARP	Agence Rwandaise de Presse
ASBL	Association sans But Lucratif
AT	Administrateur de Territoire
BADEA	Arab Bank for the Economic Development of Africa
BF	Belgian Franc
BRD	Banque Rwandaise du Développement
BUNEP	Bureau National d'Etudes de Projets

CAMP	Consortium for Africa Microfilm Project
CCCE	Caisse Centrale de Coopération Économique (Paris, France)
CDR	Coalition pour la défense de la république
CECA	Communauté Européenne du Charbon et de l'Acier (Direction Etudes et Structures)
CECA	Coopérative d'Etude Coloniale et d'Achats
CECOTRAD	Centrale d'Education et Coopération des Travailleurs pour le Développement
CEEAC	Communauté Economique des Etats de l'Afrique Centrale
CEPGL	Communauté Economique des Pays des Grands Lacs
CESTRAR	Centrale Syndicale des Travailleurs du Rwanda
CIM	Compagnie Commerciale Industrielle et Minière
CMS	Christian Missionary Society
CNKI	Comité National du Kivu
COPIMAR	Coopérative de Promotion de l'Industrie Minéral Artisanale
DM	Deutsche Mark
EC	Economic Council (either a division of the Arab League or the European Economic Community)
ECA	Economic Commission for Africa (United Nations)
EDF	European Development Fund
EEC	European Economic Community
EUA/ECU	European Unit of Account/European Currency Unit (European Economic Community)
FEDECAME	Federación Cafetalera de America (Federation of Coffee Growers of America)
FDC	Force démocratique du changement
FET	*Foreign Economic Trends* (United States Department of State)
FF	French Franc

FPR	Front patriotique rwandais
GENEX	Société Générale d'Exportation Van Santen et Vanden Broeck
GEOMINES	Campagnie Géologique et Minière de Ingénieurs Industriels Belges
GWH	Gigawatt Hour
HIV	Human Immunodeficiency Virus-I Protesafe
IBRD	International Bank for Reconstruction and Development
ICO	International Coffee Organization
ICRC	International Committee of the Red Cross/ Comité International de la Croix-Rouge (CICR)
IDA	International Development Agency
IMF	International Monetary Fund
IND	Indigène
INEAC	Institut National pour l'Etude Agronomique du Congo Belge
INRS	Institut National de Recherche Scientifique
IRCB	Institut Royal Colonial Belge
IRSAC	Institut pour la Recherche Scientifique en Afrique Centrale
ISAR	Institut des Sciences Agronomiques du Rwanda
JOC	Jeunesse Ouvrière Chrétienne
JUST	Justice
KG	Kilogram
MARC	Mouvement d'Action pour le Résurrection du Congo
MDR	Mouvement démocratique républicain
MINETAIN	Société des Mines d'Etain du Ruanda-Urundi
MNC	Mouvement National Congolais
MOG	Military Observer Group
MRND	Mouvement Révolutionnaire National pour le Développement
MRNDD	Mouvement républicain national pour la démocratie et le développement

MSM	Mouvement Social Muhutu
NRA	National Resistance Army (Uganda)
OAU	Organization of African Unity
OBK	Organisation pour l'Aménagement et le Développement du Bassin de la Rivière Kagera
OCIR-CAFE	Office des Cultures Industrielles du Rwanda, Département Café
OCIR-THE	Office des Cultures Industrielles du Rwanda, Département Thé
OCIRU	Office des Cafés Indigènes du Ruanda-Urundi
ONAPO	Office Nationale de la Population
OPEC	Organization of Petroleum Exporting Countries
OPROVIA	Office National pour le Développement et Commercialisation des Produits Vivriers et des Produits Animaux
OPYRWA	Office du Pyrèthre du Rwanda
ORTPN	Office Rwandaise du Tourisme et des Parcs Nationaux
OTRACO	Office d'Exploitation des Transports Coloniaux
OVAPAM	Office de Valorisation Agricole et Pastorale du Mutara
OVIBAR	Office de Valorisation Industrielle des Bananeraies Rwandaises
PADER	Parti démocratique rwandais
PARERWA	Parti républicain rwandais
PARMEHUTU	Parti du Mouvement de l'Emancipation des Bahutu
PDC	Parti démocratique chrétien
PDI	Parti démocratique islamique
PECO	Parti écologiste
PIP	Public Investment Program
PL	Parti libéral
PLANTANGA	Société des Plantations du Tanganyika
PLATURUNDI	Plantations du Ruanda-Urundi

PNAS	Programme national d'actions sociales
PPJR	Parti progressiste de la jeunesse rwandaise
PROTANAG	Société Coloniale des Produits Tannants et Agricoles
PSD	Parti social-démocrate
PSR	Parti socialiste rwandais
PTA	Preferential Trade Area for Eastern and Southern Africa.
RADER	Rassemblement Démocratique Ruandais
REDEMI	Régie d'Exploitation et de Développement des Mines
REGIDESO	Régie de Distribution d'Eau et d'Electricité
RF	Rwandan Franc
RPA	Rwandese Patriotic Army
RPF	Rwandese Patriotic Front
RTD	Rassemblement travailliste pour la démocratie
SAAK	Société Auxiliaire Agricole du Kivu
SABENA	Société Anonyme Belge d'Exploitation de la Navigation Aérienne
SAKIRWA	Savonnerie de Kicukiro du Rwanda
SAP	Structural Adjustment Program
SARL	Société à Responsabilité Limitée
SIRWA	Société Industrielle du Rwanda
SOBILIRWA	Société des Boissons et Limonades au Rwanda
SOCOFINA	Société Commerciale Financière et Agricole du Ruanda
SOMIRWA	Société des Mines du Rwanda
SOMUKI	Société Minière du Muhinga et de Kigali
SONARWA	Société Nationale d'Assurance du Rwanda
SONATAR	Société Nationale de Transports Aériens du Rwanda
SORAS	Société Rwandaise d'Assurances
SORWATHE	Société Rwandaise pour la Production et la Commercialisation du Thé
TABARUDI	Le Syndicat des tabacs du Ruanda-Urundi et du Congo Belge (Société TABARUDI)

TF	Texte Fiche
TRAFIPRO	Travail, Fidélité, Progrès
UMHK	Union Minière du Haut-Katanga
UNAKI	Union Agricole des Régions du Kivu
UNAR	Union National Rwandaise
UNDP	United Nations Development Programme
UNESCO	United Nations Educational, Scientific and Cultural Organization
UNHCR	United Nations High Commission for Refugees
UNICEF	United Nations International Children's Emergency Fund
UNR	Université Nationale du Rwanda
UPC	Uganda People's Congress
UPR	Union du peuple rwandais
USAID	United States Agency for International Development
WHO	World Health Organization

HISTORICAL OVERVIEW

GEOGRAPHICAL DESCRIPTION AND THE ECONOMY

Environment determines the conditions of production, but it can be a limiting factor as well. Rwanda is located in the Central African Great Rift Valley, slightly south of the equator, in one of the highest areas of the continent, equidistant from the Atlantic (2,000 km) and Indian (1,500 km) oceans. It is bounded on the east and west by the converging frontier of Tanzania and Zaire (formerly the Belgian Congo) and in the north by Uganda. Rwanda is separated from Burundi by the Akanyaru River in the south and in the extreme east by the Kagera River valley.

The climate is the tropical highland variety; the annual average temperature in the central plateau region fluctuates around 68° F. The drier tropical lowlands in the Kagera River area can be extremely hot, and the Congo-Nile dividing range in the north experiences very cold temperatures at night. The amount of rainfall varies between 40 and 50 inches a year; however, it is neither uniformly nor evenly distributed. The year is punctuated by a long dry season which extends from May or June to mid-September; a short rainy season from mid-September to January; a dry season of several weeks intervening in January; and a much longer rainy season, extending from the end of January to the beginning of May. Any interruption of the cycle causes crop failures, drought, and near-famine conditions.

East of Lake Kivu, traversing the entire region from north to south, are the giant peaks of the Congo-Nile crest, reaching a maximum of 14,000 feet in the Virunga chain. This is a region of ancient volcanoes, which are now covered with thick tropical woodlands that merge into an undulating plateau, with altitudes varying between 4,500 and 6,500 feet. The landscape consists of

1

hills and valleys scattered with eucalyptus trees and banana groves, as well as patches of luxuriant pasture. The region is quite fertile, and is used for herding and the cultivation of food crops. To the east, there are vast stretches of savanna and forest areas.

Still, Rwanda is one of the poorest countries in the whole of Africa (the twenty-first according to World Bank sources), with a per capita income of approximately $270. A major source of economic stagnation lies in the perennial pressures of overpopulation on the land. With 6.53 million inhabitants (estimate for mid-1987), Rwanda has the highest population density in Africa—248 per square mile. At the present rate of increase (3.3 percent per annum between 1980 and 1986), its population is likely to reach 10 million by the year 2000. The problem is compounded by uneven distribution of population, with heavy concentration on the central highlands, and a more sparse distribution of population on the slopes to the east and west. A smaller, but equally dense populated area, is to be found along the shores of Lake Kivu, while the northeast is a region of much lighter habitation. Because of the density of population in relation to cultivated land, the average planting surface for a family with six children is 1.47 hectares (the maximum is 2.92 hectares and the minimum 0.74 hectares). The degree of urbanization is low, however, about 5 per cent in 1985 according to the World Bank.

While the country has attempted in recent years to broaden its economic base, an arabica variety of coffee, introduced by the Belgians in 1931 under a compulsory cultivation program, is still the single most important cash crop. Arabica grows best at altitudes ranging from 1,400 to between 1,800 and 2,000 meters, which includes most of Rwanda with the exception of Virunga, the Congo-Nile crest, and the region of Byumba. While the hilly topography limits the planting surface, the yields are high around the banks of Lake Kivu, the regions of Gisenyi, Cyangugu, and portions of Ruhengeri, closest to the border of Kibuye. Superior yields in these areas are attributed to soils enriched by volcanic activity. Production, however, tends to decrease on the hills of the central plateau where the three prefectures of Kigali, Gitarama, and Butare account for nearly half of the planted surface of the country. The country's commercial agricultural production, however, is constrained by a shortage of land suitable for cultivation.

Coffee is the principal source of foreign exchange, accounting for around 70 percent, or $57 million, in 1984, and it provides monetary income for about half of the farmers (approximately 400,000). These planters cultivate about 60 million coffee plants on 37,000 hectares, or an average coffee plot of 7.7 ares per planter. These plots are widely dispersed and average about 123 coffee trees, which produce about 46 kilos of parchment coffee per planter. Rwanda produced 42,120 tons of parchment coffee in 1987.

Rwanda's major problem is its landlocked status, and as a result its commercial sector suffers from isolation and periodic stagnation, brought on by periodic conflicts with its neighbors, particularly Uganda. For example, when Uganda closed its borders to truck traffic from Rwanda in 1979, the country had to commission Air Rwanda to transport almost all of its coffee to Mombasa. Border closings occurred quite frequently in 1983 and again in 1985 when Uganda experienced its civil war. These border conflicts have siphoned off valuable currency reserves from the country; however, in recent years Rwanda has attempted to broaden its economic base by increasing cotton, pyrethrum, quinine, timber, and tea production. In fact, tea production has been the most successful, rising from 2,522 metric tons in 1972 to 10,300 tons in 1986, and accounting for 10 percent of the total export earnings for that year. Secondary commercial crops include tobacco, barley, and wheat in regions of higher altitude.

The main food crops are beans, peas, sorghum, cassava, maize, and bananas for the brewing of beer. These and tree crops are cultivated on approximately 26 percent of the land (34 percent is in permanent pasture and 6 percent is forests) and in sufficient quantities to satisfy the needs of domestic consumption. But one needs only recall the famines of 1916 and 1943, which caused 50,000 and 36,000 deaths, respectively, to realize the limits and vulnerability of the country's domestic food resources. In fact, because of the density of population in relation to arable land, only about one are per person is used for raising food for domestic consumption.

Rwandan farmers necessarily practice intense cultivation, but an even further strain on land resources is the high density of the cattle population, numbering more than 800,000 in 1984. As in most pastoral societies of East Africa, the herding of cattle has more than economic significance; ownership is an important status symbol and also an essential ingredient in the traditional sociopolitical systems of Rwanda. Although the animals play a minor role in the economy, these cattle destroy by overgrazing land that might be better used for food crops for the growing population. These cattle also accelerate the process of erosion on deforested hillsides. In fact, the country has the distinction of being the most eroded and deforested land in tropical Africa.

The overpopulation of people and animals has conspired with the difficult terrain to retard the development of industry, energy resources, and communications, even by African standards. Cassiterite is the only significant mineral resource. It yielded 1,145 tons of tin ore in 1985, and known reserves are estimated at 90,000 tons. The future of this industry is a bleak one. Profit margins have been squeezed by the high transportation costs. In 1985 GEOMINES, a Belgian company with a 51 percent shareholding in SOMIRWA, was declared insolvent, and immediately went into receivership. In May 1988, however, the government established the Régie d'Exploitation et de Développement des Mines (REDEMI), to work with the tin concession formerly held by SOMIRWA.

At independence an industrial sector did not exist. Currently, Rwandan manufacturing includes the processing of food for domestic consumption; however, foreign ownership is widespread. The Dutch brewing firm Heineken operates a brewery, Bralirwa, which also produces lemonade for the domestic market. Tabarwanda, which is partly Belgian owned, manufactures cigarettes. There is a joint venture between the Rwandan and Swiss governments to manufacture matches. At Cyangugu, there is a cement factory financed by the Chinese; the Société des Boissons et Limonades au Rwanda (SOBILIRWA), which is a subsidiary of the United Kingdom's Meyer Mojonnier, bottles Pepsi-Cola. The Anglo-Indonesian Trust manufactures agricultural tools at its factory in Kigali.

Hydroelectricity is a major source of energy in urban areas, and it augments the wood and charcoal used for fuel in rural areas. Some major development projects in this area have reduced Rwanda's need to import energy resources from Zaire. Work is underway on a $23.6 million program by Société National de Production, de Transport et de Distribution d'Electricité d'Eau et de Gaz (Electrogas), which will upgrade the power distribution network by modernizing the 11-million-watt Ntaruku hydroelectric station and by providing a series of extensions to connect with Zaire's Ruzizi II plant.

There are no railroads; of the existing 5,400 miles of poorly maintained roads, a third are classified as fair-weather roads or tracks, and virtually none was tarred until recently. The Rwandan government has, however, secured funding to modernize and upgrade existing roads. Saudi, OPEC, and ADB funds of about $50 million have been secured to construct a road between Gitarama and Mukamira on the Ugandan border. A road linking Kigali to Gatuna in the north has been funded by the Arab Bank for the Economic Development of Africa (BADEA), the World Bank, and the Rwandan government. A grant from UNDP of $12 million is earmarked for repairs to sections of the national roads from Butare to Muninya and from Gihinga to Kibungo.

Steamers on Lake Tanganyika are the principal carriers of products destined for export from Rwanda, but the paucity of transport, coupled with a landlocked position, have added to the difficulties of establishing foreign trade patterns. In short, the Rwandan economy is very weak, and without foreign aid the government would not have sufficient reserves to implement most of its ambitious development plans.

To a large extent, social change and the dominant social organization throughout much of Africa have been primarily rural; in Rwanda real villages do not exist. Today, as in the past, the hill remains the primary focus of sociopolitical and economic activity in the countryside. Beyond the hill there is relatively little sense of unity among rural communities; fragmentation and parochialism are the rule rather than the exception. And in the absence of adequate communications, the forbidding nature of the topography places further obstacles in the way of any large-scale sociopolitical or economic mobilization. The problems of ethnicity have been minimized in recent years; still the dilemma of Tutsi refugees presents political and socioeconomic challenges for the country. Rural cooperatives and development projects are devices used by the government to effect social change, balance population pressures, and achieve national integration.

ANCIENT RWANDA

Rwanda gained its present territory partly through conquest and partly through peaceful assimilation. In the fifteenth century independent lineages of Kiga hill dwellers and highly centralized Hutu state systems based on agricultural and animal husbandry began to expand. Almost simultaneously Tutsi herdsmen from the north, and east from Karagwe, entered the area. Initial contact between these groups was peaceful. Some authorities suggest that Tutsi herdsmen pastoralists and the Kiga and Hutu farmers coexisted peacefully at least until the end of the fifteenth century, when the Tutsi began to enter Rwanda in greater numbers. While the Tutsi eventually achieved domination over the socioeconomic and political systems, they never constituted the majority. In fact, they currently represent about 14 per cent of the total population, while the Hutu constitute about 85 percent. The Twa, a group of pygmoid forest dwellers and the first people to inhabit the country, now make up less than one percent of the population.

Tutsi hegemony was consolidated by the sixteenth century, when the central region of Rwanda was absorbed into the nuclear kingdom centered in Kigali. When they entered Rwanda, both the Hutu and the Twa had settled in clearly defined areas. Tutsi expansion and incorporation commenced from a small nuclear area near Lake Muhazi in the east, the cradle of Rwanda. Rugwe and his successor, Kigeri Mukobanya, increased the size of the eastern region by incorporating surrounding areas on the central plateau. With the accession of Ruganzu Ndori to power in the seventeenth century, a series of invasions were launched against formerly independent Hutu areas in the west and north, which resulted in a further expansion of Rwanda's boundaries. The final stage in the process, however, was not completed until the latter half of the nineteenth century during the reign of *umwami* Kigeri Rwabugiri, one of Rwanda's most prestigious historical figures. Rwabugiri implemented political reforms and consolidation. He also refined the patron-client relationship that would be a prominent feature in Tutsi exploitation of the Hutu and lesser nobility. Rwabugiri appointed chiefs to rule frontier regions of the kingdom—Murera, Bufumbira, Bigogwe, Buberuka, and Rusenyi. In some of these areas, the functions of chiefs were divided into land chiefs (who had authority over Hutu) and cattle chiefs (who were responsible for Tutsi tribute).

Under Rwabugiri, the *umwami* was the source and symbol of all authority in the politically centralized state. He alone could confer legitimacy upon subordinates' ranks, and because of this he could be characterized as an absolute monarch. Rwabugiri and his successor, Musinga, were able to control this polity through a highly centralized bureaucracy, in which a triple hierarchy of army chiefs, land chiefs, and cattle chiefs—all recruited from the dominant stratum—radiated from the capital to the provinces and from the provinces to the districts. Each province was entrusted to an army chief and each district to a land chief and a cattle chief (who were responsible for the collection of tithes in produce and cattle). From the triumvirate spread a vast network of subchiefs from whom tribute was exacted for the higher chiefs and the Tutsi kings. How much power the chiefs and subchiefs claimed for themselves, and for how long, was entirely dependent upon the *umwami*'s grace. Consequently the chiefs were bureaucrats in the sense that they did not claim their position by right or inheritance or by virtue of any prior connection with the area to which they were appointed, but rather served at the discretion of the *umwami*.

Rwandan society was also hierarchical: each individual was assigned a specific caste, and each caste a specific rank. Clientship served to link each layer of the hierarchy in a relationship of mutual dependence. At the core of this relationship lay a feudal institution called *ubuhake,* a cattle contract of pastoral servitude, in which an individual, either a peasant or Tutsi notable, voluntarily commended himself to a patron in return for cattle and pastureland. His rights, however, were those of usufruct: he was entitled to the cow's milk and the calves. By the same token, the pasture rights enjoyed by the client did not make him a landowner but only a tenant at the mercy of this lord. In return for these privileges, the client, or vassal, swore fealty and recognized his duties of homage to his patron.

THE COLONIAL PERIOD

The colonial period for Rwanda was comparatively short. It encompassed the reigns of three African rulers—Yuhi Musinga (1896–1931), Mutara Rudahigwa (1931–1959), and Kigeri Ndahindurwa (1959–1962)—and the colonial rule of two European powers—Germany (1898–1916) and Belgium (1916–1962). Of the three African rulers, Musinga's reign was the most contentious. He was an interloper, and his ascension to the throne in 1896 preceded a period of rivalry between two royal factions—the Bega and the Banyinginya clans. The strife commenced after the death of *umwami* Kigeri Rwaburgiri in 1895. Musinga's halfbrother, Rutalindwa, was the heir apparent, but Musinga's mother (and queen mother), Kanyogera, and his maternal uncles thought differently.

In November 1896, at Rucuncu, succession was finally settled to the advantage of the Bega clan after a brief but bloody palace revolt during which the heir apparent, *umwami* Rutalindwa, his wife, and his three children were killed. The new *umwami* took the throne, but had to accommodate one and then in 1919 a second, colonial master. The Germans, whose effective occupation began in 1898, served Musinga well, but the Belgians, who arrived in Rwanda during World War I, demanded more than Musinga was willing to sacrifice.

Musinga used German forces to extend Tutsi hegemony to the north. Lieutenant Eberhard Godowius was enlisted to lead a punitive expedition against the followers of Nyabingi in that region in 1912. The northerners were brought into the kingdom; in return for German assistance and support, Musinga gave the Germans his loyalty. The Belgians, on the other hand, proved to be less malleable. They provided Musinga with more than just military force and pacification. They had come to stay and therefore wanted Musinga to help them rule their new mandate territory. Musinga's response to Belgian requests for compliance ranged from accommodation to passive resistance and evasion. The Belgians interpreted these actions as unacceptable, but were unable to respond directly until 1931. In the interim, they were accommodating, patient, and tolerant, but these attitudes eventually crystallized into the deposition of the *umwami* when the administration saw Musinga's presence as an impediment to the economic transformation of the country. Musinga was deposed and replaced by his eighteen-year-old son, Rudahigwa.

The reign of Mutara Rudahigwa from 1932 to 1945 was uneventful. Rudahigwa and Tutsi notables were the arbiters within a dual colonial system in which the oligarchy received directives from the Belgian administration and imposed them on the masses below. In exchange for their services, the Tutsi oligarchy became members of an exclusive African bureaucracy that siphoned off surplus from the Africans below and maintained certain obligations and privileges as traditional authority figures. But the last fourteen years of Rudahigwa's reign were characterized by tremendous political, economic, and social changes, both internal and external. The Cold War and visitations by the United Nations Mission to Trusteeship Territories, beginning in 1948, accelerated political development within the country. The changing character of Catholic missionary personnel in 1948, and their support, plus economic opportunities helped to change Hutu perceptions of themselves. Those Hutu who had access to educational opportunities and jobs became more assertive and began to participate in preindependence politics and protests, exercising leadership at the national level. Rudahigwa's suspicious death in 1959 and his brother's ascension to throne occurred within this new political and social context.

Umwami Kigeri Ndahindurwa was essentially a caretaker during the political disintegration of the colony from 1959 to 1962. His brother's death and the circumstances surrounding his own enthronement in 1959 aroused suspicion from the Belgian administration, the Tutsi oligarchy, and the emerging Hutu political elite. Distrust and the violence that resulted from it ensured Hutu hegemony. Attacks by gangs of Tutsi upon Hutu subchiefs and leaders of PARMEHUTU caused a massive retaliation against Tutsi by Hutu throughout the country. Before calm was restored in early November, Rwanda was placed under a special Military Resident, and martial law was imposed by Colonel Guillaume Logiest, an officer of the Force Publique in the Belgian Congo. In its wake about half of the Tutsi incumbents were dismissed from chiefly offices and thousands were uprooted from their homes. When independence became inevitable and the republic a reality by January 1961, Kigeri Ndahindurwa was forced into exile.

EUROPEAN RULE TO 1930

German occupation began in Rwanda with the establishment of a military post at Shangi in 1898. The Germans pursued an administrative policy of indirect rule not only because the centralized political system was admirably suited to it, but because they realized that any attempt to displace Musinga would probably have met with considerable resistance from the local population. Moreover, a new government would have required far greater numbers of European administrators than were available at the time. This consideration takes on added weight when one recalls that of all colonial administrations Germany's was among the most understaffed. As late as 1913 the whole of German East Africa—a territory larger than Nigeria—was administered by only seventy European officials. Moreover, the Tutsi aristocracy was viewed with considerable sympathy by the German officers on the spot, many of whom were Prussian noblemen.

Since the Germans had earned Musinga's trust and loyalty, they made every effort to strengthen and consolidate the position

of the Crown. German punitive expeditions served also to reinforce the absolutism of the monarchy, and consequently the hegemony of the ruling caste; however, very little was accomplished
in the realm of civil administration because the entire period of
German rule was largely devoted to those punitive expeditions.
Administrative machinery set up by the Germans did not amount
to more than a few strategically located police posts.
Economically, there were some modest accomplishments. The
Germans experimented with coffee, tobacco, and rice cultivation
as commercial crops, which they believed would provide revenues that would enable Africans to pay taxes.

Central to the German economic development program was
colonization and modern transportation, especially the railroad.
The Germans believed that the railroad would bring trade, trade
would produce money, and money would enable Rwandans to
pay taxes. Rail transportation would also reduce costs of exports
from Rwanda. While the Germans planned for the economic future of the country, they failed entirely in economic development,
primarily because the war intervened before development plans
could be fully implemented. Finally, there were too few competent people to initiate developmental plans, and the administration could not depend upon Musinga to control his subjects, since
his power declined in direct proportion to the distance away from
his capital at Nyanza. Rebel chiefs could easily incite the latent
hostility of the Hutu against the Tutsi. But these were moot concerns because Rwanda fell in April and May 1916, as the
Germans forces withdrew before the concerted attack of superior
Belgian and British forces. With the German defeat went the
Imperial vision and hopes for a railroad.

The primary aim of the Belgian military effort in Africa during
World War I was to assume possession of German territory for
use as a pawn in negotiations. When the peace negotiations
opened, the Belgians hoped to trade German East Africa for
Portuguese territory on the southern banks of the Congo River.
Their hopes failed to materialize, however, and the Milner-Orts
agreement of May 30, 1919, left Belgium with only Ruanda-
Urundi, which meant that Belgium was locked out of German

East Africa and lost the southern bank of the Congo and the extreme eastern part of Rwanda to the British, who received the lion's share of the former German colonies.

The administrative status of the territory was finally settled in 1924, when the League of Nations conferred a Class A Mandate on Belgium. On August 21, 1925, the Belgian government enacted a law providing for administrative union between their newly acquired mandate and their Congo colony, but it took six years before Rwanda enjoyed the full benefits of a civil administration. Day-to-day business remained largely in the hands of the military and at first did not extend very far beyond the immediate requirements of peace and order. The Belgians were slow to initiate administrative reforms because, according to one colonial official, the "customs and institutions in Rwanda were unlike any found in the Congo." Moreover, Belgian military personnel, by virtue of their training and background, showed little concern for the social and political problems connected with the tasks of colonial administration. Rwandan institutions seemed strange to the Belgian officers on the spot. When queried by the Permanent Mandates Commission about the pace of civil administration, officials stressed repeatedly that the administrative machinery the Germans had left behind was "so rudimentary and inadequate that it could serve only as a makeshift arrangement pending the introduction of a new system."

The early years of the Belgian mandate bore the unmistakable imprint of the German legacy. The military was entrusted with a wide range of administrative functions; like their German counterparts, the Belgian Residents were forced into a variety of roles, acting as troubleshooters, judges, counselors and law-enforcement agents, relying for assistance on a handful of European deputies. They were often too few; stressed and strained to capacity because of the geographical extent of the mandate; and over-extended in terms administration.

The prime objective of Belgian colonial authorities was the development of the colony, so that it could eventually complement the economy and society in Brussels. To accomplish this task, Belgian colonial officials had to transform the traditional socioeconomic structure of the area. The Belgians were not especially innovative in this regard. They decided to follow their predecessor's example of indirect administration, and proceeded to reinforce the existing Tutsi bureaucracy but with some structural modifications. For example, in 1916 the Belgian Resident, acting as the "Government of Occupation," divided Rwanda into two separate administrative zones and instituted a policy of dealing with the chiefs in each area, as a result of which Musinga's notables became more independent and the *umwami* lost control over them, since he could neither discipline them nor protect those whom the Belgians sought to punish. Thus both his political power and his prestige were progressively undermined.

The following year the Belgian Resident, Gerard DeClerck, informed the *umwami* and the Tutsi chiefs of the administration's desire to protect the Hutu from the arbitrary powers of the oligarchy. A series of decrees passed in July and August 1917 mandated that Musinga lost the power of life and death over his subjects and that Tutsi chiefs could compel Hutu to do only two days of customary work (*uburetwa*) instead of the three or more frequently demanded by the notables. Moreover, farmers would keep all the produce from their fields and the earnings from porterage without the risk of confiscation by the chiefs. DeClerck also encouraged Musinga to implement a decree which would double the amount of land Hutu farmers were then cultivating. To eliminate disputes over the control of men and cattle, the Resident limited the *shebuja*'s (or patron's) right to recall cattle from the *abagaragu* (his client). To reduce future famines, DeClerck also ordered all Rwandans to plant manioc, a drought-resistant tuber crop, and trees which would contribute to erosion reduction. While Musinga submitted to these changes in the organization of his kingdom, neither he nor his notables implemented them. DeClerck, anticipating resistance, instructed his personnel to inform Rwandans of these administrative changes.

A major concern of the Belgian authorities was economic development. An early Resident, Georges Mortehan, and other officials agreed that economic development in Rwanda was essential, and that it could take place only if the administration gained firmer control over the kingdom. So in September 1923, Mortehan reminded the Court to reduce its demands on the Hutu and to provide security of land tenure for them. When the Court and notables ignored his requests, Mortehan began to deprive Musinga of the right to assign the responsibility for making labor requisitions for Europeans. The administration also believed that the Court's distribution of work quotas according to political criteria rather than ability to fill them led to inefficiency and delays. Administrators in post areas had been distributing quotas to notables in their own regions, while the Court retained control of the distributions within the central kingdom. After some chiefs complained that Musinga used work orders to punish them, Mortehan ordered the *umwami* to confine his demands to one small region where most of the positions were held by his favorites. In all other areas, administrators assigned work quotas to the most important chiefs; where no one chief predominated, officials named one individual to be *akazi* chief for administrative work projects.

Technically, every adult male performed *akazi,* usually for public-works projects, which became general in the 1920s. The local chief, however, decided who actually participated, and the type of work assigned to the individual for *akazi* often depended on his standing with the hill chief. Refusal to perform *akazi* was often the excuse used by a chief to dispossess a person of his land.

In establishing the position of the *akazi* chief, European officials were able to address two fundamental problems simultaneously: geographic isolation and administrative control. Before 1923, commercial trade in northern, central, and eastern Rwanda was oriented toward the Bukoba-Mombasa route, primarily because of the favorable rates merchants received for their hides. Products from southern Rwanda passed through the Bujumbura–Kigoma–Dar es Salaam route, which merchants used to avoid the inconvenience and cost of carriers from Bukoba. To transport trade goods to either terminus required numerous African carriers rather than mechanical transportation, since there were few roads, and until road construction began, Rwanda would remain isolated with trade confined to the peripheral areas where water-transport systems and railroad traffic facilitated trade. In 1923, the nearest road for automobiles went east from Mbarara in Uganda, and the telegraph had come only as far as Kbale, Uganda. The only railroad was the Kigoma and Dar es Salaam connection, and the caravan route connecting Cyangugu with Bujumbura was the only road in Rwanda.

The creation of the *akazi* chief meant that labor could be mobilized more efficiently for carrying trade goods out of Rwanda and for road construction. As a result, the administration was able to commence a road construction program, and at the end of 1923 the year major construction began, some 210 kilometers of carriage roads were built. Between 1923 and 1927 the Butare-Kansi and Butare-Lubonoa roads were constructed. In 1924 construction began on the Tanganyika-Kivu road, several bridges were repaired, and segments of the road from Kamaniola to Bukava were surfaced and enlarged. In the same year, twenty kilometers of motoring road were constructed between Kigali and Butare, on the Nyanza-Kabgayi route thirteen stone bridges were built, and three more were constructed on the route from Kigali to Ruhengeri.

Similar to the Germans, the Belgians created a dual tax system: one system was operative for European commercial and administrative centers, and a separate one operated in the rural African sector. The rationale, of course, was that the modern economy ought to assume a disproportionate share of the burden for economic development. As progress was made and more Africans were forced into the world market, the tax rates for individual provinces were increased and assessed according to ability to pay. Taxes were collected by Tutsi notables who were supervised by Europeans and a member of the clergy. Even though this procedure did not curtail abuse, tax collection was successful, primarily because of the rigorous control instituted by the Belgian administration to end the abuses of a few unscrupulous collectors and because of the elimination of large numbers of intermediaries, each of whom had taken a percentage of the tax collection.

The creation of the *akazi* chief also signaled the first step toward the establishment of a civil service to carry out the administration's orders promptly. The government consolidated its control and gained the allegiance of the chiefs by permitting them to retain 10 percent of all taxes collected. The *umwami* received 5 percent of this total, and subchiefs and chiefs shared the remaining 5 percent. Belgian officials hoped that the extra income would cause the Court and notables to lessen their demands on the people and discourage corruption.

Part of the reorganization policy also included the extension of Belgian control outside the central plateau. With an army of 650 men, the Belgians provided the power required to extend their control not only in the northeast but also in the southwest and along the eastern frontier. With the approval of Belgian officials, Tutsi notables in these areas took large but fairly unified blocks of territory, which they then parceled out to their followers. Hutu who were displaced either remained without land, sought Tutsi patrons, or appealed to their lineage heads for land.

The administration sanctioned this system of land allocation in order to prevent the complex system of overlapping commands similar to those in the central plateau. Within each command, one notable ruled the people, and where he could obtain Hutu sanction he also ruled the land. As an administrator and civil servant, he collected the taxes and requisitioned labor for the Belgians. Depending upon their size, these new domains became known as *chefferies* and *sous-chefferies*. With expansion in these areas, European officials for the first time assumed such Court prerogatives as the distribution of domains and the appointment and removal of notables. Incompetent chiefs were replaced, and officials sometimes used the death of a chief to appoint more manageable or suitable candidates, although generally the post was passed on to the deceased chief's son.

These changes indicated that the Court was no longer the real authority in the kingdom. It no longer directed the expansion of central control into the outlying regions, nor did it distribute commands or exercise authority in the settlement of disputes or in the collection of taxes. In 1926, to counter the colonial government's control, the Court began spreading rumors about an imminent end to Belgian rule. Musinga knew otherwise but hoped to diminish the desire of the notables to cooperate with Europeans by playing upon their hopes and fears. Moreover, to counteract the growing influence of the White Fathers, Musinga flirted with the Seventh-Day Adventists, the most radical Protestant group in Rwanda, an alliance which alarmed the administration because they saw the millennial doctrine of the Adventists as a dangerous invitation to social unrest. Musinga's efforts, however, merely led to more governmental reform and intervention.

The administration continued its program of regrouping and consolidating administrative units throughout Rwanda. Hundreds of scattered enclaves and smallholdings of cattle and land complicated administrative control and development projects. To restructure and reduce these areas into more easily identifiable geographical units, the administration grouped subchiefdoms of a given region into chiefdoms, generally following the boundaries of the provinces of precolonial Rwanda. Chiefdoms were grouped at the next highest level into territories, which constituted the lowest units of the European administrative structure. At the head of each territory was a European administrator (l'administrateur de territoire, AT) who was responsible directly to the Belgian Resident at Kigali. Heading each chiefdom was a provincial chief (chef de chefferie) who was usually appointed by the king with the consent of the administration, but most often the local official made the selection. Similarly, the chief or notable usually chose his own subchiefs subject to the approval of the territorial administrator. The Belgians also urged notables to exchange domains, regardless of their size or value, but those who stood to lose evaded the issue or delayed taking action. The administration did not press the issue of exchange until the famine of 1928 and 1929, when officials removed a large number of notables from their commands and merged their domains with others because they had failed to execute relief measures. In fact, it was during the famine that the Belgians rearranged the commands on a massive scale, using force when necessary, to get notables to comply.

By 1928 the Belgian administration had instituted an African civil service composed of the Tutsi oligarchy. It had also implemented a tax structure and commenced a road-building program. Its next task was to stabilize land tenure by appropriating and regulating land as a function of the state, and by dismantling the tributary mode of production in order to free African labor. For change to commence, the Belgians had to restrict the suddenly growing demands that the feudal aristocracy was making so that the Hutu could meet Belgian production quotas in commercial agriculture and requisitions, and be free for eventual employment in the developing European-dominated economy. So as early as 1924 Belgian officials began a gradual reduction of dues in kind and in labor. Their efforts were partially successful, especially in the vicinity of administrative areas, but attempts to provide security of land tenure for the Hutu never materialized, not for lack of laws or decrees but for the lack of effective implementation at the local level by both Tutsi and European officials. Nor did Belgian decrees and enactments have much effect on the hills (*collines*).

Before individual land tenure was decreed in 1961, the administration used a variety of techniques to ensure the security of tenure for peasant farmers: in 1917 the produce of Hutu fields was protected; Ordinance No. 49 of December 31, 1925, which sanctioned the compulsory cultivation of nonseasonal crops, also compelled chiefs and notables to surrender the land that their subordinates cultivated; and Regulation No. 52, in the 1930s, which permitted territorial agents to use force to compel notables to give up new areas of land for cultivation to their people, was used by the administration to secure land tenure. The bulk of the Belgian effort, however, was concentrated on freeing African productive capacity from prestations and corvée.

Belgian officials stabilized and reduced the collection of the following prestations: *imponoke,* a payment in cattle demanded by a patron to replenish herds; *indabukirano,* or dues in land and cattle demanded when a Tutsi assumed command of a hill; and *abatora,* the requisitioning of bananas. The government reduced corvée to forty-two days per year, and in 1926 the Resident suppressed three hierarchies of Tutsi authority: the *chef de l'ubuhake,* or land chief; the *chef de l'umukende,* or chief of the pasture; and the *chef d'ingabo,* or the military chief, who required dues in produce and in kind. The elimination of these hierarchical ranks, however, did not have the desired effect of reducing corvée or dues in kind. Because the functions of these ranks were invested in one chief instead of three, power became more concentrated, enabling a smaller coterie of chiefs to increase their power and influence through even more exactions and retainers. So in 1927 the government officially reduced corvée to one day out of seven.

By 1930 the administration's attempt to dismantle the tributary mode of production had achieved mixed results. Corvée had been reduced officially, but chiefs often ignored the decree and forced Hutu to work as many days as the chief desired. As a result, the administration was forced constantly to supervise its policy of reducing traditional obligations. Young and literate Tutsi tended to accept the reductions without much discussion, but the more traditional chiefs viewed the administration's policy as an attack on their prerogatives. They believed that the exercise of power had little meaning if no distinctions could be made between the rights and privileges of the ruling oligarchy and those of the subjugated Hutu. In retaliation against the more traditional chiefs for their lack of cooperation, Belgian authorities used increasingly harsh measures to try to force the more traditional authorities to comply with their wishes.

The rewards for those who complied were extremely beneficial. Compliance meant education in mission schools subsidized by the Belgian administration and political power and influence in the colonial apparatus. Those chiefs and subchiefs who were not eliminated by the transformation found themselves in a new role as agents and functionaries (civil servants) for the administration—obeying various directives to construct roads, collect taxes, plant trees, or drain swamps, and to report infractions. They had to fulfill their obligations to the Europeans or face the consequences. For the Hutu, there were new exactions calling for more than a simple exchange under the old rules of clientship. Because of the Belgian development policy, Hutu became both the impetus and the central components for the formation of development capital. They paid taxes, which provided capital for road construction and other development projects; they supplied the labor needed to exploit raw materials, to plant commercial crops, and to build the infrastructure, which would facilitate the colony's integration into the world market and the modernization of Rwanda.

GOVERNOR CHARLES VOISIN'S ECONOMIC POLICY

To modernize Rwanda would be expensive, and the government at Brussels, preoccupied with its own domestic economy, the Great Depression, and what had been the enormously profitable Belgian Congo, could no longer subsidize the Rwandan economy, which would have to support itself or sink. Therefore, the Colonial Office at Brussels sent Charles Voisin to increase economic production and to maintain the colony's solvency.

When Charles Voisin was named vice governor-general and governor of the Territory of Ruanda-Urundi on May 28, 1930, he announced the government's official development program in the preamble to the 1930 Annual Report. He included, among other objectives, the regrouping of chiefdoms for better administrative control, the improvement of livestock, reforestation, mineral prospecting, and the construction of roads. In a speech before his administrative officials in September of the same year, the governor added a program to remedy periodic famine and the under-nourishment of Rwandans, the development of markets so that Africans could get cash in return for their excess production, which would in turn stimulate their purchasing power, the participation of Europeans in the economy, and the construction of schools.

To foster agricultural development, Voisin decided to expand cotton, palm oil, coffee, and tobacco, primarily because he believed high transportation costs prohibited the development of other crops. He believed that these selected products would yield higher sales value, which would offset high transport costs. The rationale for expanding coffee cultivation was also based on the belief that coffee would greatly influence the general economic growth of the country, provided it was undertaken by Africans.

Another feature of the new, rationalized development called for European participation in the economy, a policy which the administration had sanctioned since 1925, when it agreed to grant concessions of large tracts of land to business interests. To protect the normal development of the African population and to prevent monopolies by foreign colonists and other foreigners, the administration did not permit land transfers unless an equitable payment was agreed upon, and Africans abandoned their rights willingly. Densely populated agricultural land would not be granted if African residential patterns would be upset. Furthermore, concessions in these zones were usually limited to a maximum of 500 hectares, and a second concession would be granted only after the first was in full production. Companies or owners also had to agree to build schools and quarantine stations as part of a social contract obligation.

To make investment in Rwanda more attractive and as a response to the problem of limited financial resources for new but floundering companies, the administration changed its concession policy in significant ways. First, it passed Ordinance No. 18 on June 28, 1929, creating a system of progressive renewals for agricultural leases at intervals of five years. The ordinance aimed to assist struggling companies, which were allowed to retain their profits until their holdings were in full production. Second, Voisin began to promote more vigorously the concepts of protective zones and partnership between Africans and Europeans. The concepts worked side by side. For example, in areas designated as protective zones, companies which agreed to assist Africans would be assured of a monopoly for ten years. Protective zones would enclose an area of 70,000 hectares or more, in which companies would have full access to African labor and produce. By the end of 1929, twenty-one protective zones had been leased or were on the verge of being reserved.

The final components of the developmental strategy were perhaps the most important. Voisin sought to encourage the growth of mining concessions as a means of augmenting foreign exchange. The first concession for the exploitation of six deposits of tin was awarded to the MINETAIN Society in 1930. Export production for that year was 164 tons, but by 1949 the output had risen to 2,267 tons, and mineral exports would become the second-ranking source of foreign exchange after coffee.

Then, there was the problem of insufficient pasture and Rwanda's many cattle. The government believed that cattle should be improved by breeding Rwandan animals with European stock or with cattle from neighboring colonies. Culling herds would also result in fewer animals requiring less pastureland. Tutsi notables vigorously resisted reductions, however, and the administration never made much headway except in the area of improving the health of the herds. Nonetheless, the administration's concern about insufficient pasture was a real one. Overgrazing and an excessive cattle population remains a severe problem for Rwanda. As early as 1933 there were some 80,000 head of cattle, which, at a rate of at least 2.5 hectares per head required some 300,000 hectares for adequate grazing. The total area of the country is just 265,000 hectares, and only 243,151 hectares are suitable for agriculture and animal husbandry. With 60,000 adult farmers cultivating 68,763 hectares, there was not sufficient land for pasture, unless yields on pasture lands could be increased.

To combat famine, such non-seasonal crops as manioc and sweet potatoes were introduced, and regulations were imposed for their cultivation. The Resident had the power to require each able-bodied adult male to maintain 35 ares of seasonal and 15 ares of nonseasonal food crops. The latter included manioc or (above 1,900 meters) potatoes. Manioc could be sown in bushland or on well-drained slopes apart from each household's landholdings. Since the country lacked suitable storage facilities, the selection of these durable crops was wise, and if Hutu farmers complied with the rules, famines would no longer disrupt the production cycle. Voisin strongly pursued this program, and recalcitrants were subject to fines of fifty to a hundred francs for failure to follow instructions to the letter.

Other regulations decreed the use of marshlands for agricultural purposes, a great source of irritation to the Tutsi notables, primarily because of the need for dry-season pasture. The notables found ways to circumvent the new directive, usually through benign neglect or gracious noncompliance. Finally, since land in Rwanda had been systematically depleted of its forests by farmers seeking new fields, Belgian officials instituted a forest-reclamation project, in which Banyarwanda had to plant commercial groves of fast-growing trees, particularly eucalyptus, to be used as firewood and in construction.

An important component of Governor Voisin's economic program was the extension of coffee cultivation in the African sector, which he initiated in 1931. The initial coffee campaign of 1931–1932 was restricted to Tutsi notables and administrative chiefs, and in spite of insufficient technical personnel and Tutsi reluctance and neglect, Voisin's initial trials were quite satisfactory. Subsequent campaigns, however, were restricted to Hutu farmers rather than to Tutsi. To ensure success the administration sought to simplify planting procedures, and African initiative was severely circumscribed. Monitors, assisted by a European, selected and demarcated fields and staked out the holes for plants. To facilitate supervision over geographical areas, agricultural personnel grouped individual parcels into tens or hundreds. Instead of concentrating nurseries in the principal urban centers, the Agriculture Service constructed and distributed nurseries throughout the various provinces. Generally these nurseries served one or more hills, and most were built near streams, although placement depended upon the density of the surrounding population. During planting, Hutu farmers were given between forty-nine and fifty-four plants from the local nurseries and instructed to plant them in a line near their enclosures and among their banana trees or other shade plants.

The Belgians also instituted guidelines to regulate the processing and sale of African coffee. According to the draft decree, coffee could be purchased only by those with a special license, just as processing required a separate permit. Theoretically, every processor had the right to purchase African coffee in the mandate territory, but the government reserved the right to establish a minimum purchasing price to protect Africans from unscrupulous mill owners. With the exception of the purchasing license and the minimum purchasing price, the commercialization of coffee was otherwise free.

As the government believed Africans would sell poorly processed beans, it instituted quality controls, just as it had issued Ordinance No. 90 (AE) of November 21, 1931, to distinguish white-produced coffee from that produced by blacks. The ordinance outlined the packaging and labeling procedure for coffee exported from the Belgian Congo, Burundi, and Rwanda. Coffee had to be placed in sacks of a particular dimension and marked in large letters of no less than five centimeters high with the name or mark of the planter, plantation, company, or the commercial expediter of African coffee; "IND" to indicate African brands of coffee; and finally the name of the province. The ordinance did not apply to reexported coffee, but labeling coffee in this manner was obviously designed to placate the unfounded fears of planters who voiced opposition to African coffee cultivation and who believed that the African product would lower the market value of their coffee. However, these government efforts did not stifle the opposition from European coffee planters in the Belgian Congo or in the mandate territory.

By the 1936–1937 campaign all the kinks in the program were ironed out. However, the administration was still concerned with saving man-hours and transportation time. In the interest of efficiency, a new procedure was introduced with respect to the creation and location of nurseries. One to two malthouses or hotbed nurseries were established in each chieftaincy. Seedlings or plants were placed in each hotbed a slight distance apart, 250 seedlings per square meter, in order to save space (approximately 60 percent). When this phase was completed, each taxpayer was required to build a flower bed, 2.5 to 3 meters long and 1.5 meters wide, alongside of his homestead (*rugo*). Once the flower bed was built, farmers were required to take and transplant a hundred young plants from the administration's new nurseries. Officials believed that with the creation of these individual nurseries, Africans would pay more attention to maintenance, and monitors would pay more attention to instructing farmers on the most rational way to plant their coffee. By the end of the 1936 campaign, 8.5 million coffee trees had been planted in Rwanda, and Africans received 2.50 to 3.50 BF per kilo for their coffee. By the final year of the campaign, 75 percent of all taxpayers had at least 60 coffee trees. By the end of December 1937, some 21 million coffee trees had been distributed—500,000 to notables; 700,000 to Tutsi subchiefs; and 19,000,000 to individual Hutu. Approximately 50,000 to 60,000 Rwandan planters participated in the campaigns.

AFRICAN AND EUROPEAN REACTIONS AND POST–WORLD WAR II RWANDA

Not everyone accepted Belgian colonial rule or the Tutsi position as arbiters in the colonial administration. In 1930 Tutsi chiefs in Kisenyi refused to participate in the development program and planning for the region. In the following year, some Hutu at Budaha refused to work for the administration in the district of Kibuye, while others refused to pay taxes. In 1932 and 1935 the administration had to crush tax revolts by Hutu in northern Rwanda. European *colons* who had to compete with African farmers in Stanleyville, Bukavu, the Kivu, and in the mandate territory began to organize themselves into commercial associations to lobby for their interests at Brussels and Antwerp. Africans protested against the harshness and unfairness of colonial rule and Tutsi overlordship. Europeans, in contrast, protested in order to retain the protective zones, to limit African cultivation, and to obtain protective subsidies for their agricultural commodities. Neither European nor African protest changed the focus of colonial economic policy prior to World War II.

In fact, Belgian and Tutsi exactions and supervision became more intense during World War II. When the Germany army invaded Belgium on May 10, 1940, and the Belgian army was forced to surrender on May 27, Rwandans and Belgians were affected directly. Economic mobilization for Rwanda and Burundi and the Belgian Congo commenced in the fall of 1940, when the Anglo-Belgian agreement was concluded. In order to provide the

Allies with such necessities as tin and rubber, production levels were increased and African labor mobilized. The mining of both cassiterite (which contains tin) and tin itself, were greatly extended in the west and northeastern regions of Rwanda and in the territory of Kigali. The principal mining companies—SOMUKI, Murudi, Mindfor, and Géoruanda—produced 12,454 tons of cassiterite between 1940 and 1944. African farmers were compelled to increase food production in order to feed the workers in the mineral centers throughout the eastern Congo and the mandate territory, and to provide labor for the war effort. African males living in traditional areas were obliged to devote a total of 60 days a year to paid and unpaid work of importance to their local communities. By 1944 obligatory labor had increased to 120 days a year. Europeans, on the other hand, lost valuable agricultural subsidies and had to endure restrictions on plantation acreage.

War mobilization, however, had the most devastating impact on Africans, and caused African peasant life to deteriorate. The Belgian administration demanded labor for reclamation of swamps (to make more productive land available), clearing roads, and construction. In addition to these demands there were the continuous burdens of compulsory food and cash crops. Moreover, the Tutsi continued to demand the maximum in *ubuletwa* and *corvée* from the Hutu. The oligarchy was not completely exempted; their cattle were requisitioned to provide meat and milk. In addition, all Africans had to compete for space with European colonists. The number of European agricultural settlements in Rwanda rose from 42 in 1940 to 137 in 1947. Land concessions for European agriculturalists rose from 2,679 hectares to 7,552 hectares in the same period. European colonists came to Rwanda to participate in the cultivation of pyrethrum, which was important during the war. Those who had settled in Ruhengeri, Biumba, Kisenyi, and Cyangugu produced food crops and supplied timber to Costermansville.

Wartime mobilization, the increase in customary and unofficial *corvée,* and other exactions drained and weakened Rwanda to such extent that its inhabitants succumbed in 1942 to a famine that cost the lives of at least 300,000 people. In addition, traditional foodstuffs, such as peas and sweet and ordinary potatoes, were blighted by mildew and destroyed by a severe drought and by insects. An epidemic of typhus brought Rwanda to near paralysis, and food reserves were quickly exhausted. The Belgian administration transported about 32 million francs in emergency food supplies from the Belgian Congo to Rwanda and Burundi, which comprised about 30 per cent of all receipts for both territories. By mid-1944, the famine abated, partially in response to a large manioc harvest and to a compulsory food-crop program enacted by the government in 1943, but deaths from famine did not stop until July. To prevent future disasters and to increase productivity, Belgian officials compelled Rwandans by law to plant hedges, dig ditches, and carry out other types of anti-erosion public works. The first Ten-Year Development Plan sponsored by the colonial office in Brussels in 1951 was partially in response to the severe famine of the early 1940s.

THE MOVEMENT TOWARD INDEPENDENCE

Hutu political agitation began on July 14, 1952, when a Belgian decree introduced advisory councils at all levels of government, and culminated in the infamous Bahutu Manifesto of March 1957. The Tutsi response was the Statement of Views, which followed within a matter of days. The first political party, the Association pour la Promotion Sociale de la Masse (APROSOMA) was formed later in the year, followed by the Mouvement Sociale Muhutu in 1958. Subsequent party development included the Union National Rwandaise (UNAR), Rassemblement Démocratique Ruandais (RADER), and Parti du Mouvement de l'Emancipation Hutu (PARMEHUTU). A series of events, including the mysterious death of King Mutara Rudahigwa III in July 1959 and the accession of King Kigeri V, and the rebellion by Hutu on November 1, 1959, ensured Hutu hegemony.

The Hutu made additional gains in the country's first municipal elections in June and July 1960. In fact, PARMEHUTU won the majority of seats, and after the coup of Gitarama in January 1961, in which the Hutu political elite declared a republic and choose a legislative assembly, they were able to exercise total control over the institutions of government at both the national and provincial levels. In 1962, a referendum was passed recommending the abolition of the monarchy and sanctioning the creation of a republic. Rwanda declared its independence on July 1, 1962, with the Hutu firmly in control and under the leadership and presidency of Grégoire Kayibanda, the leader of PARMEHUTU.

THE NATIONAL PERIOD

Independence did not guarantee peace and tranquillity. Efforts by the United Nations to persuade Rwanda and Burundi to remain as one political unit failed, and by the end of 1963 the two countries agreed to go their separate ways in terms of the customs and monetary union, the coffee regulatory agency OCIRU, and the central banking system. In November and December 1963, Rwanda was invaded by Tutsi *inyenzi* ("cockroaches"), who had fled the country before independence. Insurgents crossed into Rwanda from Burundi in an attempt to take Kigali, the capital. The insurgents were repulsed and forced to retreat back into Burundi; however, the invasion had serious internal and external repercussions for Rwanda. Tutsi were arrested throughout the country; an estimated 10,000 were reportedly killed, with many thousands more forced to flee the country into exile. The government reportedly executed about twenty prominent Tutsi citizens, and it accused the Burundi government of complicity in the invasion. The result was unfriendly relations between the two governments until 1966, when a republic was established in Burundi.

Grégoire Kayibanda ruled a presidential republic for eleven years, until his civilian government was toppled in July 1973, in a bloodless military coup led by the former minister of defense and head of the national guard, Major General Juvénal Habyarimana, a northerner from Gisenyi. The northern Hutu politicians felt alienated from the central and southern regions of the country. When they assumed power with Habyarimana, they dissolved PARMEHUTU, suspended the 1962 constitution, and introduced a more centralized system of administration, new economic policies, and a more moderate position toward the Tutsi. The army and police were merged into the National Defense Army. In July 1975, President Habyarimana formed the Mouvement Révolutionnaire National pour le Développement (MRND), a new ruling party of soldiers and civilians. At the same time, President Habyarimana was confirmed head of state in a national presidential election in which he stood unopposed.

After assuming control of the state, President Habyarimana attempted to stimulate economic growth and development and to provide for internal security. In June 1974, a tripartite conference was held at Bujumbura among Rwanda, Burundi, and Zaire, in which the participants agreed to improve border security and to facilitate economic cooperation. Such conferences have become a permanent feature of Rwandan foreign policy. In addition, various aid and development agreements have been made with the governments of the United States, West Germany, Switzerland, France, Belgium, and China to secure funding and support for grain storage facilities, road construction projects, and various kinds of technical assistance. In 1978 a new constitution was introduced which permitted limited suffrage and judicial reform. However, the most pressing concerns have been threats to stability and the viability of the state.

For example, relations with Uganda generally between 1976 and 1983 and most recently in 1990, and with Idi Amin specifically have resulted in frequent border closings. Because Rwanda is landlocked, these border closings have produced periodic economic stagnation. In April 1980, the government crushed a coup attempt led by an anti-Tutsi former security chief, Major Théoneste Lizende. The major and thirty coconspirators were arrested for planning the attempted coup and sentenced to death. His sentence was commuted in 1982; however, in a retrial in June 1985, he and four coconspirators were convicted for murdering more than fifty political prisoners and were again sentenced to death. Four men were released in December 1987, but Major Lizende and three others remained in prison until January 23,

1991. The major escaped from prison when the Rwandan Patriotic Front overran and released everyone from the maximum security prison at Ruhengeri.

In 1992 Rwanda became embroiled in a transport tariff dispute with Kenya which if left unresolved will prove quite devastating to the Rwandan economy. The Kenyan government imposed a subsidy of 20 percent on all exports to Rwanda from its port at Mombasa at the beginning of 1992. In retaliation, the Rwandan government in August 1992, implemented a 60 percent import charge on Kenyan goods coming into Rwanda. Neither country has yet to rescind its respective surcharges, and Rwanda has been forced to seek an alternative routing through Tanzania and Burundi to receive its exports from the Indian Ocean. Consequently, freight costs have increased tremendously.

Rwanda recognizes that its economy is quite fragile and appealed to the international community for assistance on November 9, 1990. The World Bank, IMF, in conjunction with the Rwandan government, devised the Structural Adjustment Program (SAP). The program is designed to reduced the country's dependency on coffee production and to increase efficiency in the agricultural sector, in energy production, and in the public sector. The objective is to increase real GDP by four percent, decrease inflation by five percent, and reduce the balance of payments deficit by ten percent of GDP by the end of 1993. For its part, the government devalued the Rwandan franc by forty percent and restructured its import licensing fees. It has also instituted an austerity program internally by reducing ministerial salaries and controlling access to foreign exchange by changing a 5 percent commission fee.

An additional concern for the country, and only recently recognized as pressing by the government, is the refugee problem for both Hutu and Tutsi. The problem of refugees is complex and a matter of perception. For those coming from Uganda, they number several hundred thousand and are concentrated in the southwest region, largely in Kigezi, Ankole, and Toro districts. Many have lived in these areas since the colonial period, and many have become Ugandan citizens. Others came to Uganda in the early 1960s during the turbulent years of the independence struggle. The majority are Tutsi, but included in this category are Hutu dissidents. Smaller numbers of Tutsi can be found in Burundi, Tanzania, and Kenya, as well as in Zaire. These refugees have periodically affected Rwanda's foreign policy as early as 1963. The most serious disturbance has been the invasion by a militant Tutsi faction from Uganda. Members of the Rwandese Patriotic Front (RPF) crossed the border into Rwanda from Uganda at Kagitumba on October 1, 1990. This invasion is in its third year and has had dire social, economic, and political consequences for the country.

About 7,000 Rwandan troops led by Major General Fred Rwigyema, later assassinated by his own confederates, invaded northern Rwanda from Uganda. They enjoyed some initial successes, and even inflicted heavy losses upon Rwandans and those troops sent from abroad at the battle at Lyabega on October 23. But both Majors Bayingana and Bunyenyezi, leaders of the RPF, were killed in this engagement. Major General Paul Kagame has assumed command of RPF forces. Heavy fighting took place near Gutuna, Kaniga, and Ngarama in late November and early December. If victorious, the RPF would implement democratic rule and national unity within Rwanda. It promises to end government corruption, build a self-sustaining economy, bring the refugees home, and pursue a progressive foreign policy. But in almost three years of fighting, the RPF has not broadened its political base nor has it rallied the Hutu to its side.

Nor has peace been achieved despite numerous attempts to bring the combatants to terms. Individual efforts by various African leaders and conferences called by European nations, the United States, and OAU have not produced a viable ceasefire or acceptable peace terms. What the war has done is to further divide the society, create political instability, and cause near economic collapse. The war has also exacerbated both ethnic cleavages which precipitated attacks against Tutsi in Ngorolero in Gisenyi in October 1990 and in the Bugesera in March 1992, and an internal refugee problem. About 350,000 Banyarwanda, living in the south of the war zone and RPF-held territory have been displaced for their villages and farms.

Since the invasion, the movement toward democratic rule and multi-party participation in the political process has been accelerated. In July 1990, during the 17th anniversary celebration of President Habyarimana's rule, he announced to the National Assembly that he would revise the constitution to allow multi-party participation in the political process. An interministerial working group was appointed to review the political system, and the president announced that their recommendations would be implemented by July 1992, to coincide with the 30th anniversary of the country's independence. But once the invasion began, this time table was revised. In his November 1990 address, the president informed the National Assembly that a referendum on the rules governing the operations of political parties would take place on June 15, 1991.

The first political party to become public did so before the presidential announcement. On November 8, 1990, Silas Majyambere, the former president of the Rwanda Chamber of Commerce, living in exile in Brussels, formed the Rwandan People's Union/Union du Peuple Rwandais (UPR). Several months later, the Mouvement Démocratique Républicain became active. When the National Synthesis Commission/Commission Nationale de Synthèse in its report to the National Assembly of April 10 recommended the modification of the 1978 constitution, the abolition of the single party system, and the creation of the post of prime minister the MRND, the sole party in the country, became the Mouvement Républicain National pour la Démocratie et le Développement (MRNDD) on April 28.

As new political parties emerged, new journals with an extremely critical voice entered the political fray and not without consequences. Editorials from such newspapers as *Kanguka, Ijambo, Isibo,* and *Kangura* were extremely critical of the government, peace negotiations, and the new political atmosphere, which often produced violence and death. Editors and their copy were seized, and several editors were imprisoned for short periods of time. But Pandora's Box had been opened and could not be closed. In June, the president signed a new constitution, which legalized multi-parties and reduced presidential power. He also signed a new law on June 20 that established the rules by which new political parties would function. And during the month of August, about a dozen new parties were established. The most important among them are the Democratic Republican Movement/Mouvement Démocratique Républicain (MDR), the Christian Democratic Party/Parti Démocratique Chrétien (PDC), the Social Democrat Party/Parti Social-démocratique (PSD), the Liberal Party/Parti Libéral (PL), and the ruling Mouvement Républicain National pour la Démocratie et Développement (MRND). Efforts to forge a coalition government commenced in October 1991 between the national government and the opposition. But disagreements over procedures and structure prevented an accord from being implemented. The opposition was dissatisfied with the government's objectives and wanted a provisional government composed of the opposition and led by a prime minister appointed by them rather than one appointed by the president. To their dismay, the president appointed Sylvestre Nsanzimana, the Minister of Justice, to the post of prime minister on October 10, 1991. Mr. Nsanzimana was given instructions to form a cabinet with representatives from six of the political parties. The opposition refused to comply. While the political atmosphere remained quite tense, little or no activity took place until December 18, when the president again attempted to come to grips with political reality. In the meantime, the RPF, the press, and the Rwanda Catholic church came out in support of an independent transitional government, which would be responsible for peace negotiations.

But in the December 18 meeting with the opposition, the president reaffirmed his support for his prime minister and his ability to form a transitional government. The following members of the opposition—the MDR, PSD, PL, and the PSR—withdrew from the proceedings, leaving the government to deal with the PCD, PECO, PDI, and RTD to choose ministers for the coalition government. But only PCD had sufficient portfolio to negotiate with the government. On December 30, Prime Minister Nsanzimana presented his new cabinet to the country, which was composed of one PCD member, fifteen members from the MRND, and one army officer. This transitional government had a short life; opposition to it coalesced almost immediately. On January 23, 1992, the president was forced to pursue new negotiations with the opposition to form a transitional government agreeable to all concerned.

The new year not only witnessed political compromise but also growing conflict with Uganda over its alleged complicity in Rwanda's war with the RPF and increasing internal instability. Current charges and mutual recriminations over support of the RPF and Uganda's complicity have brought them to the brink of war. Political rallies and demonstrations against the government often result in violence. New groups such as the Protestant Church and the Seventh Day Adventists have joined the opposition and have called for a negotiated settlement in the war with the RPF and the refugee issue and support for the Structural Adjustment Program (SAP).

During the last week of February and the early part of March, the president and Prime Minister Sylvestre Nsanzimana hammered out a compromise over a coalition government with twelve of the registered opposition parties. The agreement also called for elections by April 1993 at the latest and settlement of the refugee problem. A new prime minister, Dismas Nsengiyaremye, who is a member of MDR, was selected, and his new cabinet was formed on April 16 with MRND receiving nine posts, PSD three, the PL three, and the PCD one. On April 21, President Habyarimana retired from the army to head the transition government as a civilian and, it is hoped, to focus his attention on a peace settlement.

The country continued to be plagued by ethnic and inter-party political violence and conflicts between Rwandan forces and the RPF from mid-May to the end of the year. At the conference table, the issue was no longer a negotiated settlement but how final peace would be structured. In June 1992, mediation centered on the integration of the RPF into the Rwandan army and political guarantees for refugees, as well as a ceasefire. In August, a new constitution and RPF representation in the government were added to the list of issues to be negotiated. After a month of inactivity, negotiations resumed in October at Arusha, Tanzania, where the government agreed to reduce presidential power and to incorporate the RPF into the government. The only issues remaining in 1993 were a viable ceasefire and how the RPF will be incorporated into the national army.

Finally, despite the war and civil unrest, the country's most pressing problems are still economic development, food security, and population density. However, expanding the economic base and providing adequate nutrition for the society through the development of both food and cash crops is constrained by a shortage of land suitable for cultivation and by low levels of public spending. The government actively pursues foreign and private investment and has instituted a very generous code to encourage investors. It has not insisted upon a share-holding in new enterprises, but instead guarantees a five-year exception from corporation taxes. With respect to population pressures, there is no indication that the government will press officially for birth control nor seek alternative avenues such as emigration to Tanzania or Zaire to relieve population pressure. Although it has negotiated with both Gabon and Tanzania on this very issue, results thus far have been inconclusive. Consequently, it is doubtful whether the government can solve the refugee problem in neighboring countries, relieve population pressures, or provide food security for its people. Still, with the assistance of donor aid from the west, the government has sought various means to diversify the economic base of the society and to stay one step ahead, which is probably the most accurate prognosis for the rest of the 1990s.

CHRONOLOGY

6000 B.C.   Shift taking from hunting and gathering to a more sedentary habitation in the Great Lakes region.

3000   Inhabitants of the Great Lakes region begin to make iron tools and implements.

2000   Nilotes and Bantu-speakers begin to occupy the Great Lakes region.

A.D. 800   Some evidence of political and social stratification in the Great Lakes region. The iron bell with clapper and the flange bells are symbols of authority.

1000   Hutu farmers begin to settle in Rwanda.

Development of trade between the interior of the Great Lakes region and the Indian Ocean.

Cattle keeping begins to spread in the Great Lakes region.

1100   Roulette-decorated and dimple-based pottery used in the Great Lakes region.

1386   Death of *umwami* Ndahiro Ruyange; *umwami* Ndoba (1386–1410) becomes his successor.

1410   Death of *umwami* Ndoba; *umwami* Samembe (1410–1434) becomes his successor.

1434   Death of *umwami* Samembe; Nsoro (Muhigi) Samukondo (1434–1458) becomes the new *umwami*.

1458   Death of *umwami* Nsoro Samukondo; his successor is Ruganzu Bwimba (1458–1482).

     Ruganzu's nuclear kingdom is located in the region of Buganza and Bwanacyambwe.

1482   Death of *umwami* Ruganzu Bwimba; his successor is Cyilima Rugwe (1482–1506).

     Rugwe occupies Kigali, and with his son and successor, Mokobanya, conquers the provinces of Buriza, Bumbogo, and Rukoma.

     Rugwe acknowledges the *Abakoobwa* clan as "president or leader" of all the *abiiru*, while the *abiiru* from Nyamweeru is given the privilege of designating the family who would supply the successor with a queen mother.

1500   Rwanda is a small state within a confederation, or loose alliance that included Bugesera, Gisaka, and Ndorwa.

1506   On January 24 an annular eclipse is observed.

     Death of *umwami* Cyilima Rugwe; he is succeeded by Kigeri Mukobanya (1506–1528).

     Royal ideology commences with Mukobanya's acceptance of the *ubwiiru,* and he establishes the office of guardian of the royal gongs.

     Mukobanya incorporates some of the smaller Tutsi

states of the *Abongera* and the *Abatsobe* in the western region into his kingdom.

1528   Death of *umwami* Kigeri Mukobanya; his brother, Mibambwe Mutabaazi, becomes the new king (1528–1552).

1552   Death of *umwami* Mibambwe Mutabaazi; the new *umwami* is Yuhi Gahima (1552–1576).

Umwami Gahima annexes the eastern portion of the Congo-Nile ridge up the volcanoes and the regions of Bwishaza and Rusenyi. He is able to extend the kingdom to Lake Kivu.

1576   *Umwami* Yuhi Gahima dies; his successor is Ndahiro Cyamaatare (1576–1600), who inherits a kingdom that includes half of Bumbogo, the regions of Buriza, Rukoma, Ndüga, and Mayaga.

Cyamaatare's reign is challenged, and there is a bloody war over succession with his brother, Juru, even though the *abiiru* designated Cyamaatare as the legitimate ruler.

Juru is killed in battle, but another son and challenger, Bamara, and his paternal uncle, Byinshi, continue to challenge Cyamaatare's authority.

The kingdom is divided; the dynastic drum falls into the hands of the enemy, who occupy the territory for eleven years; and the prince and heir apparent, Ndoori, is forced to flee to Karagwe to live with his fraternal aunt.

1600   *Umwami* Ndahiro Cyamaatare dies; his successor is Ruganzu Ndoori (1600–1624). Ndoori is given a new dynastic drum, and is credited with reorganizing the Rwandan kingdom both administratively and through the introduction of new dynastic ceremony.

From Ndorwa, Ruganzu Ndoori launches a series of invasions against the rulers within the region of Bugesera and the formerly independent Hutu communities. The conquest of latter results in the formation of a unitary state.

Abacocori and *Bakono* pastoral groups enter Ruhengeri from the north, and establish themselves at Mulera on the Mukono Hill.

1624   *Umwami* Ruganzu Ndoori is killed in an ambush by the mountain men of Bwishaza; his successor is Mutara (Nsoro) Seemugeshi (1624–1648).

Seemugeshi conquers the kingdoms of Busanza, Bufundu, and Bungwe in Astrida territory, reforms the *ubwiiru*, and gives it the authority to interpret the king's last will and testament with respect to succession.

1648   *Umwami* Mutara Seemugeshi dies; his successor is Kigeri Nyamuheshera (1648–1672).

Nyamuheshera conquers Kigali and extends the kingdom northward to Lake Edward, to the east to Rusenyi, and to the west to Kinyaga and portions of Ndorwa.

1672   *Umwami* Kigeri Nyamuheshera dies; his successor is Mibambwe Gisanura (1672–1696).

1696   *Umwami* Mibambwe Gisanura dies; his successor is Yuhi Mazimpaka (1696–1720).

1720   *Umwami* Yuhi Mazimpaka dies; his successor is Karemeera Rwaaka (1720–1744).

1744   *Umwami* Karemeera Rwaaka abdicates; his successor is Cyirima Rujugira (1744–1768).

1750   *Umwami* Cyirima Rujugira effectively colonizes the southern part of the country, but is unable to centralize administrative and political power from the core kingdom. The boundary of Rwanda is fixed at the Akanyaru River, where it remains today.

    He also attacks Ndorwa and Gisaka, and is able to obtain territory from each of these areas. He initiates the eastern and western expansion of the Rwandan kingdom.

1768   *Umwami* Cyirima Rujugira dies; his successor is Kigeri Ndabarasa (1768–1792).

    Ndabarasa conquers Ndorwa and Nubari, but he is unable to subdue Gisaka.

1792   *Umwami* Kigeri Ndabarasa dies, his successor is Mibambwe Sentabyo (1792–1797). Before assuming power, Sentabyo has to fight his half brother, Gatarabuhura, for the throne.

1797   *Umwami* Mibambwe Sentabyo dies from smallpox; his successor is Yuhi Gahindiro (1797–1830).

    Gahindiro increases the number of *abwiiru* and sanctions the reform of the district chief, which is divided into two functions—land chief and cattle chief. He also begins the process of appointing governors for the frontier areas.

Ndorwa revolts, but the rebellion is suppressed, and Ndorwa is occupied by Gahindiro's forces.

Successful military campaigns are conducted against the Bushi and Burundi.

During the end of Gahindiro's reign, *ubuhake* (cattle clientship) and *igikingi* (land grants) become particularly strong, as does the increasing power and influence of the Tutsi notables.

1830   *Umwami* Yuhi Gahindiro dies, and is succeeded by Mutara Rwogera (1830–1860).

The *umwami* annexes Gisaka, and he begins to extend the concept of clientship.

1850   The development of a series of independent Tutsi states occurs with the kingdom of Gisaka in the east being the most powerful.

1860   *Umwami* Mutara Rwogera dies. Kigeri Rwabugiri, or the great warrior king, becomes the *umwami* (1860–1895). He proceeds to expand and consolidate his power in the central kingdom and in the western region; he builds his capital at Gisaka; and he initiates military campaigns in the eastern region against the rest of Ndorwa, Bushi, Nkore, and Ijwi Island. Ndorwa and Ijwi Island are annexed; Nkore is defeated, but he is unable to conquer Bushi.

Rwabugiri reestablishes royal control at Bygoyi, Bwishaza, Kingogo, Murera, western Buberuka, Busigi, and Nyantango, areas where Tutsi herdsmen had been autonomous. Much of the western region is incorporated administratively, except

Buhunzi, Busozo, Bushiru, and portions of Kibari. He also expands the system of clientship.

1865   On December 10, Leopold I dies; his son, Prince Leopold, becomes King Leopold II of Belgium.

1884–1885   The Association Internationale du Congo obtains recognition as a state by the European powers at the Berlin West Africa Conference.

1885   Kigeri Rwaburgiri institutionalizes *corvée,* food prestations, and *igikingi* on the central plateau. He also eliminates the right of hereditary succession of chiefs and chiefdoms among the Tutsi notables and lineages; he reduces the number of districts to twenty-one; and he establishes a series of new capitals in northern Rwanda.

Arabs appear in the Ruzizi Valley.

1889   On December 22, a solar eclipse occurs.

1890   Famine in the territory of Astrida (now Butare).

1892   On September 11, Oscar Baumann, a German explorer and participant in the Masai Expedition organized by the German Anti-Slavery Society, reaches the marshes of Akanyaru and spends four days in Rwanda.

Outbreak of foot-and-mouth disease.

1894   On May 2, the German explorers, von Goetzen, von Prittwitz, and Kersting enter Rwanda from Karagwe.

On June 14, Richard Kandt, a German geographer,

ethnologist, and poet, pitches camp at Mkingo in the Nduga region.

1895   *Umwami* Kigeri Rwaburgiri dies; his successor is Mibambwe Rutarindwa (1895–1896). His reign is challenged by supporters of the young Musinga, who is also the son of Rwabugiri and the queen mother. The latter wishes to take the throne for her own son.

Kabaare, Musinga's uncle, commences the civil war against Rutarindwa.

The outbreak of a cattle pest destroys almost all the cattle in the kingdom.

1896   Members of a Belgian military expedition pitch camp at Ishangi (Shangi) and remain in the area for several weeks.

Rutarindwa is assassinated at Rucunshu.

1897   *Umwami* Yuhi Musinga begins his reign (1897–1931).

The Belgians establish a camp at Nyamasheke.

Dhani mutineers invade the country from the north, looting and killing as they proceed southward. They engage and defeat a Belgian military force at Gaseke, but are stopped and defeated by German forces from Ujiji on December 27.

1899   Rwanda becomes part of German East Africa.

The Nyabingi movement enters the country from the west.

German military post established at Usumbura, and the German Resident, Richard Kandt, arrives at Shangi to establish his residence.

The first missionaries from the White Fathers arrive at Usumbura. Fathers Hirth, Brard, Barthélémy, Anselme, accompanied by Baganda catechists, are given carriers and a guide for their trip to Ishangi. They are met by Kandt and Captain von Bethe, who provide an escort and carriers for their journey to Nyanza.

Catholic mission station is established at Issave.

1900   At the beginning of the century, the central core of Rwanda includes the central plateau, Gisaka in the east, and all of the western region.

Monsignor Jean-Joseph Hirth's visit to Musinga at his court at Nyanza on February 2 marks the arrival of the White Fathers in Rwanda.

The Belgian-German Convention is signed on April 1.

1901   Francis Richard von Parish takes his post at Shangi.

Musinga requests German military assistance to crush rebellion led by Rukura in Gisaka.

1902   From September 15 to 26, von Parish accompanies Captain von Veringe and Dr. Engeland to the royal residence at Nyanza to visit *umwami* Musinga.

1902–1903   Famine *(kiramwaramwara)* in the territory of Butare. Drought destroys bean crops, a caterpillar infestation decimates sweet potato fields, and according to the Resident the late rains cause harvested sorghum to germinate before it can be stored.

1903   Catholic mission station established at Rwaza.

The White Fathers establish the first coffee plantation at their Nyundo mission station near Gisenyi.

1904–1905   Famine throughout Rwanda.

1905   Hutu at Bugarura refuse to pay royal tribute, and *umwami* Musinga appeals to Eberhard Gudowius to send a military expedition to the region. The Hutu are defeated at Remera; many are killed and their cattle confiscated.

The White Fathers' mission station at Mibirizi receives Guatemalan coffee seedlings from Amani, a German experimental station.

In June and August, Musinga mounts military expedition against Basebya, a Twa at Mulera, whose people refuse to pay traditional prestations. Musinga's forces are defeated, and he appeals to the Germans for assistance.

1906   Famine continues in Nyanza and Butare.

In February, von Grawert leads a military expedition against Basebya at Mulera. Basebya avoids capture.

On June 20, the military district of Usumbura (now Bujumbura) becomes the Residence of Ruanda-Burundi.

1907
Richard Kandt is appointed Resident and constructs his residence at Kigali, signaling the beginning of civilian administration in Rwanda.

Administrative services for Rwanda are transferred from Bujumbura to Kigali.

The School for the Sons of Chiefs is established at Nyanza.

On February 26, the White Fathers hold a ceremony to commemorate the completion of the church at Save. Musinga, although invited, does not attend.

In May there are measles and malaria epidemics in Nyanza.

In July there are reports of a smallpox epidemic in Bygoyi, Budaha, and Kingogo.

During July, Protestants from the Bethel bei Bielefeld mission arrive in the country.

On July 15, the Duke of Mecklenburg begins his scientific expedition, which continues until October 7.

Outbreak of foot-and-mouth disease.

1907–1908
Grasshopper infestation in Bugarura, Kiryi, and Rwaza is followed by famine.

1908
German officials open the country to commerce. Greek and Hindu merchants establish themselves at Kigali.

1909
In December, Leopold II dies. He has no surviving sons, so Albert, his nephew and the son of the count

of Flanders, becomes king of Belgium on December 23.

In March and April, a new German expedition is mounted against Basebya, but Basebya escapes.

Gudowius's June military campaign against Basebya is equally unsuccessful. Basebya escapes to Mulera.

In September, a third German military expedition is sent against Basebya, but he is not captured.

Reports of dysentery throughout the country during the year.

1910   Father Loupias is assassinated at Gahunga on April 1 by Rukara rwa Bishingwa, a Hutu. The Germans retaliate with a military expedition, assisted by Tutsi notables from Nduga. This group travels to Gahunga. Several Hutu are killed and rugo are burned, but Rukara escapes.

On April 29, a second German expedition is sent to find Rukara, but it is unsuccessful.

On May 14, the common frontiers of the Belgian Congo, British Uganda, and German East Africa, including the territory of Ruanda-Urundi, are fixed at the Conference of Brussels by representatives from Germany, Great Britain and Belgium. With the new boundaries, Rwanda loses the territories of Bufumbira, which is annexed to Uganda, and Bwishya, Gishari, and the island of Ijwi to the Belgian Congo.

In October, a third German expedition is sent to Ruhengeri to capture Rukara, but he escapes.

1911   In February, a smallpox epidemic spreads throughout the country.

In March, a dysentery epidemic begins in Nyundo.

In May, the Germans mount a punitive expedition against Nyiragahumuza, *umwami* Rwabugiri's widow, Rukara, Ndungutze, and Basebya in northern Rwanda.

In December, the dysentery epidemic continues and is accompanied by an outbreak of typhoid fever.

1912   On April 13, Ndungutze is killed.

On April 18, Rukara is captured, found guilty of Father Loupias's murder, and executed at the Ruhengeri military station.

1913   In June, an outbreak of diphtheria in Ruhengeri.

1914   On September 23, Ijwi Island, a Belgian military post, is conquered by German troops.

On October 11, Belgian forces attack the German outpost at Cyangugu.

October 20, Belgian and German forces clash at Gisenyi.

Germans levy a tax of one rupee or thirty days of labor on every able-bodied adult male.

1915   Allied-German conflicts are reported in Bukemba, Bugoyi, and Ruhengeri.

On August 31, an ordinance is passed which authorizes only Europeans with adequate guarantees to possess firearms. Non-Europeans must receive permission from the governor to possess arms.

1916   Belgian troops take control of Rwanda.

Troops enter the country from Ruhengeri.

Famine is widespread, and smallpox epidemic is reported in Nyanza, Ruhengeri, and Gisaka.

Kigali becomes a territorial unit.

1917   Belgian administration begins, and the first royal high commissioner, Malfeyt, is appointed.

Belgian administration initiates the first head tax levy of 2.50 BF per household.

Outbreak of epidemics of smallpox and cerebrospinal meningitis.

1917–1918   Famine *(rumanura)*.

1918   In February and April, territorial administration posts are created at Gakenke in Kibali and at Gashunga (both in northern Rwanda and the territory of Ruhengeri).

Louis Franck is appointed the new minister of the colonies.

Smallpox and cerebrospinal meningitis epidemics continue.

Hutu at Buhama and Bushiru refuse to perform traditional prestations and refuse to allow Europeans and Tutsi to pass through the territories.

Umwami Musinga sends a punitive expedition to the Mwiyaniki and Birembo regions, and attempts to take control of Buhama and Bushiru. These regions are brought under control after several weeks of resistance.

1919 Smallpox and cerebrospinal meningitis epidemics continue, and in March a grasshopper infestation occurs in Kigali; beans and eleusine crops are lost.

In May, the Orts-Milner Convention is signed, and the mandate is officially granted to Belgium.

1920 In February, a permanent territorial administrative post is created at Mulera in northern Ruhengeri.

Vice Governor-General Alfred-Frederic-Gerard Marzorati succeeds General J. Malfeyt.

The administration distributes coffee plants to Tutsi chiefs and subchiefs.

1921 In November, famine in Gisaka and in Gatsibo territory. Thousands die.

1922 Decree is issued to regulate work contracts between European employers and African workers. Limitations are placed upon the employment of children, terms of contracts (no longer than three years), certain reciprocal rights and obligations, and the treatment of workers. *Akazi,* or corvée, for various kinds of public works and compulsory cultivation projects becomes more generalized.

Administration begins interior road construction.

Famine continues in Gisaka and in the territory of Gatsibo.

1923   Georges Mortehan is Resident until November 21, when Oger Coubeau replaces him.

Domestic slavery is abolished on May 23. The Belgian authorities free all the slaves held by Tutsi notables and other Africans.

Akanyaru, which was part of Nyanza territory, becomes the territory of Astrida (now Butare) on December 1.

The district of Save becomes an administrative post.

Administration's road building program has resulted in the construction of 210 kilometers of motor roads.

1924   On October 20, Belgium receives official approval from the League of Nations of the mandate status of Rwanda and Burundi.

The administration creates fifteen African tribunals.

Ecole Industrielle de Shangugu (in Kamembe territory) is created.

Ordinance of December 24 directs polygamous nonindigenous inhabitants to pay a supplementary tax.

On December 26, Belgian authorities abolish three

traditional prestations—*imponake, indabukirano,* and *abatora*—and reduce some other work prestations to forty-two days per year. Certain traditional taxes in kind are also abolished.

Because of the lack of rain, the government halts the exportation of food crops and requires farmers to cultivate nonseasonal crops.

The administration publishes an official periodical, *Bulletin Officiel du Ruanda-Urundi,* which contains all the legal texts and regulations, as well as commercial regulations, related to the mandate.

1924–1925   Famine throughout the country.

1925   Administrative post is established at Butare, which is located in the center of Astrida territory.

Station Expérimentale d'Agriculture et de Sériciculture at Lusunya is established.

Government announces an economic policy focusing on agriculture and food production, as well as an emphasis on industrial crops and the improvement of potential pasture.

On August 21, the mandate territory is united for administrative purposes to the Belgian Congo and constitutes a Vice Government-General, but the territory retains its distinct juridical personality and its own finances and assets. The following is a diagram of the administrative structure of the country to the end of 1959:

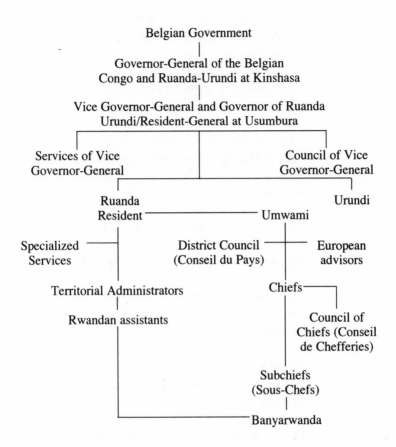

Belgian Government

Governor-General of the Belgian
Congo and Ruanda-Urundi at Kinshasa

Vice Governor-General and Governor of Ruanda
Urundi/Resident-General at Usumbura

Services of Vice
Governor-General

Council of Vice
Governor-General

Ruanda
Resident

Urundi

Umwami

Specialized
Services

District Council
(Conseil du Pays)

European
advisors

Territorial Administrators

Chiefs

Rwandan assistants

Council of
Chiefs (Conseil
de Chefferies)

Subchiefs
(Sous-Chefs)

Banyarwanda

Source: Murego Donat, Le Révolution rwandaise; 1958–1962: Essai d'interprétation (Louvain: Publications de l'Institut des Sciences Politiques et Sociales, 1975), p. 481 and Centre de Recherches Scientifiques du Ruanda-Urundi de l'Institut pour la Recherche Scientifique en Afrique Centrale, Compte-rendu des Travaux du Séminaire d'anthropologie sociale (Astrida: IRSAC, 1952), p. 73.

The administration requires all chiefs and subchiefs to plant and manage a half-hectare of industrial crops, such as coffee or peanuts.

On October 2, Prince Leopold of Belgium visits Kabgayi.

Until November 15, Royal High Commissioner Alfred Marzorati administers the mandate, but then leaves for his vacation. He is replaced by Pierre Ryckmans, Resident of Urundi.

The common currency becomes the Congolese franc.

Busozo experiences military occupation.

1926   Three hierarchies of Tutsi authority—*chef de l'ubutaka, chef de l'umukenke,* and *chef d'ingabo*—are abolished.

On March 29 an ordinance is issued by the governor-general sanctioning the establishment of separate quarters in urban areas for Europeans.

On December 17, Alfred Marzorati resumes his post as royal high commissioner and vice governor-general of the mandate. Pierre Ryckman returns to his post of Resident of Urundi.

1927   The seat of local government is transferred from Usumbura to Astrida (now Butare).

On February 25, the Station Expérimentale d'Agriculture at Lusunya closes, and is replaced by the more centralized station at Rubona, situated between Nyanza and Astrida, and a second station at Ndendezi.

Société Coloniale des Produits Tannants et Agricoles (PROTANAG) receives a concession of 7,000 hectares in the Shangugu region.

Corvée due to Tutsi notables from Hutu is reduced by the Belgian administration from two days out of five to one day out of seven.

Official reports note that the Association des Intérêts Coloniaux Belges creates the Association Belge d'Agriculture Tropicale et Subtropicale in its general assembly on February 14 at Brussels. On April 29, the Association Belge d'Agriculture Tropicale et Subtropicale holds its inaugural meeting at Brussels.

Very little rain in November and December, but some crops survive. Dryness persists in the southern part of the country. The administration announces the receipt of a credit of 50,000 BF for the residents of the mandate to purchase seed. The administration refuses to suspend the exportation of foodstuffs because the situation is not serious.

Government imposes the cultivation of coffee trees as a profitable crop.

1928   Administration reports that there has been very little rain. Central and southern regions are abnormally dry.

Coffee campaign initiated during the previous year halted on account of the famine.

In March, an insurrection led by Dungutsi, the son of Lwabugiri and half brother of Musinga, and considered by some to be the legitimate *umwami*, begins in northern Rwanda.

Dungutsi's attack comes from neighboring Uganda with about one hundred men; they occupy the area north of Lake Baferu, and the Hima. Dungutsi is proclaimed *umwami*.

On March 24, the insurgents, numbering about two thousand, attack Mukano Hill, held by the Tutsi chief Lukeratabaro. The insurgents are repulsed.

On March 25, the Resident orders a military expedition to the area.

From March 31 to April 3, the insurgents are attacked in the marshes near Kumushuri in neighboring Muyumbu and at Butoro.

From April 4 to 14 the region is calm and the revolt is contained as troops patrol the neighboring hills looking for Dungutsi, who has crossed the border into Uganda.

On April 16, six Hima notables submit to Belgian authorities; the Resident ends the military operation but not the occupation. He announces that fifty-one people were killed or missing as a result of the disturbance. Partisans of Dungutsi have burned about forty-three Tutsi farms and have stolen about one hundred head of cattle and about twenty sheep and goats. In retaliation Tutsi plunder and set fire to about a thousand granaries and homesteads near the border.

At the general meeting of administrators on July 21, they decide to settle the issue of diverse work prestations. Prestations of a general nature in the chiefdoms are reduced to a maximum of forty-eight days per year, while traditional prestations due to chiefs and subchiefs are reduced to fifteen days per year.

PROTANAG begins work in Shangugu, preparing the land for planting *black wattle (arbre à tanin)* and coffee nurseries.

Territory is administered by Vice Governor-General, Alfred Marzorati, but because of illness A. Jamoulle, the judicial advisor *(le conseille juridique),* is placed in charge after October 20.

1928–1929   Famine conditions in Rukiga; region is placed under military occupation. Gisaka, Gatsibo, Kigali, and Nyanza are also affected.

1929   Territory administered by Governor Marzorati until his departure for a holiday on February 3. Vice governor-general of the Belgian Congo M. H. Postiaux assumes the function of governor in his absence.

Belgian administrators implement various reforms. They abolish fiefs smaller than twenty-five taxpayers, or *ibikingi*. The power to condemn or sentence Africans to detention is invested in African tribunals. Corvée and work prestations are reduced from 146 days for each Hutu family to 52 days for each family per year, and they hold individual corvée to a maximum of 13 days per year for each able-bodied adult male.

Ordinance No. 18 of June 28 fixes new procedures for determining the selling price, rental fees, and location of state land *(terres domaniales).*

Royal decree of October 19 determines the property rights of individuals whose titles were conferred during German occupation.

Military presence in Rukiga in the territory of Gatsibu is increased to a platoon and one section.

Cattle at Rukiga suffer from pests.

The Groupe Scolaire is established by the Frères de la Charité de Gand at Astrida (now Butare).

According to law, each family must provide at least ten kilos of seeds for sowing and at least sixty kilos of food for each household.

Compagnie de la Rusizi introduces the cultivation of cotton in the Bugarama region of Kinyaga.

1930   Charles Voisin is appointed governor-general of the territory.

September 25, Governor Voisin begins his reform policy, meant to reorganize the traditional political structure.

Grasshopper infestation destroys crops, and the administration abolishes the coffee campaign because too many plants are neglected.

Belgian administration halts labor recruitment for the Katanga mines.

Several African farmers begin cotton production in the Ruzizi Valley.

1931   Government announces that the Ministry of Colonies' negotiations with various transport companies have resulted in tariff reductions.

Beginning January 1, la Compagnie du Chemin de Fer du Congo's charge for transporting coffee is twenty centimes per metric ton instead of forty-three centimes.

Le Comité National du Kivu's charge is reduced by 30 percent for shipment of freight on Lake Kivu, and la Campagnie Maritime Belge's (Lloyd Royal) freight charge from Matadi to Antwerp is reduced 33 percent.

Biumba (southeast of Mulera, northwest of Gatsibu, and north of Kigali) becomes a new territory.

Compulsory coffee cultivation program begins. The chief of every chieftaincy must plant 1,000 trees, each subchieftaincy must cultivate 250 coffee plants, and each farmer must plant 54 coffee trees.

Food crops are expanded considerably. Each family unit is required to plant thirty-five ares in food crops and twenty-five ares in nonseasonal crops, of which one-fifteenth must be devoted to manioc.

A polygamy tax is introduced, and on July 17 the administration initiates a head tax, or *impôt de capitation*.

On September 24, the administration passes Ordinance No. 64 (JUST) which prohibits blacks from traveling between the hours of 9:00 p.m. and 5:00 a.m.

On November 12, *umwami* Musinga is deposed by the Belgians in favor of his son, Charles Rudahigwa Mutara (1931–1959).

On November 14, a royal party consisting of the deposed king, Musinga, his mother and his wife, as well as his younger children and a number of servants, leaves for exile at Kamembe.

On November 16, Rudahigwa Mutara is proclaimed king. To commemorate his investiture, he announces that prestations in kind and in work provided by the population for the *umwami* are to be replaced by a tax payment of 1 BF (Belgian franc) annually for every taxpayer.

On November 21, the governor-general passes Ordinance No. 90 (AE), describing how African coffee from the mandate will be packaged and labeled for export.

Christian Missionary Society (CMS) constructs hospital at Kigeme.

Consolidation of chieftaincies is complete, and Port Kagera on the Kagera River in Tanganika Territory is opened for domestic and international traffic.

Administration notes that at year's end 40,510 coffee trees have been planted in the country.

1932   Charles Voisin continues as vice governor-general until June 8; G. Mortehan acts as vice governor-general from June 8 to August 8, until the arrival of Eugene Jungers, appointed vice governor-general of the territory as of June 30.

In March and April, the administration creates new coffee nurseries, estimated at 6 million seedlings. It also issues a series of decrees to regulate the commercialization and manufacture of African coffee, to include licensing, the prices paid to coffee growers, and quality controls.

Belgian administration introduces prestation reforms to relieve the burden on the Hutu and to regularize their administration.

On October 14, the administration passes an ordinance creating minimum payment of 7 or 11 BF per week for rations in kind.

Economic crisis is quite severe: custom duties and taxes are greatly reduced, receipts have declined by more than 50 percent, and requests for concessions are declining. The government is pursuing a policy of reducing expenditures, particularly in the areas of salaries and allowances to European personnel and the cost of matériel, which has produced a savings of 16 percent.

Crisis in commercial sector as well, particularly with non-African agricultural enterprises. Some have abandoned their operations in sisal and coffee; others have reduced their activities; while a few have expanded food crops because the profits are immediate.

The administration notes that the cotton crop is plagued by attacks by locusts and damage by rose worm and other parasites.

The queen mother, Kankazi, constructs her residence at Shyogwe.

The government reopens the old medical dispensary at Rugabagoba.

1933   Prestations in foodstuffs are replaced by a money payment from each taxpayer for the hill chief and the chieftain.

Kinyamateka, a fortnightly magazine devoted to economics, is founded at Kigali.

For the coffee campaign of 1934–1935, the administration plants 10 million seedlings in October, and compels each taxpayer to plant at least 54 coffee trees. It warns farmers that the Agricultural Service will examine planting very closely.

From June to December, the administration transports 560 tons of food to the chieftaincies of Kalinda and Kivu because of food shortages and notes that precipitation for the last three months of the year is irregular and insufficient.

On October 15, *umwami* Rudahigwa marries Nyiramakomari of the Bagesera clan.

In November and December, the administration distributes only 400,000 coffee plants.

Catholic mission station is established at Kaduha.

1934   Rains in January are vigorous and much longer than usual.

February 17, King Albert I dies accidentally when he falls from a high rock at Marche-les-Dames. Leopold III becomes king of Belgium.

Rainfall levels in February and March are much lower than average.

Outbreak of cattle infestation *(peste bovine)*.

Prestations in foodstuffs from the first harvest *(ibikunikwa)* are replaced by a money payment from each taxpayer for the chiefs and subchiefs.

Tribute payment *(ikoro)* due to the *umwami* is replaced by a money payment for each taxpayer.

Catholic mission station is established at Kibeho.

New cassiterite mine opens in Kibuye territory, and the administration announces the construction of the Mwogo bridge and the opening of the Mutara dairy at Nyanza.

Rains in October, November, and December abundant and regular.

The administration reports that by the end of the year it has planted 801,000 coffee trees in the country.

1934–1935   A Seventh-Day Adventist mission is founded at Rwankeri in Ruhengeri.

1935   In March, some 300 to 500 mountain folks, led by a clan elder, are arrested when they take control of Nyanza out of fear of being vaccinated with vaccine allegedly tainted by Tutsi. The *umwami* and a contingent of police are able to calm them. The provocateurs are given various prison terms for the disturbance.

In April, the coach road between Ruhengeri and Kabale (Uganda) is open to traffic. Since the road construction program began, the administration has built 6,000 kilometers of roads.

Ordinance No. 90 (AE) of November 21, 1931, pertaining to packaging and labeling of African coffee for export, becomes operative.

Catholic mission station established at Nyanza and Muyunzwe, and the Grand Séminaire is constructed at Nyakibanda, as well as a mission station at Janja in Ruhengeri.

1935–1936   Cerebrospinal meningitis epidemic.

Catholic mission post founded at Nemba in Ruhengeri.

1936   Administration reports adequate rainfall for the year.

Outbreak of aphtha-trypanosome fever (a bovine infestation) in Ruhengeri.

Rural dispensary opens at Gitare in Ruhengeri.

European colons begin to cultivate pyrethrum in the northern Kivu and Rwanda.

1937   January 1, the administration establishes the Fonds Temporaire de Crédit Agricole, to finance diverse projects, such as extension and exploitation of cultivation, the maintenance and replacement of equipment, and the purchase of materials needed for the conservation and treatment of agricultural products.

January 22, the king and Belgian parliament issue a royal decree creating an Office of Colonization as part of the Ministry of Colonies.

League of Nations expresses concern about the excessive amount of taxation in the African sector and notes that taxes on Europeans have not increased in the same proportion.

Territorial administration establishes indigenous savings banks.

The administration passes several ordinances: the

decree of September 24 maintains that mining agreements have to be obtained and approved by the government, and a second decree restricts the movement of Africans in European urban areas between 10 p.m. and 4:30 a.m. unless required by duties in a public service.

1938   Administration reports the month of May is excessively dry, and precipitation is quite irregular.

On July 22, the administration passes a decree prohibiting the creation of new coffee plantations in the European sector, including the replacement of old coffee trees. The decree does not apply to African coffee planters.

Administration studies traditional work prestations and decides to maintain some of them because they symbolize allegiance, power, and prestige for the traditional aristocracy; however, certain categories of corvée can be substituted or purchased by a money payment of thirteen francs for thirteen days of work due annually.

Catholic mission stations are established at Kamonyi, Kanyanza, and Mugambwe.

Administration reports that the month of November is abnormally dry.

Administration reports the coffee pests and infestations are declining. *Antestia, lygus,* and *volumnus* have been declining in the Kivu and Ruhengeri since the Agricultural Service introduced the cultivation of pyrethrum in the higher altitude zones in 1937.

Administration also notes that coffee prices on the world market have declined 37 percent for *café dé-parche* and 40 percent for *café en parche*.

Tilapia is introduced by the administration as a protein supplement for the population. The fish come from ponds and streams in Uganda and the Belgian Congo.

1939   Eugene Jungers is governor-general of the mandate, and A. Gille is Resident to January 24. His replacement is Maurice Simon.

Contract workers, large-animal breeders, catechists, and individuals who had been absent from their place of residence for at least nine months could purchase *corvée* or *ubuletwa* obligations.

Government passes ordinance prohibiting the transportation and purchase of damp or moist *(humide)* coffee, directed at transactions between Hindu merchants and African planters.

1940   Eugene Jungers continues as governor-general of the mandate. Maurice Simon continues as Resident until September 9; his replacement is J. Paradis.

Administration notes that World War II has increased the growth of labor migration to Uganda, and that this has strained agricultural and industrial development in the mandate.

Musinga's residence in exile is moved from Kamembe to Moba in the vicinity of Albertville.

For fiscal purposes, the regions of Kibuye and Gabiro are abolished and their chieftaincies are attached to neighboring territories.

De Vleeschauwer, minister of colonies, visits.

1941   On February 1, the government passes an ordinance, No. 26 (AE), creating the Commission des Devises et des Importations, which exercises control over commercial trade.

1942   On January 18, *umwami* Rudahigwa marries Rosalie Gicanda, a Catholic convert.

Eugene Jungers is governor-general of the territory, and J. Paradis continues as Resident to April 14. His replacement is Grauls, who serves as Resident until July 1. J. Paradis returns as Resident from July 1 to September 21, and is again replaced by Grauls.

The Algrain Bridge over the Nyabarongo River thirteen kilometers from Kigali collapses.

1943   On March 10, the governor-general's ordinance of December 26, 1942, prohibiting the purchase of beverages in excess of 4 percent fermented alcohol or 2.4 percent distilled alcohol, becomes law.

Ordinance No. 347 (AIMO) of October 4, governing the lawful absence of Africans for more than thirty days without a "transfer passport" from a chief or his deputy, is passed.

Ordinance No. 70 (AIMO) of November 20 gives the Resident the power to impose the cultivation of food, forestation, and antierosion work, and the use of natural fertilizer in the African sector.

Last quarter of the year is excessively dry.

On October 17, *umwami* Mutara Rudahigwa is baptized.

1943–1944   Famine *(ruzagajura)* conditions in Nyanza, Butare, Kibungu, Byumba, Kigali, Kisenyi, Kibuye, and Ruhengeri.

1944   Eugene Jungers is governor-general of the territory.

Outbreak of cattle infestation *(peste bovine)* in Kisenyi and Shangugu caused by bad vaccine.

Musinga dies at Moba.

Payment for *corvée* obligations becomes optional for all Africans.

The Christian Missionary Society (CMS) establishes a mission at Shyogwe.

The Catholics create a mission station at Byimana.

In December, the decree prohibiting new coffee plantations in the European sector is suspended.

1944–1945   Minor smallpox epidemic and outbreak of bacillus dysentery in Ruhengeri and Kisenyi.

1945   The post of Resident rotates between Georges-Victor Sandrart and Grauls during the year.

Military camp is constructed at Rwesero-Nyanza;

Catholic mission stations are founded at Nyumba and Gisagara.

On September 10, the Office des Cafés Indigènes du Ruanda-Urundi (OCIRU) is established to promote the growth and trade of African arabica coffee. The office is also dedicated to the improvement of production, processing, and conditioning of coffee.

On September 11, an ordinance by the governor of the mandate recognizes the division of urban districts into segregated European, Asian, and African areas and maintains that those who wish to establish a domicile or business in a quarter other than that allotted to him must secure a special permit valid for one year.

L'Ami, a periodical for Catholic *évolués,* begins publication at Kabgayi.

1946   Eugene Jungers is governor-general of the mandate to July 2 when he is nominated vice governor-general of the Belgian Congo.

Smallpox epidemic and bacillus dysentery continues in Ruhengeri and Kisenyi.

Bridge is constructed over the Kayumbu River, and piers for the Nyabarongo bridge are constructed at Mwaka.

Fonds d'Egalisation, or Coffee Stabilization Fund, is established, in order to provide technical assistance, such as free saws, pruning shears, drying trays, and to finance certain studies designed to improve farming methods and to promote coffee.

The Belgian government passes ordinances on April 6 establishing the Commission du Travail et du Progrès Social Indigène (the African labor and social progress commission).

On May 10, the government passes a decree regulating the organization of African trade unions.

The Association des Anciens Elèves du Groupe Scolaire d'Astrida begins to publish the *Bulletin de Jurisprudence des Tribunaux Indigènes du Ruanda-Urundi* on a semiannual basis.

1947   Administration notes the rainfall for the beginning of the year is regular and abundant.

Administration abolishes whipping by chiefs and subchiefs of those who have violated administrative laws.

African tribunal is constructed at Gisagara, and a rural dispensary opens at Murambi in Kibali.

On March 4, governmental decree establishes the Conseil du Vice-Gouvernement-Général for the mandate. The council is advisory and is composed of twenty-five individuals. There are no Africans on the council.

Ordinance No. 1/47 of March 7 prohibits Africans from selling peas, maize, beans, wheat, and potatoes in Kitega, Muramvya, Ngozi, and Bururi. Violations bring from one to seven days imprisonment and a maximum fine of 200 francs.

On March 17, credit facilities are established for those Africans who wish to purchase, construct, or convert homes with durable and semidurable material.

On May 16, the government passes an ordinance regulating the commercialization of African coffee, which cannot be sold or purchased by Africans without the permission of the governor.

An ordinance, No. 40 (TF) of May 22, is passed to modify the arrangements of the decree of January 10, 1940, which concerned free concessions of land granted to old functionaries and agents of the colony.

Ordinance No. 200 (AGRI) of June 24 requires importers of European coffee to obtain a special license from customs before exportation.

On July 1, the Institute for Scientific Research in Central Africa (IRSAC) is established to encourage, promote, and coordinate in Belgian Africa the study of the human and natural sciences. IRSAC is a semigovernmental institution.

Precipitation in October and November is irregular.

1948   United Nations delegation to the trust territory tours the country from July 28 to August 11.

Construction of a housing project built with durable local materials begins at Ciarwa near Butare.

On December 4, the administration creates the Fonds d'Egalisation by Ordinance No. 53/421, designed to regulate the market price of arabica coffee and to promote economic and social development in the African sector.

On December 31, the Fonds d'Egalisation takes effect.

1949   On January 1, compulsory redemption (purchase of exemption) from *corvée* (forced labor) becomes effective.

On April 25, the treaty between Belgium and the United Nations concerning the Trusteeship Agreement for Ruanda and Urundi is ratified.

On April 28, *umwami* Rudahigwa arrives in Belgium for a state visit until May 17.

Trading centers are created at Kaduba, Karamb, Remera, and Gacurabwenge.

On August 1, an ordinance is passed providing compensation to workers for injuries resulting from employment accidents and occupational diseases.

On August 16, the government issues a decree to simplify the formal requirements for establishing cooperatives, and vesting advisory and supervisory functions in the Belgian administration.

Anti-malaria campaign financed by the Indigenous Welfare Fund begins with the disinfestation of African huts.

Labor recruitment for the Katanga mines resumes. Union Minière du Haut-Katanga is the principal recruiter.

1950   Léon Pétillon is provisional governor of the territory.

On March 16 and 21, the government announces measures relating to the inspection of working conditions, industrial safety, and sanitary conditions in the workplace.

On April 28, the administration passes an ordinance subjecting the purchaser of African arabica coffee to obtain a "license of purchase" issued by the administration.

District administrative center is established at Rwesero-Nyanza, a rural dispensary opens at Gatonde in Bukonya, and in August a building for the African tribunal is constructed at Munini.

On August 1, King Leopold announces that he will delegate all royal power to his son, Prince Baudouin, thus agreeing to abdication.

1951   In February, the Ten-Year Plan is submitted to the Colonial Ministry in Brussels.

Trading center is established at Butare.

In June, the Belgian administration in compliance with the United Nations Visiting Mission's wishes, abolishes corporal punishment carried out by indigenous courts.

On July 16, Prince Baudouin becomes king of Belgium.

August 1–13, the United Nations Visiting Mission to the Trustee Territories tours the country.

The administration begins construction of a fish-breeding center at Kigembe.

1952   Léon Pétillon is governor of the territory until A. Claeys Boúúaert, the new governor of the mandate, assumes his duties as of May 27.

On July 14, a governmental decree is issued establishing four types of councils and membership—subchiefdom, chiefdom, district, and the High Council of State. Members of the subchiefdom councils are to be selected by an electoral college consisting of notables whose names will be selected from a list prepared by the subchiefs, taking into account the preference of the inhabitants. The other councils are to consist partly of subchiefs or chiefs, ex officio members (notables elected indirectly by an electoral body appointed by members of the lower council), and co-opted members. These councils have advisory powers to territorial officials. The formation of these councils leads to a surge of political activity in the country.

Bridge is constructed over the Akavuguto-Cyahinda at Mbasa. The administration also builds a medical dispensary at Gikongoro and creates a trading center at Ruhashya.

Catholic mission posts are established at Kinoni and Murama, and a Petit Séminaire is constructed at Murama in Ruhengeri.

Coffee yields are low because of bad weather and very heavy attacks of *antestiopsis* and *dieback*.

The monthly *Bulletin de la Banque Centrale du Congo Belge et du Ruanda-Urundi* begins publication.

1953   The territory of Kibuye is reconstituted.

INEAC creates a *paysannat* (farming community) at Muhero-Ntyazo.

Consumer cooperatives for mine workers are established at Rutongo and Rwinkwavu.

In the Subchiefdom Council *(conseils de sous-chef)* elections, the Tutsi retain the majority except in Ruhengeri. Hutu representation in all provinces or districts is about 25 percent, and they gain only three seats of the fifteen available.

1954   On January 30, the Impara Cooperative of African Coffee Planters is established (in Shangugu territory).

From August 1 to August 10, the United Nations Visiting Mission to Trustee Territories tours the country.

Ubuhake is abolished.

1955   Jean-Paul Harroy is appointed governor-general of the mandate territory.

L'Ami and *Bulletin de Jurisprudence des Tribunaux Indigènes du Ruanda-Urundi* cease publication. The former becomes the weekly *Temps Nouveaux*.

Hobe (or "young people"), a monthly periodical in Kinyarwanda, is established at Kigali.

World coffee prices are declining.

A decree of October 26 establishes the Université Officielle du Congo Belge et du Ruanda-Urundi at Elizabethville for students of Belgian Africa, including the mandate territory.

1956   Subchiefdom Council elections from September to December.

Jean-Paul Harroy is governor of the mandate as of November.

Aloys Munyangaju, a native of Save, publishes *Soma*, a newspaper critical of the abusive power of the Tutsi chiefs specifically and discrimination in Rwandan society generally.

1957   In March, nine Hutu intellectuals issue the Bahutu Manifesto. The document criticizes the social, economic, and political monopoly of the Tutsi.

The High Council of the State (Ruanda) issues the Statement of Views concerning the political, economic, and social development of the country.

By a royal order on March 26, the Council of the Vice Government-General is replaced by a General Council of forty-five members for the mandate territory.

In June, the Mouvement Social Hutu is formed, and on June 26 the mandate receives $4.8 million from the International Bank for Reconstruction and Development for port construction at Bujumbura and for the first section of the thirty-two kilometer road connecting Bujumbura to Kigali.

From July 29 to August 3, the General Council for the mandate territory holds its first meeting.

From September 24 to October 5, the United Nations Mission to Trust Territories visits the country.

Joseph Habyarymana Gitera creates the Association pour la Promotion Sociale de la Masse (APROSOMA) and uses the association's newspaper, *Ijwi rya rubanda rugafi* (The Voice of the Common People) to attack the social system, the privileges of the Tutsi, the court of the *umwami*, and the Kalinga (drum).

The Nkora African Coffee Cooperative is formed in Kisenyi territory.

1958   In January, Joseph Gitera of APRSOSOMA asks the *umwami* to have the High Council of State study the relations between the Hutu and Tutsi.

Le Mouvement Social Muhutu is formed with its seat at Kabgayi (in Nyanza territory) and focuses on economic, social, and moral development. Its leader is a Hutu journalist.

The administration also reports on the formation of the Association pour la Promotion Sociale de la Masse (APROSOMA) which calls for independence.

Its seat is at Save and its leader is Joseph Gitera, who is also an editor.

Umwami Mutara Rudahigwa consents in April to establishing a special commission on social relations, consisting of Tutsi and Hutu, to study social problems and to submit recommendations to the High Council.

In June, the High Council of Ruanda considers the recommendations of the report of the Hutu-Tutsi Committee, which include administrative and judicial appointments for Hutu, as well as educational opportunities for Hutu children.

Umwami Mutara Rudahigwa visits Belgium.

The administration abolishes the cultivation of compulsory food crops, and it announces the formation of four new cooperatives—the Bandaga African Coffee Cooperative, the Bukago African Coffee Cooperative, the Nyamuswaga African Coffee Cooperative, and TRAFIPRO.

The country's economy is separated administratively from that of the Belgian Congo.

Chemical fertilizer is used on a trial basis in the cultivation of arabica coffee, particularly in the regions of heavy coffee density and in areas that show promise.

1959   On January 1, Gitarama becomes a distinct territory, created from a portion of Nyanza territory.

The Hutu rebellion against Tutsi overrule begins.

On April 16, the Working Group is formed in Belgium to study the political and social problems in the mandate.

On April 22, the Working Group arrives in the trust territory.

On April 28, the report from the Commission on Political Reform is approved by the High Council and is submitted to the Working Group.

Members of APROSOMA and the Hutu Social Movement meet with the Working Group.

The Working Group leaves the country for Belgium.

In June, an anonymous leaflet is distributed and signed by "the Warrior-Defenders of Rwanda." It denounces Hutu leadership and announces the death of APROSOMA and of Joseph Gitera, "who have sold [out] Ruanda."

On July 25, Mutara Rudahigwa, the *umwami*, dies mysteriously in Bujumbura. News accounts note that after attending a showing of the film *The Lords of the Forest* at Usumbura, he went to see his medical adviser and during the visit was given an antibiotic injection. He died shortly afterward.

On July 28, the burial of *umwami* Mutara Rudahigwa takes place on *Mwima* Hill, near Nyanza in an atmosphere of extreme tension.

Rudahigwa died without a descendant; thus he is succeeded by his brother, Kigeri Ndahindurwa

(1959–1960), who is declared the new *umwami* by the *abiru* and without the consent of Belgian authorities.

In August, Union National Rwandaise (UNAR) becomes the first political party in the country. It is pro-monarchy, pro-Tutsi, and anti-Belgian.

On September 13, UNAR holds its first meeting at Kigali, with about 2,000 people in attendance.

On September 14, Rassemblement Démocratique Ruandais (RADER) is established at Kigali. President of the central committee is Prosper Bwanakweri.

On September 20, UNAR holds a meeting at Astrida, and a large number of APROSOMA supporters hold a counterdemonstration against the UNAR leaders.

On September 24, monsignors Birgir*umwami* and Perraudin, the apostolic vicars of Nyundo and Kabgayi, respectively, in confidential circular letters to their respective Catholic priests warn them against the UNAR party, which according to their letters wishes to have a monopoly on patriotism and represents a trend closely resembling national socialism. The party wishes to remove the schools from mission control and advocates national service for young people. The pastoral letters make references to the party's alleged pro-communist and pro-Islamic sentiments.

On September 27, UNAR holds a meeting at Gitarama.

In October, the administration notes that the political situation in the country is deteriorating.

On October 9, the all-Hutu Parti du Mouvement de l'Emancipation Hutu (PARMEHUTU) is formed at Kigali from the Mouvement Social Hutu, and it issues its manifesto. Its president is Grégoire Kayibanda.

On the same day, *umwami* Kigeri Ndahindurwa is sworn in at Kigali.

On October 10, the governor of the mandate issues an order prohibiting political meetings, because of increasing tensions and the potential for conflict.

On October 11, monsignors Birgir*umwami* and Perraudin issue a second pastoral letter warning against APROMOSA. They believe that the party's statements inflame racial hatred. The two bishops also reproach the party for distorting certain remarks regarding the Kalinga (the royal drum of Rwanda).

On October 17, from 200 to 300 people demonstrate against the decision made by the vice governor-general to discipline three chiefs whose "attitudes and speeches constitute a grave lack of respect to their offices."

On October 25, an anonymous leaflet is posted on trees in the Nyanza district denouncing the "enemies of Ruanda, of the kingdom and of the Kalinga." It lists the names of ten RADER and Hutu leaders, saying that their chief was Monsignor Perraudin of Kabgayi, and "all of these [people] are traitors to Ruanda [because they wished to maintain colonial rule and wanted] the death of H.M. Kigeli V and the overthrow of the kingdom of Ruanda." It asks that the people unite and "whatever the cost, seek out these enemies of Ruanda and their off-spring and purge Ruanda of this bad seed. Let us march forward and exterminate all these snakes, the enemies of Ruanda."

In November, Joseph Gitera transforms APROMOSA into a political party.

The government periodical in Kinyarwanda, *Imvaho*, is published by the Service d'Information from the Belgian residence of Kigali.

The disturbance of November 1 begins when Dominique Mbonyumutwa, a Hutu subchief and leader of PARMEHUTU is attacked at Byimana in Gitarama by a band of young Tutsi, who are supporters of UNAR. In retaliation, Hutu attack a Tutsi chief who belongs to UNAR. Across the country, Hutu bands set fire to thousands of Tutsi huts. The Tutsi retaliate, killing several Hutu leaders. By the end of the year, several hundred people have been arrested or killed.

On November 2, groups of Hutu begin to demonstrate at Gitarama in front of the quarters of Swahili merchants known to be supporters of UNAR. Other groups of Hutu attack the house of Chief Haguma, a Tutsi, destroying his banana and coffee plantations. A platoon is sent from Kigali to Gitarama to restore order.

On November 3, rumors circulate that Mbonyumutwa has died; Hutu demonstrators, protesting in front of the home of Chief Gaashagaza, attack and kill two Tutsi notables visiting the chief and wound several others. The same day another band of Hutu pillage the house of Tutsi subchief Biriguza of

Ndiza after beating him and several Tutsi visitors. Hutu begin to pillage and set fire to thousands of huts throughout Ndiza. District administrator from the residency of Kigali arrives in Gitarama to assess the situation.

On November 4, the Tutsi subchief Ruhinguka is attacked and killed in the neighboring chiefdom of Marangaza. Pillaging and fires continue at Ndiza, and reports indicate they have spread to Marangaza and Rukoma in the Gitarama district and to Bumbogo in the district of Kigali.

On November 5, fires spread to Kingogo, to Kanage and Bushivu in the Kisenyi district, and to Kibali in the Ruhengeri district.

On November 6, fires are observed in the chiefdoms of Buberuka, Bugarura, and Bukonya in the Ruhengeri district and in those of Bwishaza and Budana-Nyantango in the Kibuye district. Tutsi leaders mount an offensive, and by November 10 they arrest or kill Hutu leaders, including Secyugu, a Hutu trader and known supporter of PARMEHUTU. Others are assassinated.

On the same day, reinforcements arrive from the Belgian Congo, bringing the strength of the security forces to seventeen platoons, and the governor places the entire country under a state of "military operation" *(opération militaire)*. All the civil and military authorities are under the command of Colonel Guillaume Logiest.

On November 7, rioters are operating in the Bugoyi chiefdom in the Kisenyi district and moving out from Ruhengeri to the Biumba district.

On November 8, fires spread to Mulera and Rwankeri in the extreme northern portion of the Ruhengeri district. Troops at Mabanza, in an attempt to disperse rioters, kill two and wound two others. At Nyondo, where the Tutsi organize their defense, several people are wounded and six are killed. Innocent Mukwiye Polepole, a councillor of APROSOMA, is attacked and killed.

On November 9, the Governor and *umwami* Kigeri Ndahindurwa issue jointly the proclamation of military operation, which places a ban on all gatherings, restricts road traffic, applies a curfew between 6 p.m. and 5:30 a.m., and pacifies the interior by authorizing security forces to use arms. The governor requests additional companies from the Belgian Congo, including two companies of Belgian paratroopers.

On November 10, Joseph Kanyaruka, secretary and treasurer of APROSOMA, is attacked and killed in Urundi, where he had fled with his family and livestock. In Ruanda, Belgian authorities take military action to restore order.

The governor declares a state of emergency in all the districts and provinces of the country and appoints Colonel Guillaume Logiest as Military Resident in place of the Resident. Under the state of emergency, the military could sentence people to house arrest and ban publications, meetings, and associations.

On the same day, the Belgian government publishes the report of the Working Group formed to study the political problems of the mandate territory.

On November 12, the country is placed under military rule (*régime militaire*).

On November 17, Military Resident Colonel Logiest prohibits all meetings, both public and private, because of mounting tensions in the country.

On November 27, two companies of paratroopers leave the territory.

On November 30, Colonel Logiest cancels the curfew and restores freedom of movement.

On December 5, the governor announces in a special communiqué the Belgian government's decision to place the country under a special Resident system and its appointment of Colonel Logiest as Special Civilian Resident.

On December 25, in an interim decree, the government announces a political reorganization program designed to give a progressive measure of autonomy to Rwanda. Under the reform, subchiefdoms would be enlarged and, along with extratribal centers, would be reintegrated into the administration as communes. The existing subchiefdoms, extratribal centers, and urban *circonscriptions,* would become provisional communes which would elect their councils by universal suffrage during the first half of 1960. At the state level a new state council would be established and would exercise, jointly with the *umwami*, the local legislative powers which would be progressively assigned to it. The majority of the members of the new state council would be elected by indirect suffrage by an electoral college composed of the councils of the provisional communes. The election of councils of the provisional communes would take place early enough for the council to take office in the second half of 1960. Alongside of the state legislature, a government would be set up whose head and departmental heads would be appointed or removed from office by the *umwami* in agreement with the Resident. The *umwami* as constitutional head of the state would remain outside of the government and above political parties. He would not govern, and his public enactments would have to be countersigned by the government. Judiciary powers would remain with the colonial authorities.

Political disturbances during the past year and the abolition of compulsory food crops have resulted in a dangerous decrease in food reserves.

About 100 tons of tea are exported.

1960   Administration reports that the distinction between the traditional system and the administration has been abandoned.

From January to April, about 22,000 Tutsi are displaced by ethnic conflict.

On January 15, military rule ends.

On January 19, the resident-general in a public speech to the people of the mandate maintains that the proposed political reform program under the decree of December 25, 1959, shows "Belgium's determination to act [in good faith and] promptly [with] reform and . . . to bridge the gap between the past and the future."

On February 6, the government issues Ordinance No. 221/51, which abolishes the High Council of the State and its permanent delegations to the General Council. The powers of these bodies will be exercised by a Provisional Special Council composed of six members appointed by the Resident-General.

On February 14, the inauguration of the Provisional Special Council takes place at Kigali.

On February 28, the Provisional Special Council with the sanction of the *umwami* issues a circular recognizing the legality of the four largest political parties and appeals for calm.

From March 8 to 21, the United Nations Visiting Mission to the Trustee Territories tours the country.

On June 30, Belgium grants independence to the Belgian Congo, and it becomes the Democratic Republic of the Congo, under the leadership of President Joseph Kasavubu and Prime Minister Patrice Lumumba.

In June and July, the Rwanda's first local elections are held amid violence. PARMEHUTU emerges from the elections with an overwhelming victory, winning 2,390 out of the 3,125 legislative seats, and taking 210 of the 229 newly created administrative units.

July 13, Moise Tshombe announces the secession of the Katanga province from the Democratic Republic of the Congo.

One hundred tons of tea are exported.

The *Bulletin de la Banque centrale du Congo Belge et du Ruanda-Urundi* ceases publication.

On October 18, a legislative ordinance sanctions

the formation of communes, and a second announces the dissolution of the Provisional Special Council created in February, and establishes in its place the Council and the Provisional government of Ruanda.

Administration reports very little rain for the year.

On December 29, the General Assembly of the United Nations recommends that legislative elections for the country be established at some future date.

Umwami Kigeri Ndahindurwa is deposed.

1961   In February, Patrice Lumumba is assassinated while in the custody of Moise Tshombe.

On January 25, Colonel Logiest, the Special Resident of Rwanda grants autonomy to the Provisional Government, which had been formed in October.

On January 28, the newly elected mayors and local officials meet at Gitarama to declare a Republic and to choose a legislative assembly.

On February 1, the Belgian government at Brussels sanctions the autonomous powers of the Rwandan government proclaimed at Gitarama on January 28.

On March 13, UNAR militants and refugees organize themselves into guerrilla bands, called *inyenzi* (cockroaches), and mount attacks on Hutu officials from Uganda, Burundi, Zaire, and Tanzania.

On December 9, Tanzania receives its independence from Great Britain.

1962   February and March, the *inyenzi* attack Biyumba from Uganda, killing a number of Hutu officials. In retaliation, Hutu massacre between 1,000 and 2,000 Tutsi.

On June 15, the *Bulletin Officiel du Ruanda-Urundi* ceases publication.

In July, Colonel Michel Micombero of Burundi creates a "government of public safety."

On July 1, Rwanda becomes independent with PARMEHUTU firmly in control of the political apparatus; Grégoire Kayibanda is the country's first president. Burundi achieves its independence on the same day.

On October 9, Uganda is granted independence from Great Britain and becomes a member of the British Commonwealth.

In November, *umwami* Charles Ndizeye of Burundi is deposed by Colonel Michel Micombero, and Micombero becomes president.

On November 24, a new constitution replaces the Rwandan constitution formulated during the *coup d'état de Gitarama.*

New international coffee agreement fixes coffee sales at 20,400 tons for the 1962–1963 season.

TRAFIPRO, a commercial cooperative originally established by the Catholic church, is currently being staffed and financed under a Swiss foreign aid program.

The information bulletin *Butare-Rwanda,* published by the Belgian friends of the Catholic diocese, begins publication.

1963   President and Prime Minister Grégoire Kayibanda presents his resignation to the legislative assembly in June, but the assembly refuses to accept it.

Racial clashes occur between Tutsi and Hutu in November and December, particularly on the nights of December 20 and 21. Conflict stems from the armed actions of *inyenzi* from Burundi. Troops from both countries gather at the frontier. *Inyenzi* conduct isolated raids from Burundi into the southern portion of the country. These incursions are repulsed, but in retaliation Hutu kill an estimated 1,000 Tutsi, with many more fleeing the country.

The government executes about twenty prominent Tutsi.

Banque Commerciale du Rwanda SARL is established at Kigali.

Tea emerges as a significant export crop with the exportation of 300 tons.

December 31, the economic union with Burundi, particularly the Customs Union, OCIRU and the Central Bank, is officially dissolved.

Catholic diocese at Butare sponsors the publication of the review *Etudiants en Vacances*.

The Université Radiophonique is established at Gitarama.

1964   Special representative of United Nations secretary-general notes that a quarter of a million Tutsi still reside in the country after the "troubles," and that some 45 percent of all of Rwanda's administrative services are still staffed by Tutsi. They also form the majority of all secondary school teachers.

Banque Nationale de la République Rwandaise and the Caisse d'Epargne du Rwanda are established at Kigali.

PARMEHUTU moves to consolidate its power: the principal leaders of RADER are eliminated; those from APROSOMA are excluded from leadership positions.

Government establishes the Office des Cultures Industrielles du Rwanda (OCIR), and in April it begins to publish the quarterly, *Bulletin de Statistique du Rwanda*.

Tea exports amount to 320 tons.

The country's economy is officially separated administratively from that of Burundi.

A research center, the Institut pour la Recherche Scientifique en Afrique Centrale (IRSAC) becomes the Institut National de Recherche Scientifique (INRS).

1965   Grégoire Kayibanda is reelected as president, and the Parti du Mouvement de l'Emancipation Hutu emerges as the unchallenged victor. In essence, the country becomes a single-party state.

On February 16, a technical aid agreement is signed with West Germany. The aid package is worth 5 million DM in the form of capital equipment and 2.8 million DM in technical assistance.

On February 17, the border with Uganda is closed. The initiative is taken by Uganda because of its quarrel with the Democratic Republic of the Congo.

On November 24, General Joseph Mobutu seizes power in the Congo, and ousts Joseph Kasavubu in a bloodless military coup.

1966   Rwanda announces devaluation of the currency.

In March, the United States agrees to send food shipments and to grant financial credits to Rwanda to help with the stabilization of the economy. Aid agreement includes the shipment of flour, edible oil, and powdered milk, with an estimated value of $1.5 million.

In April, the International Monetary Fund announces a credit of $10.5 million to back the stabilization program. Belgium's participation under IMF auspices will provide 75 million BF to be used for importing Belgian products. About 30 million BF will be provided as a gift, and the remainder as a loan repayable in five years.

On September 27, technical and financial assistance agreement with Belgium is renewed in order to finance agricultural and other development projects (22 million BF), the installation of a system of radio controls at Kigali airport (56 million BF), and the construction of houses for civil servants (32 million BF). Other projects include the improvement of tourist facilities, aid for teaching, and hospital construction.

In November, the paving of 150 kilometers of the road between Kigali and Butare begins, as well as the construction of a hydroelectric power station at Moukungwo in the southern portion of the country.

Banque de Kigali SARL is established at Kigali.

In December, two thousand Tutsi attempt to invade the country from Burundi. Several hundred are killed in the fighting with the Rwandan National Guard.

Le Diapason, a journal published by the students of the National University of Rwanda, begins publication. The university administration begins to publish its own review, *L'Informateur.*

1967   New Five-Year Plan for 1967–1971 is designed to secure economic independence; social development for the country is introduced. The total value of the program is $113 million, of which 61 percent comes from the central government, 24 percent is derived from private sources, and 15 per cent emanates from industrial investment. In terms of allocations, 5.7 percent will be devoted to the productive sector, 28 percent to social investment, and 15 percent for economic infrastructure.

The International Monetary Fund grants an additional credit of $2 million for the stabilization program announced in April 1966, bringing the total credit at the IMF to $12.5 million, of which $5 million has already been withdrawn.

Banque Rwandaise de Développement SARL (BRD) is established at Kigali.

Urunana, published three times a year by the Grand Séminaire de Nyakibanda at Butare, is established.

In March, the bimonthly review *Dialogue,* which is edited at Kigali by Abbé J. Massion, a Belgian priest, is established.

On July 5, a price-control law is passed, intended to establish prices and profit margins for all products, domestic and foreign, traded in Rwanda, as well as to set charges for road transportation.

1968   OCIR (Office des Cultures Industrielles du Rwanda) and the Ministry of Agriculture and Animal Husbandry begin to publish the *Bulletin Agricole du Rwanda,* a quarterly periodical.

1969   In January, the European Development Fund approves a grant to finance an initial study of the plans for the hydroelectric complex at Mukengwa.

Legislative elections are held, and PARMEHUTU candidates are elected unopposed. President Kayibanda is the sole candidate for president.

1970   King Baudouin of Belgium makes an official visit to Rwanda.

1971   The coffee market is stagnant, and as a result the economy is depressed. Prognosis for an adequate coffee harvest is poor.

With coffee prices low, the quota for the 1971–1972

season has been changed from 216,000 bags to 195,000 bags.

The European Development Fund approves a second grant of one million RF to finance the second part of a study for the planned hydroelectric complex at Mukengwa. The fund also approves a 24.5 million RF grant to be used for technical assistance at the Gitarama agricultural and crafts center, built with French aid.

Government has initiated discussion with Republic of Zaire (formerly the Democratic Republic of the Congo) about the possibility of air service.

Border with Uganda is closed, and appeals have been made to the Organization of African Unity to intercede with President Amin.

La Source, published by the Christian community of the National University of Rwanda, is established at Butare.

1972   Tea production reaches 2,522 tons.

The *Trait d'Union,* to be published about ten times a year, is established by the vicar apostolic of Rwanda.

The April uprising of Hutu in Burundi, which stemmed from purging Hutu from government jobs and from systematic attacks and killings, is suppressed violently by Colonel Micombero.

Between 80,000 and 200,000 Hutu (many of them with formal education) and Tutsi die in the fighting.

About 100,000 Hutu are forced to flee abroad, mainly to Tanzania.

In October, members of PARMEHUTU begin campaign to verify if the 9 percent quota allotted for Tutsi representation in education holds for the schools throughout the country.

1973   Resurgence of ethnic conflict and mounting antagonism between Hutu from Ruhengeri in the north and Hutu from the central region at Gitarama.

In February, PARMEHUTU's campaign to verify the number of Tutsi in schools ends.

On July 5, Major General Juvénal Habyarimana, a Hutu from Gisenyi in the north, seizes power from Grégoire Kayibanda in a bloodless coup. The former president is tried and sentenced to death, but his sentenced is commuted to life imprisonment.

August 1, Major General Habyarimana assumes the presidency and forms a government with a majority of civilian members but with officers from the north holding the key portfolios. President Habyarimana also assumes a more moderate stance toward Tutsi under a slogan of "Peace and National Unity."

On October 15, the government periodical, *La Relève*, is published by the Service d'Information at Kigali.

The 1962 constitution is suspended, the national assembly is dissolved, and the Office National du Commerce is abolished.

Société des Mines du Rwanda (SOMIRWA) and the Office Rwandaise du Tourisme et des Parcs Nationaux (ORTPN) are established at Kigali.

1974　　In June, a tripartite conference is held at Bujumbura and attended by the heads of state of Rwanda, Burundi, and Zaire; participants agree to improve border security in each state and to take steps to facilitate economic cooperation across national boundaries.

Aid agreement is signed with the United States Agency for International Development (USAID) to build six storage depots with a total capacity of 2,000 tons (four of 250 tons and two of 500 tons) at six strategic locations in the country (Byumba, Kibungo and Kigali in the first phase, and Nyabisindu, Ruhengeri, and Cyangugu in the second phase), for a total cost of 80 million RF, including operating capital and the training of managers.

Coffee trees suffer from infestation of *antestiopsis*. Damage to coffee beans is estimated at 13 percent and losses amount to 3 percent.

Government reports that climatic conditions are the worst in thirty-five years and expects food production to decline. It has requested food assistance relief from the UNDP.

1975　　In July, the National Revolutionary Movement for Development is formed as a new party by President Habyarimana. The new party also commemorates the second anniversary of the creation of the Second Republic.

Agence Rwandaise de Presse, the Société Nationale d'Assurance du Rwanda (SONARWA), and the Société Nationale de Transports Aériens du Rwanda (SONATAR) are established at Kigali.

A bilingual periodical, *Bulletin d'Information de la Chambre de Commerce et d'Industrie du Rwanda/ Ubucuruzi bwa Kijyambere,* begins publication by the Chamber of Commerce and Industry.

Government agency (OPROVIA) (National Office for Development and Marketing of Foodstuffs and Livestock Products) is created to promote and organize regional specialization in farming and livestock production on a national level.

National Price Commission is created in August.

Coffee trees suffer from heavy infestation of coffee bugs (*antestiopsis*). Administration believes that 18 percent of the beans are affected and estimates losses at 6 per cent.

Weather conditions are normal, and food production is expected to rise.

1976   West German scientists estimate that methane gas in Lake Kivu has the energy capacity of 60 million tons.

The Swiss government approves a 21-million-Swiss-franc grant for technical assistance over the next three years, and the government approves a 12-million-Swiss-franc interest-free loan.

In mid-July, Idi Amin orders Ugandans to seize thirty oil tankers destined for Rwanda and Zaire, because the Kenyan government ordered a complete cutoff of fuel supplies to Uganda. Amin's refusal to allow goods for Rwanda to pass through his territory has brought industries to a standstill.

President Michel Micombero of Burundi and President Habyarimana of Rwanda meet at Kigali and agree to strengthen commercial, economic, cultural, and social ties, and to participate jointly in agricultural and fisheries projects.

Tripartite summit is held at Kigali among Zaire, Rwanda, and Burundi. The three presidents—Mobutu, Micombero, and Habyabimana—pledge support for the South African liberation struggle and issue a communiqué about the signing of legal agreements covering border security. The summit sanctions the formation of the Economic Community of the Countries of the Great Lakes (CEPGL). The community's headquarters will be in Gisenyi.

Colonel Michel Micombero is overthrown by Colonel Jean-Baptiste Bagaza in Burundi. The new president promises to work toward intercommunal harmony and to revolutionize Burundi society.

1977   The government's development plan for 1977–1978 announces the resettlement of inhabitants in unoccupied areas in an effort to restrict the exodus to towns from the countryside and to make better use of unexploited land in the east of the country and in the marshy areas.

Etudes Rwandaises, a quarterly devoted to pure and applied science, literature, and human sciences, is established at the Université Nationale du Rwanda at Butare.

In October, the Ugandan government limits the maximum weight of commercial vehicles transiting Uganda to thirty-five tons. This action causes inflationary pressures in Rwanda and makes access to international suppliers and buyers more difficult.

1978   Rwanda, Burundi, and Zaire establish the Organisation pour l'Aménagement et le Développement du Bassin de la Rivière Kagera to develop the water power and mineral resources of the Kagera basin.

Société Rwandaise pour la Production et la Commercialisation du Thé (SORWATHE) SARL is established at Kigali.

On December 17, a new constitution, establishing a five-year term for the National Development Council (Conseil pour le Développement National) by universal adult suffrage, and reorganizing the judicial system, is approved by almost 90 percent of the electorate in a referendum.

Under the reorganization, the judicial system includes a Council of State with administrative jurisdiction, a Supreme Court of Appeal, a Constitutional Court consisting of the Supreme Court of Appeal and the Council of State sitting jointly, a Court of Accounts responsible for examining all public accounts, and courts of appeal, courts of first instance, and provincial courts.

A decree of May 8 establishes the Rwandan Pyrethrum Office with its headquarters at Ruhengeri.

Office des Cafes (OCIR-CAFÉ), which is devoted to the development of coffee and new agricultural industries, is established at Kigali.

On December 20, the revised constitution becomes the law of the land.

On December 24, President Habyarimana is confirmed in office by vote of almost 99 percent.

1979   President Habyarimana officially sworn in for another five-year term. In his inaugural address at Kigali, he announces a general amnesty, commuting all death sentences to life imprisonment, reducing all current life terms to twenty years, and halving all sentences longer than three months.

In February, the Rwandan army arrests two groups of mercenaries in Gisenyi near the border of Zaire. Government maintains that at least twenty soldiers were carrying a large number of weapons. Twelve are believed to be Belgian citizens. Both Belgium and Zaire have requested their extradition, but the government maintains that the mercenaries will be tried in Rwandan courts.

From February to May, the border with Uganda is closed because of civil war and Tanzania's support of rebel forces. Rwanda's access to the Indian Ocean is disrupted and as a result there are stockpiles of coffee and tea, as well as shortages of petroleum and cement.

New reports note that Idi Amin's forces are in retreat in eastern Uganda.

Economic forecast is bleak: world tin and coffee prices at an all-time low. To assist the economy, the EEC Commission provides a grant of 300,000 EUA to finance an airlift from Mombasa of 7,500 tons of fuel and 17,000 tons of miscellaneous products for a period of three months.

In April, the EEC increases its grant for the air bridge from Mombasa to Kigali. Fuel, food, and other kinds of merchandise are airlifted.

Idi Amin's forces are routed by Tanzanian troops, and the roads are now open through eastern Uganda to Kenya.

The Sixth Franco-African Conference is held at Kigali; President Giscard d'Estaing attends opening ceremony.

In June, the twelve Belgian mercenaries arrested in February are put on trial. Ten are sentenced to jail terms ranging from three to nine years; the other two are deported to Belgium. Apparently, they planned to seize the town and airport of Goma in eastern Zaire, in order to allow reinforcements with ammunition from Sweden to land. The landing was to coincide with separate actions by troops of MARC, the Anti-Mobutu Movement, in Kin-shasa, Angola, Zambia, Sudan, and Uganda.

Serious outbreak of meningitis in northern Rwanda. At least 3,000 people are affected.

In August, the ten imprisoned Belgian mercenaries are deported to Belgium.

1980   April witnesses an unsuccessful coup attempt known as the Lizinde Affair. Théoneste Lizinde, a former security chief and a Mygoyi (from Bugoyi in the north), is arrested with about thirty others for planning the attempted coup.

Elections for a fifty-member parliament and for

president are held; Juvénal Habyarimana is the sole presidential candidate.

Refugees from Burundi mass along the border.

Rwanda, Burundi, and Zaire admit Uganda as member of the Organisation du Bassin de la Rivière Kagera.

The Bishops' Conference *(Conférence Episcopale du Rwanda)* is established with its seat at Byumba.

Milton Obote is elected president of Uganda.

To facilitate private investment, the government has devised an investment code for various kinds of enterprises. For those enterprises designated as first class *(régime de faveur),* generally with capital assets of not less than 10 million RF ($107 million) for Rwandan companies and at least 20 million RF ($214 million) if foreign, an express order is required from the minister of finance. The order permits the company to have a foreign exchange account within and outside of the country. Profits earned by foreign investors, and foreign directors'and employees'emoluments, can be converted into foreign currency at the official rate and remitted abroad. In addition, foreign exchange is supplied by the national bank for the importation and exportation of goods, the transfer of profits and remittance of capital is guaranteed, and exemption from duties on equipment and goods, and from export levies and payment of profit tax for the first five years. Companies considered to be important to the country's development are given contractual status *(régime de la convention)* which, among the other concessions mentioned, provides them protection from competition.

The Bureau National d'Etudes de Projets (BUNEP) is created under the Ministry of Planning.

The Kigali-Ruhengeri-Cyanika road is under construction. Once completed, it will give Kigali better access to Uganda and Zaire, and it will comprise Rwanda's portion of the Mombasa-Lagos Transafrican Highway.

1981   In June, the government introduces a new business tax, to which all persons in private commerce and in business, but not salaried employees and small farmers, are subject. The tax is graduated in regional zones and calculated according to estimated business turnover. Company taxation ranges from a tax on profits of 20 percent up to 250,000 RF, up to 45 percent on profits above 1 million RF. Tariffs range from 5 percent for chemicals to 20 percent for agricultural products. Import taxes range from 10 percent to 150 percent according to product, and according to concessionaire terms granted by the minister of finance.

On September 17, the trial for former security chief Major Théoneste Lizinde and his cohorts begins at the criminal court at Ruhengeri. The accused is on trial not only for plotting to take over the government but also for fomenting anti-Tutsi hatred.

On November 25, twenty-five of the accused plotters are sentenced and twenty-four are acquitted. The two leaders, Major Théoneste Lizinde, the former chief of security, and Alphonse Ndegeya, are sentenced to death. The remaining twenty-three are sentenced to terms of imprisonment ranging from two to twenty-three years.

The EEC has announced plans to finance the development of northern and central transport corridors to the Indian Ocean. The project will cost 20 million ECU, and will consist of a road linking Rwanda to Burundi by way of Bujumbura, then a lake transport link to Kigali from Tanzania, and a refurbished rail link from Tanzania to the port of Dar es Salaam. A second road will be upgraded between Rusomo in Rwanda and Isaka in Tanzania, so that Rwandan traffic can get to the Isaka rail terminus. The northern corridor involves road and rail transport through Uganda and Kenya to Mombasa.

Drought in the eastern part of the country is quite severe toward the end of the year. There is a shortage of drinking water and some reports of starvation because of crop failure. The government has initiated food relief and has made appeals for foreign aid.

Because of increased exports of coffee, Rwanda's overstocking problem has declined.

On December 2, Alexis Kagame, perhaps Rwanda's most outstanding writer on African culture, dies in Nairobi, Kenya.

On December 28, parliamentary elections are held, and the first elected legislature (the Conseil National de Développement) since 1973 returns. Although a single party system prevails, the legal requirements of the Mouvement Révolutionnaire

National pour le Développement (MRND) permits a choice of two candidates for each seat. No choice exists for the election of the president.

1982   On July 1, the country celebrates its twentieth anniversary of independence. President Habyarimana announces that Banyarwanda refugees can return provided they make personal applications and are positively vetted by Kigali authorities. He also commutes the death sentences of Théoneste Lizinde and Alphonse Ndegeya, alleged coup plotters, to life imprisonment.

In October, members of the youth-wingers of the Uganda People's Congress and a unit of the paramilitary special forces destroy the homes of Banyarwanda living in southwest Uganda, forcing 40,000 refugees to cross the border into Rwanda.

In mid-October, a Rwandan delegation headed by Felicien Gatabazi, the minister of social affairs, arrives in Kampala to discuss the refugee problem with the Ugandan government.

On October 25, Rwanda closes its border with Uganda to prevent a further influx of Banyarwanda refugees. The government also appeals to the international community for assistance in coping with some 50,000 refugees from the Ankole district of southwest Uganda.

Toward the end of October, the Ugandan government agrees to prevent Banyarwanda refugees from crossing the border into Rwanda, and the Rwandan government agrees to resettle its nationals currently in refugee camps in Rwanda and to examine requests by Rwandans living in Uganda for eventual repatriation.

In mid-November, United Nations officials report that thousands of refugees in camps still lack food; that the EEC is considering an emergency relief grant of 2 million ECU to aid refugees in Rwanda; and that the United Nations High Commission for Refugees (UNHCR) has asked some fifty donor governments for an additional $8 million in emergency relief aid.

The government's five-year development plan for 1982–1986 gives priority to resettling Banyarwanda in unoccupied areas in the eastern region of the country and in marshy plains. It also seeks to improve self-sufficiency in food production, with progress in the industrial sector being confined to providing basic infrastructure in support of the country's primary development.

Chambre de Commerce et d'Industrie du Rwanda is established.

On December 19, Major General Juvénal Habyarimana is reelected president.

On December 28, Rwandans elect for the first time the sixty-four members of the National Development Council, or parliament. Five women were successful candidates, while two Tutsi and two Twa candidates stood for election, but failed to win.

1983   The government agrees to resettle more than 30,000 refugees. The French government in response to requests for aid from the Rwandan government and UNHCR has agreed to send 900,000 FF worth of medical and material aid, including medicines, blankets, two vehicles, and tents. The EEC has also made an emergency grant of 2 million Ecu.

The government announces an austerity program which also includes restricting personnel in public administration.

On June 30, President Habyarimana is reelected president of the MRND for another five-year term.

On July 5, the nation celebrates the tenth anniversary of the Second Republic.

During the 1982–1983 season, some 28,000 tons of coffee are produced, but the ICO export quota is set at 25,800 tons.

Major aid agreement of 15.6 million FF with France is concluded in September. The grant will fund the construction and the equipping of a retraining center for primary and secondary teachers, a nurses' school in Ruhengeri, a medical care facility in Gisenyi prefecture, and a rural health care facility and the second phase of the eastern Kigali rural development project.

USAID has agreed to contribute $500,000 to a reforestation project of at least 400 hectares of communal land and about 15,000 hectares of private forests.

In October, the government and Zaire hold talks with the EDF about a joint project to extract methane gas from Lake Kivu.

On December 19, President Juvénal Habyarimana

is reelected for another five-year term. He receives 99 percent of the popular vote.

Some 6,000 Banyarwandan refugees from Uganda are forced to leave their homes in the Rakai district, west of Lake Victoria and some sixty kilometers from the Ankole district, because of ethnic hostilities in Uganda. Some cross the border into Rwanda, while others enter northwestern Tanzania.

On December 26, parliamentary elections are held. Some 2,390,000 voters go to the polls to choose between two rival candidates for each of the seventy seats. Of the nineteen women candidates, nine win election. Two Tutsi candidates participate; one obtains a seat.

1984   With severe drought conditions in the country and transportation disruptions in Uganda, the economic outlook is bleak.

Government refuses to assume responsibility for the 4,000 refugees who fled Uganda in December into the Kagera region of Tanzania, despite requests from the Tanzanian government to do so.

In April, President Habyarimana introduces a program of "rigor and austerity," despite the best coffee prices in the last six years. Many nonessential projects are suspended, and priority is given to agriculture, water conservation, energy, and infrastructure.

On June 4, the minister of foreign affairs and cooperation declares a food emergency, and appeals to the international community for emergency food aid. He notes that the food deficit ranges from 30 to

60 percent in some areas of the country, and that the Bugesera region, containing some 4,000 refugees from Burundi, is the most seriously affected.

In August, the government announces that it has received pledges of 24,250 tons of foodstuffs and some $1.3 million to cover the transportation and distribution of relief aid to famine and drought victims. According to United Nations sources, about three million people are affected by the drought, and it estimates that the national food deficit will approach 140,000 tons.

Société Rwandaise d'Assurances (SORAS) is established at Kigali, while Centrale d' Education et de Cooperation des Travailleurs pour le Développement (CECOTRAD) succeeds the Confédération Syndicate des Travailleurs du Rwanda (COSTRAR).

On October 31, Minister of Justice Jean-Marie Vianney Mugemana announces that twelve prisoners who were convicted in 1981 and 1983 for taking part in the abortive 1980 coup attempt led by Major Théoneste Lizinde will be released unconditionally because of "good behavior and serious evidence of social rehabilitation."

Tea production reaches 8,669 tons.

1985   Théoneste Lizinde, leader of the attempted coup in 1980 is retried and, on this occasion, charged with the murder in mid-1970s of a number of politicians of the First Republic. He, along with five others, is convicted and condemned to death.

On July 5, the anniversary of independence, of the foundation of the Second Republic, and of the creation of the MRND, President Habyarimana grants a general amnesty for all categories of crimes other than antistate activities, murder, and armed robbery. Eleven political prisoners who have been jailed for more than twenty years are released. Eight of them had been members of a small monarchist cell, the inyenzi, and were originally sentenced for insurrection against the republic.

On July 27, Milton Obote is ousted as president of Uganda by an army coup; he seeks sanctuary in Kenya.

On July 29, Lieutenant General Tito Okello assumes power in Uganda.

Since mid-September, internal conflict in Uganda has disrupted Rwandan trade, and the country has to depend more upon the route through Tanzania to Dar es Salaam.

In October, government announces that because of civil war in Uganda, Air Rwanda will inaugurate a weekly flight to Mwanza in Tanzania, so that truckers en route from Dar es Salaam can unload their vehicles there.

The UNHCR in Kampala reports that in late November the Rwandan government repatriated 30,000 Banyarwandan refugees from Uganda over a three-month period.

Ico sets Rwanda coffee quota for the 1985–1986 (October-September) season at 28,200 tons.

In December, at the fifth MRND congress, President Habyarimana announces plans for a radical reorganization of the party to include a school of ideology for party workers and salary increases for party officials. The congress also announces the resignation from the MRND central committee of the Roman Catholic archbishop of Kigali.

Tea exports reach 8,463 tons.

Economic austerity program is implemented with priority given to agriculture, water conservation, energy, and infrastructure. An additional factor in the economy's decline is civil disorder in Uganda and disruption of transportation through that region.

Dian Fossey, the U.S. naturalist, is found dead.

1986   In January, Air Rwanda begins service to Goma in eastern Zaire. This new route will facilitate travel to West Africa by way of Kinshasa.

The MRND Central Committee's membership is enlarged from twenty-two to twenty-five.

On January 25, the National Resistance Army (NRA) of Uganda takes Kampala.

On January 29, the commander of the NRA, Yoweri Museveni, becomes the president of Uganda.

The export quotas of the International Coffee Organization are suspended in February. The tea market is reported to be in a depressed state as well. Figures published by the Rwandan National Bank show inflation currently running at a negligible 1.7 percent.

On February 4, the government commemorates the twelfth anniversary of the introduction of *umuganda*, the system of civic good works which each citizen is required to provide one day each week.

Economic austerity program continues with priority given to agriculture and water conservation, and includes the project to improve rural water supplies in the Lava district, as well as energy and infrastructure.

In April, Minister of Justice Jean-Marie Vianney Mugemana presses the government to deal swiftly with 200 Rwandans detained for membership in religious sects not recognized by the government. Of those arrested, members of some of the smaller religious groups are charged with disrespect for the national flag, the anthem, and the system of community service *(umuganda)*. The government also takes legal action against Jehovah's Witnesses, *Abantu b'Mama* (men of God), and *Abarokore* (God's Elect).

The Lava district water project receives funds from the World Bank, the EEC, and the Arab Bank for Economic Development in Africa (BADEA).

Civil conflict in Uganda still disrupts transportation from the north, but in April a general cooperation agreement with Uganda, covering security, trade, industry, transport, and communications, is concluded.

On July 27, the central committee of the MRND issues a declaration announcing it will not allow the immigration of large numbers of refugees because the country's economy is incapable of sustaining their numbers.

A new international airport serving up to 500,000 passengers per year opens at Kigali.

In August, a second agreement with Uganda is concluded; trade between the two countries is to be conducted on the basis of specific contracts between them and by individuals empowered to carry out specific activities.

On October 1, a trial opens at the state security court in Kigali for the 296 members of the Jehovah's Witnesses, Temperates, Seventh Day Adventists, *Abantu b'Imana Bihana* (Men of God Who Repent), and *Abarokore* (God's Elect). The state prosecutor has asked for prison sentences ranging from eight to fifteen years for the accused. He has asked that Phocas Hakizumwani, a prominent Jehovah's Witness, be sentenced to fifteen years, and twelve years for five other members of the sect. All of the accused have pleaded not guilty.

On October 17, the *Abantu b'Imana Bihana* (Men of God Who Repent), *Abarokore,* the Jehovah's Witnesses, and the Temperates are convicted of inciting rebellion against the authorities, dishonoring the national flag, and encouraging violations of the law. They receive very harsh prison sentences, ranging from four to twelve years. Two Jehovah's Witnesses—Augustin Murayi Nduhira, the former director general of the Ministry of Primary and Secondary Education, and his wife, Rachel Ndayishimiye—are given the maximum sentences. In announcing the sentences, Minister of Justice

Jean-Marie Vianney Mugemana sanctions religious freedom as long as religious sects respect the law and receive official recognition from the state.

Rwanda's coffee quota for the 1985–1986 season is set at 28,200 tons.

On December 4, 1986, Air Rwanda begins regular twice-weekly service, to Entebbe, Uganda.

1987   In January, a meeting is held with the minister of internal affairs for Uganda to discuss the problems of border security and refugees.

Minister of Agriculture, Livestock, and Forestry Anastase Nteziryayo announces at a meeting at Kigali that this is the year of self-sufficiency in foodstuffs, and that policy would be directed toward the improvement of antierosion measures, the production of organic and mineral fertilizers, the development of enterprises aimed at import substitution, the restructuring of livestock management, and the conservation of Rwanda's forests.

The International Coffee Organization (ICO) meets in London from February 23 to March 2 and fails to reach an agreement on the reintroduction of export quotas. The coffee producers are divided and will not accept the demand of consumer nations for an allocation according to "objective criteria," that is, past export performance and the level of verifiable stocks.

On March 11, the government announces that an agreement has been made with Warner Bros. for exclusive rights over a two-year period to shoot a film on the life of Dian Fossey, the U.S. naturalist, killed under suspicious circumstances in Rwanda in 1985. The film is budgeted at $17 million.

On June 3, President Habyarimana and Burundi's president, Jean-Baptiste Bagaza, visit Cyangugu for the first meeting of a joint commission on bilateral relations and border security.

On June 16, President Habyarimana forms a special high-level commission to manage the economic crisis confronting the country. The commission includes ministers attached to the presidency, the director of the Central Bank, ministers of finance and the economy, and of industry and mining. The commission will give priority to import management, export promotion, transportation, debt management, and food aid.

On July 1, 296 members of unregistered religious sects and about 4,000 other prisoners receive pardons from the president under a general amnesty to commemorate Rwanda's twenty-fifth anniversary of independence. King Baudouin and Queen Fabiola attend the twenty-fifth anniversary celebration.

From July 24 to 31, Dr. Casmir Bizimugu, the minister for health, social affairs, and community development, holds a retreat to study social and demographic problems in the country. Dr. Bizimugu calls upon the Office Nationale de la Population (ONAPO) to take measures to reduce voluntarily the rate of population growth in the country. He reminds the participants at the retreat that the ruling Mouvement Révolutionnaire National pour le Développement (MRND) has called upon Banyarwandan families to have a maximum of four children.

In August, there is a military coup in Burundi; President Bagaza is overthrown; Pierre Buyoyo comes to power.

On August 20, Charles Nyandwi, minister for higher education and scientific research, announces that university students at home and abroad will now pay scholarship fees of 20,000 RF, and that those students at the national university who fail their examinations risk losing state financial support.

On October 22, President Habyarimana in an address before the MRND Central Committee, outlines a bleak picture of the country's economic prospects and announces a freeze on employment in the civil service.

Tea production reaches 11,619 tons.

Economic austerity program is still in effect, with priority given to agriculture, water conservation, energy, and infrastructure.

1988   In February, President Habyarimana visits Uganda to participate in a joint ministerial commission on the problems of refugees.

In March, the Office Rwandais du Thé (OCIR-THE) suspends all projects not directly related to increasing output because of the declining world prices.

In June, a program of privatization was announced by the president; the state will sell its equity in three companies in the service and industrial sectors to private interests.

In August, ethnic tensions in Burundi lead to the flight of some 38,000 Hutu refugees into the southern part of Rwanda.

In October, the government increases civil service salaries by 3 percent after a nine-month freeze.

The Société de Boissons et Limonades au Rwanda (SOBILIRWA) establishes a plant which will produce 96,000 bottles of Pepsi-Cola per day for the United Kingdom's Meyer Mojonnier company.

1989   In September, government reports that the production of haricot (beans) in Kibuye in the west and Gikongoro in the south has been badly affected by heavy rains which followed a period of prolonged drought.

In an attempt to resolve the refugee issue, Rwanda and Uganda ask the United Nations High Commission for Refugees to survey the refugee settlements in both countries to determine the private wishes of the Banyarwandan refugees regarding their permanent settlement in Rwanda or their continued residence in Uganda.

Beginning in December, President Habyarimana launches an appeal for 250,000 tons of emergency food aid because of severe food shortages in the southern region of Mayanga (in Butare prefecture).

On December 14, Vincent Ruhamanya, the former minister of finance, is sentenced to six years in prison. He is charged with having embezzled 30 million RF ($380,000) from the fraudulent sale of a gas station while head of Rwanda's state oil corporation, PETRORWANDA.

1990   At the end of January, Agence France-Presse reports that one in six of the population are affected by famine.

At the end of January, the sixth conference of the ten-member Communauté Economique des Etats de l'Afrique Centrale (CEEAC) is held at Kigali. Among priorities discussed are the upgrading of the road linking Rwanda with Burundi and Zaire and the creation of a bank at Kigali specializing in the financing of intracommunity trade.

In February, the EC donates $6.25 million in food aid, and the United Nations World Food Program approves additional emergency food aid. The International Red Cross and the Red Crescent grant 30.5 million RF ($395,000) to the Rwandan Red Cross, plus supplies of sorghum, beans, and cooking oil, for food relief.

On February 23, the Rwandan government signs an agreement with the OPEC Fund in Bonn for a low-interest loan of $4 million toward the cost of the Gitarama-Kibuye road construction project. The seventy-five-kilometer all-weather road would link Gitarama with Kibuye on Lake Kivu, as well as facilitate the marketing of agricultural produce.

In March, President Habyarimana visits villages in Butare, Gikongoro, and Kibuye, areas hit hardest by the famine. Government estimates that at least 250 people have died of starvation.

On March 21, the government reduces the price paid to domestic coffee planters for green beans from 125 RF ($1.60) per kilogram to 100 RF ($1.30), and reduces the price paid for coffee delivered to the factories to 105 RF per kilogram. This reduction represents the first change in producer prices since 1986.

On March 23, President Habyarimana establishes the National Commission on Agriculture. The commission will provide long-term solutions to the famine in southern Rwanda by devising ways to increase agricultural production.

In April, the West German government grants 1.5 million DM ($890,000) for the purchase of maize and beans for the food-relief program.

On April 1, the National Commission on Agriculture releases figures indicating that 303 people died as a result of the famine. Most of the deaths occurred in Gikongoro. The commission requests additional food relief aid, and notes that only 10,000 tons of food pledged by international donors has been received, out of the 138,000 tons requested in December.

The Tanzanian government expels 400 Rwandan refugees.

In mid-May, some 5,000 refugees arrive in Rwanda from Tanzania. Most had entered the country illegally in 1986, but their numbers have increased because of famine conditions in southern Rwanda. Authorities estimate that about 18,000 Rwandans have crossed the border into Tanzania between January 1986 and March 1990. The Rwandan government is seeking international aid to assist with their resettlement.

On May 20, Rwandan and Tanzanian officials meet in the Kagera region of Tanzania to discuss appropriate measures for identifying and facilitating the resettlement of Rwandan refugees.

On May 31, government reports that one student is killed and five seriously injured in a riot at the National University at Butare. The disturbance occurred during a concert performed by a popular Zairian band when a student allegedly used force to gain entry to the concert. The local police opened fire and used tear gas in an attempt to quell the disturbance.

At the end of May, President Habyarimana attends a summit meeting of the Communauté Economique des Pays des Grands Lacs (CEPGL) in Gbadolite in northern Zaire to discuss the free movement of goods and people among the three countries.

On June 1, students on the campuses at Butare and Ruhengeri go on strike to protest the shooting and request a meeting with President Habyarimana to present their version of the events.

On June 3, a follow up meeting of CEPGL is held at Kigali involving the foreign ministers of Zaire, Rwanda, and Burundi.

On June 6, the president meets with a student delegation. They demand the resignation of those officials responsible for ordering the shooting. The president urges the students to end their strike and return to classes. He promises a judicial inquiry into the shooting and agrees to send one of the injured students abroad for medical treatment.

On June 7, the students end their strike.

On June 12, President Habyarimana convenes a meeting of the country's prefects to discuss agricultural diversification and development of marshlands, particularly for such crops as coffee, tea, pyrethrum, French beans, peppers and ornamental plants.

In the second week of July, Frédéric Karangwa, the prefect of Butare, and Commandant François Muhirwa, head of the local police force, are suspended from their duties following an investigation into the student riot at the National University at Butare on May 31.

On July 3, Vincent Rwabukwisi, the editor in chief of *Kanguka,* an independent bimonthly, is arrested on charges of subversion and endangering state security for allegedly working in collusion with Rwandan refugees living abroad. The government is asking for a sentence of twenty years in prison.

On July 5, during the seventeenth anniversary celebrations of his coming to power, President Habyarimana announces his intentions to revise the country's constitution in order to separate the party from the state. He appoints an interministerial working group to review the existing system, with the intention of implementing the revisions by July 1992, which will coincide with the thirtieth anniversary celebrations of the country's independence.

On July 6, Hassan Ngeze, the editor in chief of *Kangura,* an independent bimonthly, is arrested on charges of subversion and endangering state security, because he wrote in a recent column that 70 percent of Rwanda's wealth is in the hands of the Tutsi minority. The government is demanding a sentence of ten years in prison.

On September 7, Pope John Paul II arrives in the country, and to commemorate his visit, President Habyarimana declares a graded amnesty for all convicted prisoners in the country, except those serving terms for political offenses or for corruption against the state. Those who were sentenced to death will have their sentences commuted to life in prison. Those who are serving prison terms of greater than ten years will have their sentences reduced. Women, young offenders, and all those who were condemned for less than ten years are freed.

Around 10 a.m. on October 1, the Rwandese Patriotic Army (RPA) of 7,000 troops and the military arm of the Rwandese Patriotic Front (RPF), led by majors Peter Bayingana and Chris Bunyenyezi, invade Rwanda from Uganda at Kagitumba.

President Habyarimana in response to the invasion by the RPF in northern Rwanda from across Uganda's border requests assistance from his allies.

On October 3 and 4, the government announces that the garrison and resort at Gabiro, as well as the trading center at Nyadatare, has been recaptured from RPF forces.

Between October 4 and 5, some 350 Belgian paratroopers, 300 French Legionnaires, and a large contingent of Zairian soldiers from the Special Presidential Division arrive in Kigali to protect foreigners and to assist with their evacuation.

In October, the United Nations High Commission for Refugees begins its survey to determine Banyarwandan residential preference for repatriation.

On October 7, oficial reports note that Zairian troops had engaged RPF forces in the north and that they had suffered heavy losses. Government also enforces a strict curfew and restricts the movement of civilians.

On October 8, a formal declaration of a state of siege is proclaimed by the government.

Rwandese Patriotic Army captures the tourist resort and barracks of Babiro and the town of Nykatare.

There are reports of ethnic violence in the subprefecture of Ngorolero in Gisenyi; Hutu civilians reportedly have killed from 50 to 335 Tutsi in attacks which began on October 11 and lasted for several days. The government arrests 400 people for taking part in the killings, including the deputy subprefect head and the mayor of Kibirura for their failure to stop the killings.

On October 13, the minister of justice reports that 2,582 rebel sympathizers have been arrested.

On October 15, diplomatic efforts to resolve the conflict begin when Belgian Prime Minister Wilfried arrives in East Africa.

On October 17, a diplomatic meeting is held at Mwanza in Tanzania among presidents Habyarimana, Museveni, and Mwinyi. The participants agree to an October 24 cease-fire to be monitored by neutral troops and to a regional conference to solve the refugee problem.

Zairian troops leave the country.

On October 18, President Habyarimana announces from Paris his willingness to talk to any opposition leaders either inside or outside of the country.

President Mobutu sponsors talks between warring factions at Goma and Gbadolite.

The Rwandese army mounts an offensive, and on October 23, ambushes RPA forces. Majors Peter Bayingana and Chris Bunyenyezi of the RPA are killed, along with some 320 of their soldiers. There are also reports of civilian casualties at Baliza, Chonyo, Bushoga, Chapayaga, Mihingo, Gahiragye, Kanyeganyege, Gitengure, and Kiboga.

On October 23, it was announced that government troops won a major victory at Lyabega. Majors Bayingana and Bunyenyezi of the RPF are killed in an ambush along with 320 of their troops.

The October 24 cease-fire is cancelled. Each side accuses the other of violating it.

The RPA abandons conventional fighting and reverts to guerrilla warfare.

Estimations are that by the end of October, some 5,000 rebel sympathizers will be detained.

The Belgian government withdraws its military forces.

The October 24 ceasefire is violated by both sides. Diplomatic efforts also fail to produce positive results, except for the Rwandan team which successfully monitors the Ugandan side of the border.

President Habyarimana takes a hard line and maintains that no negotiations will take place as long as rebel forces continue to shoot at government troops, and they must withdraw before talks can commence. The RPF refuses.

Conflict between government forces and RPF precipitates mass arrest of some 5,000 civilians inside Rwanda. Most are screened and released, but Amnesty International and some western nations register strong protest. Complaints from the west cause the public opinion in France and Belgium to pressure their respective governments to withdraw their military troops, but only Belgium complies by withdrawing its forces.

On November 1, Belgian paratroopers return to Belgium; French forces remain to guard the Kigali International Airport.

RPF under the command of Major Paul Kagame, former acting head of the military intelligence in Uganda's NRA, moves south along the Tanzanian border and west along the Ugandan border to engage Rwandan troops.

On November 8, Silas Majyambere, the former president of Rwanda's chamber of commerce and presently living in exile in Brussels, Belgium, announces the formation of a new political party, the Rwandan People's Union/Union des Peuple rwandais (UPR).

On November 9, the World Bank with IMF approval urges the Rwandan government to adopt the Structural Adjustment Program (SAP). SAP was to be implemented on October 1, but it was delayed by the invasion. As part of its own austerity measures, the government devalues the Rwandan franc by 40 percent to 188 BF=$1.

France's CCCE grants loan worth 84 million FF ($3 million) to fund the first five years of a multi-donor project to develop irrigated rice and other crops on 1,810 hectares of land in the Mutara region of the country.

In an address before the National Assembly on November 13, President Habyarimana announces that the political reform process set in motion on July 5 would be stepped up. To accomplish this, he urges that those who wish to form political parties should do so immediately. Even refugees would be given assistance to return home to present their views. Ethnic identity cards would be discontinued, and the country would move toward multi-party politics or could begin the process of forming political parties. He also informs the National Assembly that the referendum on the "national political charter" or the rules governing the operations of political parties would begin by June 15, 1991.

On November 15, the government reports heavy fighting between RPF forces and its own troops in the vicinity of Gatuna.

In mid-November, Colonel Alexis Kanyarengwe, the former minister of internal affairs and a Hutu, becomes president of the RPF.

A November 18 report notes that Major Fred Rwigyema, commander for RPF forces in the north, had died in an ambush at Gabiro along with several other high ranking officers.

Heavy fighting between RPF and Rwandan forces reported during late November and early December around Gutuna, Kaniga, and Ngarama. Also a late-November report notes that only 150 French paratroopers remain in the country. The majority are stationed at Kigali.

In December, the government announces that 1,556 rebel sympathizers face trial for their participation in the "October War."

The Rwandan government signs aid agreement on December 4 with France's CCCE worth 49.7 million FF (of which 8 million FF is a direct grant) for various development projects, including agricultural development at Masaka, which is east of Kigali, and the mapping of principal towns, like Kigali and Butare. Additional projects include the computerization of customs services, improvements in air traffic control at the Kanombe International Airport. More than half of the aid, 36.5 million FF in combination with 26.5 million FF from the Rwandan government funds will be used to fund and extend the Kibuye sugar factory.

In mid-December, Major Paul Kagame, a Tutsi refugee, and Colonel Alexis Kanyarengwe, a Hutu and former minister of internal affairs, emerge as leaders of the Rwandan Patriotic Front.

Radio Rwanda announces on December 27 that 5,540 RPF troops were killed in Byumba prefecture. The high casualties stem from air attacks and the efforts of local civilians armed with machetes and spears. Government also reports that 50 or more civilians were killed in the vicinity of Kibuye by RPF forces, and it confirms heavy fighting in the northwest between RPF and its own forces around the strategic Virunga volcano chain and in the border areas of Gatuna, Kaniga, and Rwempasha.

Of the 5,000 alleged civilian sympathizers and supporters of the RPF arrested during the October invasion, the government announces that 1,566 will stand for trial. Amnesty International protests announced trials on procedural grounds, charging that lawyers appointed to defend those to stand trial were not given adequate details of charges. Lawyers were notified on the day prior to the trial. The government is forced to postpone the first group of trials until January 3.

Relations with Uganda are strained because government suspects Ugandan complicity in RPF attacks and acts as a safe haven for them. It also believes that Ugandan National Resistance Army supplies both sympathy and materiel. President Yoweri Museveni denies Uganda's complicity and insists that no weapons are crossing the border or that there are RPF camps in Uganda. He also informs Rwandan authorities that RPF and NRA deserters who cross back into Uganda will be placed under arrest and sent to Lubiri Barracks in Kampala, where independent reports confirm that large numbers of RPF/NRA deserters now reside.

1991   On January 3, thirteen rebel sympathizers are brought to trial. Amnesty International's observers at the trial of the alleged RPF supporters and sympathizers conclude that it is "summary and unfair" and remark that most were not represented by counsel. Also most of the accused were forced to make confessions of guilt under duress. One member of the International Commission of Jurists estimates that only 40 percent of the 5,000 or so arrested had some kind of connection with the RPF.

On January 7, one rebel sympathizer is sentenced to death and nine others receive long prison terms.

Reports note that between January 8 and 14, the RPF occupied the strategic Virunga volcano chain in the northwest region of the country, where the borders of Rwanda, Uganda, and Zaire meet. The RPF established a base camp in the area.

On January 23, RPF forces attack and capture Ruhengeri. They rob the local bank of 13 million RF and release 1,780 prisoners from the maximum security prison. Among those released are Major Théoniste Lizinde, the former head of intelligence, who was imprisoned in 1980 for plotting against President Habyarimana; and Commandant Stanilas Biseruka and Captain Donate Muvumanyambo, two Hutu who had been in the prison for a decade.

Because of the conflict and the disruption in trade that comes through Katuna or is carried on across the border, there are serious signs of a food shortage.

During the first couple of days in February, the government reports that their forces had achieved three successful victories against RPF camps on the Muhavura and Mgahinga volcanoes. But reported later in the week that a ceasefire agreement, effective February 18, had been signed in Zanzibar.

The February 18 ceasefire fails to materialize.

On February 19, President Habyarimana and the heads of state of Rwanda's four neighbors sign the Dar es Salaam declaration, in which Rwanda agrees to accept back its refugees and to work toward a ceasefire and dialogue with the armed opposition, with President Mobutu serving as referee.

During the first week of March, the government announced the release of 1500 prisoners who were accused of being supporters and sympathizers with RPF and were brought to trial in December. It also announced that those who were sentenced to death will not be executed.

On March 14, President Habyarimana announces the establishment of four amnesty centres at Kinigi, Cyanika, Rwempasha, and Kaniga. RPF troops were given fifteen days to report to these respective locations.

A new political party, the Mouvement Démocratique Républicain, emerges in response to the promised political reforms scheduled for June of this year.

On March 29, the government announces the signing of a ceasefire agreement with the RPF military commander, Paul Kagame, at N'sele, Zaire. Brigadier General Hashim Mbita of the Organization of African Unity (OAU) will head the monitoring forces, composed of Barundi, Rwandan, Zairian, Ugandan, and RPF officers. In addition, the RPF and the Rwandan government will begin talks by April 12.

President Habyarimana also offers amnesty to RPF forces and extends an invitation to them to become a political party under the new political reform program.

In early April, the Belgian government donated 7,000 tons of wheat as emergency food aid. This donation amounted to a third of the country's annual wheat consumption and will be used primarily by secondary schools and in the war-affected areas of the north.

On April 10, the National Synthèsis Commission/ Commission nationale de synthèse, charged with preparing the political reform program, recommends the following to the president: modification to the 1978 constitution, the abolition of the single party system, and the creation of the post of prime minister.

Announcement made on April 12 that the ceasefire agreed to on March 29 has failed; both sides violate the terms of the agreement by continuing hostilities. Nor has a dialogue between the warring factions commenced. The OAU officials and auxiliary forces are unable to monitor the ceasefire. Some say that the RPF has been unwilling to cooperate.

On April 17, seven alleged RPF collaborators, sentenced to death, receive commuted sentences. Government also releases 1500 others, detained since the start of the October war as RPF sympathizers. Among those released was Vincent Rwabukwisi, editor of *Kanguka,* who had received a 17-year-sentence the previous July for subversion.

On April 18, curfew hours and travel restrictions in

effect since the October invasion are lifted everywhere except the northern region.

On April 21, President Habyarimana presents the political reforms to his cabinet.

On April 25, the minister of finance announces a "national solidarity tax" in order to make up for the budget deficit for 1991. All wage earners in the public and private sectors will pay 8 percent of their monthly net salary, parastatals will pay 5 percent, and private companies 1 percent of their 1990 financial turnover. Salary increases for 1991 financial year have been frozen and the corresponding amounts are to be paid to the treasury by public and private companies.

Burgomasters, councilors, and other public and private figures were in attendance when this announcement was made and responded by calling for the cancellation of the benefits to political officials. They also called for the creation of a commission to examine and investigate the causes of the war, capital flight, and illicit enrichment or war profiteering.

On April 28, President Habyarimana presents political reform recommendations to an extraordinary congress of the Mouvement Révolutionnaire National pour le Développement (MRND). The MRND uses the meeting to change its name to Mouvement Républicain National pour la Démocratie et le Développement (MRNDD).

On May 1, the Rwandan army mutinies throughout the north over the issue of promotion, with some claiming that senior officers favored performance in battle over seniority.

On May 3, the government resolves problems with its military in the north.

National Assembly discusses the political reform recommendations on May 7 and decides on a number of solutions: first, that a new law on political parties is required, and second, that the constitution should be amended to reflect a multi-party system. The latter produced a debate on whether or not parties should be allowed to form on sectarian basis. While the president opposed ethnically based parties, the Assembly issues a compromise, which allows sectarian parties but with open membership.

On May 13, the United Nations High Commissioner for Refugees (UNHCR) and the Organization of African Unity (OAU) meet at Geneva to draw up a plan for the repatriation of Banyarwanda refugees, including a budget which will be presented to potential donors.

Four journalists are arrested in June. Vincent Rwabukwisi of *Kanguka,* who had been released from a 17-year-sentence, two of his staff, and the editor of *Ijambo,* Francois-Xavier Hagimana, were among those detained. The government also seized several issues of *Isibo, Ijambo,* and the pro-Hutu *Kangura* for printing copy deemed demoralizing to the army.

On June 10, President Habyarimana signs a new constitution, legalizing multi-parties and reducing presidential power with the addition of a new post of prime minister as head of government business. It prohibits army officers from joining political parties. The new constitution allows the president and the current National Assembly to remain in power until new elections are held.

President Habyarimana signs a new law on June 20 that sets out the rules by which new political parties will function.

On July 5, the reformulated Mouvement Républicain National pour la Démocratie et Développement holds its first constituent assembly and declares the old MRND as dead. The minister of interior instructs all heads of prefectures and communes to serve all parties.

During the month of August, about a dozen new political parties begin to operate in the country with party platforms and broadcasts over Radio Rwanda. The most influential are the Democratic Republican Movement/Mouvement Démocratique Républicain (MDR), the Christian Democratic Party/Parti Démocratique Chrétien (PDC), the Social Democrat Party/Parti Social-Démocrate (PSD), the Liberal Party/Parti Libéral (PL), and the ruling Mouvement Républicain National pour la Démocratie et Développement (MRND). Included in this group is Partima, a grouping that represents the *métises,* people of mixed Hutu-Tutsi parentage.

National census begins.

On September 5, the secretary general of the MRND relinquishes to the minister of public works all the property and other assets that it had at its disposal. The property is said to be worth 1.53 billion RF ($12.6 million) and credits worth 4.38 billion RF ($36.2 million).

On September 7, official reports indicate that President Ibrahim Babangida of Nigeria, representing OAU, and the region's heads of state from Burundi, Rwanda, Uganda, Zaire, and RPF officers met recently at Gbadolite in Zaire to dissolve the first monitoring team, made up of the countries bordering Rwanda. A new team of monitors, consisting of 15 Nigerians and 15 Zairian officers and headed by the Nigerian General Oparey, was created.

Between September 15 and 17, official reports note that Rwandans and RPF delegation met at Gbadolite for discussions.

Official reports in early October note that the economy is in decline. Government documents submitted to the donor roundtable describe the country's 1990 economic performance as having been severely weakened by the war. They predict that a small upturn will resume as a result of the Structural Adjustment Program (SAP).

On October 2, President Habyarimana addresses the CND and presents two amnesty bills. He urges all the legal political parties to meet at a consultant meeting in order to establish a joint management for the current transition period.

On October 3, the MDR, PSD, and the PL respond to the president's request in the negative, citing that the framework and objectives of the meeting of parties are unclear. They argue that the transitional period to the elections could be better managed by a provisional government which included all legal parties and headed by a prime minister appointed by the opposition parties. They call for the suspension of the CND, and they support a mutually agreed upon prime minister to chair a new cabinet.

The minister of justice, Sylvestre Nsanzimana, is appointed as prime minister by President Habyarimana on October 10, with instructions to establish a new cabinet with representatives from six political parties. The Committee of Consultation, however, objects to Mr. Nsanzimana's appointment and refuses to participate in the new cabinet.

During the early part of November, there is widespread inter-ethnic violence, with deaths occurring under mysterious circumstance in eastern Rwanda and at Kanzenze where, according to Agence France Press, eight people were taken from their homes at night and found dead several days later. Rumor has it that the MDR, the PSD, and the PL are responsible for inciting the killings.

By November 16, tension between Uganda and Rwanda grows, as Rwandan artillery hits the district headquarters in Kisoro in southern Uganda and twelve people are reported killed. The Ugandan government claims that some 70,000 of its citizens have been displaced by the shelling of suspected RPF positions. It accuses Rwandan soldiers of looting Ugandan homes, located on the border of the two countries. The Rwandan government accuses Ugandan president, Yoweri Museveni, of supporting the RPF by permitting communications and food supply lines through his country.

The Committee of Consultation holds a mass political rally in Kigali before a crowd on November 17. Attendance is estimated at 25,000, and those present are told why the Committee blocks the implementation of a transitional government and refuses to participate in a new cabinet. The central issue is the appointment by the president of Sylvestre Nsanzimana, as prime minister. The Committee also criticizes MRND's privileged access to Radio Rwanda, and the party's use of government vehicles. It accuses government officials of misusing state property. The latter, along with the Hutu/Tutsi problem, regional tensions between the north and south, and the refugee issue with respect to the resettlement of Tutsi refugees, should be the subject of examination by a national conference.

The MRND holds a counterdemonstration and rally on November 24 in order to answer the Committee's charges and respond to its proposals.

Ethnic unrest among the Hutu of Burundi occurred later in the month. Some 5,000 are reportedly killed by government troops in response to an attack from Palipehutu, a Hutu opposition group within the country. Because of increased tensions, the diplomatic representatives from both countries are recalled. A key Palipehutu leader, Etienne Karastasi, is permitted to broadcast over Radio Rwanda. Barundi forces arrest and deport 18 Banyarwanda; 230 Rwandans in Bujumbura are forced to seek refuge in the Rwandan Embassy. Official reports estimate that about 10,000 Barundi of Hutu origin have sought sanctuary in southern Rwanda.

During the first week in December, the Rwandan Catholic Church takes a political stance with respect to the new political atmosphere, the civil war, the RPF, and the government's "pseudo-negotiations." It calls for serious talks with RPF and sanctions a new and independent transitional government, which would be responsible for peace negotiations.

World AIDS Day celebration held on December 1. Minister of Health, Francois Xavier, uses the occasion to state that in Kigali an adult becomes infected with HIV every 50 to 90 minutes; a baby with HIV is born every six hours. His solution is the creation of a national association or council, either voluntary or state sponsored, to fight the disease. He notes that coordination is essential.

Around the 15th, the government accuses Uganda with complicity in RPF attacks launched against its forces in Butaro commune. The RPF offensive was launched from the Echuya forest, which straddles the border between the two countries.

Census figures are released, but there are accusations of underreporting by 600,000. At any rate, the new census figures indicate that the rate of population growth is 3.3 per cent and that the total population is 7,164,994. The government had anticipated figures of 3.7 per cent and 7.6 million respectively. Ruhengeri is reported to have the highest population density with 462 persons per square kilometer, with Butare registering the lowest—415. More men than women inhabit the urban areas, with a ratio of 110 to 100 and more women than men live in the rural areas and in the country as a whole, the ratio being 100 to 95.

Despite the war, the Kagera Basin Organization met for two days, December 16 and 17, in Kigali to settle arrears and to focus on road and railroad construction projects. The construction of the hydroelectric dam over the Rusumo Falls in eastern Rwanda was also discussed.

President Habyarimana and representatives of seven opposition parties hold a meeting on December 18, where he rules out a national conference and reaffirms his support for Prime Minister Nsanzimana. He informs those present of his confidence in him to form a transitional government.

On the following day, the MDR, PSD, PL and the Parti Socialiste Rwandais (PSR) inform the president that they opposes his choice of prime minister and therefore, would not participate in the government. PSR withdraws from the meeting, leaving the government to deal with the Parti Démocrate Chrétien (PDC), the Parti Ecologiste (PECO), the Parti pour la Démocratie Islamique (PDI), and the Rassemblement Travailliste pour la Démocratie (RTD) to choose ministers. Of these four, only the PDC was sufficiently organized to offer a portfolio; the rest had not announced their programs or memberships.

On December 30, Prime Minister Nsanzimana presents his new cabinet, which is composed of one PDC member, fifteen members from the MRND, and one army officer.

1992　　In January tensions between Rwanda and Uganda have grown. Current charges and mutual recriminations over support of the RPF and Uganda's complicity in the conflict have brought these countries to the brink of war.

On January 1, Mr. Kanyabugori, a member of the Bagogwe and the legal representative of *Kanyar-*

wanda, a human rights group, and some survivors of the Bagogwe massacre appeal to President Habyarimana to conduct an independent investigation into the massacre.

On January 8, the MDR, PL, PSD, and PSR hold a mass rally in Kigali to protest the new government. Violence occurs. Other party members demonstrate in Gitarama and Butare.

Ugandan foreign minister arrives in Kigali to discuss growing tensions between the two countries over the civil war in the north.

On January 15, the opposition parties hold a second rally in Kigali to protest the new government. Turnout is reported to be much lower than for the first rally. The rally turns violent.

Two days later, President Habyarimana and the cabinet announce bans on demonstrations on weekdays for economic reasons and for fear that RPF might use demonstrations as an opportunity to infiltrate southward. The government maintains that the opposition would be liable for damages resulting from its rallies. Peace negotiations held in Tanzania on January 19 between presidents Habyarimana, Museveni of Uganda, and Mwinyi of Tanzania.

On January 23, President Habyarimana meets with the opposition and forms a committee of three government officials to pursue negotiations over the formation of another cabinet that would be agreeable to all parties.

During the end of the month, the Rwandan government again accused Uganda of supporting the RPF, particularly in the recent attack against Rwandan defensive positions near Butaro commune. The RPF attack was launched from the Echuya forest region.

An official report notes that the promised Nigerian monitoring team, which was to be sent by President Babangida of Nigeria has not arrived. Nor has President Mobutu, because of internal problems, been able to exercise his role as mediator in the peace talks. The French have stepped into the vacuum: a team of soldiers to monitor the border has arrived; and the parties have been invited to Paris for talks. But the RPF are suspicious of the French, who they say have allied themselves with the Rwandan government.

During the early part of February, a news release from *Marches Tropicaux* reports that the Communauté Economique des Pays des Grands Lacs (CEPGL) is experiencing financial difficulties. Personnel have not been paid for three months, and almost all members are in arrears.

At an ecumenical summit held on February 6 in which the Catholic, Protestant, and Seventh Day Adventist churches and opposition parties were in attendance, the participants release a statement calling for a transitional government which would negotiate with the RPF, handle the refugee and resettlement issue, and pursue the Structural Adjustment Program (SAP). The churches call upon the parties to conduct dialogue and a tolerant campaign; they also urge the president to respect the decisions taken jointly by the opposition.

Government announces a general amnesty and

5,871 prisoners are freed from jails; included among these, according to Africa Watch, are people responsible for communal violence and human rights violations.

On February 8, the National Conference of Bishops declares its support for a national conference to resolve the issue of transitional government.

The minister of planning signs a financial agreement worth 50 million FF ($9.3 million) on February 12 to rehabilitate Rwanda's telephone system.

Rwandan foreign minister arrives in Dar es Salaam in mid-February to discuss joint power, transport, and communications projects. The participants also discuss the pipeline connection project for petrol from Dar es Salaam to Mwanza and the hydroelectric dam at Rusomo with the Kagera Basin Organization.

The African, Caribbean, and Pacific (ACP) of the European Community passes a resolution urging the RPF and the Rwandan government to settle their differences. It also calls upon French troops to withdraw from the conflict and urges the Rwandan government to respect human rights.

A February 25 news release notes the death of Renee Popaa, an 87-year-old French nun, who was killed along with a Rwandan nun at Rushaki near the Ugandan border. They are the newest casualties of the civil war in the north.

Africa Watch issues a report on February 27 accusing the government of committing a number of human rights violations since the October 1990 invasion. The report accuses the government of doing very little to stop the ethnic violence and killings. It describes the Rwandan military as constituting a threat to civilian life, because it lacks training and discipline. There is also widespread intimidation by the government and the military of political opposition, outspoken journalists, and the clergy. Africa Watch also accuses the RPF of killing hundreds of civilians, pillaging and attacks on civilian targets, refugee camps, and health centers.

During the last week in February and the early part of March, President Habyarimana and Prime Minister Sylvestre Nsanzimana negotiate with twelve registered political parties over the formulation of a genuine coalition government.

In the first few days of March, reports circulated that there was tremendous amount of unrest and violence in the country. In Kigali and Butare, editors and journalists were rounded up, arrested, and detained. People were killed and injured in some mysterious bombings or mine explosions. Eyewitnesses reported that these bombs or mines exploded in or under minibuses and in restaurants in various urban centers. The national government acknowledged at least two bombing attacks in Kigali, two in Butare, three in Bugesera, and one in Nyabisindu. Some blamed the RPF; others, including the press, accused the government, citing that President Habyarimana is in an *"après moi, le déluge"* frame of mind. But no group has claimed responsibility.

On March 2, reports circulate in Kigali that the French government will recall the controversial Lieutenant Colonel Chollet.

A March 3 broadcast over Radio Rwanda announces that an anonymous source in Nairobi has
word of planned assassinations of 20 or more
prominent Hutu leaders by Tutsi living in Rwanda.
The broadcast is repeated several times during the
day.

On March 4, groups of Hutu attack Tutsi and burn
and loot their homes in the communes of Kanzenzi,
Gashora, and Ngenda in Bugesera prefecture. Some
observers blame the Radio Rwanda broadcast from
the previous day.

The Kuwait Fund for Development has agreed to
loan the government 1.7 million KD ($5.8 million)
to finance the Ngororero-Mukamira portion of the
Gitarama-Mukamira road. The KFD has previously
loaned 3 million KD to the project.

On March 6, a new opposition political party is
formed—the Coalition pour la Défense de la
République (CDR)—but is formed too late to take
part in current discussions between the opposition
and the government.

The Parti Démocratique Rwandais (PADER) is
formed on March 7, but it will not participate in
current discussions between opposition parties and
the national government about new emerging democratic process, multiparty government, and the
new coalition government.

Because of ethnic violence, looting, and killing, the
government declares a state of siege in Bugesera
prefecture on March 8.

On March 9, a 55-year-old Italian nun is killed by

Rwandan security forces in Kanzenze commune, Bugesera prefecture. Reports indicate that her death occurred during the evening hours.

Breakthrough occurs and a genuine transitional government is formed on March 13. The MDR, PSD, PCD, Parti Libéral (PL) and the Mouvement Révolutionnaire National pour le Développement (MRND) sign a memorandum of understanding about the objectives of the new transitional government. According to the terms of the memorandum, the participants agree to the following: to negotiate peace settlement with the Rwandan Patriotic Front (RPF); to improve internal security; to review and evaluate the performances of current and future political appointees and reshuffle or remove them as necessary; to settle the refugee issue; to press on with structural adjustment program (SAP); to prepare for the elections to be held by April 1993 at the latest; and to organize a national debate on whether a national conference should be held. The latter is opposed by the MRND on the grounds that it might lead to the undemocratic removal of the current president and others in leadership capacities.

The Bugesera massacre becomes official by mid-March, when the national government acknowledges a death toll of 60. The opposition parties place the figure at several hundred and the Rwandan Human Rights Association claims at least 300. Unofficial estimates claim that between 6,000 and 9,000 people may have taken refuge at the Nyamata Roman Catholic Church, and more than a hundred are being sheltered at the Institute for Agricultural Science. The government estimates that about 15,000 people have been displaced. It acknowledges that the broadcast was misleading, including its assertion that the Parti Libéral was its source. It announces that the director of information has been transferred to the post of first counsellor in the Rwandan embassy in Bonn.

The weekly, *Isibo,* reports for the period March 20 to 27 that the government imposed a MRND *bourgmestre* at the Nyakabanda commune in Gitarama prefecture, despite protest from the opposition. It went on to say that it took 40 soldiers to secure his placement. *Isibo* also reports that the *bourgmestre* of Nkuli has prevented people from joining opposition political parties.

On March 29, Fidele Kanyabugori, who comes from the Bagogwe group of Tutsi and is the legal representative of Kanyarwanda, a human rights group, is arrested in Kigali. Amnesty International protests.

Reports filtering into Kigali in late March and early April note that the countryside has been quite tense and violent. They report that Tutsi have been killed in Gisenyi and elsewhere, and that conflicts are occurring between the people and MRND *bourgmestres* and *préfets* in outlying areas, particularly when they seek to join opposition political parties. They note that the people complain that MRND officials have used intimidation and have even threatened them with forced removal from their lands if they attempt to register with the opposition.

Prime Minister Nsengiyaremye forms a new cabinet on April 16. MRND receives nine posts; the PSD three, the PL three, including the premiership, and the PCD one. Two new ministries were added to the cabinet—Tourism and the Environment, and Women and the Family. For the first time the cabinet contains two women.

The New Coalition Government

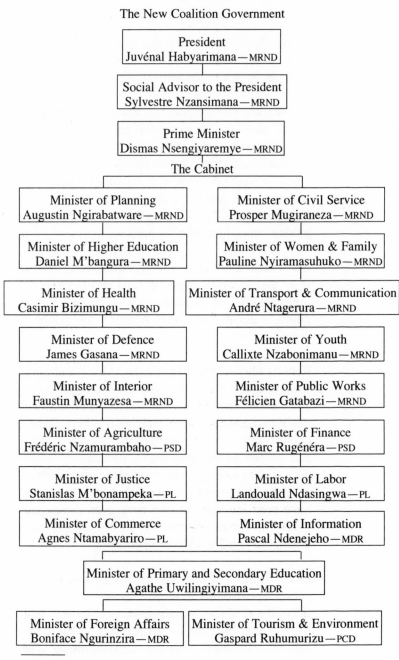

President
Juvénal Habyarimana—MRND

Social Advisor to the President
Sylvestre Nzansimana—MRND

Prime Minister
Dismas Nsengiyaremye—MRND

The Cabinet

Minister of Planning
Augustin Ngirabatware—MRND

Minister of Civil Service
Prosper Mugiraneza—MRND

Minister of Higher Education
Daniel M'bangura—MRND

Minister of Women & Family
Pauline Nyiramasuhuko—MRND

Minister of Health
Casimir Bizimungu—MRND

Minister of Transport & Communication
André Ntagerura—MRND

Minister of Defence
James Gasana—MRND

Minister of Youth
Callixte Nzabonimanu—MRND

Minister of Interior
Faustin Munyazesa—MRND

Minister of Public Works
Félicien Gatabazi—MRND

Minister of Agriculture
Frédéric Nzamurambaho—PSD

Minister of Finance
Marc Rugénéra—PSD

Minister of Justice
Stanislas M'bonampeka—PL

Minister of Labor
Landouald Ndasingwa—PL

Minister of Commerce
Agnes Ntamabyariro—PL

Minister of Information
Pascal Ndenejeho—MDR

Minister of Primary and Secondary Education
Agathe Uwilingiyimana—MDR

Minister of Foreign Affairs
Boniface Ngurinzira—MDR

Minister of Tourism & Environment
Gaspard Ruhumurizu—PCD

Source: EIU, Country Report, No. 2 (1992), pp. 21–22.

On April 21, President Habyarimana retires from the army, but as president remains as commander-in-chief of the army and head of MRND.

Heavy fighting between government forces and RPF is reported in the vicinity of Mutara and in the Byumba province in late April. The RPF claim that they have captured three-quarters of the province, killed 200 soldiers, and seized 60 pieces of government artillery. Official reports indicate that 220,000 people have been displaced within the country as a result of the war.

First couple of weeks in May characterized by violence and political instability. Bombings are reported throughout the country, particularly in Ruhango, south west of Kigali, and in Butare. No one has claimed responsibility.

On May 8, party militia violence develops in Kigali, giving rise to attacks on rival party members and counterdemonstrations by supporters. In the inter-party violence, the new education minister is attacked in her home by twenty armed men.

In a press conference on May 10, President Habyarimana denounces looting by the army and announces the removal of a number of senior army and political personnel, including the chief of staff of police and the army chief of staff.

Reports out of Kigali note that relations with Burundi have improved. Hutu who had taken refuge in Rwanda are returning to their homes in Burundi; respective prime ministers have visited one another's country; and each has reopened its borders.

Between May 10 and 11, Herman Cohen, the

United States assistant secretary of state for African affairs, visits Kigali and announces that he made contact with Mr. Kanyarengwe of the Rwandan Patriotic Front (RPF) and held discussions with President Yoweri Museveni in Kampala. In his discussions with President Habyarimana and the new cabinet and in a recent press conference, Secretary Cohen maintains that he has France's support for peace talks and that the United States is prepared to provide observers and assistance to facilitate the peace process.

RPF representatives and Rwanda government officials assured Secretary Cohen that they wished to negotiate a ceasefire in line with the N'Sele accord, proposed in March, 1991.

During mid-May, reports of random violence circulate throughout the country. Thirty people are killed in separate incidents in Ruhengeri and Gisenyi. A local bank in Kibuye is reportedly robbed by Rwandan soldiers, and there are numerous reports that travellers are being harassed and kidnapped by military personnel. In the Lake Kivu region, the availability of weapons have become quite commonplace, since Zairian soldiers have been selling their weapons and equipment in return for goods unavailable in Zaire.

RPF reports capture of the military base at Rukomo on May 19, but government claims that attack failed.

Tutsi and Hutu students clash at the Nyakinama campus of the National University of Rwanda, the Protestant Seminary at Gahini, Saint André College in Nyamirambo, and the secondary school in Nyaminshaba.

New Rwandan government and RPF hold talks on May 24 in Kampala, while foreign ministers of France and Belgium attempt to mediate a ceasefire. The new government also asked President Yoweri Museveni to use his influence to bring about a negotiated settlement and to do whatever possible to reopen the main roads between his country and Rwanda.

3,000 women demonstrate in support of the education minister who was attacked in her home in Kigali on May 8.

Inter-party militia fighting broke out in Kigali between May 28 and 29. The fighting occurred when MRNDD marched against the Parti Libéral (PL), the predominantly Tutsi party. Marchers reportedly attacked each other with sticks, stones, and machetes for several hours until the army intervened and dispersed them. One person was reportedly killed in the melee. The government has promised an enquiry because of the length of time it took for the army to disperse the crowd.

On May 29, members of the political opposition within Rwanda meet with the RPF in Brussels. The RPF signs a communiqué stating that armed struggle must pave the way to political reform; it encourages all political parties to work together to expose the misdeeds of the Juvénal government and calls for national unity within Rwanda.

From June 2 to 6, there were reports of renewed fighting between RPF and Rwandan government forces.

Rwandan government and the RPF held peace talks in

Paris from June 5 to 7. Among the items discussed were the role of outside mediators, an agenda, which would include the integration of RPF forces into the Rwandan army and political guarantees for refugees, and the selection of advisors and a timetable for talks to be held between July 10 and 12.

On June 15, official reports note that heavy fighting has resumed in Byumba.

As part of its Structural Adjustment Program, the government announces the following measures: a tax increase on beer and cigarettes; less red tape in obtaining import and export licenses; and the devaluation of the Rwandan franc by 15 per cent, from 171.2 RF=1 SDR to 201.4 RF=1 SDR. Rwanda's IMF structural adjustment arrangement will run for three years to April 1994, and at the end of June, 21.9 million SDR ($31.6 million) of the original credit of 30.1 million SDR had not been dispersed.

Ceasefire agreement is signed in Arusha, Tanzania. The agreement is essentially an updated version of the N'Sele Accord and should go into effect in two weeks. Monitors of the ceasefire will include soldiers from OAU and Rwanda, RPF personnel, and a political-military commission drawn from representatives from Uganda, Kenya, Burundi, Zaire, the United States, England, France, Belgium, and Senegal.

Also the Rwandan government guarantees the right of refugees to return and agrees, in principle, to the integration of RPF forces into the Rwandan army.

From July 4 to 8, several prisoners in Kigali went on strike to protest the abduction by the military of certain prisoners. The strike ended only when guards used tear gas to restore order.

A new ceasefire agreement is signed on July 13 by the Rwandan government and the RPF.

Official reports of July 21 note that inter-party violence and rivalry continues. About 21 people are killed and 12 are injured in fighting between the supporters of the MRNDD, and those of the Parti Libéral (PL), and the Mouvement Démocratique Républicain (MDR).

The Coalition pour la Défense de la République (CDR) and the MRNDD organize counterdemonstrations demanding the resignation of the prime minister, who is a member of MDR. These demonstrations result in the death of two people, and scores of demonstrators have been arrested.

The Rwandan government announces on July 26 that its delegates to the ceasefire conference sponsored by OAU in Addis Ababa should finalize the ceasefire agreement in a couple of days.

A ceasefire agreement is finalized on July 30 at Addis Ababa. It calls for a military observer group (MOG) of OAU member states to monitor the ceasefire, and the establishment of a neutral corridor between the areas which would be controlled by both countries. The agreement stipulates that prisoners of war should be released through the agency of the International Committee of the Red Cross.

Economic forecasts during the month of August note that the country is on the verge of bankruptcy.

They note that the country's GNP has declined by 6.8 percent between 1988 and 1990; the Rwandan franc has been devalued by an additional 14.9 percent; and prices have increased between 40 percent and 60 percent since January.

The war in the north is also an enormous drain on the economy, costing the country some $100 million a year, with military spending increasing from 2 percent GDP in 1989 to 6.9 percent in 1991. They note that coffee harvests will be much lower than last year's, primarily because of a lack of rainfall during the months of January and February. The government also expects a 12,000-ton shortfall in food requirements and will have to rely upon food aid, some 14,000 tons which have been pledged by international donors.

The trade war with Kenya over the issue of the Kenyan government's export incentive of 20 percent on Rwandan goods is an additional factor. The Rwandan government has charged that this constitutes an export subsidy, and has retaliated with a 60 percent import charge on Kenyan products. In its complaint to the PTA, the Rwandan government charged that this export incentive constitutes dumping, which is a breach of the East African Preferential Trade Area (PTA) rules. This dispute has forced Rwanda to use an alternative routing from the Indian Ocean. Trade goods must flow through Tanzania and Burundi, which is much more expensive and incurs increased freight charges.

The International Development Agency (IDA) will contribute $19 million to support various food security and social projects as part of a coordinated relief program with UN Development Program (UNDP). UNDP has pledged $3.1 million, and the World Food Program will contribute $16 million. The Rwandan government's share is $8 million. The coordinated relief program will include public works projects, such as the improvement of rural roads, assistance to small businesses, food planning developments, and food aid.

Peace talks between RPF delegates and the Rwandan government resume on August 11 in Arusha, Tanzania and reports note that there have been ceasefire violations.

RPF and Rwandan government sign an accord on August 18 in Arusha which sanctions a pluralistic, transitional government. Still unresolved are the issues of a new constitution, the refugee problem, and the inclusion of the RPF in the government.

The MOG monitoring the ceasefire complain of the absence of a stationary front. They identify three combat zones—Byumba, Mutara, and Ruhengeri, which makes establishing a neutral corridor difficult. Plus they had no enforcement provision other than to report violations.

Inter-party violence and rivalry continued during late August. Violence erupted and death occurred in Gishyita, in Kibuye province, where Tutsi villages were attacked. Six people were killed; scores wounded; and nearly 3,000 left homeless.

During the first week of September, the RPF presented a new proposal at the peace talks at Arusha, calling for the resignation of the present coalition government, including the civil service. It also proposed a national reconciliation committee of ten members with full executive and legislative powers. The prime minister and vice-prime minister would be filled by RPF; the defense minister would come from either the MRNDD or the RPF. The committee would come to power within three months. Refugees would be allowed to return within six months, and elections would be held once this was accomplished. The proposal was rejected out of hand by the Rwandan government. The RPF countered by proposing a seven-member presidential council, which was also rejected by the government. Talks were then terminated and the N'Sele accord collapses.

A new International Coffee Agreement (ICA) is currently being negotiated. Participants have agreed upon a definition of a "universal export quota" and have made some progress on the issue of selectivity. But they have not come to terms on control mechanisms and implementation.

United States government pledged $10 million for a non-governmental organization project designed to improve the productivity of small- and medium-sized enterprises in the non-agricultural sector. The project has a five-year implementation span.

Joint military commission, consisting of RPF delegates and Rwandan military brass, met in Addis Ababa between September 25 and 27. But talks have stalled over the issue of integrated military forces and disarmament.

Peace talks between RPF and Rwandan government resume at Arusha, Tanzania on October 5. The government delegates concede to the reduction of presidential power and agree that it can be transferred to a
government council composed of the RPF. But it re-
jects the proposed seven-member presidential council.
The RPF makes a counterproposal, calling for the president to be excluded from the executive and transfer-
ring his power to the prime minister during the transition period.

Official reports note that more than 300,000 people
live in refugee camps around Byumba. Infant mor-
tality is high; malnutrition and disease are severe;
and facilities are nearly nonexistent. There are few
clinics, bathrooms, or showers. Welfare agencies
have made appeals to the international community
for assistance.

Representatives at the peace conference at Arusha
arrived at a consensus in late October. In the transitional government and during the transitional period, executive power will be shared and the office
of the prime minister will have many of the duties
previously reserved for the former president. The
prime minister will call the meeting of the Council
of Ministers, and the president will be able to attend
cabinet meetings and place items on the agenda.
But he will no longer have the power of veto. He
will still represent the country in the international
arena but only with the approval and consultation
of the cabinet. The prime minister will declare state
of emergencies but in consultation with the cabinet.
The president will still appoint the prime minister
and the cabinet, but the prime minister will have the
power to appoint local administrative personnel to

the offices of prefects and sub-prefects and the heads of state industries.

General Opalaye of Nigeria and commander-in-chief of the military monitoring force reprimanded the French government for failure to withdraw its forces from Rwanda.

To assist the refugee effort, the EC provided 700,000 ECU ($854,000) during the first week of November for housing and medical supplies to be used for the refugees camped in northern Rwanda near the combat zones and in RPF-held territory.

Government-reported epidemic of bacillary dysentery, which has spread through Byumba. About 120 people have died from the disease in the Muhara commune. Some 1800 cases have been reported in the region thus far.

Minister of Health announces on December 1 that the country had 8,483 hospitalized cases and perhaps as many as 500,000 cases of AIDS for the entire country as of June 30.

1993   During the first of the year, two very broad groups have emerged in the political arena. The MDR, PSD, and PL formed a coalition, the Forces Démocratique du Changement (FDC). The MRNDD, the CDR, which is perceived as the MRNDD's extremist wing, and three other minor parties have joined forces to become the Alliance pour le Renforcement de la Démocratie (ARD).

In some circles, ARD is supposed to be responsible for much of the violence currently sweeping the country.

An international commission of enquiry arrives on January 7 to investigate the alleged atrocities committed by a domestic terrorist group called Network Zero. The squad, believed to have ties with the MRNDD, is accused of killing a Catholic priest and murdering several members of the political opposition.

A compromise is achieved on January 9. The competing political parties and RPF agree upon a power-sharing formula and the transitional composition of the Conseil pour le Développement National or the CDN-parliament. The structure of the transitional government is apportioned in the following ways: the MRNDD secures six cabinet seats, including the presidency and the ministry of defense; the RPF gains five posts, including the interior ministry; the MDR gains four posts, including prime minister; the Parti Libéral (PL) secures three positions; the Parti Social-Démocrate (PSD) three; and the Parti Démocratique Chrétien one. With respect to the composition of parliament, all of the major parties get 11 seats, except for the PDC, which receives four. Eleven other parties gain one seat each. The agreement schedules local elections for six months after the end of the transitional period, which by most estimates should last for only one year. Until that time, local government appointments will be by nomination only.

On January 10, the general secretary of MRNDD denounces the agreement achieved the previous day as treasonous and charges the prime ministers and foreign ministers, who come from the same rival political factions, with usurping power. He demands the removal of the foreign minister from the peace negotiations.

On January 11, President Habyarimana removes the foreign minister and appoints the defense minister as his replacement on the grounds that he would be more suitable, since the next topic in the peace negotiations were military matters.

The following day, the new prime minister refuses to accept President Habyarimana's replacement and the peace talks in Arusha come to a halt over the replacement issue and the government's refusal to accept the January 9 agreement.

With the failure of the agreement, the Force Démocratique du Changement (FDC) tells its members to prepare for the defense of the motherland.

There are unconfirmed reports of a massacre of 300 Tutsi by government troops in the north.

A February 8 report confirms fighting between government military forces and the RPF has resumed in northern Rwanda. The RPF successfully overruns ten government outposts.

Fighting in the north has forced the staff at the Karisoke Research Station to flee. They report that buildings were looted and that the anti-poaching squads, introduced by Dian Fossey in 1967, were also forced to leave the area.

In mid-February, an OAU representative accused the French of prolonging the conflict by supporting Rwandan forces militarily. He also accused the French of firing upon RPF positions in Ruhengeri, which the French strenuously deny.

On February 20, Paris announces that two more

companies of French troops will be sent to Rwanda, bringing the total number of troops in the country to about 800.

In late February, the French government attempted to establish a new ceasefire initiative and to reinstate peace talks. Among the new conditions for resumption of peace talks would be supervision of the ceasefire by the United Nations. The French has approached the United Nations Security Council on this issue.

On March 4, the RPF announces that it would withdraw from some of the territory that it currently holds in the north and abide by the rules of the ceasefire, if the French were to withdraw their troops from the country.

On March 7, an announcement from Dar es Salaam maintains that the Rwandan government and the RPF were close to establishing March 15 as a new ceasefire date. Also, the RPF would withdraw its forces to the position held as of February 8 and that peace talks would resume. Both sides anticipate that a new agreement, amending that of January 9, would be in place by the first week of April.

Four international human rights groups release a 100-page report on March 8, which implicates the government in many of the 2,000 civilian deaths that have occurred since 1990. They also criticize the RPF for its flagrant disregard for the lives of the civilian population near the combat zones.

Peace talks resume in Arusha, Tanzania on March 15.

By mid-April the government was able to announce

that the mandate for the transitional government would be extended for another three months. The extension would allow for the conclusion of the peace talks currently taking place in Arusha. The problem in negotiations appears to be the composition of the new 13,000-manned national army.

THE DICTIONARY

-A-

ABACHUZI. Traditional blacksmiths. They ordinarily supplied a hoe to each adult male and they were exempted from all other prestations.

ABAGARAGI. Clients, either Hutu or Tutsi, who have usufruct in cattle. Their obligations to their Tutsi patrons (*shebuja*) include accompanying them on voyages, providing produce and guard duty, cutting wood, carrying water, cultivating the *shebujas'* fields, and constructing their houses. The patrons could reclaim cattle at any time to invalidate the contract, but disputes were generally taken to the African traditional courts. Prestations in this category were extremely complex, because the client arrangement could extend over generations and the obligations could be passed from father to son.

ABAJA. Servants or slaves in Rwandan society.

ABAKAMYI. Young men responsible for performing the traditional obligation of milking cows. They were forbidden to live with women during the times they were exercising their duties. They were exempt from all other corvée, and they received a cow after one or two years of service.

ABAKARAANI. European-educated Rwandan clerks or civil servants, who were sons of chiefs. They attended one of the official schools to learn reading, writing, and elementary arithmetic.

ABAKUTSI. A traditional corvée, or work obligation, performed by Hutu farmers living near a Tutsi notable. Those who performed *abakutsi* were responsible for keeping the kraal clean. They received part of the manure as compensation.

ABAKUZI. Suppliers of honey as a traditional work obligation. The *abakuzi* received in compensation either cattle or exemptions from all other prestations or corvée.

ABALIMYU. Rwandans required to perform corvée as laborers. They had to plant the chief's field, and he was required to house and feed them.

ABANTU B'IMANA BIHANA. "Men of God Who Repent," a fundamentalist religious sect not officially recognized by the government. The sect refuses to pledge allegiance to the national flag, sing the national anthem, or allow their children to attend school on the Sabbath (Saturday). They believe that the end of the world is imminent and therefore work is futile. Their beliefs brought the sect into conflict with the government policy of *umuganda,* or community service and good works, which each citizen is required to perform one day each week. In April 1986, members were detained for membership in the sect, disrespect for the national flag, and failure to perform *umuganda.* Members were brought to trial on October 1, 1986. The state prosecutor demanded prison sentences of between eight and fifteen years for the accused. All of the accused pleaded not guilty. A verdict was rendered on October 17, with the accused receiving sentences ranging from four to twelve years.

ABANYABUTAKA. "Men of the land." An administrative unit created in the eighteenth century by the *umwami* in order to reduce the power of the *abatwaare,* a powerful Tutsi lineage and contenders for royal power in the country. The *abanyabutaka* served the Royal Court at the various royal residences throughout the country; they had the right to assign vacant lands to those who sought new or increased holdings. These administrators began to interfere in the distribution of land within areas previously controlled exclusively by other lineages, including the appropriation of pasturelands. As a result of control over landholdings, this group of officials became quite powerful.

ABANYAMUKENKE. "Men of the grass." A traditional administrative unit created by *umwami* Yuhi Gahandiro in the nineteenth century in order to curb the power of the *abanyabutaka*. The *abanyamukenke* controlled the distribution of pasturelands and collected payments in kind for its use.

ABANYIGINYA. The royal lineage to which the *umwami*, or king, belonged. The name signifies "princes of royal blood" (*princes de sang royal*), and was given to the Nkore, Ndorwa, Rwanda, Bugesera, and to the parent dynasties that governed these countries. It is credited with establishing the original kingdom. According to tradition, the *abanyiginya* arrived in the country by crossing the Kagera River at Mubare.

ABAROKORE. "God's Elect," a fundamentalist sect not officially recognized by the government. Like the *Abantu b'Imana,* they did not allow their children to attend school on the Sabbath (Saturday). Its members were arrested in April 1986, along with members of the *Abantu b'Imana* (Men of God) and the Seventh-Day Adventists for failure to acknowledge the national flag, sing the national anthem, or perform *umuganda* (community service) on religious grounds. Their interpretation of the Bible permits them to sing only religious chants and hymns. The government arrested 296 in all. They were brought to trial on October 1, 1986, in Kigali, where the government's prosecutor asked the court for prison sentences of between eight and fifteen years. The accused pleaded not guilty. In the verdict delivered on October 17, sentences ranged from eight to twelve years.

ABASANGWABUTAKA. Members of major lineages, such as the Singa, Zigaba, and Gesera who form the subclans and were considered to have been the first to occupy the country.

ABASENYI. Suppliers of wood as a traditional obligation. The *abasenyi* conducted their fagoting in the evening, and they were required to draw water and sink wells for the chief.

ABASUKU. Hutu who had to perform the traditional obligation as cooks. They also repaired cooking utensils, supervised the preparation of honey and beer, and cared for the sleeping mats and quarters. They were always men and often became trusted and responsible companions to their notables. They were treated well and often received personal gifts, including cattle.

ABATARA. Notable tax collectors in the traditional administrative structure who, after the administrative reform program of 1924, were restricted to collecting only the tribute due to the *umwami*.

ABATERAMYI. A traditional work obligation that was owed to a notable. Those who performed *abateramyi* were guards responsible for the safety of a notable's home, or *boma*. They received food and were replaced after two or three days of guard duty.

ABATWAARE. A powerful Tutsi lineage whose power frequently threatened the Royal Court.

ABAZUNGU. *See* UMUZUNGU.

ABIIRU. The royal clan, or lineage, in charge of the esoteric code (*ubwiiru*) and therefore able to influence succession.

ABUNGERE. A traditional work obligation that was owed to a Tutsi notable. Those who performed *abungere* were guardians of cattle, both night and day. At night they had to bring a bunch of herbs to fumigate the kraal against flies and mosquitoes during milking. For compensation, they received milk and food, and sometime a cow.

ACQUIRED IMMUNE DEFICIENCY SYNDROME (AIDS). According to the World Health Organization, about 14 million people have been infected with the AIDS virus worldwide. Of this total, sub-Saharan Africa has more than 8 million infected people with some parts of Asia now spreading at the highest rate. For Rwanda, the WHO reported 3,407 AIDS cases in 1991, and government figures on HIV show that 25 percent of the women attending ante-natal clinics in the larger towns are infected, and clinics for sexually transmitted diseases are finding 50 percent infection rates among their clients. Moreover, a UNICEF study of Rwandan young people found that most were ignorant about AIDS transmission routes and the gravity of the disease. The study noted that rural women were the least informed.

ADMINISTRATEUR. Well-educated Belgian stationed at headquarters and responsible for the overall administration of the territory. He reviewed reports submitted by the district commissioner, and he was required by law to maintain constant communication with traditional African authorities and to guide the development of African institutions. He was required to spend twenty days in each month touring the territory.

ADMINISTRATEUR-ADJOINT. Substitute for the territorial administrator in the latter's absence.

ADMINISTRATION GENERAL DE LA COOPERATION AU DEVELOPPEMENT (AGCD). A recent survey of the Belgian governmental organization's involvement in Africa shows that its major preoccupation has been directed towards its former colonies. In 1990, Burundi, Rwanda, and Zaire made up 41.6 percent of its total aid budget, while other African countries received no more than 5 percent. The report notes that the Belgian aid commitment to Rwanda and Burundi is likely to diminish.

ADMINISTRATIVE REFORM PROGRAM (1924). The first Belgian attempt to reform the traditional political and economic structure of the country. The administration abolished the collection of certain dues in kind associated with cattle, goods, or land.

ADMINISTRATIVE REFORM PROGRAM (1927). An edict issued by Belgian administrators limiting *ubureetwa* service for each Hutu adult male to one day per seven-day week. It represented the first attempt on the part of the administration to come to grips with labor issues. Under this edict, no chief could legally compel an individual to perform unremunerated work for him for more than 52 days annually. The administration believed that this edict represented a significant reform, since previously *ubureetwa* had consisted of 2 days out of each 5-day week or approximately 146 days annually.

ADMINISTRATIVE REFORM PROGRAM (1929). Belgian order consolidating traditional chieftaincies, reducing traditional corvée, and equalizing traditional prestations in work details by the Hutu that were due to Tutsi notables. These measures were designed to provide some relief for the Hutu majority, who carried the burden of the system.

ADMINISTRATIVE REFORM PROGRAM (1930). A major Belgian reform program. Traditional administrative units (such as the offices of the land chiefs and cattle chiefs) were fused into a single position. The position of army chief was abolished outright. Reforms were designed to reduce the number of clientship arrangements, and as a means to change traditional socioeconomic and political structures.

Restructuring of these chieftaincies meant the suppression of *ibikingi,* which was essential because it would continue to impede the reforms introduced in the areas of corvées and prestations. But more importantly, *ibikingi* was utilized by chiefs to gain additional wealth, since it gave these categories of chiefs the right to allocate land to new clients.

A court system was established so that the Hutu could redress grievances. Agricultural improvements were implemented in order to overcome periodic famines and food shortages. Coffee cultivation was introduced; reforestation of eroded hillsides was intensified. There were also improvements made in livestock production, and mineral prospecting and mining operations were facilitated. New roads were constructed and trade reorganized.

ADMINISTRATIVE REFORM PROGRAM (1932). An amendment to the reorganization of traditional chieftaincies in 1930. It provided for the redemption of traditional taxes, or prestations, in kind rather than in work. These were replaced by annual money payments of 1 BF. This tax was designed to free Africans from a series of additional corvées, such as tribute in the form of produce or the housing and provisioning of prestation workers.

ADMINISTRATIVE STRUCTURE. The country is divided into the following central and local governmental institutions: the *préfecture,* the *sous préfecture,* the *commune,* and the *cellule,* which is the lowest echelon. Prefectures are divided into subprefectures, followed by communes, and then by cells. Each prefecture is headed by a prefect, who is appointed by the central government. The commune is directed by a mayor and an elected communal council. Both are elected by direct popular vote. The cell is headed by a *chef de cellule,* who is elected by a five-member *comité de cellule*. The latter is elected by the local community, which consists of twenty-five to thirty families.

AFRICAN CIVIL SERVICE (1921). Appointments made by the governor-general that included teachers, postal clerks, assistants in the customs and medical departments, and public works foremen.

AFRICAN/NATIVE TRIBUNAL. Tutsi political institution founded in 1924 as part of the Belgian administrative reform program to consolidate Tutsi authority. Fifteen tribunals were initially created.

AGENCE BELGE DE L'EST AFRICAIN. A Belgian commercial brokerage from Antwerp with interests in transportation, customs clearance, and insurance from 1936 to about 1951. It operated out of Kigali and had branch offices at Dar es Salaam and Kigoma. Its activities included the direction of Belgian concessions in Dar es Salaam and Kigoma and operations dealing with the movement of travelers and merchandise. The agency was also responsible for managing the Belgian government's port facilities at Dar es Salaam and at Kigoma on Lake Tanganyika.

AGENCE FRANCE-PRESSE (AFP). The foreign press bureau located in Kigali.

AGENCE RWANDAISE DE PRESSE (ARP). Rwandan national press agency, founded in 1975. It publishes a daily bulletin.

AGENTS. A grade within the colonial administrative and technical services, which was further subdivided into highly competitive categories: principal, first, and second classes. The governor-general was authorized to appoint agents. The appointment to an initial rank depended upon educational qualifications. A second-class agent did not need a university degree, but might attend classes in technical instruction at the Ecole Coloniale in Brussels. An agent's tour of duty overseas after 1935 was for three years, with a six-month leave after the completion of service. The first tour was generally probationary.

AGRICULTURAL CALENDAR. There are four seasons: October to December (a small rainy season and the first planting season); January to February (a small dry season); March to May (the second planting season); and June to September (the large dry season). A third planting season occurs only in the marshlands in the eastern region of the country.

AGRICULTURAL CREDIT. Ordinance No. 126 (AIMO) April 27, 1942, modified by Ordinance No. 226 (AIMO) September 1, 1947, which authorized the governors of each province to allow African district and traditional authorities to grant loans of 5,000 BF or less to their inhabitants. These loans could be used to extend cultivation, harvest, preparation, and conservation of coffee or other produce. The interest rate for these loans was 5 percent annually.

AGRICULTURAL EDUCATION. During the colonial period the teaching of agricultural theory and practice was stressed. The itinerant staff of the Agricultural Service, when visiting Africans in the rural areas, held on-site practical demonstrations to illustrate problems of cultivation. A school for African agricultural assistants, part of the responsibility of the Groupe Scolaire in Astrida, provided a four-year course. Three years were devoted to theoretical training and one year combined theory and practice. Those who obtained a diploma were engaged by the colonial administration.

AGRICULTURE ET ELEVAGE AU CONGO BELGE ET DANS LES COLONIES TROPICALES ET SUBTROPICALES. A Belgian periodical and the official voice of the Association Belge d'Agriculture Tropicale et Subtropicale, published by the Association des Intérêts Coloniaux Belges. The magazine was devoted to the agricultural interests of European planters in Belgian Africa during the 1920s and the 1930s.

AGRICULTURAL SERVICE. *See* SERVICE DE L'AGRICULTURE.

AGROTIS SEGETUM. A cutworm that attacks coffee plants.

AIR RWANDA (SOCIETE NATIONALE DE TRANSPORTS AERIENS DU RWANDA). National airline, established in 1975, operating domestic passenger and cargo services and international cargo flights to Bujumbura (Burundi), Goma (Zaire), and Entebbe (Uganda), as well as flights to Tanzania, Kenya, and destinations in Europe. As of 1989, the airline's holdings included one Boeing 707–320C, two Twin Otters, one Islander, and one Aztec.

AKANYARU. A major river system in the southern region of the country, which borders on Burundi. Also the name of a territory, created in 1923 out of Nyanza territory, too heavily populated to be administered as a single unit.

AKAZI. Forced labor, usually done for little or no pay, for the German or Belgian colonial government. Nonelite Tutsi were required to perform *akazi,* and failure to comply could result in the confiscation of a person's land by the local chief. A significant decline in security of tenure for African cultivators occurred when some chiefs used *akazi* to arbitrarily expel landholders.

AKINKAMIYE, MADELEINE. The first Rwandan woman to hold a ministerial office in the national government. She was born in Ntarama, Ruhengeri, in 1942. As a member of PARMEHUTU she served in the Ministry of Social Affairs. She was responsible for women's services. In January 1964, she was appointed to head the Ministry of Social Affairs, and she directed the ministry until October 1965.

ALBERT I, KING OF BELGIUM (1875–1934). Albert was born at the palace at Laeken to the Count and Countess of Flanders. He succeeded his uncle, Leopold II, on December 23, 1909, and was very popular with his people because of his leadership during World War I. His reign coincided with a period of greatness and prosperity such as Belgium had never known before. The young prince took extensive trips to Belgian Africa and demonstrated great interest in the welfare of Africans and other colonial problems. He died on February 17, 1934, as the result of an accident, falling from a high rock at March-les-Dames.

ALBERT NATIONAL PARK. An area of 34,500 hectares in northern Rwanda set aside in 1933.

ALBERTVILLE-STANLEYVILLE-MATADI ROUTE. An international trade route for merchandise imported and exported from Rwanda, used primarily in the 1930s.

ALLIANCE POUR LE RENFORCEMENT DE LA DEMOCRATIE (ARD) The Alliance for the Reinforcement of Democracy is a political coalition of like-minded groups, generally conservative and supporters of the status quo, that emerged at the beginning of 1993. The alliance included the dominant political party in the country, the MRNDD, and four other minor parties, including the CDR. The ARD was formed in response to the democratic and multi-party movement and what members of the coalition believed was a diminution of their influence in the country's political affairs. Members of the coalition were also dissatisfied with the direction of peace negotiations to end the civil war. Most observers feel that the ARD is responsible for much of the violence against political opponents that have ocurred in recent months.

AMABANGA. Communal pastureland in the traditional system, primarily for cattle.

AMBLYGONITE. A lithium ore mined in Rwanda and exported overseas for foreign exchange since the 1950s.

AMI, L'. A Catholic review devoted to the évolués of Rwanda; it began publication at Kabgayi in 1945. It ceased publication in January 1955 to become the weekly *Temps Nouveaux.*

ANGLICANISM. A Protestant faith practiced in Burundi, Rwanda, and Zaire. Approximately 120,000 Banyarwanda are practicing Anglicans. The dioceses of Rwanda have two bishops, one stationed at Kigali, and the second at Shyira near Ruhengeri.

ANIMISM. Traditional African religions practiced by about 42.5 percent of the African population.

ANTESTIA. A parasitic infestation that often plagues coffee. There was a major outbreak in 1937 in Kivu, Mulera, and Ruhengeri that reduced coffee yield by one-third. Another infestation occurred during the 1974–1975 coffee season. About 30 percent of the coffee beans were affected.

ANTHRAX. A bacteria that attacks cattle.

ANTIEROSION PROGRAMS. Early colonial economic programs for Rwanda enacted in order to retain groundwater. Terrace antierosion ditches and quickset hedges to protect soil on hilly ground or on slopes were used systematically. The Belgian administration also increased the amount of cultivable land available by draining marshy areas in eastern Rwanda and the Cyamwakize marshlands in Akanyaru, the province of Astrida (Butare).

ARABICA COFFEE. Bourbon and Guatemala varieties were introduced by Catholic missionaries (the White Fathers) into

Rwanda from their mission station at Mibirizi. Only the Guatemala variety survived, and by 1931, Rwandans were persuaded to cultivate coffee.

A minimum price was fixed by the Belgian government for African coffee planters. It was assumed by Belgium that this crop would one day be a great source of wealth. The government provided both technical and scientific assistance and facilitated efforts for its exportation. *See also* COFFEE CULTIVATION.

ARABS IN RWANDA. During the period of German rule, the government decreed on March 10, 1905, that Arab merchants had to obtain special permission in the form of a license to enter Ruanda-Urundi before they could conduct trade. The decree was designed to protect Africans from unscrupulous methods, and it was a temporary measure designed to last until "specified" markets could be built where trading could take place. The difficulty was that the Germans were too few to ensure fair trade between the Africans and the Arab merchants, who concentrated on two products—salt, which they imported from Uganda, and dried fish (*ndakala*), which came from Kigoma.

ARMY CHIEF. Leader of the *umwami*'s army, as well as arbitrator of disputes involving cattle and other livestock.

ASIANS IN RWANDA. The March 10, 1905, German decrees concerning Arabs also regulated Asian traders. Before they could participate in trade, they also had to obtain a license. Asian and Indian traders dealt with items such as salt, dried and smoked fish, tea, and jute bags. They usually catered to Africans; very seldom did they import items used by Europeans or participate in the export trade, which was reserved for European traders. In the interior regions of the country and in African areas, Asians and Indians controlled the retail trade.

ASKARI. Foreign troops—either Africans, Arabs, or Asians

from German East Africa—who accompanied the Germans when they entered Rwanda.

ASSOCIATION BELGE D'AGRICULTURE TROPICALE ET SUBTROPICALE. A lobby for European planters in Belgian Africa created in February 1927 in the general assembly of the Association des Intérêts Coloniaux Belges. Its membership included persons from scientific organizations, educational societies, and commercial companies interested in agriculture. The association frequently petitioned the government at Brussels in the interest of planters, and it conducted campaigns against African coffee cultivation and for tariff reductions in transportation rates for the shipment of coffee during the 1930s.

ASSOCIATION DES COLONS DU KIVU ET DU RUANDA-URUNDI. Planter trade association established in September 1929 in Brussels. It was affiliated with the Association des Intérêts Coloniaux Belges.

ASSOCIATION DES INTERETS COLONIAUX BELGES. The official publisher for the Association Belge d'Agriculture Tropicale et Subtropicale, a Belgian lobby for the colonial planters, created in 1927. The association published the periodical, *Agriculture et Elevage au Congo Belge et dans les Colonies Tropicales et Subtropicales*.

ASSOCIATION DES PLANTEURS DE CAFE. An association created in Brussels in 1935 and concerned with the cultivation of robusta and arabica coffee, tariff rates, technical assistance to European planters in Belgian Africa, and the marketing of their coffee in Belgium. Its membership included individuals from UNAKI, and its first chairman was Professor Edmond LePlae.

ASSOCIATION POUR LA PROMOTION SOCIALE DE LA MASSE (APROSOMA). A political party established in

November 1957 by Joseph Gitera, a former member of the Mouvement Social Muhutu (MSM). Its program included the democratization of traditional institutions and the elimination of caste or ethnic distinctions and privileges. The party was successful in and around Butare, but on the whole its achievements were insignificant. In the Communal Council elections in 1960, it received 233 seats out of a total of 3,125.

ASTRIDA (BUTARE). A territorial unit and educational and commercial center during the colonial period; currently a prefecture, as well as a principal town with a population of about 21,000. The prefecture region is approximately 265,000 hectares, or 1,830 square kilometers, situated on the central plateau, about 6,000 feet above sea level. It has a population of approximately 603,000 inhabitants. The town was named for Queen Astrid of Belgium, and its location was selected because of its altitude and its agreeable and healthy climate. The town became the temporary seat of local government in Rwanda in 1927, and eventually the educational and commercial center for hides, coffee, and cassiterite during the colonial period. Astrida was also the home of Groupe Scolaire, where Africans were educated for the colonial civil services.

ASTRIDA (BUTARE)-SHUNGUGU ROAD. A road of about 150 kilometers, extending from the south central region to the southwest of the country.

ATHENAEUM. An educational institution created by the Belgian colonial government and located in Bujumbura for children of mixed parentage from the mandate.

AUGUST 1988 MASSACRES. Between 2,000 and 3,000 Tutsi were reportedly killed by Hutu in Burundi in mid-August. In retaliation, the Burundi army, mobilized "to stabilize" the situation, killed between 5,000 and 10,000 Hutu, and forced another 60,000 to flee to Rwanda and to other neighboring countries. The massacres stemmed from efforts by President Pierre Buyoya of Burundi to moderate discriminatory practices toward Hutu and to give them more power. Hutu had been disenfranchised. The president urged more economic and political freedom for the Hutu, but his appeal had little impact on the attitudes and practices of local officials, who continued to discriminate against Hutu. The Hutu in frustration apparently lashed out in anticipation of an attack by the Tutsi.

-B-

BACOBOZI. *See* PARTY YOUTH WINGS.

BAGARAGAZA, THADDEE. A Rwandan politician and member of PARMEHUTU. He was born on June 6, 1936, at Muvumo in Byumba. He was educated at a mission school in Rulindo and attended the Petit Séminaire at Kabgayi and the Grand Séminaire at Nyakibanda for one year. He spent two years at Lovanium University at Leopoldville in the Belgian Congo. He held a variety of political offices, including chef de service and later secretary-general of the Department of Social Affairs. In October 1961, he headed the Ministry of Social Affairs and served as the national delegate from Ruhengeri for the MDR-PARMEHUTU. From 1963 to 1969, he was minister of international cooperation and planning, and president of the National Assembly from 1969 to 1973, when he became minister of education.

BAGAZA, JEAN-BAPTISTE. A Tutsi army officer who became president of Burundi in 1976. He seized power from his Tutsi kinsman, Michel Micombero, who had been president since 1966. As president, Bagaza ruled through a thirty-member Supreme Revolutionary Council. He promised an eventual return to civilian rule and inter-communal harmony, and he revolutionized Burundi society. The new constitution of 1981 sanctioned democratic elections for 1982; however, Bagaza continued to rule through the military and a one-party system. UPRONA (Unity for National Progress) is the only party in the country. In recent years he attempted to relieve Hutu oppression.

BAGOGWE MASSACRE (JANUARY 1991). The Bagogwe are a group of people of Tutsi origin living in the province of Ruhengeri. In October 1991, domestic and international sources report that several hundred Tutsi called the Bagogwe had been killed by government troops and civilians after the January 1991 attack on Ruhengeri. The January attack involved government and RPF forces. The Bagogwe were accused of acting as RPF scouts by those involved in the massacre. As a group, the Bagogwe are traditional cattle keepers with very little education.

BAHUTU MANIFESTO (1957). *See* MANIFESTE DES BAHUTU.

BANANA. The banana tree is the most valuable and useful plant in the eyes of the Banyarwanda. The fruit is used to make the local beer, which is consumed in large quantities.

BANQUE BELGE D'AFRIQUE. With its home office in Brussels, the bank operated in Rwanda during the 1930s.

BANQUE COMMERCIALE DU CONGO. A Belgian bank with branches in Usumbura (now Bujumbura) and Kigali, providing services for the colony and mandate during the 1930s.

BANQUE COMMERCIALE DU RWANDA SARL. One of the three commercial banks in the country. It was founded in 1963 and has reserves and capital of 375.2 million RF and

9,079.8 million RF in deposits, according to 1985 figures. There are eleven branches throughout the country.

BANQUE CONTINENTAL AFRICAINE RWANDA SARL. A commercial bank operating out of Kigali with capital and reserves of 208.5 million RF and deposits of 3,391 million RF, according to 1986 official reports.

BANQUE DE KIGALI SARL. A commercial bank founded in 1966 with ten branches throughout the country. Capital and reserves amount to 425.7 million RF, with deposits of 7,745 million RF, according to 1985 estimates.

BANQUE DU CONGO BELGE. A Belgian bank that provided service for the colony and the mandated territory as early as 1925. Its main branch was located at Usumbura (now Bujumbura), and the bank was initially responsible for placing European currency into circulation.

BANQUE NATIONALE DU RWANDA (DE LA RE-PUBLIQUE). The National Bank of the Republic was created in 1964. The main branch is located at Kigali, and it has capital and reserves of about 3,000 million RF.

BANQUES POPULAIRES DU RWANDA (BANKI Z'ABAT-URAGE MU RWANDA). Banques Populaires, located in the capital, Kigali, is the country's second development bank. It has capital and reserves of 394.3 million RF and deposits of 3,195.8 million RF according to 1988 official estimates. Also, according to an official report, Rwandan farmers contribute 50 percent of the deposits held by the bank, but receive only 13 percent of the loans. Merchants and civil servants receive 42 percent and 17 percent respectively.

BANQUE RWANDAISE DE DEVELOPPEMENT SARL (BRD). This development bank is one of two in the country. It was founded in 1967, and it has capital and reserves, according to 1985 estimates, of 2,783.9 million RF and deposits of 3,491.3 million RF.

BANYAMBO. An ethnic group of several thousand living in Rwanda.

BANYARWANDA. The Hutu, Tutsi, and Twa inhabitants of Rwanda.

BARLEY. A basic food crop, which is also used in the brewing of the local beer.

BARTHELEMY, PAUL (1872–1943). Member of the Missionnaires d'Afrique, or the White Fathers. Father Barthélémy was born in Leberau-Alsace, France, on July 10, 1872. He attended secondary school in Strasbourg and received a degree in rhetoric at Saint Eugene in Algiers. He became a novice on October 7, 1894, and was ordained on March 13, 1899. He was assigned to southern Nyanza in September, but as soon as he arrived he joined a group of White Fathers, including fathers Brard and Anselme, who were traveling by caravan to Rwanda. The caravan arrived at Bujumbura on January 8, 1900, on its way to Ishangi in Rwanda. On February 2, the caravan arrived at Musinga's court, where they were given permission to establish their first mission at Save (Issavi). Father Barthélémy was also instrumental in the establishment of the mission at Zaza, south of Lake Mohazi, and a third mission station at Bugoye, on the shores of Lake Kivu, where he remained until his return to Europe in 1909. The following year, Father Barthélémy was nominated the general bursar (*économe général*) for the vicariate of southern Nyanza at Bukoba. He remained in this position until 1937, when he returned to France, where he lived at the sanatorium of the White Fathers at Pau-Billère. He died on August 24, 1943.

BASEBYA. A legendary Twa figure of the early twentieth century. His exploits are recounted in songs and folklore. He organized a Twa band in Buberuka, a marshy region in northern Rwanda, gave protection to emigrant members of the royal family who were enemies of *umwami* Musinga, and refused to pay tribute to the king. *Umwami* Musinga's armies, sent in June and again in August 1905, were unable to dislodge Basebya and his band. Musinga asked for German assistance, and a military expedition was sent in February 1906. The Germans burned numerous villages while searching for Basebya, but were unable to find him. He was finally caught and executed in 1911 by the Germans, when he fell into a trap laid by a Tutsi chief.

BAUDOUIN I, KING OF BELGIUM (1930–1993). Albert-Charles-Leopold-Axel-Marie-Gustave Baudouin was born in Brussels on September 7, 1930—the son of King Leopold III and Queen Astrid, princess of Sweden. He became king in July 1951, when his father abdicated. King Baudouin visited Rwanda in 1970, as well as for the 25th anniversary celebration of independence on July 1, 1987.

BAUMANN, OSCAR. An Austrian and the first European to enter Rwanda. Baumann had been sent to Africa by a German antislavery group. In addition, he was supposed to report on the geographical and economic potential of the northwest region of German East Africa. He left Europe in October 1891 and arrived at Tanga on January 14, 1892. His expedition reached Ruvubu on September 4, and six days later he reached the marshes of Akanyaru. He spent four days (September 11 to 15) in Rwanda.

BAYINGANA, PETER. An army officer in the Rwandese Patriotic Army (RPA) who participated in the invasion of Rwanda from Uganda on October 1, 1990. Major Bayingana took command of the invading force on October 2, the day after Major General Fred Rwigyema, the leader of the attack, was killed in battle. According to Major Bayingana, the invasion had been planned for three months, and the major challenge had been "how to evacuate the Rwandese Patriotic Army troops from Uganda's National Resistance Army (NRA)." Major Bayingana was killed in an ambush along with some 320 other RPA fighters on October 23.

BEANS. A basic food crop and a major source of protein for the population.

BEER. Social obligations in Banyarwanda society are expressed in terms of visits, and beer is an important component of the ritual. Prior to independence visits were especially important in the nuclear feudal clusters, and to be seen was very important. Afternoons were usually given over to visits. Generally gifts were exchanged. Both visits and gift giving were controlled by custom, and the Belgian administration prohibited most of the *redevances* associated with custom, except for giving either banana or millet beer, which was allowed at all levels.

BELGIAN MANDATE. The League of Nations conferred mandatory status upon the Belgian acquisition of Ruanda-Urundi on August 23, 1923. Its confirmation made Belgium responsible "for peace, good order, and good administration" of the territory. Belgians were to abolish slavery, protect all inhabitants against fraud, and enhance, "by all means in her power," the material and moral well-being and social progress of the inhabitants.

BELGIAN THESIS. The Belgian defense of colonialism and its responsibility as a trustee are outlined in this thesis, and also designed as a counteroffensive against the criticism and attacks from members of the United Nations Trustee Council and Visiting Mission, who had accused Belgium of exploiting its African charges.

The thesis maintains that Belgium had the moral obligation to bring civilization and self-government to its African dependents. It claimed that the trust should be exercised not only over indigenous peoples residing in non-self-governing territories but also over indigenous and underprivileged peoples of sovereign states.

BICAMUMPAKA, BALTHAZAR. A Rwandan politician and member of PARMEHUTU. He was born in Mukono, Ruhengeri, in 1920. He was a teacher, and in 1958 he was nominated as a *sous-chef*. In 1960, he was vice president of PARMEHUTU, a member of the Provisional Council, and minister of agriculture and the *paysannat*. In February 1963, he became minister of the interior and social affairs and served as president of the National Assembly from 1965 to 1969.

BIRARA, JEAN. Rwandan lawyer, politician, and banker. Jean Birara was born in Mudende, Gisenyi, in 1937. He received a doctorate in law and a license in economics at the University of Louvain, as well as taking special courses at the Direction Etudes et Structures de la CECA at Luxembourg and the Université Internationale d'Economiques Comparatives. He was administrator of the National Bank of Rwanda in 1964, the vice-governor in 1967, and governor after 1971.

BISERUKA, COMMANDANT STANILAS. Commandant Stanilas Biseruka is a former Hutu army officer, who was imprisoned in the maximum security prison in Ruhengeri for nearly a decade but was freed when RPF forces captured and overran Ruhengeri on January 23, 1991.

BIZIMUNGU, PASTEUR. Pasteur Bizimungu was a prominent Rwandan businessman, who was active in the underground movement against the country's only ruling political party, the MRND. Pasteur sought refuge in Uganda at the beginning of 1990, and the government has been seeking his extradition, and that of his son, Vlen since September 1990.

BORGERS, EDGARD. Administrator at Mulera in 1923, he

pacified the territory and helped to extend Tutsi control in this region.

BOURGEOIS, RENE. Territorial administrator from 1933 to 1935.

BOURSES DU TRAVAIL. Belgian colonial agencies responsible for regulating the recruitment of African laborers by private firms and individuals in the Katanga and the Kasai provinces since 1910.

BRACHYTRYPES MEMBRANACEUS. A disease that attacks coffee plants.

BRALIRWA. A subsidiary of Heineken, the Dutch brewing firm. Bralirwa manufactures and bottles beer in Gisenyi and soft drinks in Kigali. It is the largest agroindustrial company in the country in terms of turnover, some 6.7 billion RF in 1986. The company produced 641,000 hectoliters of beer and 169,000 hectoliters of lemonade in 1986.

BRARD, ALPHONSE (1858–1918). Member of the Missionnaires d'Afrique, or the White Fathers. Father Brard was born in La Chapelle-Biche on April 4, 1858; he was ordained a priest at the Maison-Carée in Algiers on September 21, 1883. He was posted to East Africa in 1887 and arrived at Kigua, which is near Tabora, on September 17. He spent much of the 1890s at various mission stations in Uganda. In 1899, he accompanied Father Barthélémy and Father Anselme to Rwanda, where they eventually established the first Catholic mission station at Save (Issavi) on February 6, 1900. He remained in Rwanda until 1905, when he was designated a representative at the general chapter house of the Société des Pères Blancs. He remained there for one year, and eventually obtained permission to enter the Carthusian monastery of *Lucques* (Lucca) in Italy, where he died in 1918.

BROTHERS OF CHARITY OF GENT (FRERES DE LA CHARITE DE GAND). Religious order responsible for establishing the Groupe Scolaire at Astrida (now Butare) in 1929. They also encouraged the publication of the journal *Servir* by their African students.

BUGESERA. A province located in the southeastern portion of the country that was divided into two sections in 1933 as part of the administration reorganization program. The province was overpopulated and overgrazed. In 1933 and even today, Bugesera contains the largest percentage of Tutsi residents of any province in the country.

BUGESERA MASSACRES (MARCH 4, 1992). The massacre occurred the day after Radio Rwanda's broadcast without confirmation that an unknown group in Nairobi, associated with the Parti Libéral, intended to kill 20 or more prominent Hutu living in Rwanda. As a result, on the night of March 4, a number of Hutu civilians began to attack Tutsi and burn and loot their homes in the communes of Kanzenze, Gashora, and Ngenda in the Bugesera prefecture. According to one of the Rwandan human rights organizations, about 300 civilians were killed. The government, however, put the death toll at a much lower figure, between 60 and 150. A few of the opposition parties claim that the numbers killed were at least several hundred. Unofficial estimates place the numbers made homeless between 6,000 and 9,000. Many of these sought sanctuary at the Nyamata Roman Catholic Church, where the Italian nun, Antonia Locatelli, was shot early during the year. The church was overwhelmed; the numbers seeking sanctuary outstripped the church's capacity to assist them. Many suffered from hunger and exposure, as well as from harassment from local security forces. But hundreds more with the assistance of government forces were able to find refuge at the Institute for Agricultural Science. Others fled into Burundi. Unofficial estimates note that 15,000 people have been displaced.

Both the Parti Libéral and the MDR accused the government of complicity in the massacres. Eyewitness accounts maintain that those taking part included MRND youth wingers, and report that many of those wounded in Bugesera were brought to Kigali for treatment. They also report that Tutsi who tried to defend themselves were disarmed by government soldiers. The MDR for its part called for the dismissal of the ministers of the interior and information and the *préfet, sub-préfet,* and the *bourgmestre* at Bugesera. The government's response was to transfer the director of its information service to the post of first counsellor in the Rwandan embassy in Bonn, and it arrested 392 people for participating in the murder and looting.

BUJUMBURA. *See* USUMBURA.

BUKOBA-MOMBASA ROUTE. A secondary international trading route used as early as 1925, but not preferred, because of the high freight costs, the rising prices for carriers to Bukoba to make the connection to Mombasa, and the increasing commerce from large firms at Usumbura and Kigali.

BULERA. River and lake in the eastern region of the country.

BULETWA. A traditional prestation in kind that was collected by the sous-chefs. A portion of the *buletwa* was eventually forwarded to the *umwami* as *ibihunikwa* and to the hill chief as *imisogonero.*

BULLETIN AGRICOLE DU RWANDA. A quarterly periodical published by the Office des Cultures Industrielles du Rwanda (OCIR) Café, near Kigali-Gikondo. Publication began in 1968 under the auspices of the Ministère Rwandais de l'Agriculture et de l'Elevages. At that time, it had a domestic circulation of about 800. The bulletin covers the problems of agriculture and animal husbandry in tropical countries generally and in Rwanda specifically. It also contains statistical information about agricultural production, commerce, consumption patterns, agricultural cooperatives, demography, as well as the human and social aspects of agriculture and animal husbandry.

BULLETIN DE JURISPRUDENCE DES TRIBUNAUX INDIGENES DU RUANDA-URUNDI. A biannual bulletin published from 1946 to 1955 by the Association des Anciens Elèves du Groupe Scolaire d'Astrida and by the governor of the mandated territory. The bulletin contains articles about customary law in Rwanda and its development, as well as judicial decisions made by traditional and Belgian colonial authorities.

BULLETIN DE LA BANQUE CENTRALE DU CONGO BELGE ET DU RUANDA-URUNDI. This periodical was published monthly from 1952 to 1960, and it contained information about the budget, economic conditions, commercial activity, and the finances of the African territories administered by the Belgians.

BULLETIN DE STATISTIQUE DU RWANDA. A statistical bulletin that began publication in April 1964 by a department in the Ministry of State responsible for national development planning. It began as a quarterly, but publication has been irregular. It contains statistical information on demography; foreign commerce; transportation; public finances; agricultural, mineral, and industrial production; consumer prices; tourism; the school population; and public health.

BULLETIN D'INFORMATION DE LA CHAMBRE DE COMMERCE ET D'INDUSTRIE DU RWANDA/UBUCURUZI BWA KIJYAMBERE. A bilingual periodical in French and Kinyarwanda that has been published irregularly since 1975 by the Chambre de Commerce et d'Industrie du Rwanda.

BULLETIN OFFICIEL DU RUANDA-URUNDI (RWANDA-BURUNDI). The official journal of the mandated territory, published from 1924 to 1962. It was a bimonthly from 1924 to 1931; from 1932 it was published as a monthly until 1955, when it returned to a bimonthly periodical. It contains all of the official legislation associated with the mandated territory, as well as the actions (*actes*) of commercial companies and certain judicial rulings, such as petitions and investitures, assignations, and other kinds of judgments.

BUNYENYEZI, MAJOR CHRIS. One of the leaders of the October 1990 invasion of Rwanda from Uganda. Major Bunyenyezi took command after Major General Fred Rwigyema died on October 2. Major Bunyenyezi was killed in an ambush on October 23.

BUREAU NATIONAL D'ETUDE DU PROJETS (BUNEP). BUNEP was established in 1980 under the Ministry of Planning to design Rwandan development projects and to assemble, train, and utilize personnel.

BUTEGANA AFRICAN COFFEE PLANTERS COOPERATIVE. This cooperative and several others were part of the Belgian government's initiative to increase coffee production during the 1950s. The cooperative at Butegana received a five-year loan of one million BF from the government, which charged no interest during the first year, but assessed interest during the second year at 2 percent, and at 4 percent after the third year.

BWANAKWERI, PROSPER. Tutsi chief of Nyanza territory and a member of the Banyiginya, the ancient royal lineage of Rwanda. In 1954, he became a member of the opposition with *umwami* Mutara as cofounder and president of Parti RADER, which he represented in the Special Provisional Council.

BWIMBA, RUGANZU, UMWAMI OF RWANDA. Ruganzu reigned from 1458 to 1482. He conducted raids in the western part of the country and established a small nuclear kingdom in the vicinity of Buganza and Bwanacambwe.

BYUMBA. A territorial unit during the colonial period, and a prefecture since the national era. Byumba is situated in northern Rwanda, and located southeast of Mulera, northwest of Gatsibu, and north of Kigali. It is approximately 4,987 square kilometers and has a total population of 522,000 inhabitants. The territory was created in 1931 during the administrative reorganization program. Pyrethrum, peas, and sorghum are grown in the region. The country was considered rather isolated and too mountainous for coffee cultivation, but it became a thriving economic center and a food reservoir later in the colonial era.

-C-

CAISSE CENTRALE DE COOPERATION ECONOMIQUE. The Central Bank of Economic Cooperation is a French development bank, similar to the World Bank in its mission and inception. It was established in 1941 and was given its present name in 1958. The French development bank lends money to member states and former members of the Franc Zone. It is also committed to supporting developmental projects, either through modest loan agreements or outright grants to Third World countries. In the past, the CCCE loaned significant sums to the Rwandan government to support development projects in the Masaka region. A recent loan agreement of 49.7 million FF (including a grant of 8 million FF) was signed with Rwanda on December 4, 1990 to support the mapping of Rwanda's main towns, beginning with Kigali and Butare, to computerize customs services, and to improve air traffic control at Kanombe international airport. Over half of the amount, 36.5 million FF will be used to modernize and extend the Kibuye sugar factory. The Rwandan government will contribute 26.5 million FF to the Kibuye project as well.

CAISSE D'EPARGNE DU CONGO BELGE ET DU RUANDA-URUNDI. Bank established to encourage savings among Africans by offering them the guarantee of the State. The institution used part of its capital for loans to individuals and private organizations concerned with economic development within the African community. It granted mortgage loans to private individuals at 7 or 8 percent annual interest.

CAISSE D'EPARGNE DU RWANDA. Savings bank created in 1964 and currently having nine branches and thirty-five sub-branches throughout the country. Its capital and reserves amount to 162 million RF with deposits of 1,724.3 million RF, according to 1984 official estimates.

CAISSES DE TRESORERIE. African savings fund created in 1937 and managed by the territorial administrator. This institution assessed every able-bodied adult male 2 BF annually, collected fees from the cost of legal proceedings before the African/Native Tribunal, as well as fines and funds collected from seizures pronounced by the tribunal. Funds could be allocated for expenses for administration and development projects only within African communities.

CAISSES DU PAYS. An institution formed after World War II and augmented by contributions from the head and supplementary taxes, as well as the fees from cattle injections, contributions from the *umwami*'s tribunal, receipts from the African Territorial Tribunals, fines imposed by notables, interest from deposits, and gifts and subsidies from the government. The institution's funds could be used for general administration and construction, including the improvement of local roads. The Service d'Agriculture could also use its resources for salaries, matériel, and the purchase of pyrethrum for its insecticide program.

CASSITERITE. The major mineral mined in western Rwanda as early as 1928, from which tin is extracted. Estimated reserves in 1935 were about 2,900 tons. Cassiterite was mined in the west and northeast regions of Rwanda and in the province of Kigali. During the colonial period, the principal mining societies were MINETAIN, SOMUKI, Mirudi, Mindfor, and Georundi. Tin mining was expanded during World War II, from 1940 to 1944. In 1985 yields were 1,145 tons and it was the third highest export earner after coffee and tea. It has recently fallen upon hard times.

CASTOR OIL. The castor oil plant grows wild, and Hutu occasionally used the oil in the absence of butter to anoint their bodies.

CATERPILLAR CONTROL. A regulation of December 21, 1935, made caterpillar control compulsory on African farms.

CATHOLICISM. *See* RELIGION.

CATTIER, FELICIEN. Honorary professor at the University of Brussels, former member of the Colonial Council, director of the Société Générale de Belgique, and president of the Compagnie du Congo Belge pour le Commerce et l'Industrie. Cattier was a proponent of colonial enterprises in the 1920s.

CATTLE CHIEF (UMANYAMUKENKE). As a member of the traditional administration, this Tutsi notable took care of dues from livestock.

CATTLE MARKETS. Markets organized by the Belgian administration to provide meat for the African population. The markets were patronized by butchers who supplied the territory's main centers, by traders who supplied live cattle or meat in bulk to the mining companies, and by African traders who exported live cattle to Kivu province.

CATTLE TAX (IMPOT BETAIL). A source of revenue for the Belgian administration and a category within the ways and means budget of the State and the chieftaincy funds. The tax varied according to levels of economic development within a particular region. It was enacted by an ordinance which established a tax per head of cattle. In 1931 the cattle tax was 4 BF per head. It was considered a tax on wealth, and was also designed to decrease the size of herds.

CEASE-FIRE AGREEMENT (MARCH 29, 1991). In an attempt to resolve the conflict precipitated by the October 1990 invasion, three formal ceasefire agreements were arranged and signed between the Rwandan government and the Rwandan Patriotic Front (RPF). The first agreement occurred on February 17, 1991. The February conference took place in Zanzibar. Among those present were the presidents of Rwanda and Uganda. The terms called for the cessation of hostilities on February 18. The ceasefire failed to materialize. The second agreement was supposed to begin within two weeks of the signing of the Dar es Salaam agreement on February 19, but this one failed as well. The third was the ceasefire agreement of March 29, 1991, which was signed in N'sele, Zaire, between Rwanda's foreign minister, Casimir Bizimungu, and the RPF military commander, Paul Kagame. It called for a monitoring team headed by Brigadier Hashim Mbita of the Organization of African Unity (OAU) with Barundi, Rwandan, Zairian, Ugandan, and RPF officers participating. Article 5 of the March 29 agreement stipulated that both sides were to stop using the media to insult and defame each other. The March agreement failed as well.

CENTRALE D'EDUCATION ET DE COOPERATION DES TRAVAILLEURS POUR LE DEVELOPPEMENT (CECO-TRAD). The only trade union currently operating in the country. It was founded in 1984 to succeed the Confédération Syndicale des Travailleurs du Rwanda (COSTRAR).

CENTRE D'INFORMATION ET DOCUMENTATION DU CONGO BELGE ET DU RUANDA-URUNDI. Center responsible for collecting and disseminating information about Belgian Africa. George Sandrart was its assistant director for a short period in 1951.

CHAMBRE DE COMMERCE ET D'INDUSTRIE DU RWANDA. Government agency established in 1982 and designed to coordinate commerce and industry on a national level. Its activities originate from Kigali.

CHARTE COLONIALE. The Colonial Charter was formulated on October 18, 1908, when Belgium assumed the administration of the Congo Free State. It contains the administrative procedures for the Belgian Congo and eventually for the mandated territory of Ruanda-Urundi. Under the charter, legislative power for the colony was delegated from the Belgian parliament to the king. The latter exercised legislative power by decree, while parliament retained certain rights in connection with financial matters and the granting of concessions.

   The charter also stipulated that no one could be compelled to work for individuals or companies; it outlined the responsibilities and duties for the minister for the colonies, the Colonial Council, Temporary Expert Commissions, the governor-general, the vice governor-general, Provincial Councils (Conseils de Province), Governmental Council (Conseil de Gouvernement), Administrators (Administrateurs, Fonctionnaires, Agents), and Commissioners (Commissaires).

CHEF. Chiefs were important servants of the *umwami* and had ownership rights to products from parcels of land (*ibikingi*) conferred on them by the king. Chiefs received their chiefdoms at the favor of the king. Under Belgian administration, they became agents and functionaries who carried out directives to impose cultivation, drain swamps, plant trees (including coffee), construct roads, collect taxes, and report infractions.

CHEF DE CHEFFERIE. An administrative unit in both the traditional and colonial administrations, comparable to a district, and commanded by a Tutsi notable.

CHEF DE COLLINE. The hill chief was part of the traditional administrative structure; he had the power to distribute land to newcomers.

CHEF DU SERVICE DES AFFAIRES INDIGENES ET DE LA MAIN-D'OEUVRE (AIMO). Agency that functioned during the colonial period and maintained statistical data on the emigration of Africans from Rwanda and Burundi to the Belgian Congo and the countries of British East Africa.

CHEFS DU BUNETSI. Chiefs of forced labor, and a temporary administrative title used by the German officers at Gisenyi in 1913 to reward Africans who had converted to Christianity and facilitated requisitions.

CHEMIN DE FER DU BAS-CONGO AU KATANGA. A privately owned railroad used to facilitate the flow of international freight to and from the interior. As the leading rail operator in Belgian Africa in both ton-mileage and freight volume transported, this railroad also had financial ties with the Union Minière du Haut-Katanga. Both were subsidiaries of Société Générale.

CHEMIN DE FER DU CONGO SUPERIEURS AUX GRAND LACS AFRICAINS. Rail line used to facilitate the flow of international trade to and from the interior of Belgian Africa.

CHEMIN DE FER DU KIVU. A fifty-eight-mile-long rail line operated by the freight company OTRACO. The line runs from Uvira on Lake Tanganyika to Kamaniola.

CHRISTIANITY. *See* RELIGION.

CHURCH MISSIONARY SOCIETY. Since the 1930s, this Protestant missionary society has operated a mission station at Shyira and has conducted a number of nongovernment schools for Africans.

CIVIL AVIATION. The country has airfields at Butare, Gabiro, Ruhengeri, and Gisenyi, which serve internal flights. A new international airport, the Grégoire Kayibanda airport, opened at Kigali in July 1986, and has the capacity to handle 500,000 passengers annually. There is also an international airport at Kamembe.

CLAESSENS, JOSEPH. A member of the Belgian administration in the Agriculture Service. Claessens was born on October 15, 1873, and received his first promotion within the colonial service on February 15, 1912.

CLAEYS-BOUUAERT, ALFRED-MARIA-JOSEPHUS-GHIS-LENCUS. Vice governor-general of Ruanda-Urundi from 1952 to 1955.

CLASSE, MONSIGNOR LEON-PAUL (1874–1945). A member of the Missionnaires d'Afrique, or the White Fathers, and the vicar apostolic of Rwanda. The monsignor was born at Metz on June 28, 1874, and spent more than forty years in Rwanda. Before going to Africa, he studied humanities at Saint Nicolas of Chardonnet and the Petit Séminaire of Versailles. Later, he entered the Grand Séminaire Sulpicien at Issy. On October 11, 1896, he become a novice of the White Fathers at the Maison-Carrée in Algiers. He was ordained a priest at the cathedral of Carthage on March 11,

1900. When he received his appointment to Rwanda, he was serving as secretary to Monsignor Livinhac, the superior general of the White Fathers. Both he and Father Paulin Loupias, who would be murdered in Rwanda, departed from the port of Marseilles for their assignment together. When Father Classe arrived in Rwanda, Monsignor Hirth was in charge. His first assignment was to establish a fourth mission station, at Ruaza in northern Rwanda among the Balera. In October 1907, Monsignor Hirth appointed Father Classe deputy vicar (*vicaire délégué*) of Rwanda, when he was only thirty-three years old. The next decade and a half was devoted to the organization, consolidation, and extension of church activities in Rwanda.

In 1920, Father Classe returned to the home office in Algiers and then to Belgium. He was serving as bursar at Antwerp, when he received the news on April 26, 1922, that he had been appointed the bishop of Rwanda. This appointment marked a new phase in Classe's career and church activities in Rwanda in terms of influence and the visibility of the church. Monsignor Classe hoped to use the *umwami* and his court to benefit the Catholic Church at the expense of Protestant sects, which were becoming quite competitive during his absence. He was also instrumental in the deposition of *Umwami* Musinga, who was exiled to Kamembe in 1931. Monsignor Classe personally approved Musinga's successor, his son, Charles Mutara III Rudahigwa. Several cathedrals were built during the 1930s, at Rulindo, Kigali, Kiziguru, Rambura, Mibirizi, Rwamagana, and Butare.

On December 2, 1944. Monsignor Classe aggravated an old fracture of the right collarbone in a fall. His doctor recommended that he be transported to Leopoldville for consultation. The examination at Leopoldville revealed a double fracture of the upper and lower femur and that nothing could be done for him. The Monsignor returned to Bujumbura on January 2, 1945, and died on January 30. His body was transported to Kabgayi, where it was buried.

CLIENTAGE SYSTEM. A traditional institution in which a client asked for the protection of a more wealthy patron in exchange for whatever goods and services had been agreed upon beforehand. It was a bond of reciprocal loyalty, which permeated the entire sociopolitical structure, from the *umwami* to the lowest vassal. The giving of a cow confirmed the patron-client relationship.

CLIMATE. Rwanda is situated on the edge of the zone influenced by the Indian Ocean. It can best be described as tropical highland. The daily temperature range may exceed 25 degrees, while the annual range is about 5° F.

The summers and winters are dry, and springs and autumns are wet. The equatorial pattern persists, but with less rainfall and a climate resembling that of the Sudan with its characteristic droughts rather than the genuine equatorial climate of the Congo variety.

Rwanda is a region of heavy rainfall, though the average annual precipitation is far lower than that of many areas in the Congo basin. Altitude, the proximity of the mountains, and the strength and direction of the prevailing winds are all factors influencing the climate.

The central plateau, where rainfall is relatively abundant, has a temperate climate. Rainfall and fertility decrease progressively in the eastern part of the country, where the altitudes are lower, the temperature higher, and precipitation rarer.

COALITION GOVERNMENT (MARCH 13, 1992). After repeated attempts, the character and composition of the transition government, pending new elections to be held at the latest by April 1993 (the date had been scheduled for December 1993), was resolved when the MDR, PSD, PCD, the Parti Libéral, and the *ex-parti unique*, the Mouvement Révolutionnaire National pour le Développement (MRND) signed a memorandum of understanding, which underlined the objectives of the government to be created. The memo-

randum signed outlined seven aims of the coalition government: a negotiated peace; improved internal security; conduct performance evaluations of political appointees and remove them if need be; the settlement of the refugee issue;
support for SAP; preparation for the elections scheduled for
April 1993; and the organization of a national debate on
whether a national conference should be held. On April 2, a
new prime minister, Dismas Nsengiyaremye, who was
agreeable to all the political parties, was appointed. Mr.
Nsengiyaremye is a member of MDR, and he replaced
Sylvestre Nsanzimana, who was considered the president's
man and the focus of a great deal of opposition from the new
political parties.

COALITION POUR LA DEFENSE DE LA REPUBLIQUE
(CDR). The Coalition for the Defense of the Republic is a
new political party that came into existence on March 2,
1992, much too late to participate in political discussions,
which took place in late February and early March, between
the government and the other opposition parties to determine the composition of the coalition government. The
CDR's orientation is pro-Hutu, and its founders are senior
government officials and businessmen, such as Mr. M.
Bucyana, head of Papeterie de Zaza, Ferdinand Nahimana,
head of ORINFOR, the information bureau which has close
ties to the president, and Mr. T. Nahimana, head of the tax
bureau.

Mr. Ferdinand Nahimana was recently transferred from
his post as head of ORINFOR to that of first counselor in the
Rwandan embassy in Bonn for his role in permitting the
anti-Tutsi broadcast over Radio Rwanda on March 3, 1992.
Many believed that this broadcast caused the massacres in
Bugesera. Moreover, many observers believe that the CDR
has contributed much to the current political instability now
plaguing the country. For example, on July 21, 1992, the
CDR in concert with the MRNDD organized a series of demonstrations demanding the resignation of the prime minister, a

member of MDR. These demonstrations resulted in two deaths and scores of arrests.

COFFEE CULTIVATION. An arabica variety was introduced officially under a compulsory cultivation program by Belgian colonial authorities in 1931. The administration believed that coffee would contribute to the general economic growth of the country. The general cost to African producers would be much lower than those of European planters, since Africans had recourse to family members for planting, maintenance, and harvesting.

The campaign was implemented in seven distinct phases. The campaign for 1931–1932 was the initial trial run. Model fields of 250 to 1,000 plants were given to Tutsi notables and subchiefs. These plots were located in poor pasturelands and on denuded hillsides, far from individual *rugos*. The results of the 1931–1932 campaign were mediocre. Belgian authorities discovered that the Tutsi neglected their coffee fields. Trees that were planted on hillsides died from being exposed to drying winds.

Of the total number of plants distributed, approximately 50 percent perished and another quarter had to be destroyed. Those which survived were placed in an artificial environment with intercalary plants, such as *albizzia, tephrosia,* and banana trees. The Agricultural Service cultivated some leguminous plants for covering. Terracing was used on high slopes. Mulching was employed during the dry season, and a considerable amount of organic material was distributed at the base of the coffee trees.

In the 1932–1933 campaign, Hutu farmers were used instead of Tutsi notables. The Agricultural Service provided assistance in the selection of fields, and African monitors assisted by Belgians inspected coffee fields periodically, staked out the holes for planting, provided nurseries, and grouped the coffee parcels of fifty-four plants. Coffee trees were planted in bottomless baskets made from bamboo laths tied with banana leaf fibers. Young trees were protected by shade plants. The results were much better than in the first campaign.

For the 1933–1934 campaign, the administration provided more intense supervision and technical assistance in the form of new nurseries and flowerbeds, maintenance materials (such as poles for cloches and papyrus-mat covers for shade), and the collection and distribution of thousands of baskets filled with decayed manure. The campaign was designed to increase yields and to instruct the populous in proper maintenance procedures.

The 1934–1935 campaign extended coffee cultivation to other regions of the country. For example, about 500,000 coffee plants were planted in Kigali territory. The 1935–1936 campaign emphasized the proper maintenance of coffee nurseries and the training of the African cadre. Nurseries were positioned on the slopes and the summits of hills, and instruction was given in the proper methods of transplanting coffee trees from nurseries to the fields.

The final campaign, of 1936–1937, dealt with the technical and marketing aspect of coffee production, as well as the extension of production to the rest of the country. African farmers were instructed in washing, shading, plowing, and weeding techniques. Coffee nurseries were established in each chieftaincy. Approximately 70 percent of African taxpayers throughout the country had on average 60 coffee trees.

Today Rwandan coffee is grown by over 500,000 smallholders, and production is approximately 41,000 metric tons.

COFFEE STABILIZATION FUND (CAISSE DE COMPENSATION). The fund, created on June 26, 1954, by Ordinance No. 53/218, regularized the purchasing price of African coffee in Rwanda and Burundi and promoted the social and economic development of coffee in African areas. The fund was financed by a tax deduction from marketable coffee for export, which was deducted by OCIRU. The administration used the interest from the fund to purchase coffee driers and pruning shears. The fund was suspended in 1958.

COLLEGE INTERRACIAL. College established by the Jesuit order as a "free subsidized school" at Bujumbura in 1954. The boarding school was designed to accommodate forty boarding and 200 day students.

COLON; COLONAT. Terms used in the context of the controversial policy of European colonization in Belgian Africa during the 1930s. Some Belgian authorities believed that white settlers would transform the social and economic realities of Belgian Africa; others believed that their presence would cause only discord and problems.

COLONIAL COUNCIL. Created by the colonial charters to advise the minister for the colonies. It was composed of fourteen members: eight were nominated by the king, three were elected by the Belgian senate, and three by the Belgian chamber of deputies. The council recommended legislation on administrative measures and was consulted on all decrees. The minister for colonies had the power to override the council and could issue decrees without consulting it, particularly in emergencies. The council could censure the use of emergency procedures, however, if it felt that they had been implemented unnecessarily.

COLONIAL TRANSPORT OPERATIONS SERVICE. A transport company that monopolized navigation on Lake Kivu.

COMITE NATIONAL DU KIVU. Created in 1928 to organize European colonization and to develop the infrastructure of the Kivu. The commission later turned to other activities, such as commercial agricultural development in 1929 and the recruitment of Rwandan laborers under one-year contracts during the 1930s. This commission was indicative of the close cooperation between the State and the industrial sector.

COMMISSAIRE DE DISTRICT. With the reorganization of 1933, the holder of this administrative post served as an inspector. The district commissioner made a detailed inspection of every territory in his district at least twice a year and reported on the operations of the various services.

COMMISSAIRE DE PROVINCE. Administered the province and the local technical services and visited every district in his province at least once a year.

COMMISSION DES DEVISES ET DES IMPORTATIONS. An agency created by Ordinance No. 26 (AE) of February 1, 1943, and Ordinance No. 21 (AE) of January 25, 1946, which exercised control over and regulated commercial import activities. It was composed of a regional director from the Banque d'Emission du Congo Belge et du Ruanda-Urundi and a delegate from the Belgian administration. The commission was located at Bujumbura, where it met weekly.

COMMISSION NATIONALE DE SYNTHESE. The National Synthesis Commission was established in September 1990 by President Habyarimana and was charged with preparing the country's political reform program for the national government. In its report to President Habyarimana on April 10, 1991, the Commission recommended that the 1978 constitution be modified rather than rewritten. It called for the abolition of the single party system and the creation of the post of prime minister.

COMMISSIONS ON LABOR AND INDIGENOUS SOCIAL PROGRESS. An advisory group that was formed in the 1950s. It was composed of five senior governmental officials, five representatives of employers, and five representatives of the African workers' interests—one European missionary and four African clerks. The group advised the government on the minimum rates of wages, and discussed and adopted recommendations on questions affecting labor, such as eligibility for benefits other than money wages and measures to be taken to check absenteeism.

COMMITTEE FOR CONSULTATION (AUGUST 1991). The Committee for Consultation, which was formed in August, 1991, is composed of the MDR, PSD, and the PL. The Committee is actually a political alliance in opposition to the MRND, the government's party, which it feels has the clear advantage in the new political climate and the movement toward representative government. In fact, it believes that the current government is unconstitutional and the new constitution, signed by President Habyarimana on June 10, 1991, is invalid and refers to it as an "MRND document." The Committee wants to delay the elections, scheduled for December 1993, until the war in the north is resolved. It also demands a "sovereign" national conference, which would establish a transitional government and a new legislature. The national conference's decisions would also be binding and above the constitution. MRND, as well as the PDC, reject the idea of a national conference as undemocratic and support the December 1993 elections.

The government, however, presented its own version of the Committee for Consultation, when President Habyarimana addressed the CND on October 2, 1991. At the CND meeting, the president urged all the legal political parties to meet in consultation in order to establish a joint management plan for the current transitional period. The Committee for Consultation responded with a resounding no the next day, maintaining that the government's framework and objectives of the meeting were unclear. It countered by maintaining that a transitional period to the elections could be better managed by a provisional government. The latter would include all the legal parties and would be headed by a prime minister appointed or acknowledged by them. The government was undeterred, because on October 10, 1991, President Habyarimana appointed his party's minister of justice, Sylvestre Nsanzimana, as prime minister and instructed him to establish a new cabinet with representatives from the six major political parties.

The Committee objected and refused to participate in the transitional government. On November 17, the Committee held a mass rally at Kigali with some 25,000 in attendance. It explained its position to the assembled and criticized the appointment of Mr. Nsanzimana as prime minister, MRND's privileged access to Radio Rwanda, and the party's use of government vehicles. In addition, the Committee called for the establishment of a national conference, which would examine the several issues, including the misuse of state property by government officials, the Hutu/Tutsi problem, the issue of regional tensions between the north and the south, and the problem of refugees and their resettlement. A week after the Committee's rally, the MRND held its own counter-demonstration.

COMMITTEE OF NINE. Signatories of the Bahutu Manifesto of 1957. It included M. Neyonzima, Grégoire Kayibanda, Claver Ndahayo, Isidore Nzeyimana, Calliope Mulindahabi, Godefroid Sentama, S. Munyambonera, Joseph Sibomana, and Juvénal Habyarimana.

COMMUNAL COUNCIL ELECTIONS (JUNE–JULY 1960). Rwanda received its independence on February 2, 1961. In preparation for a more widely based African electorate, a series of communal elections were held between June 26 and July 31 prior to the plebiscite for independence. Of the total number of eligible voters, 78.21 percent turned out to vote, and of the total of 3,125 councillor vacancies at the communal level, PARMEHUTU won 2,201 seats, for a total of 70.4 percent, APROSOMA won 233 seats, or 7.4 percent, RADER won 209, or 6.6 percent, UNAR 56, or 1.7 percent, while a splintering union of APROSOMA and PARMEHUTU won 190 seats, or 6 percent. The remaining 7.9 percent was divided among several minor parties and individuals. The election was an overwhelming victory for the Hutu and for their principal party, the Parti du Mouvement de l'Emancipation des Bahutu (PARMEHUTU). The Hutu victory also culminated in the persecution of and exodus from the country by Tutsi for nearly eighteen months. Their lands were confiscated and some were arrested.

COMMUNAUTE ECONOMIQUE DES ETATS DE L'AFRIQUE CENTRALE (CEEAC). The Economic Community of Central African States was formed by ten mostly French-speaking countries in 1983 at the suggestion of Omar Bongo, the president of Gabon. Rwanda, Burundi, and Zaire are members. The group meets periodically to discuss mutual issues, such as tariff reductions, as well as to coordinate economic policies. The sixth conference took place in Kigali in January 1990, where participants discussed the upgrading of the road linking Rwanda with Burundi and Zaire as a priority project for submission for consideration by financial institutions.

COMMUNAUTE ECONOMIQUE DES PAYS DES GRANDS LACS (CEPGL). The Great Lakes Economic Community is made up of Rwanda, Zaire, and Burundi. These countries hold periodic summits to discuss the free movement of goods and people across their borders.

COMPAGNIE COMMERCIALE INDUSTRIELLE ET MINIERE (SOCIETE CIM). A prospecting Belgian company, with interests in Kanyarira. The Belgian administration expected the company and others like it to contribute to the financial prosperity of the country. Société CIM received the right to prospect in 1927, but did not begin exploration until 1932. In 1934, it employed 4 mining engineers and 80

African workers. Two years later, it had a staff of 7 Europeans and employed 250 Africans. CIM ceased general prospecting in 1936 and concentrated most of its activity in Kanyarira. In 1937 it created Société Mirudi, which dabbled in the mining of gold and the production of cassiterite.

COMPAGNIE DE RUZIZI. The parent company was based in the Ruzizi Valley in Urundi, near Bujumbura. The company purchased cotton from African planters and planted coffee in Shangugu territory during the 1930s.

COMPAGNIE DES CHEMINS DE FER DES GRANDS LACS. A commercial company that provided service on Lake Tanganyika during the colonial period.

COMPAGNIE DES CHEMINS DE FER DU CONGO SU-PERIEUR AUX GRANDS LACS AFRICAINS. The company monopolized lake transportation from the ports of Rwanda, Burundi, the Belgian Congo, and Tanganyika territory during the colonial period.

COMPAGNIE DES CHEMINS DE FER DU KIVU. The company transported commodities, such as coffee, tin ore, pyrethrum, and construction materials, on Lake Kivu during the colonial period.

COMPAGNIE DES TABACS DU RUANDA-URUNDI ET DU CONGO BELGE. The company cultivated tobacco in its concessions at Kisenyi and Ruhengeri as early as the 1930s, and collaborated with neighboring population centers by supplying them with tobacco plants and purchasing their harvests in order to supply its own factory, which manufactured cigarettes at Bujumbura.

COMPAGNIE DU CHEMIN DE FER TANGANYIKA-KIVU. A company that recruited labor in Rwanda under one-year contracts during the 1930s.

COMPAGNIE DU KIVU. A Belgian firm from Antwerp that began operations in Rwanda in 1927 and participated in the import and export of African commodities, such as hides, coffee, and palm oil. It conducted activities in Bujumbura, Kitega, Uvira, Bukavu, N'Goma, Kisenyi, Butare, and Kigali.

COMPAGNIE GENERALE DE L'EST AFRICAIN BELGE. A Belgian import-export firm that began operations in 1926. The company traded in African hides and furs and conducted its activities in Bujumbura, Kitega, Kigali, Ruhengeri, Bukavu, and Shangugu.

COMPOST. Under Ordinance No. 70 (AIMO) of November 20, 1944, the Resident of the colony could require able-bodied African farmers or herdsmen to save all products (such as ash, cow dung, and household refuse) which would normally be thrown away, and to use them to fertilize their fields. The use of fertilizers, chemical or otherwise, among African farmers was very limited, owing both to the high costs and to low yields.

COMPULSORY CULTIVATION. Legislation enacted in 1917 and formally sanctioned by the Belgian government through Legislative Ordinance No. 52 of November 7, 1924, authorized the Resident of Rwanda to compel African inhabitants to plant food and exportable products. A revised ordinance, No. 21/81 of July 10, 1953, stipulated that every able-bodied adult African male residing in a chiefdom and not regularly employed in the service of the State or with a European establishment had to plant and maintain under cultivation (a) 35 ares of seasonal food crops, and (b) 25 ares of non-seasonal food crops, of which at least 15 ares had to be planted in cassava at all times of the year. Exemptions were extended to those whose land was situated in altitude zones over 1,900 meters. In this particular case, the 25 ares had to be planted in sweet potatoes, or any other tuber recommended by Belgian administrative authorities. The revised law also required the inhabitants of Buganza, Buyogoma, and those near mining areas to plant twenty banana trees each. These measures were designed as safeguards against famine. Compulsory cultivation was terminated in December 1958.

COMPULSORY LABOR. At the very beginning of the colonial experience, collective work obligations by Africans were required by the Belgian colonial authorities in cultivation of food crops on the hills and in valleys, as well as in drainage, irrigation, and reforestation projects.

CONCESSIONS. Land units granted by the Belgian government to Europeans and commercial concerns in order to stimulate the development of the colony. Agricultural concessions were about 75 hectares in populated areas, and the maximum was fixed at 200 hectares in nonpopulated regions of the country. A European farmer could own on the average from 25 to 75 hectares of land, while an African family was usually allotted from 1 to 2 hectares. Mining concessions varied depending upon the size of the mineral deposit.

CONFEDERATION SYNDICALE DES TRAVAILLEURS DU RWANDA (COSTRAR). The union confederation of workers of Rwanda was the country's first trade union. It was government sponsored, and membership was open to all, even self-employed agricultural workers. COSTRAR was succeeded by the Centrale d'Education et de Coopération des Travailleurs pour le Développement (CECOTRAD) in 1984.

CONGO FRANC-STERLING EXCHANGE RATE. Parity varied throughout the colonial period and affected the number of francs obtained for money earnings taken into Rwanda, the relative prices of goods in Uganda, and the magnitude of Banyarwanda migration to British territories. In fact, any change in the fixed rate of exchange between the franc and pound sterling was generally followed by broad movement in the size of the flow in the direction that might be expected: an increase in years when the franc depreciated in comparison with sterling, and a decrease in times when sterling was depreciated. Therefore, the late 1920s, a period of famine and food shortages in Rwanda and of heavy immigration into Uganda, was also a period when the franc was considered to have been undervalued.

The sharp drop in immigration between 1931 and 1935 was also accompanied by a sharp decline in the wages paid by Ugandan employers. After the Belgians abandoned the gold standard in 1935, the British Annual Report of the Labor Department of 1936 noted that immigration into British territories was far in excess of previous years. Similar broad changes in the flow of immigration occurred when the franc-sterling parity changed in September 1939, June 1940, and September 1949.

CONSEIL DE GOUVERNEMENT. As constituted in 1933, it included as ex officio members, the vice governor-general, the state inspectors (*inspecteurs d'état*) or senior officials responsible for general supervision of administration throughout the country, the procurator-general, and the secretary-general. Six provincial commissioners or their representatives were added in 1934.

CONSEIL DU VICE GOUVERNEMENT-GENERAL. The Vice Government-General's Council was established by decree on March 4, 1947 as part of the administrative reorganization of 1947–1948. The council was purely advisory; it examined budgetary proposals, considered questions submitted to it by the governor of Ruanda-Urundi, and submitted recommendations to the government. It contained twenty-two members, of whom five were high-ranking officials; three were officials selected by the governor of the mandate; nine were representatives of settlers' associations, chambers of commerce, employers' organizations, and associations of professional employees; and five were representatives of the African population, usually missionaries or government officials. One or more of this last group could be an African after 1950. The *umwami* became a member in 1949. The Council of the Vice Government-General became a general council in 1957.

CONSEIL POUR LE DEVELOPPEMENT NATIONAL. Until the new constitution of 1991, the national legislature, first elected in 1973 after the old national assembly was dissolved, was a unicameral body elected for five-year terms by universal suffrage. It had a membership of 70, elected by voters from 140 candidates nominated by the MRND, and it exercised legislation on its own. The council could censure the president by a vote passed by four-fifths of its members but could not dismiss him. It discussed financial matters, made changes to proposed legislation, and formed committees for specific national problems.

CONSEILS DE PROVINCE. In the administrative reorganization of 1933, the provincial council replaced the much older comité régional. It was attached to the commissioners of the six provinces and was an advisory body, unofficially sanctioned by Belgian administrative authorities. The council's membership consisted of the procurator-general, the district commissioner, officials nominated by the provincial commissioner, and (at his discretion and by nomination) residents in the province of Belgian nationality. Members of the Provincial Council created the provincial budget, and they were consulted on all questions related to defense, the police force, African welfare, public works projects, and general administrative policy.

CONSTITUTION (NOVEMBER 24, 1962). The text of Rwanda's first constitution was proclaimed during the *coup d'état de Gitarama* on January 28, 1961, by an assembly of the newly elected mayors and communal representatives.

The constitution consists of eighty articles and one chapter of provisional information acknowledging the official trusteeship of the United Nations that was assumed by Belgium.

CONSTITUTION (DECEMBER 20, 1978). The National Development Council (Conseil pour le Développement National), elected for a five-year term by universal adult suffrage, replaced the previous National Assembly. Under the new constitution, the judicial system was also reorganized to comprise a Council of State with administrative jurisdiction, a Supreme Court of Appeal, and a Constitutional Court consisting of the Supreme Court of Appeal and the Council of State, sitting jointly, a Court of Accounts responsible for examining all public accounts, and courts of appeal, courts of first instance, and provincial courts.

CONTRAT SCOLAIRE. A legal agreement between the Catholic church and the Belgian colonial state, concluded by Bishop Classe in 1923. Under the contract, the Catholic church assumed responsibility for the entire educational system in the mandate. Government schools were phased out by the early 1930s, and the Catholic church received a subsidy from the government for each pupil and teacher.

COOPERATIVE DE PROMOTION DE L'INDUSTRIE MINERALE ARTISANALE (COPIMAR). A cooperative formed by the government in 1986 after the collapse of SOMIRWA, the Rwandan mining company. The government hoped to use COPIMAR as a cooperative for the country's 10,000 miners who lost their jobs with the demise of SOMIRWA.

COOPERATIVE D'ETUDE COLONIALES ET D'ACHATS (CECA). A cooperative established in 1929 by Comité National du Kivu. It acted as a purchasing and leasing agent for materials.

COOPERATIVE TRAFIPRO UMUNYAMULYANGO. A monthly periodical that contains information about the import-export business, published in French and Kinyarwanda, with a circulation of about 10,000.

COOPERATIVES. A decree of August 16, 1949, granted Africans the right to organize cooperatives. For those who lacked funds, the Belgian colonial government provided financial assistance to cover the initial operating expenditures. There was no interest payment on the government's contribution for the first year; however, after the second year a 2 percent interest fee was charged, and it was raised to 4 percent for the next year. Cooperatives also enjoyed full exemption from personal and income taxes for three years following the date of approval. For the next two years, they were granted a 50 percent reduction in these taxes. The government had the power to approve the selection of directors and the terms of the contracts, as well as the disposal of surplus. By 1958, there were six cooperatives throughout the country.

CORVEE. Customary work obligations and a source of complaint by the Hutu against their Tutsi patrons and chiefs. Prior to reform in 1929, customary labor obligations were levied on the Hutu for Tutsi notables at the rate of three days out of five throughout the year. These were gradually reduced to thirteen days per year—of these days, three were to benefit the provincial chief and ten days were reserved for the *sous-chef* (subchief)—and redemption became optional. Initially the latter was restricted to certain categories of Africans, but in 1945 it was extended to all Africans. On January 1, 1949, redemption of contributions in the form of labor was made compulsory. Corvée obligations were difficult to eliminate, primarily because traditional chiefs saw their reduction as an attack on their prerogatives, and felt that their power had very little meaning if one could not distinguish between their rights and privileges and those of the Hutu.

COTTON CULTIVATION. The Belgian administration encouraged the cultivation of cotton by African producers during the 1930s.

COTTON RESERVE FUND. Established in 1943 to regularize the production of cotton and to promote the economic and social development of the crop in African areas.

COUBEAU, OGER. A Belgian colonial civil servant, born on September 8, 1885, he entered colonial service in September 1917, served in Rwanda in an administrative capacity in 1924, and in 1930 became district commissioner, second class. He was the Resident of Rwanda from 1931 to November 17, 1932.

COUNCIL OF FOUR. On May 6, 1919, members of the council—Great Britain, the United States, France, and Italy—decided that the German colonies would be administered as mandates by the "Great Powers," which meant that Great Britain received the lion's share—German East Africa and the eastern part of Rwanda. Great Britain also came to terms with Belgium, which had hoped to gain the southern bank of the Congo River in exchange for the territory it occupied in East Africa. Instead, Belgium received Ruanda-Urundi and dropped the issue of negotiating for the southern bank of the Congo with the Portuguese.

COUNCIL OF THE GREAT CHIEFS. Part of the traditional African administrative hierarchy that was summoned and consulted during periods of crisis. It also acted as the sounding board for the *umwami*'s ideas and actions.

COUP D'ETAT (GITARAMA, 1961). The political emergence of the Hutu. On January 28, Hutu political leaders met at Gitarama, abolished the monarchy, and proclaimed the Rwandan republic. It was actually a peaceful takeover. At the meeting, Jean Baptiste Rwasibo asked all the mayors and communal councilors to take "certain measures in the domain of pacification and maintenance of order," and he called for a republic and the election of a president. Of the 3,126 delegates present, 2,873 voted to elect a president and to declare Rwanda a republic. On February 1, 1961, the Belgian government recognized the autonomous powers of the Rwandan government as constituted at Gitarama.

All of these actions were in violation of United Nations Resolutions 1579 and 1580. The former challenged the Belgian action of arbitrarily suspending the power of the *umwami,* the legitimate authority, who had left the country during its most turbulent period. The resolution called for his return and the resumption of his functions until such time as his future could be decided by referendum. Resolution 1579 called upon the Belgian government to delay legislative elections until there was a spirit of "peace and harmony" in the country, following riots and massacres the previous year. The resolution requested that the Belgian administration grant a general and unconditional amnesty to permit all the political leaders, exiled and imprisoned, to participate in "normal and democratic political activities." The resolution created a three-member commission to observe and assist in the forthcoming election.

At the Ostend Conference from January 7 to 12, the United Nations, the Belgian government, and various representatives from Banyarwandan political parties and interest groups discussed the future of the Rwandan state and the two United Nations resolutions. The Belgian government announced on January 20 that it would postpone the elections in accordance with the UN resolution, even though "the large majority of the representatives of the [country]" favored holding the election as scheduled.

COUP D'ETAT (JULY 5, 1973). Major General Juvénal Habyarimana assumed control of the state and became its new president. The coup stemmed from mounting conflicts and antagonism between the Hutu from the north of the country and those from the central region. The northerners incited the army, whose higher-ranking officers were predominantly northern, to seize power through a bloodless coup.

COW. An animal with unique prestige value in traditional society. It was used to record marriage transactions and, more importantly, was considered the property of a nobleman. The effective disposal of the cow was the main institutionalized means of achieving power. The acquisition of wealth was another reason to possess a cow, which enabled a person to secure labor and agricultural produce through the clientage structure. Wealth was figured in terms of cattle ownership. Cattle were not slaughtered for meat unless sick or injured; however, meat could be eaten on very special occasions, with pride and respect. Horns were used as containers for drawing water and were acclaimed for their durability. Hides were used for clothing and were available to wealthy notables only. Milk was a valuable product and a supplement to other foods during the hard times. It was believed to possess medicinal qualities as well.

CREDIT AGRICOLE D'AFRIQUE. A society that managed PROTANAG (Société Coloniale des Produits Tannants et Agricoles) and several other companies in the Kivu in the 1930s.

CRICKETS. Their larvae attack coffee plants.

CRYPTOGAMICAL DISEASE. It attacks cotton plants.

CYAAMATARE, NDAHIRO, UMWAMI OF RWANDA. Ndahiro reigned from 1576 to 1600. His kingdom included Bumbogo, portions of Buliza, Rukoma, Nduga, and Mayaga. He had to defend his throne against his brother, nephew, and paternal uncle. Civil conflict resulted in the division of the kingdom and forced the heir apparent, Ruganzu Ndoori, into exile.

CYILIMA RUGWE, UMWAMI OF RWANDA. *See* RUGWE, CYILIMA.

CYILIMA RUJUGIRA, UMWAMI OF RWANDA. *See* RUJU-GIRA, CYILIMA.

CYIMANA, GASPARD. Rwandan politician and member of PARMEHUTU, born in Rulindo, Kigali, in 1930. Cyimana attended the Grand Séminaire at Nyakibanda for three years, where he majored in philosophy. Afterward, he spent four years at the Ecole d'Administration of Kisantu. Then he attended Saint Ignace at Antwerp where he obtained a license in commercial science and finance. From October 1960 to June 1968, he was minister of finance, and from 1961 to 1969 national delegate to MDR/PARMEHUTU from Byumba.

CYSTICERCOSIS. A parasite that attacks cattle and humans, and since 1960 has affected approximately 50 percent of those living in less densely populated areas. Some 95 percent in the more densely populated areas are affected by it.

-D-

DARDENNE, J. The territorial administrator and supervisor of Akanyaru territory, which was created from Nyanza territory in 1923. He was in colonial service until 1927. He constructed the post at Butare, as well as the Astrida-Kansi and Astrida-Lubona roads.

DAR ES SALAAM–KIGOMA ROUTE. One of the two main commercial transportation routes. The eastern route was by lake steamer to Kigoma, and then by Tanganyika Railways to Dar es Salaam. The western route crossed the lake to Albertville, and continued by Belgian rail and river route to Matadi. In each instance, all of the traffic passed through

Bujumbura. The import trade and the exportation of coffee took this route into and out of Rwanda during the 1940s. However, most of the coffee was shipped via Matadi.

DE BOCK, F. The acting vice governor-general from December 1935 to July 1936, while E. Jungers, the vice governor-general vacationed. De Bock was actually assistant provincial commissioner.

DECEMBER 1963 MASSACRE. Abortive attempts by Tutsi rebels to overthrow the Rwandan national government between November and December. Armed Tutsi refugees, who had fled to Burundi after the 1959 revolution, crossed the border into Rwanda and conducted a few isolated raids. The Rwandan national army repulsed the invaders, but large numbers of Tutsi inside of Rwanda were killed in retaliation for the raids. The figures range from as low as 1,000 from government sources to as high as 20,000, with many more fleeing the country. Sporadic hostilities occurred after that, straining relations between Burundi and Rwanda.

DECLERCK, GERARD (JEAN-FRANCOIS) (1878–1919). Military commander and Resident of Rwanda. DeClerck was born in Molenbeek-Saint-Jean on February 14, 1878. He served more than two years in the Congo as a first sergeant. He was eventually promoted to *sous-officier* in the Force Publique in 1899. He returned to Belgium in 1904 before accepting an assignment in 1905 to campaign against the Sultan of Engwetra. Once this assignment was complete, he was awarded a frontier post at Dilolo. He returned to Belgium in 1909, was awarded the rank of captain, and returned to Africa in 1910 to administer the Sankuru district. Two years later he was again in Belgium, where he reenlisted in the Force Publique as *capitaine-commandant,* and returned to the Congo for the fourth and final time. He was assigned to the district of Lomami, where he conducted several policing actions.

When war was declared, he was given command of the M'Toa post, where he repelled a German offensive. He commanded the Fourth Battalion of Group II until the arrival in February of Lieutenant Colonel Moulaert. During Belgian occupation of Rwanda, he was made Resident in 1917. In this position, he encouraged the establishment of schools throughout the country. DeClerck believed that education would transform traditional society by eliminating superstition and providing skills needed by the colonial administration. However, *umwami* Musinga resisted DeClerck's efforts to send the sons of the notables to these schools. He did not relent until DeClerck and the White Fathers convinced him that education would serve the interest of the Tutsi ruling class. They also threatened Musinga by stating that they would reserve education to the Hutu if he did not consent. Musinga finally agreed to allow the sons of notables to attend an institution created specifically for them at Nyanza in 1919. DeClerck left Rwanda in June 1919. He was injured in a railroad accident and died in a hospital in Durban, South Africa, on July 30, 1919.

DECREE LIMITING NEW COFFEE PLANTATIONS. This prohibition to limit the creation of new coffee plantations, including the replacement of old plants that were nearing exhaustion, was issued in 1938. It applied only to European planters in Belgian Africa. African coffee planters were not affected. The prohibition was not lifted until December 1944.

DECREE OF JULY 14, 1952. An attempt on the part of the Belgian administration to democratize the African/Native Tribunals. Four councils were created: subchiefdom councils, chiefdom councils, district councils, and high councils of the states. Representatives in each of these categories were elected by popular vote, except members of the district council. Chiefs at the district or subchief level were selected by each subchief, after taking into account the preferences of the people in the subchieftaincy. A list was compiled, and each subchief council designated three notables to serve as members of the electoral college, which selected among its members representatives to sit on the chief's council. In addition, the district council included an equal number of subchiefs "elected by their peers" and notables equaling the total number of chiefs and subchiefs.

At the top level of the African government was the High Council of the State, presided over by the *umwami*, and composed of the chairman of each district council; six chiefs elected by their peers; a representative of each district council chosen from notables in the council; and eight others chosen for their special knowledge, merit, or contributions to society.

The decree did little to further mass participation, since the Hutu were excluded from the whole affair, as was noted by the 1957 United Nations Visiting Mission to Trustee Territories. However, the administrative change intensified political activity, the formation of political parties, and propaganda, as well as vocal agitation.

DEFAWE SYSTEM. A plan to extend the zone of influence introduced in the 1930s, whereby an association would be formed between European enterprises and African producers in a specific geographical zone. Africans would supply the land and labor, and European concessions would supply the capital. Africans from neighboring villages would be paid for their labor; Europeans would provide counsel, competence, and supervision about farming. Both parties would share equally in any profits from joint ventures in coffee production. The system would also ensure an adequate supply of African labor.

DEFORESTATION. A major problem for the country, especially in the eastern region, where extensive deforestation had been occurring for the last three hundred or four hundred years, since the Tutsi herdsmen entered the country. Since then, the forests on the hilly slopes have been destroyed at a steady rate. In 1953, the Belgian colonial administration put a stop to deforestation by designating the remaining forests as reserves and assigning their administration to IRSAC.

DEPRIMOZ, LAURENTII (1883–1962). A member of the Société des Pères Blancs. He was born in France in 1883 and became a priest in 1908, when he was appointed to a post in the apostolic parish of Unyanyembe, which was part of Tanganyika and Burundi. From 1908 to 1912 he served in Tanganyika, and from 1912 to 1915 he was assigned to a mission post in Burundi. In 1912 he also helped to establish in Rwanda the parish of the Kivu. Three years later he was placed in charge of the Petit Séminaire and the Grand Séminaire at Kabgayi. This appointment lasted until 1932. In 1936 he was posted to Nyakibanda, and in 1943 he became the assistant to Monsignor Leon Classe. He became the apostolic vicar of Rwanda in 1945. He resigned from this position in 1955 for reasons of health. In the interim, he was consecrated as bishop in 1952.

DERSCHEID, J. M. Chef de section at the Musée de Tervuren in 1928, and a critic of the colonial agricultural policy in Rwanda and Burundi. A collection of clippings at Michigan State University in East Lansing bears his name.

DE RYCKMAN DE BETZ PROPOSAL. J. De Ryckman de Betz, as representative of the Syndicat Agricole des Cafés du Kivu, presented an alternative proposal to the Defawe System. While his proposal sanctioned the zones of influence, he insisted that concessions be separated from one another by a radius of fifteen kilometers. Rather then have concessions granted to African-European associations or partnerships, he introduced the concept of stewardship instead. Under stewardship, concessions would be responsible for a number of African farmers within a particular zone, preferably in areas where Tutsi notables could provide Hutu labor for both Africans and Europeans involved in agricultural production. A state-controlled bank would provide credit to African farmers. He believed that stewardship would provide greater scrutiny of African agricultural production within the zone and act as a hedge against plant diseases from the African sector.

DESSAINT, MARCEL-EDOUARD-ANTOINE. Provincial commissioner and Resident of Rwanda. Marcel Dessaint was born on August 26, 1903, in Scheit-Tinlot, Liège. He received a degree in engineering from the University of Liège and joined the colonial civil service in 1928 with an assignment as territorial agent at Muhinga in the Belgian Congo. He served as Resident of Rwanda in 1951 and was promoted to provincial commissioner in 1957, with an assignment with the vice governor-general of Ruanda-Urundi.

DEUTSCHE WELLE RELAY KIGALI. One of the major radio stations in the country. It broadcasts daily in German, French, English, Hausa, Swahili and Amharic.

DEVELOPMENT BANK OF RWANDA. Established in 1968, it extended credit primarily to small tea, sugarcane, and tourism projects in the private sector.

DE VLEESCHAUWER, ALBERT. Minister for colonies in 1940, while the Belgian government was in exile in London during World War II.

DIAPASON, LE. A periodical published by the Université Nationale du Rwanda; it has a circulation of about 300.

DIEBACK. A disease that causes plant shoots to die gradually, starting at the tips. The disease is partly due to careless cultivation and partly to unsuitable climatic conditions. Coffee plants are the most susceptible to the disease.

DUNGUTSI REBELLION. An insurrection in northern Rwanda in March 1928 led by Dungutsi, the son of Lwabugiri and half brother to Musinga. Some believed that Dungutsi was the legitimate ruler of Rwanda rather than Musinga. Dungutsi's attack originated from neighboring Uganda and it included about a hundred men. They occupied an area north of Lake Baferu, where his followers proclaimed Dungutsi the umwami. On March 24, the band had grown to 2,000 men, and they attacked Mukono hill, which was held by Chief Lukeratabaro, who was able to force Dungutsi's forces to retreat. The following day the administrative Resident ordered a military expedition against Dungutsi's forces, and they were attacked in the marshes near Kumushiri in neighboring Muyumbu on March 31 and at Butoro on April 3. While the patrol was in the area for the next ten days, Dungutsi and his forces managed to elude the troops by escaping across the border into Uganda. The military operation was called to a halt, but the forces remained in the area during the rest of April.

-E-

ECOLE COLONIALE. An institution located in Brussels, Belgium, responsible for training low-level Belgian colonial civil servants. The school offered technical courses of short durations for those who had not studied at the Université Coloniale. The curriculum was fixed by the minister for colonies.

ECOLE INDUSTRIELLE DE SHANGUGU (KAMEMBE). A professional school established in 1924.

ECONOMIC COMMUNITY OF THE GREAT LAKES COUNTRIES (CEPGL). An attempt on the part of Rwanda,

Burundi, and Zaire to achieve closer economic cooperation. The three heads of state met in June 1974, at a conference at Bujumbura, and agreed to improve border security in each state and to take immediate steps to facilitate economic cooperation across national boundaries. The accord was signed in 1976.

In 1978, its members decided to form a joint development bank to cooperate on a number of projects, including the development of a transport system, the construction of a hydroelectric power station (the Ruzizi II project) on the Rwanda-Zaire border, the exploitation of methane gas deposits beneath Lake Kivu, and the promotion of a fishing industry. The bank was formally established in 1980 with its headquarters at Goma in Zaire.

EDITIONS RWANDAISES. One of two publishing companies in the country. It publishes religious, educational, and general materials.

EDUCATION. During the colonial period, nearly all the scholastic institutions were administered by religious missions and were considered private, subsidized schools. The colonial government paid a large share of their costs—from 50 percent to 100 percent—provided that the institutions conformed to the regulations and followed the curriculum drawn up by the Belgian administration.

In the postcolonial period, primary education, which begins at age seven and lasts for eight years, is officially compulsory. Secondary education, which is not compulsory, begins at age fifteen and lasts for about six years of two equal cycles of three years each. Schools are administered by the state and by Christian missions. In 1985, approximately 61 percent of the children were enrolled at the primary level, while only 2 percent of the school-age population were enrolled in secondary education.

There are plans to extend primary education with support of the World Bank. In 1990, there were about 790,000 students enrolled at the primary level and 45,000 at secondary schools, of whom some 30,000 received agricultural and vocational training, while 14,000 pursued higher education. The national government in 1984 spent 27.5 percent of the national budget on education; in 1986, the government received $15.6 million loan from the World Bank for the construction of a vocational training center and a technical school.

Rwanda has a national university with campuses at Butare and Ruhengeri, as well as several other institutions of higher learning. However, a large number of students go overseas for university training, particularly to Belgium, France, and Germany.

According to estimates from UNESCO in 1985, the average rate of adult illiteracy was 53.4 percent (males 38.8 percent, females 67.3 percent).

ELIZABETHVILLE-JADOTVILLE ROUTE. The most densely used portion of the link in the flow of international road-traffic to and from the interior of Belgian Africa. Food suppliers coming from the Kasai and Lake Tanganyika area to the mining and industrial centers of the region and the transporters of heavy minerals used this road and accounted for about 50 percent of the total volume.

ELLIOT REPORT OF 1937. J. R. McDonald Elliot, senior administrative officer of the British Colonial Office, was appointed by the Ministry of Labour in Uganda in 1937 to study labor conditions and to investigate the issue of adequate inspection of labor in the colonies. Elliot visited Rwanda and Burundi and from personal inquiries concluded that the Banyarwanda immigrated to Uganda primarily to obtain money for the payment of colonial taxes and to escape unpaid, or *akazi,* labor. Banyarwanda were also compelled to undertake road construction, maintenance, and other kinds of government work. Elliot also noted that the mines were the main private employers of Banyarwandan labor outside of Uganda. In

1935, these mines employed 8,259 unskilled laborers with an average daily turnout of 5,636. In six representative mines visited by Elliot in 1936, 40 percent of the laborers were Banyarwandan. His report also contained various recommendations for the improvement of labor conditions, information on methods of payment, rations and feeding arrangements, housing, sanitation, water supplies, and medical facilities. His report outlined a camp-building program on the northern route used by Africans in the western Nile region and on the southwest route used by the Banyarwanda.

ENTEBBE CONFERENCE (1916). Great Britain and Belgium met to discuss the future of the occupied territories of German East Africa. The conference took place on July 20 and 21, 1916. It declared provisionally, subject to ratification by the two countries, that Ruanda-Urundi and the Ujiji district would be administered by Belgium. Mwanza and Mpwapwa would be administered by Great Britain. Bukoba and Tabora were to be administered jointly by British and Belgian officials. The provisional arrangement was accepted by the two governments, but no joint administration ever occurred in Bukoba and Tabora. Tabora was handed over to the British in February 1917, and the region along the southwest shore of Lake Victoria remained under Belgian control.

ESSOR DU CONGO, L'. A journal that reflected the Belgian colonial interest and was published during the 1950s.

"ESTAF" VAN SANTEN ET VANDEN BROECK. A Belgian import-export firm operating out of Antwerp. It was established in 1926 and had offices in Bujumbura and Butare. The company sold food, wines, liqueurs, clothing, and toiletries to Europeans, and hardware and articles of trade to Africans. It also purchased animal hides from Africans.

ETHNIC CONFLICT (1966). Clashes occurred between Tutsi and Hutu in December, when 2,000 Tutsi attempted to invade the country from Burundi. It was reported that several hundred Tutsi were killed in the fighting when the Rwandan National Guard took the offensive.

ETUDES RWANDAISES. A quarterly periodical founded in 1977 by the Université Nationale du Rwanda. It has a circulation of about 1,000 and deals with the pure and applied sciences, literature, and humanities.

EUCALYPTUS TREES. An important component in the Belgian reforestation and reclamation programs during the colonial period. Forests within the country were systematically depleted by farmers seeking new land and by herdsmen seeking grazing areas for their cattle. Therefore, an important part of the Belgian economic policy was to reclaim the forest. Eucalyptus trees were ideal primarily because they grew to maturity quite quickly. The Banyarwanda were obliged to plant communal groves of eucalyptus, which they could use as firewood and in construction.

EUROPEAN CREDIT SOCIETY. The decree of July 1, 1947, modified by the decree of January 29, 1953, provided long- and short-term grants of credit to individuals and associations. Loans were approved to create, improve, and transform small and medium-size agricultural undertakings, particularly those which dealt with coffee production. The annual rate of interest was 3 percent for the first three years and would vary between 4 and 6 percent a year thereafter.

EUROPEAN ECONOMIC COMMUNITY (EEC). Rwanda is an associate overseas member of the EEC.

EVERAERTS, M. Provincial director of the Agricultural Service in Rwanda and Burundi and the guiding influence in agricultural development from 1929 to 1954. He was responsible for the coffee cultivation campaigns from 1931 to 1937.

EVOLUE. A "civilized" African. The term was used by the Belgian colonial administration to describe Africans who had made greater progress toward civilization than the mass of the indigenous population. Colonial officials and some private employers established at various places clubs for évolués, such as the Cercle des Evolués at Butare where Africans met regularly to play table tennis, chess, or cards, and to discuss organizational, social, and moral questions on a monthly basis. Each week a European gave a lecture to the group on a selected topic. The center usually contained a well-stocked library. The term did not connote change in legal status.

EXPORTS. In the African sector, exports were hides, cattle, palm nuts and oil, cotton, coffee, butter, tobacco, and African food products, which were transported to the Kivu and Katanga.

EXTRATRIBAL POPULATION. Those inhabitants who, together with their families, have left their hills permanently to live in urban areas. A sociopolitical and economic distinction used during the colonial period.

-F-

FAMINE. Famines have occurred quite frequently throughout the country since 1867. The most serious occurred in 1927–1928 when some 300,000 died. Famines were central to Belgian economic planning. To forestall the danger of famine, all able-bodied adult Africans living in traditional areas were required to cultivate thirty-five ares of seasonal crops and twenty-five ares of nonseasonal food crops. The Belgians' ambitious road construction project in the 1920s was designed to facilitate food distribution in times of famine. The famine of 1942–1944 occurred when rains failed to appear, and it affected the entire country. Drought was followed by an attack of insects that destroyed most of the potato crop and by an epidemic of typhus. Those famines which have occurred since independence have compelled the government to construct grain storage facilities and to implement food self-sufficiency programs. A famine affected the southern region of Mayanga, in Butare prefecture, and Gikongoro and Kibuye in 1989–1990. Food production—particularly the production of haricot (beans), the country's basic food staple—was badly affected by heavy rains which followed a prolonged period of drought. The government had to appeal to international donors for emergency food aid.

FISH AND FISHING. An important source of protein and food. Fisheries were encouraged by the Belgian administration, which believed that through fishing and fish breeding Africans could easily and inexpensively supplement their diet. The administration introduced a thousand young fish from Uganda in 1936 and stocks from the Belgian Congo in 1937, and in 1941 from the internal lakes of Mohazi, Luhondo, and Birira. Fishing gradually became an important source of income for some 2,500 Africans, and annual production in 1959 was 17,500 tons, valued at more than 100 million BF.

FLEMISH. A language and group of people from Flanders, often discriminated against by the French-speaking Walloons of Belgium. Those who were members of the colonial service tended to be relegated to Rwanda, especially after 1940. Flemish administrators and young Catholic missionaries tended to have much more in common with and sympathy for the Hutu intellectuals and peasantry. Together, according to one well-placed source, they "took to their protégés, the Hutu leaders, more readily than to the Tutsi," and therefore may have been biased in their favor during the push for independence.

FONCTIONNAIRES. Belgian members of administrative and

technical staffs. They did not usually need a university degree to become members of the colonial civil service. They were placed on probation for their first tour of duty and divided into two main classes—*administrateurs* and *commissaires*—by royal *arrêté* of 1934.

FONDS D'ADVANCES. A loan-granting institution divided into two sections: one that made home loans to the African inhabitants of the community, and the other granting cash loans to individuals living in extratribal centers. Loans were repayable within twenty years and could not exceed 125,000 BF.

FONDS D'ASSISTANCE AUX COLONS. An assistance fund created by Royal *arrêté* of August 24, 1937, for European settlers. The fund granted advances and mortgage loans to new colons, or immigrants, for agricultural enterprises in Belgian Africa. It was designed to ease their entry into the region.

FONDS D'EGALISATION. Created in 1948, and designed to regularize the purchase price of coffee produced by African planters in the event of a sharp decline on the world coffee market and to cover the cost of advertising. Contributions to the equalization fund were made from taxes on exported coffee. Interest accrued by the fund could be used for technical assistance programs, such as the free supply of elementary tools (saws, pruning shears, drying trays and screens) or the financing of certain studies undertaken to improve farming methods.

FONDS D'IMMIGRATION ET DE COLONISATION. A fund created to encourage Belgian immigration and settlement in Belgian Africa.

FONDS DU BIEN-ETRE INDIGENE (AFRICAN WELFARE FUND). An endowment fund established on July 1, 1947, by an order of the regent, and financed by the Belgian Congo and Belgium. The initial contribution was 2.1 billion BF, consisting of a reimbursement by Belgium of Congolese war debts of about 1.78 million BF and partial profits from the Loterie Coloniale for 1946 and 1947 of 220 million BF. Annual revenues of 300 million BF were derived from interest on the initial endowment of 2.1 billion Belgian francs, annual deductions from the endowment, and annual profits from the Loterie Coloniale. Funds could be used for all kinds of projects associated with the material and moral development of African society in the Belgian Congo, Rwanda, and Burundi.

In 1948, the United States donated 50 million BF to the fund to build thirty storage facilities for grain. In 1957, the fund sponsored a water supply program to ameliorate water shortages in Kisenyi and Ruhengeri territories and to improve water supplies in other African areas.

Similar funds were created in all of the provinces and chieftaincies in 1941. They were designed to give the African administration, the *umwami,* and his advisers the financial means to meet expenditures in the general interest of the population. These funds, while directed by the *umwami,* were often supervised by the Belgian administration.

FONDS DU ROI. Essentially a fund to subsidize African housing. It was established by royal decree on October 18, 1955, to provide easy credit to improve middle-income housing in traditional African areas and in extratribal centers. The fund was capitalized at 2 million BF, which was contributed by the colonial government.

FONDS SPECIAL DE CREDIT AGRICOLE INDIGENE. An African agricultural credit fund established on August 5, 1941, by Ordinance No. 365 (AGRI) and made applicable to the Belgian Congo, Rwanda, and Burundi by Ordinance No. 53/217 of December 17, 1954. The funding came from advances from the Colonial Treasury and from voluntary contributions from the treasuries of the African districts and extratribal centers.

The fund granted loans of more than 5,000 BF to African districts, to Africans living in extratribal centers, to cooperatives, and to legally recognized African agricultural associations. Private loans to individuals could not exceed 10,000 BF and were restricted to agricultural development and stockbreeding, the harvesting, preparation, and preservation of products from farming and stockbreeding.

Allocation of funds was controlled by the governor general's office, especially loans of more than 10,000 BF. This office also ruled on requests submitted by the African Agricultural Credit Committee. The loan period was ten years with an annual interest rate of 4 percent.

FONDS TEMPORAIRE DE CREDIT AGRICOLE. An agricultural loan fund established in 1931 to provide mortgage loans to those who had created plantations of at least twenty hectares in the Belgian Congo and in Rwanda and Burundi before January 1, 1940. The fund was administered in each of these regions by an Agricultural Credit Commission, but it favored Belgian nationals and the improvement of their ventures.

The fund financed various kinds of farming ventures, repairing and replacement of tools and equipment, building or purchase of structures, and the matériel required for the preservation and treatment of products. Loans could be relatively small amounts, since an individual could secure a loan for weeding work. In this case, the loan amount could not exceed per hectare the total annual salary and maintenance of a worker in a designated area. Loans for tools and labor could not exceed 1,000 BF per hectare planted, nor could loans for mills, industrial buildings, or work camps be more than a third of the value attributed to them by the Agricultural Credit Commission. These various loans carried an interest rate of 4 percent, and in each case the terms were fixed by the commission.

FORCE DEMOCRATIQUE DU CHANGEMENT (FDC). The Democratic Force for Change is a coalition between the MDR, PSD, and the PL. It was formed in early January, 1993, and is one of two political power blocks to emerge in the country during the year. The other is the ARD. While the ARD opposes the current direction of the peace negotiations and the conditions for the various ceasefires, the FDC advocates inclusion, compromise, and peace. It denounces the intransigence of the ARD and has instructed its members to focus their efforts on the protection of the motherland.

FORESTRY. An important component of Belgian colonial economic policy and planning. The administration sought to protect forests by placing them under the protection of the government in the form of reserves and requiring Africans to plant eucalyptus for timber and firewood. An ordinance passed on October 1, 1931, required African communities to carry out an annual planting of communal timber, consisting of African and foreign species, at the rate of one hectare per unit of three hundred taxpayers. In 1952, the system of commutation of the planting obligation was introduced, and the rate per able-bodied male adult was set at twenty Belgian francs.

FORMINIERE. A mining company established in 1906 in the Belgian Congo with interests in the mandate territory.

FOSSEY, DIAN (1932–1985). American naturalist and director of the Karisoke Centre for Mountain Gorilla Research in the Virungas mountain chain in northern Rwanda and Zaire. She was initially trained as an occupational therapist, but in 1964 she visited East Africa to see wild animals and visit friends in Zimbabwe. She returned in December 1966 when Louis Leakey asked her to become his "gorilla girl." She was found brutally murdered in the morning hours of December 27, 1985.

FRANCK, LOUIS. Minister for the colonies from 1918 to 1924 and also a member of the Liberal Party. Franck favored private investment, industrialization, and the development of indigenous institutions in Belgian Africa. In fact, he believed that the *tribunal indigène* was the cornerstone of African administration.

Described as strong willed, he was the colonial minister for almost six years. Though hostile to state socialism, he was innovative with respect to the colonial service. He founded the Colonial University at Antwerp, which resulted in better-trained administrative personnel. Even though training at the university was authoritarian and the curriculum stifled critical thinking, the university's graduates were quite professional.

Franck favored indirect rule for Belgian Africa generally and for Rwanda specifically. The latter had a highly centralized political structure, which he believed had to be transformed. His solution was to initiate a restructuring of the African administration. The legislative basis was the decree of 1926 creating the *tribunaux indigènes* and the decree of 1933 creating the *circonscriptions indigènes*. He reduced the number of *chefferies,* or chiefdoms, as well. As for European administrators, the Belgians were to act as counselors and tutors for the Tutsi notables, and the emphasis was to be placed on continuity and the maintenance of the existing traditional structures, with limited and careful reforms. Franck believed that change had to be accomplished gradually.

Franck encouraged the Belgian government at Brussels to provide loans to white colonists and subsidies for railroad construction and other infrastructure from the Lower Congo to Katanga, for the Matadi-Leopoldville line, for the enlargement of the port of Matadi, and for the construction of the port of Leopoldville. Infrastructure would facilitate the export of raw materials from the interior of Belgian Africa to Belgium.

FRERES DE LA CHARITE DE GAND. *See* BROTHERS OF CHARITY OF GENT.

FRONT NATIONAL DE RESISTANCE (FNR). The national Resistance Front was an illegal political party, organized by Innocent Ndayambaje, a student at the National University at Butare. The party was formed in 1986 as a protest against regional and ethnic injustice. Since the Rwandan constitution bans all political organizations apart from the ruling MRND, the new party was declared illegal, and the student organizer was sentenced to prison for five years for distributing political literature considered to be inflammatory at the national university. At the time of his arrest and trial, Ndayambaje claimed that he was the sole active member of the party.

"FULL STOMACH" POLICY. The United Nations Visiting Mission to Trust Territories in East Africa in 1954 noted that Africans in Rwanda referred to the administration's economic policy as the "full stomach" policy, because the administration placed undue emphasis on improving the material welfare of the people. The mission warned that such an emphasis would eventually outstrip the productive capacity of the country. It also noted that the economy had an artificial character, in that Africans did not appear to have a positive stake in the development of the country.

-G-

GAFUKU, BALTHASAR. One of the first Rwandans to be ordained a Catholic priest. The ordination occurred at Kabgayi on October 7, 1917.

GAHAMANYI, MONSIGNOR JEAN-BAPTISTE. A Rwandan Catholic priest, born in Kaduha, Gitarama, in 1930, he received his ordination in 1951. He taught at the Petit Séminaire at Kabgayi and studied at Lovanium University. He became the bishop of Butare in 1961.

GAHIMA, YUHI, UMWAMI OF RWANDA. Yuhi reigned from 1552 to 1576 and extended the empire to the west and eastward to the Congo-Nile ridge to include the regions of Bwishaza, Rusenyi, and the kingdom of Lake Kivu.

GAHINDIRO, YUHI, UMWAMI OF RWANDA. An *umwami* who ruled the country from 1797 to 1830 and in consolidating his control, curbed the power of the *abanyabutaka,* or "men of the land." He obtained wealth and influence for the Court from the use of pastureland, by creating a new set of officials, the *abanyamukenke,* or "men of the grass," who controlled the distribution of pasturelands and collected payments for its use. He granted *ibikingi* to his favorites as an additional measure of consolidation. He increased the number of *abiiru* in a proportion of one to ten. During his reign, he fused the religious and political aspects of his office by controlling the growth, prestige, and prerogatives of the *abiiru.* By the end of his reign, Yuhi Gahindiro had created devices, such as *ubuhake,* to establish personal dependency. He also occupied Ndorwa and conducted a campaign against the Bushi and Burundi.

GARAGU. Usufruct right with respect to cattle, which a client received from his patron. The person endowed with it could dispose of the milk, the male offspring of the cattle, as well as the dead cow.

GARDE TERRITORIALE. An emergency police and national security patrol formed by Colonel Guillaume Logiest in 1960 during the movement toward independence. According to his instructions, the 650-man security force was recruited based on the ethnic composition of the country. Recruits had to have at least a primary education, and recruitment occurred throughout the country. An officers' school was created in the same year under the same guidelines. In the final analysis, however, Colonel Logiest created a Hutu police force, since they were the majority in the population.

GASHONGA, DEOGRATIAS. Rwandan politician and national delegate to MDR/PARMEHUTU from Kibuye. He was born in Rwamatamu, Kibuye, in 1937, received a degree in economic science from Lovanium University, and became director and later director-general in the Kayibanda administration. He was also Kayibanda's deputy minister, charged with heading the Ministry of Coordination of Economic, Technical, and Financial Affairs in 1971.

GASINGWA, GERMAIN. Rwandan politician who was a member of APROSOMA He was born in Save, Butare, in 1927, and worked as a medical assistant. He represented APROSOMA on the Provisional Council in October 1960 and became its president in December of the same year. He served as assistant secretary of state in foreign affairs and was a national delegate from 1961 to 1965. In 1962 he headed the Ministry of Public Health.

GATUMBA. The principal tin-mining center, located in the northeastern portion of the country. It began operation during the colonial period.

GECAMINES. Belgian mining company that until 1985 held a 51 percent share in conjunction with SOMIRWA, the national tin-mining company of Rwanda. GECAMINES was declared insolvent in Brussels in October 1985, following heavy losses suffered in 1984.

GENERAL COUNCIL OF FORTY-FIVE MEMBERS. A royal order of March 26, 1957 replaced the Council of the Vice Government-General with the General Council of Forty-five Members for the mandated territory. It was composed of seven senior official and ex officio members, the procureur du roi, the provincial commissioners, the provincial secretary, and the Residents of Rwanda and Urundi. The two kings were ex officio members, two members were chosen by the High Council of Ruanda from among its membership, and two others by the High Council of Urundi.

Thirty-two members were chosen by the governor of Ruanda-Urundi as follows: six representatives from industrial and commercial companies appointed on the nomination of industrial associations and the Chamber of Commerce (in 1957 all were European directors of trading or mining companies); six representatives from the middle classes appointed on nomination by various middle-class groups, including the Chamber of Commerce representing individual enterprises (in 1957 all were Europeans, either lawyers, colonists, or individual owners of various enterprises); six representatives of labor, of whom five were appointed on the nomination of occupational associations of workers and employees in the public and private sectors, and one appointed on nomination of the worker members of the Commission on Labor and Indigenous Social Progress (in 1957 four were European officials and two were African clerks); six notables chosen on the basis of "general ability and independence of mind" (in 1957 there was one African chief, one European colonist, one European merchant, one European vicar apostolic, one Asian merchant, and one African abbot); four representatives from extrarural communities (in 1957 there was one European company manager and three indigenous inhabitants, including the chief of the Bujumbura extracustomary center, a medical assistant, and a clerk); four representatives belonging to either the general or the indigenous administration (in 1957 there was one African vicar apostolic, a European Protestant missionary, an indigenous manufacturer, and an indigenous business employee). The *umwami*'s advisers also sat on the General Council, but were not entitled to vote.

GENEX. *See* SOCIETE GENERALE D'EXPORTATION VAN SANTEN ET VANDEN BROECK (GENEX).

GEORUANDA. Mining company operating in Kibungu in 1947. The company was labor intensive, employing 3,000 African workers. In 1954, it produced about 1,000 tons of cassiterite from the open-cast method. Its operation lacked electricity and therefore production costs were fairly high.

GERMAN COLONIAL RULE. German claims to the territory began in 1885, but occupation of Ruanda-Urundi did not begin until 1899, when the military station was created at Bujumbura. German administration and rule lasted until 1916, when they were replaced by the Belgians.

German administrative personnel in the territory never exceeded ten men and therefore the German presence could not be called colonization but rather military occupation, which was limited to pacification and security measures. Ruanda was made a separate territory in 1908, and the Germans adopted a development policy that relied upon European capital. Its objective was the exploitation of products rather than large-scale white settlement. The Germans also encouraged Asian and Indian commerce.

GIHANGA. The mythical founder of the Tutsi royal dynasty, his name means "founder." According to tradition, he created cattle, the drum, and the ubwiiru as royal symbols for ceremony. His three children—Gahima, Sabugabo, and Mugondo—ruled three kingdoms in the country—Rwanda, Ndorwa, and Bugesera, respectively. Their children in turn created the ruling clans in the tenth century.

GIKONGORO. A prefecture where coffee yields are relatively low. The total area is 2,192 square kilometers, and it contains a population (figures from 1978) of 370,596.

GISANURA, MIBAMBWE, UMWAMI OF RWANDA. Reigned from 1672 to 1696 and reported to have been a just and wise king.

GISENYI. One of ten prefectures in the country. It has a total area of 2,395 square kilometers and population (as of 1978) of 468,882. It is also the name of one of the principal towns in the country, with a population (as of 1978) of 12,436. It is an area of volcanic soils near the banks of Lake Kivu, where coffee yields are the best in the country.

GITARAMA. A prefecture that was created January 1, 1959, and a principal town located on the central plateau, where nearly half of the arable land of the country is located, but where the yields are much lower and the soils are of lower quality. Before 1959, Gitarama was a part of the Nyanza territory. The total area is 2,241 square kilometers and the population is 606,212, according to 1978 census figures.

GITERA, JOSEPH. A former member of the Mouvement Social Muhutu who, in November 1957, established the political party called the Association pour la Promotion Sociale de la Masse (APROSOMA). He was elected president of the Provincial Council in October 1960, and was dismissed from the post in February 1961. He later joined PARMEHUTU and became the national delegate to MDR/PARMEHUTU from Butare in 1969. He was born in Save, Butare, in 1919, attended the Petit Séminaire and later the Grand Séminaire at Kabgayi.

GITWE. A town located in Nyanza province; home of the Seventh Day Adventist mission founded in 1919.

GOAT BREEDING. A prerogative practiced widely among the Hutu, for whom it is a source of real income. A small number of goats are owned by the Twa.

GOATS. To own and breed goats was a social prohibition in traditional times. Their existence was not recognized, though they were eaten in times of crop failure. Their milk was drunk by the ill, and their skins were used as slings (*ingobyi*), in which babies were carried. Few male goats and unproductive females were kept.

GODDING, ROBERT (1883–1953). In his obituary, published in the December 11, 1953, issue of *L'Essor du Congo,* a commemorative piece announcing his unexpected death at Leopoldville, Godding was referred to as the "grand colonial." At the time of this death the former minister for colonies was living in Panzi in the Kivu region of the Belgian Congo.

A graduate of the Université Libre de Bruxelles in 1908, Godding volunteered for duty in World War I and was awarded the Croix de Guerre. At the end of World War I, he became director of the Kreglinger firm, one of the oldest colonial businesses in Antwerp. The company had warehouses and large plantations in the Belgian Congo. He became a member of the Colonial Council at Brussels in 1932, but remained at the position for only a couple of months, when he was elected as the representative from Antwerp to the Belgian senate at Brussels. He became a member of the Finance Committee and the Committee for the Colonies, which selected him as their president.

In 1938, Godding succeeded Louis Franck as the president of the Administrative Council of the Colonial University of Antwerp, which became the Institut Universitaire des Territoires d'Outre-mer. At the beginning of World War II, Godding settled at Leopoldville. At the request of Governor-General Ryckmans, he participated in Belgian war mobilization and presided over several commissions in association with the Belgian government in exile at London.

A member of the Liberal Party, Godding became the minister for the colonies from 1945 to 1947. His election was a break with tradition, in that the dominance by the Union National, or the Catholic, party in this post had been broken. The Catholics had controlled this post since 1914.

As minister, Godding supported autonomy for the white minority in the Belgian Congo, and favored controlled European colonization and secular education in Belgian Africa, where he sought to minimize the influence of large companies.

GOETZEN, COUNT GUSTAV-ADOLF VON (1860–1910). German explorer, staff officer, diplomat, and the governor of German East Africa from 1901 to 1906. Count von Goetzen was born in Schloss Scharfeneck, Silesia, on May 12, 1860. On his first voyage to Africa in 1891, he was a lieutenant of the Imperial Guard at Uhlans. He also accompanied von Prittwitz and Kersting on their transafrican expedition in 1893 and 1894. The first Europeans to enter Rwanda, they explored Nyragongo and Lake Kivu on an essentially scientific and military expedition that stretched from India to East Africa and the Atlantic Ocean. The explorers remained in Rwanda for several weeks. From 1896 to 1898, von Goetzen replaced the German military attaché in Washington, D.C. He was appointed civilian governor of German East Africa in 1901. While governor, he spent a great deal of time trying to convince authorities in Berlin to provide funds to regularize the position of chiefs in district administration, to expand European settlement in the northern territory, and to extend the participation of the European community in public affairs. He returned to Europe in 1906. He died in Berlin on December 1, 1910.

GONOCEPHALUM SIMPLEX. A larvae that attacks coffee plants.

GOOD ADVENTURE. A British ship with a carrying capacity of forty tons chartered by Mavricas Limited of Kigoma. The ship transported Rwandan export produce destined for the port of Dar es Salaam from the port of Bujumbura across Lake Tanganyika to the port at Kigoma during the 1930s. It also transported imported goods in the opposite direction.

GOUBAU, ANTOINE (1895–1935). Catholic priest and member of the Missionnaires d'Afrique, or the White Fathers. Father Goubau was a member of the military before becoming a priest. He received the Croix de Guerre for distinguished service at Yser. After demobilization, he entered the Petit Séminaire of Saint Nicolas, where he majored in philosophy.

Later, he transferred to the Grand Séminaire at Gent for two years of theological training. In 1922, he became a novice of the White Fathers and was ordained a priest at Carthage in June 1925. In September, he left for Rwanda, where he was placed in charge of language studies. He served at the missions of Kabgayi and Muramba. He was also instrumental in launching the first periodical in the country, *Kinya-Mateka*. He died at Kabgayi on March 25, 1935.

GOVERNMENT TECHNICAL SERVICES. This branch had the responsibility for assisting and facilitating economic development within Belgian Africa. It supervised and directed the activities of State monopolies (*régies*) by chieftains in African territories. It provided all the public services required by the African population for the maintenance of public order, social security, social welfare services, public health, and education.

GOVERNOR-GENERAL. The king's representative in Belgian Africa and the highest-ranking authority, possessing very extensive executive power, which he exercised through ordinances. The royal *arrêté* of June 29, 1933, reorganized the administration of Belgian Africa, and stipulated that the governor-general be consulted on all decrees before they were submitted to the Colonial Council, but the right to exercise legislative powers remained limited by the terms of the charter to instances of emergency. In such cases, he could implement ordinances that temporarily suspended existing decrees and could introduce new legislation by *ordonnance loi*. These *ordonnances lois* were good for a period of only six months, if they had not been approved by decrees before the expiration dates. He could appoint agents, as well as post officials. In Rwanda and Burundi, he was one of two vice governor-generals of the Belgian Congo.

GRAND SEMINAIRE DE KABGAYE. Mission at Kabgayi established in 1905.

244 / **Group of Seven**

GROUP OF SEVEN FOR EUROPEAN PRIVATE SECTOR COOPERATION WITH AFRICA, THE CARIBBEAN AND THE PACIFIC/GROUPE DES SEPT POUR LA CO-OPERATION DU SECTEUR PRIVE EUROPEEN AVEC L'AFRIQUE, LES CARIBES ET LE PACIFIC (ACP), RESOLUTION OF FEBRUARY 20, 1992. The ACP is a multinational association and a component of the European Community; it was established on June 6, 1975 in Georgetown, Guyana. It is composed of the EEC and 46 African, Caribbean, and Pacific countries with a general secretariat and staff stationed in Brussels, Belgium. ACP concerns itself with investment, commerce, banking, industry, and agriculture in third world areas. It encourages a sense of partnership and closer trade, economic, and social relations among ACP member states, while promoting investment opportunities. It provides advice to its members, coordinates exchange of information in the fields of trade, technology, industry, and human resources. It maintains contact with Common Market Organizations.

On February 20, 1992, the ACP group of the European Community passed a resolution, urging the RPF and the Rwandan government to negotiate the civil conflict resulting from the October 1990 invasion of the country. The resolution called for the withdrawal of French troops, estimated to be about 300 and stationed at Kigali, but believed by some authorities to be actively engaged in military campaigns alongside of government forces against RPF troops. The RPF has also accused the French government of supplying Rwanda with large quantities of military hardware. The resolution also urged the Rwandan government to respect human rights.

GROUPE SCOLAIRE. Educational institution founded by the Brothers of Charity of Gent in 1929 and located in Astrida (Butare). The institution and the brotherhood were responsible for educating African civil servants, primarily Tutsi notables, when the Nyanza school for chief-candidates was transferred as a special section to the school in 1931. Future African functionaries and agents for service in the various administrative secretariats, as well as medical and veterinary assistants and agricultural monitors had course instruction, ranging from three to ten years in science, medicine, administration, agriculture, and teacher training. The school served both territories and was funded by the Belgian government.

The agricultural curriculum began in 1938. It involved four years of study and accepted only those who had completed the lower cycle of secondary studies. The primary aim of the school, according to Belgian officials, was the creation of a "new social class." Hutu enrollment was prohibited until after World War II.

GUDOWIUS, EBERHARD. German military officer, colonial administrator, and the interim Resident of Rwanda in 1911. He led a punitive military expedition against the Hutu at Bugarura, and as Resident experimented with the appointment of chiefs in administrative positions with approval from the *umwami,* because he believed that these appointees would be more efficient.

-H-

HABIMANA, BONAVENTURE. One of the earliest university-trained political leaders in the country. He received his degree in social sciences from the Université de Bruxelles in 1968 and was secretary-general of the Mouvement Révolutionnaire National pour le Développement (MRND). Between 1956 and 1961, he was a teacher at the Zaza primary school, and from 1962 to 1965 he studied at the Ecole Sociale de Bruxelles.

HABYARIMANA, JUVENAL. A member of Rwanda's Hutu

majority from the north of the country, one of the members of the Committee of Nine, he became president of Rwanda in 1973. He was born in Rambura, Gisenyi, in 1937, attended a one-year preuniversity program at the Lovanium University before entering officers' candidate school at Kigali, where he graduated with distinction. Upon graduation, he became the aide-de-camp of the Belgian commander. He became head of the National Guard in 1963 and was promoted to major in January 1964. He headed the Ministry of the National Guard and Police in 1965 and came to power in a bloodless coup d'état on July 5, 1973.

In coming to power, Major General Juvénal Habyarimana was able to capitalize on the basic weaknesses of former president Kayibanda's government. Authoritarian rule, coupled with a resurgence of conflict between Hutu and Tutsi in early 1973, and mounting antagonism between Hutu from the north of the country and Hutu from the center (or the Gitarama faction), enabled Habyarimana to overthrow the government with the assistance of higher-ranking officers, predominantly northerners.

On August 1, Habyarimana formed a government with a majority of civilian members, but with officers from the north holding the key portfolios. PARMEHUTU was dissolved, and the 1962 constitution was suspended. Habyarimana introduced a more centralized system of administration, reversed the trend toward economic nationalism inaugurated by Kayibanda, initiated the Mouvement Révolutionnaire National pour le Développement (MRND), and instituted a more moderate stand on the issue of Hutu-Tutsi relations than had been the case under the previous administration. He won reelection as president for consecutive five-year terms, beginning December 24, 1978.

HAGURUKA. The word for "stand-up" in Kinyarwanda, is the name of a new women's group that was established in 1992. Its founder, Eugènie Kanzayira, notes that Rwandan society is male-dominated and that the status of women in the country is quite low. Banyarwanda women gain status through their children and through the number that they have. The ideal number is eight. Children, she notes, are the only measure of status that a woman has. She cannot inherit property under Rwandan law; nor is she treated equally in divorce proceedings. Women also have fewer chances for education, employment, and promotion. Men prefer that they remain in uneducated, traditional roles at home. Therefore, for sheer survival a woman must marry and have children, who become her strength and protection against her husband. They are also her security in old age. *Haguruka* intends to improve the status of women throughout the country.

HAKIZIMANA, JACQUES (1924–1971). A Rwandan politician, born in Kansi, Butare, in 1924. He was trained in medicine and was medical assistant at Butare. From 1948 to 1955, he held a variety of medical posts, including medical assistant at Butare. From 1948 to 1955, he was professor at the Ecole d'Infirmiers of Ruhengeri. He began work with the national government in 1961, when he headed the Ministry of Refugees and Social Affairs. In 1965, he served as secretary-general in the Ministry of Public Health.

HARROY, JEAN-PAUL. Belgian university professor, ecologist, and former colonial administrator, born in Brussels on May 4, 1909. A French-speaking Freemason with academic degrees in commercial engineering and science, he was director of the Institut des Parcs Nationaux du Congo, and in 1948 he became the secretary-general of IRSAC. He was governor-general of Ruanda-Urundi from 1955 to 1962, the most turbulent years for the mandate, guiding both countries to independence. After colonial service, he became a professor at the Université Libre de Bruxelles and director of research and member of the Conseil Scientifique de l'Institut de Sociologie. Professor Harroy is the author of numerous articles and books, including *Rwanda: Souvenirs d'un compagnon de la marche du Rwanda vers la démocratie et l'indépendance* (1984).

HEAD TAX (IMPOT DE CAPITATION). A source of revenue for the mandate, particularly for the ways and means budget and the chieftaincy funds. It was a colonial tax paid by all able-bodied adult African males, except those exempt by law, such as chiefs, district chiefs, soldiers and noncommissioned officers, persons residing in the country only after October 1 of the current year, and those who had been ill for at least six months. The head tax varied from region to region, and depended upon the available resources and the degree of economic development of the population. For example, Banyarwanda whose verified income exceeded 9,000 BF net were exempt from the head tax and were subject to income tax. In 1948, 604 Africans were subject to income tax. The tax assessment was somewhat imprecise, based on an estimate of the total resources of the Banyarwanda, such as the sale of traded products, wages, and so on. Administrative officials estimated that the tax corresponded on the average to something less than one-month's income, or 8 or 9 percent of the annual income. The administration also claimed that it was not too high because it was gathered without difficulty. The tax was paid in cash.

HELOPELTIS. A parasite that attacks and seriously damages coffee plants.

HEMILEIA. A black rust fungus that attacks coffee plants.

HIINZA. The supreme agriculturalist. The *hiinza* in the traditional hierarchy of the Hutu principality, prior to Tutsi conquest and incorporation, was an individual of great power. He could work magic and make rain, and was the guardian of the harvest. He was usually the most powerful of the lineage chiefs, and his position was hereditary.

HILL CHIEF (CHEF DE COLLINE). Under traditional customs, he was called the *umutware w'umusozi,* whose counterpart under Belgian administration was called subchief, or *ibisonga.* This particular Tutsi notable could allocate a new piece of land to a new tenant, and he was often referred to as the work chief, or *chef pour le travail.* He had jurisdiction over both the cattle and land chiefs, and he had the right to keep a portion of the tribute of agricultural produce collected from the hill, or *colline.* He was also responsible for gathering tribute in labor.

HIMA. The singular and plural forms are *Muhima* and *Bahima,* respectively. The Hima are a group of several thousand people, closely akin to the Tutsi. They live in northern Rwanda, near the frontier of Uganda, and they are distinguished by their language and physical characteristics. They practice agriculture.

HINDU. An ethnic group that entered the country from India during German occupation and were given special commercial licenses to engage in trade. Their status changed when the Belgians took over the administration of Rwanda. Belgian authorities attempted without much success to reduce their influence in commercial trade.

HIRTH, MONSIGNOR JEAN-JOSEPH (1854–1931). Member of the Société des Missionnaires d'Afrique, or the White Fathers. Monsignor Hirth was born in Niederspechback in Alsace on March 25, 1854. The family moved to France after the Franco-Prussian war, and in October 1873, Father Hirth entered the Grand Séminaire at Nancy. He became a novice in the order of the White Fathers in 1875. In 1882, he was sent to Jerusalem to work with children. At the turn of the century, he became the monsignor at the Vicariate of Southern Nyanza, which extended from Lake Kivu to Mount Kilimanjaro. He took personal charge of the missionary activities in Rwanda and was responsible for the creation of most of the mission stations in the country and the Petit and Grand Séminaires at Kabgayi. He was buried in the cathedral of Kabgayi in 1931.

HOBE. A bilingual monthly periodical published in both Kinyarwanda and French. It was established in 1955 as a magazine for young people, and has a circulation of about 95,000.

HOE. A multipurpose instrument and a medium of exchange. Before the arrival of the Europeans, the hoe was the basis of all purchases, primarily because it was everywhere in abundance. Important Tutsi had several hundred hoes in reserve, considered their security. A new hoe was called *isuka* and the used one *ifuni*. Three used hoes were equivalent to one new hoe. A hoe was equivalent to ten days of work; during the 1930s the hoe was worth five francs, and a day's work was therefore equal to fifty centimes.

HOE CLIENT (CLIENT DE HOUE). According to traditional practice, a poor farmer could obtain a hoe by working for a client for two days out of five, or by performing some similar kind of corvée for a land client or notable on the hill. A Tutsi was more inclined to use this method than a Hutu. A poverty-stricken peasant would often offer his services in order to gain a hoe for his sons who were old enough to marry.

HUREL, EUGENE (1878–1936). Catholic priest and member of the Missionnaires d'Afrique, or White Fathers. His first mission assignment in Africa was to the Vicariate of Southern Nyanza in 1902. He served there until he was transferred to Rwanda in 1908, where he served in various administrative positions, including general steward (*économe général*) at Kabgayi. In 1917, he was nominated superior of the petite mission of Nyaruhengeri. Two years later, he returned to Belgium to enroll in a course in tropical medicine. His second tour of duty in Rwanda occurred in 1922. He was reas-

signed to the mission post at Nyaruhengeri until his nomination as superior to the mission at Save, from 1927 to 1935.
During his career, he published several editions of Rwandan
grammar, recorded oral traditions and literature, and compiled a historical dictionary. He returned to France in 1936
because of medical problems and died the following year in
Algiers. His body was returned for burial at Sel-de-
Bretagne, his birthplace.

HUTU. The singular and plural forms are *Abahutu* and *Bahutu,*
respectively. They were the second group of people to inhabit the country after the Twa. They are culturally related
to the Bantu, and they arrived in Rwanda during the first
millennium, probably from the south or southwest. While
they are primarily agriculturalists, they also raise cattle. The
Hutu were eventually subjugated by the Tutsi, and they provided both corvée and prestations in the daily work that
Tutsi notables required for the construction of kraals, roads,
and pontooning over marshes, as well as military service
under the traditional feudal system. The Hutu gained their
independence literally and figuratively, in 1962; they constitute 85 percent of the total population of the country.

HUTU PRINCIPALITIES. Bushiru, Buhoma, Bukonya,
Bugamba-Kiganda, Itare, Cyingogo, Ruhengeri, Kibali,
Rwankeri, and Bwamamwali were independent Hutu king-
doms in the north, eventually incorporated into the central
Tutsi kingdom by second decade of the twentieth century.

-I-

IBIGABIRO. Regions where the *umwami* had residences, including all the land that was used for kraals. These areas could
never become the property of an ordinary individual or Tutsi
notable.

IBIKUNIKWA. Tribute in produce, or "provisions," due to the chief at each harvest. This particular prestation became a regular payment in the eighteenth century, as the *umwami* sought to increase his political control over the country. Before the change, Banyarwanda supplied the Court with what it needed under the supervision of the *abanyabutaka* (sing. *ummyubutaka*), or "men of the land," when the roving Court was in a particular area.

IBIRONGOZI. A new rank of Tutsi official created in Kinyaga, under Belgian administration, to assist in collecting traditional prestations and labor from the people. They usually assisted the hill chiefs, and some could be Hutu. These new officials usurped many functions that were previously performed by lineage heads in the area, many of whom were Hutu, and therefore reduced their political participation.

IBITEKEREZO. Officially composed Court histories. Twenty or more have been recorded from an informant in Nduga, located in south central Rwanda, and published in Kinyarwanda with parallel French translation. *Ibitekerezo* cover the period from the origin of the royal clan, Nyiginya, to Kigeri Rwaburgiri's conquests.

IBUHUTU. A traditional rural zone devoted primarily to agricultural production and located on the summit of hills, plateaus, or crests. This zone was inhabited primarily by Hutu. The Tutsi who lived there were impoverished herders or members of the administrative hierarchy nominated by superior authorities.

IBUTUTSI. A traditional rural zone, sparsely populated and supporting large herds that required extensive pastures. Some agricultural production was practiced by Hutu farmers, usually clients of the cattle owners.

IGIKINGI (pl. IBIKINGI). An administrative innovation established during the end of *umwami* Yuhi Gahindiro's reign

(1797–1830) in order to extend his control over the kingdom. It was the smallest unit of command granted by the Royal Court and included land and pasture rights over several pieces of territory, or hills, given to a favored individual. Relatives, friends, or others who would pay prestations (as in the case of a hill chief) might have been granted *igikingi*.

When a Tutsi arrived on a new hill, he paid court to the chieftain by giving him a cow. In return, the chieftain provided the newcomer with *amarembo* over a certain number of households. These households were included in a geographical area which was called, as a whole, *igikingi*. The rights of a Tutsi over these households were limited to *igisigati,* or the rights to pasture his cows on sorghum stubble during the dry season. These land grants were suppressed in the Administrative Reform Program of 1931, essentially because they impeded the reforms introduced in the area of corvées and prestations. *Igikingi* was utilized by notables as a way of gaining more wealth by allocating grants to favorites, who in return provided goods and services.

IJAMBO. The newspaper *Ijambo* emerged in the new political climate of the 1990s. For the most part, *Ijambo* and others like it are devoted to political commentary. Its editor, Francois-Xavier Hangimana, was arrested and imprisoned in May for writing articles which allegedly "injured" two ministers and three colonels. His editorial was deemed demoralizing to the army. Mr. Hangimana was provisionally set free on September 24, 1991.

IKORO. A traditional tribute payment in produce due to the *umwami*. It was replaced by a cash payment and fixed at 1 BF in 1932 and 1933.

IMBURABUTURO. Land areas that were unoccupied because of superstitious fear. These areas were "je ne trouve pas ou m'installer."

IMIKENKE. Traditional land designation in rural areas for land unsuitable for agriculture, or for land that had not been touched by a hoe but could be used as pasture for the herds of the *umwami* or chiefs in charge of pasture.

IMISEZERO. Areas of the country where the *umwami*, the queen mother, or someone of great influence was buried. These areas could not become the property of an ordinary individual or Tutsi notable.

IMMIGRATION. Rwanda has the highest population density in Africa. During the colonial period, both German and Belgian officials considered excess population to be a labor pool that could be exported to neighboring countries. Before 1914, German East African officials envisioned Rwanda as a labor reservoir for the plantations in the region from Kilimanjaro to the Indian Ocean.

In addition to the labor component, the Belgian administration from time to time promoted emigration to relieve the population pressures on the land. In 1927, the government proposed a massive emigration plan and created a Belgian commission to study the feasibility of resettling Banyarwandan families in Mokotas, located west of Baraka and Uvira, and in the Mugila and Markungu mountainous areas. *See also* MOKOTAS RESETTLEMENT PLAN.

Rwandan immigrants began to appear in Uganda in 1923–1924, particularly in Buganda and western Busoga. These areas attracted migrants initially because of favorable geographical position. Their arrival also coincided with the economic revival that followed the economic crisis of 1921, the expansion of cotton production, and the abolition of colonial corvées in Buganda in 1922, as well as the introduction of compulsory cultivation in Rwanda. Immigration increased in 1926–1927 with the encouragement of British authorities, and it became more massive in 1928–1929, following the great famine in Belgian Africa. By 1948, there were 289,051 Banyarwanda living in Uganda; about 192,844 were migrants. Most settled or worked in Buganda, followed by Ankole and the Busoga district, where they worked on the Kakira Sugar Plantation or as porters to Soga farmers. Those in Buganda were employed by industries and in agriculture, while those in Ankole worked in the mines. The rate of increase between 1948 and 1959 was 43.5 percent, or 82,955. The main concentration was in Buganda, which had 216,896 Rwandans in 1959.

The flow toward Katanga occurred between 1925 and 1930 and stemmed from efforts on the part of the Belgian government to diminish the flow to English territories. During World War I, the Banyarwanda favored immigration to Uganda rather than the Belgian Congo. A report from the *Economist* in 1963 notes that about 80,000 Banyarwanda were migrant laborers outside of the country, and almost all went to the Belgian Congo.

IMPARA COFFEE PLANTERS' COOPERATIVE. Organized on January 30, 1954, in the territory of Shangugu. In 1955, it received a loan of one million Belgian francs from the Fonds Spécial de Crédit Agricole Indigéne. The cooperative had the capacity to treat its own coffee.

IMPONAKE. A traditional prestation involving cattle demanded as replacement from a Tutsi by his patron when his herds had been stricken or experienced unusually high death rates. The Belgian Resident abolished *imponake* in 1924.

IMPOT DE CAPITATION. *See* HEAD TAX (IMPOT DE CAPITATION).

IMPRIMERIE DE KABGAYI. One of two publishing companies in the country.

IMPRIMERIE NATIONALE DU RWANDA. The government's publishing house.

IMVAHO/THE TRUTH. A Kinyarwanda weekly published by

the Office Rwandaise d'Information and established in 1960. Circulation is about 23,000.

INAMA. Councils of leading Christians that functioned at several of the missions. Their members were converts who had come together before World War I and were organized by the White Fathers in the 1920s. Initially, these councils were concerned with the regular performance of Christian duties by converts and catechumens, but in the 1920s they were involved in settling disputes among Christians. They also supported one another in disputes with Tutsi notables, and they organized funds to provide financial aid in times of distress. Those at Kabgayi were consulted by the *umwami* on matters concerning Christians.

INCHOREKE. Young Tutsi or Hutu girls who were traditionally servants to the wives of Tutsi notables.

INCOME TAX. During the colonial period, Africans from non-Belgian territories were exempt from income tax. However, Asians engaged in commerce were subjected to personal income tax on a quarterly basis, as were salaried and employed personnel with disposable annual income over 9,000 BF.

INDABUKIRANO. Cattle or some other form of special prestation (such as hoes or sheep) that was given to Tutsi notable (or the army chief) from his subjects when taking command of a hill. The Belgian Resident abolished *indabukirano* in 1924.

INDIAN QUESTION. The *Inder Frage* under German administration resulted in efforts to control Indians' participation in trade in Rwanda. A governor's ordinance was passed on March 10, 1905, maintaining that "until further notice the entrance to the sultanates of Ruanda and Urundi [was] permitted only from the military station of Usumbura and only with written permission." The role that Indians would play in the development of Rwanda was discussed at Berlin and Bonn, but each German Resident in Rwanda was left to devise his own policy. By 1913, the policy toward Indians had become more liberal in the Colonial Office at Berlin.

INDIRECT RULE. During the German and Belgian colonial eras indirect rule meant rule from above—by Tutsi notables and by the Belgian administration at the top of the hierarchy.

INDUGARUGA. A regiment of Rwandan soldiers created by the German Resident in 1914 after war was declared in Europe.

INDUSTRIAL CROPS. Products intended for export—coffee, tea, spices, cotton, cotton oil, barley, cinchona bark—in order to secure European currency for exchange.

INDUSTRIAL PRODUCTION. Products primarily for local consumption—the principal articles being bricks and tile, furniture, ready-to-wear clothing, soap and insecticide, beer, and processed tea.

INFORMATEUR, L'. A review published by the National University of Rwanda since 1966. It became *Etudes Rwandaises* with volume 10 in 1977. The review contains information about the university and scholarly articles from its faculty and students.

INFURA. *Infura* is a Kinyarwanda term for notables.

INKOTANYI. A Kinyarwandan term which means the "indefatigable ones" and refers to the tenacity of the RPF troops that invaded Rwanda from Uganda in October 1990.

INKIKE. *Inkike* is a Kinyarwanda term for the residence of Tutsi notables.

INKUNGU. A parcel of land that was already prepared for cultivation, from which the former tenant had been evicted by a Tutsi notable, or had left, or had died without heirs. The right to cultivate *inkungu* could be assigned by the land chief.

INSPECTEURS D'ETAT. A senior official and member of the governmental council, an ex officio member after 1933. The state inspector was responsible for the general supervision of administration throughout the country.

INSTITUT DES SCIENCES AGRONOMIQUES DU RWANDA (ISAR). The Institute of Agronomical Sciences of Rwanda (located at Rubona in the province of Butare) is a state agency created in 1962 to replace the pre-independence INEAC, which served all of Belgian Africa. ISAR continues the crop experimentation begun before independence in six subcenters located throughout the country. The institute conducts soil sampling at higher altitudes (such as Rwerere), creates agricultural settlements (such as Bugesera at Karama), and establishes livestock improvement centers (such as Songa). It also provides support services for subsistence and export agriculture.

INSTITUT NATIONAL POUR L'ETUDE AGRONOMIQUE DU CONGO BELGE (INEAC). The institute was established in 1933 to coordinate virtually all biological and animal research in Belgian Africa. It was an independent entity that operated under royal decree, and it received its funding and administration from Brussels. It succeeded the Régie des Plantations de la Colonie. Its work included selection, improvement, and introduction of plants of possible economic value; reforestation; social maintenance and care; new food crops for the African agricultural sector; acclimatization and improvement of cattle, tropical veterinary research and study; and the introduction of new agricultural industries.

It also engaged in the analysis and classification of soils and created regulations for soil conservation and regeneration. The institute devised programs for the preservation of foodstuffs, campaigned against disease and parasites, established mechanical processes for cultivation of tropical soils, and collected varieties of forest and fruit trees and plants for the extraction of perfume.

The central office and experimental station were located at Yangambi in the heart of the Belgian Congo. There was an additional experimental station at Rubona in Rwanda (which still exists) and a branch office at Bujumbura. The experimental stations fulfilled an educational function by training Africans as specialized workers, some of whom became assistants to agricultural agents and African advisers. The Duke of Brabant (later King Leopold III) served as its first president, followed by Pierre Ryckmans and Auguste-Constant Tilkens.

INSTITUT POUR LA RECHERCHE SCIENTIFIQUE EN AFRIQUE CENTRALE (IRSAC). A scientific research institute, created by decree on July 1, 1947. The institute conducted demographic research, physical and social anthropology, linguistics, and nutritional studies in Belgian Africa. It had three research stations, one each in Butare, Uvira, and Luwiro.

INSTITUTE UNIVERSITAIRE DES TERRITOIRES D'OUTRE-MER. The university for colonial civil servants, which was formerly the Colonial University at Antwerp. Past presidents included Louis Franck, minister for colonies from 1918 to 1924, and Robert Godding, minister for colonies from 1945 to 1947. Godding served as president in 1938.

INTERAHAMWE. *See* PARTY YOUTH WINGS.

INTERFINA. A private company that operated during the colonial period, it was the largest buyer of African produce. Its large cadre of small traders obtained food crops with trinkets. To circumvent government control, these traders also secretly engaged in labor recruiting.

INTERIM DECREE (DECEMBER 25, 1959). The decree, signed by King Baudouin, was designed to stabilize political turmoil in the country. The decree was later implemented by Regulation No. 221/51 of February 6,1960. It called for political reorganization by replacing the African Native Administration by communes, each of which was provided with a mayor and a council elected directly by universal male suffrage. The chiefdoms were transformed into transitional and purely administrative units. The power of the *umwami* was suspended until procedures could be established for governing the country. The decree also abolished the Mwami's Grand Council, and replaced it with a Special Provisionary Council composed of three Tutsi and three Hutu with a Belgian administrator acting as chairman. The *umwami* was free to send a nonvoting delegate.

INTERNATIONAL COFFEE AGREEMENT (1968). Limited coffee exports by establishing a quota of 150,000 bags (or 9,000 metric tons) as compared with 212,000 bags (or 12,720 tons) under the old agreement.

INTERNATIONAL COFFEE CONFERENCE (RIO DE JANEIRO, BRAZIL, 1958). At the international meeting on May 20, the conference discussed the crisis of surplus stocks, declining coffee prices, and the possibility of stockpiling to increase prices.

INTERNATIONAL COMMITTEE OF THE RED CROSS. ICRC, the private, Geneva-based, multi-national humanitarian organization, was founded in 1863. Its primary mission is to provide protection and assistance for military and civilian victims of armed conflict and to serve as a neutral presence during periods of conflict in the international arena. It also maintains the principles of the Red Cross and ensures the application of the Geneva Conventions. ICRC aids in the protection and care of the wounded; it seeks to ban torture, summary executions and mass murder, deportations, hostage taking, pillage, and the destruction of civilian property. It works to protect political prisoners and has developed a large-scale program of visits to political detainees in many countries. It has publicized its findings through petitioning, hearings, and publications. It maintains a medical division, which evaluates the medical needs within crisis areas and provides hospital service during periods of conflict.

With respect to Rwanda, the ICRC has turned its attention to the 600,000 or more refugees in the northern region, especially those who have been displaced by the civil war and are camped south of the war zones of RPF-held territory. ICRC describes the conditions and needs in these camps as being second only to Somalia in urgency. It has called upon the international community for assistance, particularly for food aid, housing, and medicine. ICRC warns that famine in these camps is imminent and that severe malnutrition has been detected in children under the age of five. ICRC has estimated that the camps will need at least 13,000 tons of food per month. The agency's own response for 1993 has been to increase its budget for Rwanda from $10.5 million to 85.6 million.

INTORE. The "chosen ones." The *intore* were young men, sons of the *umwami*'s Tutsi clients, who were requested to come to Court for military training. When about 150 to 200 young men were gathered, they constituted a company (or *itorero*). The *intore* lived at the Court or with a chief who had been allowed to recruit an army. Under the direction of an officer called the chief of the king's residence (*umutware w'urugo rw'ummwami*), or its counterpart at a chief's court, they were trained for several years in military skills. They learned war dances and how to memorize and to recite the poems in which deeds of extraordinary bravery of past warriors were exalted.

INYANGARWANDA. A term used to describe Christian converts and currently characterizing haters or repudiators of Rwanda.

INYENZI. "Cockroaches," a group formed by François Rukeba and other UNAR militants and Tutsi refugees, who had left Rwanda during the "troubles" in 1960. They formed themselves into guerrilla bands and on March 13, 1961, crossed the border into Rwanda and mounted attacks from Uganda, Burundi, Zaire, and Tanzania on Hutu officials. They were repulsed by the Rwandan National Guard, but the retaliations by Hutu inflicted heavy casualties on innocent Tutsi within the country. The *inyenzi* mounted additional attacks into Rwanda in 1962 and 1963, with the same result. Thousands of Tutsi were killed or forced to flee Rwanda to neighboring countries for sanctuary. In 1985, the government offered amnesty to eight members of the *inyenzi,* imprisoned twenty years earlier.

INZU. The traditional hut or dwelling within the compound, or *rugo.* It also was used at the end of the nineteenth century to designate the patrilineal kinship group, including all those who traced their agnatic relationship through usually no more than four or five ascendant genealogical links to an ancestor recognized as the original ancestor of the group. This patrilineal kinship group had no collective rights over particular areas except in the north of Rwanda—in the provinces of Mulera, Rwankeri, Bushiru, and Bigogwe— where Tutsi occupation was not yet secured and where the soil belonged to the group and there was no land or cattle chief. Some Rwandan scholars use the term to designate the nuclear family, consisting of the father, mother, and children.

ISAMBU. A traditional form of individual land tenure introduced by the Tutsi, marking their initial efforts at political incorporation and consolidation of the country. *Isambu* applied to unoccupied or abandoned land that could be granted to individuals. With its introduction, two types of arable land existed in the rural area—*ingobyi y'igisekuru,* or collective or lineage lands, and *isambu,* or land granted or conceded to chiefs (*chefs de ménage*).

ISHYANGA. The designation for the Hutu patrilineal subclan that is quite common in the northern and northwestern region of the country. It also signifies a subbranch of the *abasangwabutaka,* or lineage members who were the first to occupy these regions.

ISIBO IJAMBO. *Isibo Ijambo* was one of the several newspapers suppressed and censored in June 1991 during the government's harassment spree. Several of its issues were seized. The newspaper emerged in the political climate of the 1990s, but it has been a precarious tenure.

ISLAM. About 0.5 percent of the population practice Islam.

ISSAVI. A Catholic mission station of 250 hectares, about 20 kilometers from Nyanza. The mission was established in 1900 by Monsignor Jean-Joseph Hirth and a group of White Fathers and their Ganda catechists. They received the station from *umwami* Musinga. In January and February 1907 the Save Cathedral was built. It became the home of the Soeurs Blanches in 1908. The White Sisters ran a medical dispensary and school for children on the premises. Before 1920, missionaries at Issavi distributed several thousand coffee trees to their catechists, but these were destroyed because the chiefs objected to utilizing land that could be used for grazing.

ITAC. A ship with a capacity of 300 tons that flew the Belgian flag and was chartered by Mavricas Limited of Kigoma to transport Rwandan goods destined for Dar es Salaam from the port of Bujumbura across Lake Tanganyika to the port at

Kigoma during the 1930s. This ship also transported imports to the port at Bujumbura.

-J-

JASPER, HENRI (1870–1939). Belgian lawyer, judge, diplomat, and colonial civil servant. Jasper worked in the Ministry for the Colonies from 1928 to 1930. In the spring of 1929, he devised a strategy against possible famine first by compelling the African farmer to enlarge his planting surface and by encouraging him to plant manioc; second, by granting 50 million Belgian francs for the construction of roads in Rwanda and Burundi; and third, by advocating migration of Africans to the Kivu region to work on the plantations of Europeans and to the Belgian Congo to work in the mines. He also introduced a pension program for African military personnel.

JASSIDES. An insect that attacks and seriously damages coffee plants.

JESUITS. Catholic order responsible for education in Belgian Africa.

JEUNESSE DEMOCRATIQUE REPUBLICAIN. *See* PARTY YOUTH WINGS.

JEUNESSE LIBERAL. *See* PARTY YOUTH WINGS.

JOHANSSEN, ERNST. A Lutheran pastor and member of the first Protestant sect to enter the country, in 1908. Pastor Johanssen was from the Bethel bei Bielefeld mission. He was given land by *umwami* Musinga at Zinga, about five hours from Zaza.

JUDICIAL SYSTEM. Under the provisions of the 1978 Constitution, the judicial system was reorganized to include a
Council of State with administrative jurisdiction, a Supreme
Court of Appeal, a Constitutional Court consisting of the
Supreme Court of Appeal and the Council of State sitting
jointly, a Court of Accounts responsible for examining all
public accounts, and courts of appeal, courts of first instance, and provincial courts.

JUNGERS, EUGENE-JACQUES-PIERRE-LOUIS (1888–?).
Lawyer and member of the Belgian colonial civil service,
vice governor-general of the mandate territory from 1932 to
1946, and governor of the Belgian Congo from 1946 to
1952. He was born on July 19, 1888, and entered colonial
service in April 1911 with an assignment at Boma. He
served as Resident of Burundi before becoming vice governor-general of the mandate on June 30, 1932. When he succeeded Voisin, as vice governor-general, Jungers continued
the compulsory coffee cultivation campaign with the assistance of the Agriculture Service. He also conducted a campaign against the famine of 1942–1944.

-K-

KABALO-KABANGO RAIL LINE. A 152 mile rail line that
linked the colonial commercial traffic of Rwanda and
Burundi with that of the Belgian Congo.

KABAYA. A territory designation in the northwest region in the
1930s; presently a prefecture and township.

KABGAYI. A Catholic mission station established in 1905. It became the residence of the papal curate of the White Fathers
and contains the Grand and Petit Séminaires, as well as a

primary and professional school run by the Soeurs Blanches (White Sisters). The mission sponsored basket making and had its own carpentry shop during the colonial period.

KAGAME, CARDINAL ALEXIS (1912–1981). A Tutsi Catholic priest, historian, and writer. Kagame came from a family of *abiiru,* or court ritualists, in charge of the esoteric code who therefore had influence over royal succession. He attended the school for sons of chiefs at Ruhengeri and from there the Petit Séminaire at Kabgayi in 1929. He became the assistant editor of *Kinyamateka* while a seminarian and as a professor of French at the Noviciat des Frères Josephites in 1938. He was ordained as a Catholic priest in 1941. In 1952, he traveled to Rome to begin university studies at the Pontifical Gregorian University of Rome, where he earned a doctorate of philosophy. His thesis, which was later published, was on the Bantu philosophy of being. When he returned to Rwanda, he was appointed professor of general history and philosophy at the Groupe Scolaire at Butare and taught Rwandese literature at the Petit Séminaire at Kansi. After the creation of the national university at Butare, he became professor of Rwandan literature, history, and language. In 1967, he was also professor of history and philosophy at the Grand Séminaire of Nyakibanda while maintaining his teaching duties at the National University at Butare.

Abbé Alexis Kagame wrote extensively about traditional Rwanda and its poetry, some of which was composed in Kinyarwanda. He was probably the earliest African to write about the philosophical nature of Africa's traditional thoughts and beliefs. Among his most important works are *La philosophie bantu-rwandaise de l'être* (1956); *La langue du Rwanda et du Burundi expliquée aux autochtones* (1960); *Introduction à la conjugaison du verb rwandais* (1962); and *La philosophie bantu comparée* (1976). Besides his teaching assignments, he was also a member of the

UNESCO committee in charge of the editing and publication of the *General History of Africa.*

KAGAME, PAUL. Major Kagame is a former Tutsi refugee who lived in Uganda and is currently the third chairman of the high command of the RPF. As a refugee in Uganda, he became head of the Uganda National Revolutionary Army's military intelligence from November 1989 to June 1990. He also spent seven years fighting guerrilla campaigns with Yoweri Museveni, the president of Uganda. Major Kagame is considered to be a brilliant military strategist and was enrolled in the United States Army Command and General Staff College at Leavenworth, Kansas, to learn how to become a general when the October invasion of Rwanda began. As chairman of the high command, Major Kagame established his base of operations in the heavily forested Virunga mountains in northwest Rwanda. He has reportedly rebuilt the RPF from a rag-tag band of 2,000 men to a 15,000-efficient guerrilla army.

By December 1991, his forces controlled a strip of territory along the Ugandan border, stretching about 20 miles inside Rwanda. Kagame's strategy is to pick away at the government's forces. An offensive against Rwanda, he maintains, isn't necessary, but he feels that if the RPF can increase the pressure points in the northern part of the country, then the contradictions within President Habyarimana's regime will cause the government to self-destruct. Major Kagame also participated in the signing of the March 29, 1991 ceasefire agreement.

KAGERA. A port city on the Kagera River in Tanganyikan territory, opened in 1931, to compete with Dar es Salaam and handle merchandise to and from eastern Rwanda.

KAJEGUKAKWA, VALENS. Valens Kajegukakwa, a former Rwandan businessman who on June 11, 1990 with his son,

Christian, received a suspended prison sentence of three years at a court hearing in Gisenyi for allegedly defaming prominent members of the security forces. Kajegukakwa owned a private petrol company, called Enterprise Rwandaise de Pétrole. He accused the head of the armed forces and the gendarmerie of attempting to poison his son and of organizing an attack on his family in April. In bringing Valens to court, the government accused him of refusing to appear in court when summoned. But Valens claimed that he never received the summons. Both father and son also claimed that their house had been placed under surveillance by the government. Their case was being monitored by Amnesty International. This incident follows a series of court hearings that had occurred earlier in the year when several people were prosecuted for allegedly conspiring to upset public order.

KALINGA. The sacred drum and the symbol of the *umwami*'s authority, from which were hung the genitals of the enemies killed by the *umwami*.

KAMALI, SYLVESTRE. Rwandan politician, member and national delegate from Gisenyi, his birthplace (in 1935). Kamali attended the Grand Séminaire at Nyakibanda for three years with a major in philosophy. He became a functionary in the national government from 1965 to 1969. He was named the Gisenyi's national deputy for MDR/PARMEHUTU in 1969.

KAMEMBE. *See* SHANGUGU.

KAMINA-KABALO ROUTE. A commercial route with both strategic and economic significance. It offered an alternative route to the eastern Congo, Lake Kivu, and Rwanda and Burundi, thus reducing the number of transshipments from the last two areas via the route to Matadi from seven to five and the transport distance from 2,244 to 1,957 miles.

KAMOSO, AUGUSTIN. Augustin Kamoso, a Rwandan politician and member of PARMEHUTU, was born in Kirambo in 1924. He attended the Petit Séminaire at Kabgayi. After completing his education, he worked in the Belgian colonial administration and with several private enterprises from 1943 to 1957. From 1957 to 1959, he was propagandist for the Mutualités chrétiennes au Rwanda. In 1965, he joined the national government as minister of family and community development until 1969, when he was appointed minister of posts, telecommunications, and transportation. He also became the national delegate or representative from Changugu to MDR/PARMEHUTU that same year.

KANDT, RICHARD. Richard Kandt, the German poet, explorer, scientist, and staunch free trader, arrived in Rwanda in 1907. He became the first German Resident of Rwanda, serving from 1908 to 1913. In terms of an economic program, he supported the cultivation of coffee for Africans as a cash crop and railroad construction for comprehensive development. Kandt also planned the new capital at Kigali.

KANGUKA. *Kanguka* is one among several new periodicals that have been harassed by the government in a general effort to censor the press for what it deemed as writing copy that was demoralizing to the armed forces curently fighting the civil war in the northern region. Its editor, Vincent Rwabukwisi, who was recently released from a 17-year sentence, was arrested again in June 1991. He was released on September 12 without going to trial.

KANGURA. *Kangura* is another of the new newspapers censored by the government in a move directed against the press that occurred in June 1991. A number of journalists and editors were arrested for printing copy that the government said was demoralizing to the armed forces currently fighting the civil war in the northern region of the country. Several issues of *Kangura* were seized by the government and its editor, Hassan Ngeze, was arrested for writing articles which the government maintained caused tension with Burundi. He, along with several other fellow journalists who had been arrested in June, was released on September 12 without going to trial.

KANYAMAHANGA, CHARLES. Rwandan politician and chemical engineer. A native of Gishyita, Byumba, he was born there in 1935. He attended the University of Louvain in Belgium and earned a degree in chemical engineering. He joined the national government in 1962 with service in various ministries, including minister of public works and energy in 1965 and minister of family and community development from 1969 to February 1972.

KANYARENGWE, COLONEL ALEXIS. Colonel Alexis Kanyarengwe is Hutu and a former Rwandan minister of internal affairs. Kanyarengwe was forced to leave the country for sanctuary in Tanzania in 1980, when he was accused of plotting a coup against the Rwandan government. He joined the RPF and became its president in mid-November 1990. Kanyarengwe was promoted to the rank of major shortly thereafter. In a news conference in 1991, he told reporters that the October invasion was a war of liberation, designed to implement democratic change in Rwanda and to facilitate the return of all refugees, both Hutu and Tutsi. As a military strategist, he argues that the presence of RPF forces within Rwanda's northern terrain and constant military pressure will cause the national government to self-destruct. This particular line of argument is commonly held by most of the RPF leadership.

KANYARWANDA. Kanyarwanda is the name of a new human rights organization which monitors violations against civilians within Rwanda. Its legal representative is Fidele Kanyabugori, who was arrested in Kigali on March 29, 1992. His transgression was a petition, in which he asked the government to carry out an independent investigation of the Bagogwe massacres.

KANZENZI RESETTLEMENT PLAN. An elaboration of a plan envisioned by Heeven, a former district commissioner from Lomami, who sought to create a modern type of African farming settlement with a labor-recruitment component. The plan was supported by Union Minière du Haut-Katanga and the Franciscan mission at Kanzenze. It involved the resettlement of Rwandan immigrants who would produce food products and provide labor for the mine. In fact, Banyarwanda under contract with UMHK would be given tracts of lands after the termination of their first contract in the mines as an inducement to remain and renew their labor contracts.

KAREMEERA RWAAKA, UMWAMI OF RWANDA. *See* RWAAKA, KAREMEERA.

KARISOKE RESEARCH STATION. The Karisoke Research Station was established by Dian Fossey in 1967 and supported by the U.S.-based Dian Fossey Gorilla fund, based in Denver and with a supporting branch in London. The station is located on the southwest slope of Visoke in the northwestern corner of Rwanda, and it was established to protect and to conserve the mountain gorilla and its unique ecosystem. On February 13, 1993, its European and American staff were forced to abandon the station because of fighting between the government forces and RPF. A few, as of May, 1993, have since returned to the station. The African staff, which includes the anti-poaching squad, and was left behind, reported that buildings and valuable equipment were looted, doors were broken, and windows shot out only a week after the initial party had left.

KARUZI STATION. An agricultural experimental station that

ceased operation in 1935 when its staff was transferred to the stations at Rubona and Kisozi.

KAYABACUZI, HORMISDAS. Hormisdas Kayabacuzi, a Hutu activist from Kinyaga and a member of APROSOMA, served the local subchiefdom and chiefdom council in 1953 and in 1959.

KAYIBANDA, GREGOIRE (1924–1976). Member of the Committee of Nine, leader of PARMEHUTU, and Rwanda's first president, in 1962. Kayibanda was born in 1924 near Kabgayi. It is believed that his father was a Mushi from the Belgian Congo and his mother a Hutu. He attended the Petit Séminaire at Nyakibanda and entered the Grand Séminaire at Nyakibanda in 1943. He subsequently found employment as a primary school teacher at the Institut Classé, near Kigali, where he stayed until 1952. While at the institute, he became secretary of the literary committee in charge of awarding prizes for the best essays written by Rwandese students. He was also secretary of the Amitiés Belgo-Congolaise, a cultural association founded in Kigali by J. F. C. Gossens, a Belgian settler.

In 1952, Kayibanda went to Kabgayi as a prospective seminarian, where he also became editor of *L'Ami,* a modest newspaper printed at Kabgayi (*L'Ami* ceased publication after 1956) and was editor-in-chief of *Kinyameteka* in 1954. In 1960, he became president of TRAFIPRO, a consumer co-operative, and the personal secretary to Monsignor Perraudin, as well as a member of the chiefdom council of Marangara. His mentors, Fathers Dejemeppe and Ernotte, were Christian Socialists and sponsored his visits to Belgium in 1950 and 1957, and may have influenced in collaboration with Kayibanda the wording of the manifesto. In June 1957, he formed the Mouvement Social Muhutu (MSM). At the invitation of the Catholic church, he studied journalism in Brussels and worked for the missionary press center there from 1958 to 1959. When he returned home, he found his countrymen poised for revolution and commenced to build upon their discontent.

He became president of the country in 1962 and leader of the Parti du Mouvement de l'Emancipation Hutu (PARME-HUTU), the dominant party in the country. Kayibanda was re-elected unchallenged to a second term in 1965. As political power became increasingly concentrated in the hands of a few politicians from the Gitarama region in central Rwanda, the government became increasingly isolated and authoritarian. His economic policies did not bring prosperity to all segments of society. His policies for governing the country included the regulation of price and production, the development of communications, monetary stability, and the encouragement of foreign investment. He was overthrown in a bloodless coup led by a military faction from the northern part of the country in 1973. His defense minister, Major General Juvénal Habyarimana, led the coup and placed Kayibanda under house arrest. He was tried and sentenced to death in July 1973, but his sentence was commuted to life imprisonment for fomenting ethnic discord. Kayibanda died of a heart attack three years later.

KAYONZA-KAGITUMBA ROAD PROJECT. Part of a comprehensive roadbuilding program designed to resolve the problem of transport throughout the whole country generally, and to Tanzania, Kenya, and Uganda specifically. New roads to Tanzania have been constructed, and the major road leading to Kenya has been upgraded. In 1985, a new project, estimated to cost some $50 million, was launched to upgrade the Kayonza-Kagitumba road leading to the Ugandan border. Financial assistance for the project was provided by the Saudi Fund for Development, the OPEC Fund for International Development, and the African Development Bank (ADB). In 1986, tenders were invited for a project, costing an estimated $80 million, to reconstruct another section of the main route to Uganda, the Kigali-Gatuna road. The Butare-Cyangugu line to Zaire was completed in 1987.

KDOBA, UMWAMI OF RWANDA. Reigned from 1486 to 1510.

KENYA EXPORT INCENTIVE SURCHARGE, 1992. The Kenyan government instituted an export subsidy of 20 percent on exports to Rwanda from its port at Mombasa. The Rwandan government retaliated in August 1992 and imposed a 60 percent import charge on Kenyan goods coming into Rwanda. The government claims that the Kenya Incentive has led to dumping, which it says is a breach of the Preferential Trade Area for Eastern and Southern Africa (PTA) rules (for further information, see the entry, PTA). In a countercharge, the Kenyan government maintained that the Rwandan special import levies violated the rules as well.

Experts suspect that the real issue here is Rwandan indebtedness. Since the start of the October 1990 invasion by RPF forces, Rwanda has accumulated large unpaid port charges at Mombasa worth $15.6 million. Experts also maintain that Rwanda may be the loser in this trade war in the long run. It cites that Kenya is Rwanda's largest trading partner, and maintains that 95 percent of Rwanda's imports and exports go through Mombasa. Since the dispute erupted, Rwanda must take an alternative route through Tanzania and Burundi. This routing, while it is much safer, is quite arduous and very expensive. Freight charges have increased tremendously.

KIBUNGU. One of ten prefectures in the country. It has a total area of 4,134 square kilometers and a population, according to the 1978 census, of 361,249 inhabitants. During the colonial period, this area contained the mining company Georunda, which had operations at Kugurama and Bugarula, and the customhouse at Katitumba on the border with Uganda. Soil is relatively poor, and therefore agricultural yields are quite low.

KIBUYE. A prefecture with an area of 1,320 square kilometers and population, according to the 1978 census, of 336,588 inhabitants. During the colonial period, it contained one of the most important commercial ports on Lake Kivu, vital in the westerly flow of goods to the Belgian Congo and the Atlantic Ocean. The territory also contained cassiterite mining, and it supplied workers and porters for the Gatumba mine in neighboring Kisenyi.

KIGALI. A prefecture, the capital, and one of the principal towns of the republic. As of the 1978 census the prefecture has an area of 3,321 square kilometers and total population of 698,442. The capital's population was 117,749. During the colonial period, it was the home of the German Resident from 1908, and of the Belgian Resident from 1916 to independence. It served as the crossroads for the caravan trade, as well as an important market center for hides and coffee and the center for the export of cassiterite. In 1934, the mines at Buliza employed 1,800 African workers, 4,000 at the end of 1935, and 6,000 in 1936.

KIGERI MUKOBANYA, UMWAMI OF RWANDA. *See* MUKOBANYA, KIGERI.

KIGERI NDABARASA, UMWAMI OF RWANDA. *See* NDABARASA, KIGERI.

KIGERI NYAMUHESHERA, UMWAMI OF RWANDA. *See* NYAMUHESHERA, KIGERI.

KIGERI RWABUGIRI, UMWAMI OF RWANDA. *See* RWABUGIRI, KIGERI.

KIGOMA-DAR ES SALAAM ROUTE. One of the principal routes for the import-export trade of the country. The eastern route was by lake steamer to Kigoma and then by Tanganyika Railway to Dar es Salaam. Prior to 1925, the routing was through Bukoba and then to the coast by steamer from Lake Victoria-Nyanza and by railroad to Uganda.

The port at Kigoma, located in British territory, contained

a concession that was held by the Belgian government. In 1921, the British government leased to Belgium in perpetuity and at the annual peppercorn rent of 1 BF sites in the ports of Dar es Salaam and Kigoma. Consequently, Belgian imports transported by this route escaped British customs. The Kigoma port was well built, with a railroad and a marshaling yard alongside.

KINDU-ALBERTVILLE RAILROAD. A portion of the easterly route of commercial traffic for Belgian Africa. This rail link was 443 miles long.

KINYAMETEKA. A widely read, vernacular newspaper published fortnightly since 1933 by the Catholic press at Kabgayi. The newspaper covered economic matters, but in the 1950s it was used by the Hutu elite in their nationalist struggle for independence. At that time it had a circulation of 20,000. In 1956, Grégoire Kayibanda, the first president of the country, served as its editor-in-chief, and the newspaper documented Tutsi abuses.

KINYARWANDA (IKINYARWANDA). A Bantu language spoken by all Rwandans.

KISENYI (GISENYI). A prefecture and town situated on the northeastern shore of Lake Kivu; during the colonial period it was, therefore, a major port for the entry and exit of commodities. Because of its excellent beachfront, the territory served as an important tourist resort for Europeans and the departure point for excursions to the volcanic areas of the Albert National Park. Because local missions held a tobacco monopoly, it became an important tobacco-marketing center. It was also an important coffee-growing region. The territory is 2,488 square kilometers in area.

KISENYI-RUHENGERI-KIGALI ROAD. A principal road in the country, about 265 kilometers long.

KISOZI STATION. An agricultural experimental station charged with the selection of wheat, potatoes, and food plants specifically suited for areas of high altitude (above 2,000 meters). The station tested coffee plants as well.

KITEGA STATION. An agricultural experimental station and a territorial unit which in 1925 contained the Ecole Pratique d'Agriculture. The school and agricultural station distributed some of the first Guatemalan coffee seedlings—about 100,000 to African farmers as early as 1917. In addition to coffee nurseries, the station distributed seeds for reforestation. The school was staffed by a European agronomist who advised African farmers. The station trained agricultural monitors and raised steers. In 1926, it distributed about 500 kilograms of experimental varieties of seeds, plus 100 kilograms of peas and 150 kilograms of maize.

KONFIGI COOPERATIVE. A commercial cooperative established in 1966 by a group of unemployed members from the Jeunesse Ouvrière Chrétienne (JOC) of Gihindamuyaga in the Mbazi district. They decided to go into business manufacturing confitures, using bananas, papaya, rhubarb, oranges, Japanese prunes, guavas, Cape gooseberries, and pineapples. The region grew very few fruit trees, however; so with some assistance from the Institut des Sciences Agronomiques du Rwanda (ISAR), they began to grow their own fruit trees. The cooperative received its official charter in 1968, and it was officially inaugurated by the president of the republic on June 28, 1969, when it had about thirty members. From 1969 to 1979, its production rose from six tons to forty tons annually, and its membership more than tripled from thirty to one hundred. In 1978, the cooperative divided more than one million Rwandan francs among its members.

KWIHUTURA. Kwihutura is a process by which a Hutu sheds

his Hutu-ness. The process reflects an upwardly mobile Hutu who has worked his way into the Tutsi aristocracy. The term has its antecedents in the past and reflects a pre-1959 political consciousness.

-L-

LABOR CODE (1967). The labor code of 1967 established working conditions and regulated wage rates although minimum wage legislation had been introduced in 1949. The Code stipulates that those working outside of urban centers should be paid about 90 cents per day. According to the Code, the legal work week is 48 hours, with a compulsory rest day and 50 percent addtitional wages for overtime over 2 hours. The Code sets the conditions for labor contracts, the conditions for labor recruitment and dismissal, fringe benefits, pension rights, and medical and health services. Pensions and employment injury benefits are covered by Social Security legislation enacted in 1962 and administered by the Social Fund.

According to the Code, children under 18 are not permitted to work without parental consent, and they may not work at night except under exceptional circumstances on a temporary basis. But a special dispensation from the minister of labor affairs can be obtained to permit a child under the age of 14 to work. Under the Code, labor has the right to organize, and if a collective bargaining agreement between the union and employer could be achieved, then the union could negotiate salaries and terms of employment. The right to strike is circumscribed; permission must be secured from the confederation's executive bureau, a government entity.

LABOR RECRUITMENT. A major component of Belgian colonial economic policy, which began as early as 1917. Labor contracts which were not fulfilled were liable to result in penalties, including imprisonment. With respect to the Belgian Congo, labor recruitment for the mines was halted in 1930 and reinstituted in 1949. The major direction for labor migration was to Uganda. Banyarwandan immigrants became an important component of Buganda's labor force in 1923, with many entering from the southwest. Their arrival coincided with the decree of 1924 by Belgian authorities to compel Africans to carry out the cultivation of food and cash crops. British labor statistics for 1948 showed that 75 percent of the immigrants from Rwanda and Urundi worked for African farmers and 25 percent in European and Asian enterprises. Their labor was crucial to the sugar and cotton industries.

There were essentially three main immigrant routes into Buganda: the southwest route from Tanganyika and Ruanda-Urundi; the northern route from the west Nile and the Sudan; the eastern route which carried the immigrants from the eastern province of Uganda and the Kavirondo district of Kenya. The heaviest traffic went along the southwest route. Travelers from Tanganyika and Ruanda-Urundi entered Uganda by one of four main roads. They could use either of the three main crossings over the Kagera River or the Kakitumba River which joins it at the junction of the Ruanda-Urundi, Tanganyika, and Uganda borders. These were, from east to west, Kyaka Ferry, under the control of the Tanganyikan government, and Mutukula camp, a short distance over the Uganda border; Murongo Ferry, also in Tanganyika; or Katitumba bridge. Further north there was the Kabale road over the mountain pass coming from Ruanda-Urundi into Kigezi and then to Mborara. All of these routings converged on Masaka township, which led to the main road to Kampala and to Kyagwe.

In 1949, official records indicated that there were 41,967 temporary emigrants (14,371 to the Belgian Congo and 27,596 to Uganda and Tanganyika), to which must be added an unknown number of permanent migrants directed mostly

toward British colonies. The report from the United Nations
Trusteeship Council for 1957 noted that workers to British
territories were recruited mainly for sugarcane and sisal
plantations, whereas emigrants to the Belgian Congo were
mainly workers engaged under long-term contracts, generally for three years, by mining and agricultural enterprises.
Emigrants to the Belgian Congo were mainly inhabitants
from the frontier regions of Usumbura, Buganza, Shangugu,
and Kisenyi. Emigrants in other regions preferred to go to
the British territories of Uganda and Tangan-yika.
Emigrants to the Kivu were not just workers but whole families transferred from their chiefdoms in Rwanda.

LAKE KIVU. A waterway important in the flow of commercial
traffic from the Belgian possessions in the east to the Congo
and the Atlantic Ocean and on to Belgium. Belgians pur-
posely directed the commercial flow and consequently developed traffic on lakes Kivu and Tanganyika, equipping
ports at Costermansville, Bukavu, and Albertville to receive
commodities in transit from the eastern territories. The two
lakes were joined along the Ruzizi by a double carriage road
of 105 kilometers, one on each shore, and by a Uvira-
Bukavu railroad link, which by 1939 had only reached mid-
way to Kamaniola.

Steam vessels plied between the two coasts and the is-
lands of the lake, calling at ports in Ngoma, Kisenyi, Kibuye, and Tshyangugu in Rwanda. Heavy merchandise,
minerals, food, and cattle taken on at Bugoyi, Bgishaza, and
Kinyaga were transferred at Costermansville and shipped by
truck or wagon to Tanganyika, where they were then shipped
to Albertville. Portions of the traffic from central and eastern Rwanda traveled the dirt roads across Urundi, reaching
Bujumbura and from there went by steamship from Tanganyika, arriving at Kigoma where the Tanganyika railroad took
it to Dar es Salaam.

LAKE TANGANYIKA. Entry and departure point for goods

shipped between Rwanda and the Indian Ocean, a route secondary to that via Lake Kivu. *See also* LAKE KIVU.

LAND CHIEF. A traditional administrative rank created during the reign of Kigeri Rwabugiri, who ruled from 1860 to 1895. The office of land chief was devised in order to extend royal control into local areas. The land chief was appointed to collect land prestations from specific districts. He could requisition labor and tribute from cultivators under his authority, and was entitled to keep a portion of the tribute for his own benefit. He acted as judge in land disputes with the Hutu of his district.

LAND TENURE. Both traditional and modern practices varied and were quite expansive and definitive. Under German administration, an imperial decree of November 26, 1895, declared that all land was Crown land, but recognized the rights of the traditional authorities by maintaining that the right of the Crown was subject to the rights of private and juristic persons or of chiefs and African communities. A local land commission decided what lands were unoccupied and available for allocation by the State to Europeans. Direct grants from the State were the only way freehold could be obtained. Land could be leased from Africans, but the period was limited to five years. Europeans could, however, arrange directly with Africans to vacate their land in exchange for compensation. Only when the State was satisfied that this had been done was it prepared to grant freehold title. German alienations were few, primarily because their colonial administration was so short.

Belgian administration restricted the alienation of land to non-Africans. At the beginning of its colonial period, it made provisions only for leasing up to five and then ten years, increasing this to twenty years in 1925. In 1927, it placed in force the Congo Decree of September 14, 1886, which made the validity of sales by Africans dependent on the sanction of the administration, and prohibited any measure which would result in their expulsion from the land or would deprive them directly or indirectly of means of subsistence. Private property was instituted by the Belgians in 1958.

Under Belgian rule, the land policy was to stabilize tenure for African farmers indirectly rather than through legal means. They sought to persuade the traditional authorities to ensure stable occupation, and when that did not work resorted to stronger measures, such as suspension, termination, and threats to ensure compliance. In principle, cultivated land and forest areas were never ceded. Where cession or concessions occurred, some fairly equitable compensation, fixed by a joint agreement between the administration and the African involved, was granted in exchange for rights that the latter consented to surrender. A system of personal land ownership, however, governed by the Congolese Civil Code, did exist. According to article 2 of the Royal Decree of September 14, 1886, and applicable to Ruanda-Urundi by Ordonnance Loi of March 8, 1927, "contracts concluded with Africans in contemplation of the sale or lease of land shall not be recognized by the State and shall not be registrable until they have been approved by the Administrative General of the Congo."

During the colonial period, unoccupied land (*terres vacantes*) belonged to the State, and transfers and concessions of state property (*bien domaniaux*) were governed by special regulations. According to the decree passed on July 24, 1956, only land owned by non-Africans, or by Africans who had acquired land under noncustomary title, was subject to formal registration. Large land concessions required parliamentary approval. Concessions over 10 hectares in urban areas and 500 hectares in rural areas had to be approved by decree. Alienation was not authorized in densely populated areas or in areas where development potential was limited.

Under customary law, the *umwami* had absolute right of property over all land, but customary law was not always observed. After the Tutsi had secured social and political domination, there was no longer any provision for the distribution of land among the Hutu. As holders of the land in usufruct, Banyarwanda inhabitants had only a precarious right of occupation as tenant at the will of the *umwami* and his notables. The best land was reserved for pasture, and small plots for cultivation were granted sparingly. Noncultivated land that did not belong to anyone could however be claimed indefinitely if an individual settled his family on the land, and planted and harvested crops. After the first harvest, and if the individual wished to remain on the land permanently, he had to offer a gift to the local chief.

Land uncultivated but used previously and turned over to the chief was called *nkungu*. In this situation, an interested party would have to ask the chief for permission to occupy the land by offering him a gift. The value of the gift depended upon the importance and fertility of the land, but the gift usually consisted of a pot of mead beer, considered the best the country produced, plus a pot of honey.

Efforts by Belgian authorities to secure tenure for farmers occurred in 1934, when the judicial system was reorganized. This reform and subsequent amendments of the decrees of 1937, 1938, and 1949 gave African inhabitants the fullest guarantees of protection for their land system.

LAVIGERIE, CHARLES MARTIAL ALLEMAND (1825–1892). A Frenchman, who founded the Société des Missionnaires d'Afrique, or the Pères Blancs (White Fathers), in Algiers in 1868. He insisted upon courting traditional authorities in order to facilitate Catholic conversion.

LEBERAHO, ABBE DONAT. Rwandan Catholic priest and the first of two Africans to be ordained in the country, on October 7, 1917.

LECOINDRE, CHARLES. Belgian priest associated with early missionary activity in Rwanda at the beginning of the twentieth century.

LEGAL SYSTEM. The country system of jurisprudence is based upon Belgian procedures and precedents, and much of it has been codified. Still uncodified, customary law is practiced in certain administrative jurisdictions. The judicial system is hierarchical, with a Supreme Court at the top. It is composed of a president and has five departments, each of which is headed by a vice president. Sitting together, the six justices act as both a constitutional court and an appellate court. The Supreme Court's Department of Courts and Tribunals supervises the work of all lower courts, while the Courts of Accounts act as an audit review and accounting office. The Supreme Court sits at Nyabisindu, the ancient Tutsi capital.

The three lower jurisdictions are ten courts of first instances (is one for each prefecture); the courts of appeal in Kigali, Nyabisindu, and Ruhengeri; and cantonal or communal courts, which dispense justice according to traditional law. There are also a number of police courts; these and the cantonal courts try only minor cases, and they do not maintain records of cases tried.

The judiciary is statutorily independent and is supposed to apply the Penal Code impartially, but it should be noted that the president has the right to name and dismiss magistrates. A January 1982 law, however, strengthened the independence of the judiciary by improving the nomination process and by closely defining the functions of judicial personnel.

Rwanda has three separate court systems for criminal/civil, military, and state security cases. All but the security cases may be appealed to the Supreme Court. The State Security Court has jurisdiction over national security charges such as treason. Under the Rwandan judicial system, all defendants have a constitutional right to representation, but the country has a shortage of lawyers. Family and other nonprofessional counsel is permitted.

LENAERTS, LOUIS. An administrator at Nyanza in the early 1920s. Lenaerts was trained as an educator, and had been recruited to direct the school at Nyanza.

LEOPOLD II, KING OF BELGIUM (1835–1909). King of Belgium from 1865 to 1909 and head of state of the Congo Free State from 1885 to 1908. Leopold was thirty years old when he ascended the throne. He was a business promoter and a leader in financial enterprises, primarily because he had inherited a fortune of 20 million gold francs (over $10 million) from his father. He was a self-possessed king and was never in exact harmony with the temperament of his people. His private life shocked the moral standards of his subjects. He believed that the acquisition of colonies was essential to national prosperity and greatness, but Belgium's parliament wanted no part of his dreams until international criticism of abuses in the Congo forced it to acquiesce in 1908. Consequently, Leopold used his own resources and diplomacy to obtain the Congo Free State.

LEOPOLD III, KING OF BELGIUM (1901–1983). The Duke of Brabant, who later became the king of Belgium from 1934 to 1951, except for the period after World War II when he lived in exile in Switzerland. His brother, Prince Charles, served as regent during this period. Leopold III surrendered the Belgian army to Germany during World War II, and it was his conduct during the war that forced him to abdicate in favor of his son, Prince Baudouin, on August 11, 1951. Leopold had been criticized for being too friendly to the Germans, but the straw that broke the camel's back was his visit to Hitler at Berchtesgaden on November 19, 1940. His critics maintained that he was not aloof enough during the visit, and that he should never have sent birthday greetings to Hitler in 1941, or condolences to the Italian king in 1942 upon the death of his son. Leopold also traveled to Austria during the war, and he aroused a great deal of suspicion when he was deported to Germany shortly after the Allied invasion, which he insisted was made against his will.

During his reign and before the war, Leopold visited the Congo and the mandate territory several times. He was also influential in directing economic policy and African agriculture in Belgian Africa. In fact, in a speech before the Belgian senate in July 1933, he renounced the tradition inaugurated by his great-uncle, King Leopold II, of exploiting the productive labor of Africans. He called for more intense efforts toward increasing agricultural production, supported the development of the African *paysannats,* and condemned the granting of large land concessions. His pronouncements had a profound effect on Belgian agricultural policy in the 1930s. He was also the first president of INEAC, which was created in 1933. He died at Louvain University hospital in Brussels on September 25, 1983, after heart surgery.

LEOPOLDVILLE (NOW KINSHASA). One of the principal urban centers in the Belgian Congo during the colonial period. It served as both the center of distribution of imported merchandise and the point at which export goods from Belgian Africa converged.

LEPLAE, EDMOND (1868–1941). Agricultural engineer and director-general and manager of the Direction de l'Agriculture in the Ministry for Colonies beginning in 1917. He was born on September 13, 1868, at Furnes. He received degrees in philosophy and letters (1887) and later in agricultural engineering (1891) from the University of Louvain and its Institut Supérieur d'Agriculture de l'Université. He was professor at the University of Louvain in 1894, appointed to develop courses in rural engineering and economics. In January 1910, he was appointed by Jules Renkin to organize the agricultural services of the Belgian Congo, which Belgium had taken charge of under King Leopold. He was a strong supporter of colonization by white farmers and African cultivation of tropical agricultural products, including commercial crops, such as coffee and palm oil. During the economic crisis of 1928, Leplae was able to obtain funds from the Ministry of Colonies for agricultural credit and to implement tariff reductions for transporting agricultural produce. Leplae left colonial service in October 1933. Among his greatest accomplishments was serving as president of the Eighth International Congress of Tropical and Subtropical Agriculture in Tripoli in March 1939. Leplae died in Louvain on February 2, 1941.

LEVESQUE, GEORGES HENRI. Canadian citizen and priest in the Dominican order. Levesque received his doctorate in social science from the University of Lille and was professor at the University of Montreal. Later, he established and was dean of the faculty of Economic and Social Sciences at the University of Laval. In 1955, he was superior of the Monmorency house, and from 1963 to 1971 rector and cofounder of the National University of Rwanda at Butare.

L'INKEME ZA KURINDA. A minor political party, founded in August 1959 in Mugambezi, Kigali.

LIZINDE AFFAIR. The Lizinde affair began in April 1980 when Théoneste Lizinde, a former security chief and a Mugoyi, was arrested with about 30 other people for allegedly planning a coup against the Rwandan government. At his trial, Lizinde was sentenced to death, but later received a reprieve in 1982, when his sentence was commuted to life imprisonment. He was retried in 1985, charged on this occasion with the murder in the mid-1970s of a number of politicians of the First Republic. Lizinde and five others were convicted and condemned to death. In December 1987, four fellow conspirators were released for their roles in the coup, but Major Lizinde and three other coconspirators remained in prison until January 23, 1991, when the RPF launched an offensive against Kisenyi and Ruhengeri. The latter was captured.

Besides robbing the local bank, RPF forces released 1,780 prisoners from the maximum security prison. Major Lizinde was among those released, along with Commandant Stanilas Biseruka and Captain Donate Muvunanhambo. Both of these men had been imprisoned for at least a decade. Also released was Captain Aggrey Kayitare, the former aide-de-camp to the late Major General Fred Rwigyema. Major Lizinde has subsequently become a member of the RPF.

The Lizinde affair also reflects the long-standing traditional antagonism which has existed between two northern Hutu groups: one in Gisenyi and a second in neighboring Bugoyi. There is also the regional conflict between the Hutu in the north and those in the central region. The latter or the regional centrism of the First Republic under Kayibanda was brought to an end in the 1973 coup. The coup brought to power the northern elite under General Habyarimana. However, the north is far more homogenous, and the latent rivalry between the Gisenyi and Ruhengeri regions should become apparent. Favored by President Habyarimana, the Gisenyi region gained the ascendancy in terms of patronage and political influence. But President Habyarimana's supremacy had barely been secured when Gisenyi was itself divided by conflict between Bushiru (the president's own district) and neighboring Bugoyi, which is where Lizinde hails from.

LOGIEST, COLONEL GUILLAUME. A significant personality in the events leading up to independence in Rwanda. A Belgian citizen, Logiest was born in Ledeberg in 1912. In 1933, he was war officer in the Ecole Royale Militaire, and in 1937 he joined the Force Publique in the Belgian Congo. From 1947 to 1951, he attended the Belgian War College and the Command and General Staff College in the United States before gaining a staff command in the Force Publique that covered the areas of Kisangani, the Provinces Orientales, the Kivu, and the mandate of Ruanda-Burundi. On December 5, 1959, Colonel Logiest was appointed the Special Civilian Resident in Rwanda because of the "troubles." He was charged with maintaining law and order during the transition to independence. In May 1960 Colonial Logiest formed the *Garde Territoriale* and issued instructions that the 659-member force be recruited according to the proportion of ethnic composition in the general population—15 percent Tutsi and 85 percent Hutu. The recruits were required to have completed at least primary school. An officers' school was created, and its composition was supposed to reflect the same ethnic proportion as the general population.

LOUPIAS, PAULIN (1872–1910). A French Catholic priest and member of the Missionnaires d'Afrique, or the Order of the White Fathers. Father Loupias became a novice in 1897, was ordained in 1898, and before leaving for Africa in 1900 served in various capacities in missions in France. He spent three years at the mission at Ukerewe Island near Lake Victoria. In 1902, he was assigned to the mission at Nyundo in Rwanda until 1905, when he was transferred to the mission at Save and later to Ruaza as director. It was at Ruaza that Father Loupias lost his life. On April 1, 1910, chief Lukara (Rukara rwa Bishingwe) had apparently revolted against Musinga, and the Tutsi at Gahunga had asked Father Loupias to mediate while an envoy was sent to the capital for help. Chief Lukara wounded Father Loupias with a lance, and Father Loupias died of his wound. Lukara managed to elude the German troops sent to capture him for two years before he was captured and executed in 1912.

LUMUMBA, PATRICE (1925–1961). African nationalist and the first prime minister of independent Congo Republic (the Belgian Congo) in 1960. The independence struggle in the Belgian Congo corresponded to that in the mandate of Ruanda-Urundi. The result for this Belgian colony was equally traumatic. Lumumba, a native of Kasai province, was mission educated. Before becoming a national political figure, he worked in the colonial civil service and served as assistant postmaster in Stanleyville. In 1958, he was co-founder of the Mouvement National Congolais (MNC). In 1960, he was asked to form a government as prime minister.

His rival, Joseph Kasavubu, became president. The Belgian Congo gained its independence in July 1960; almost immediately, the new country began to fragment. In September Lumumba and Kasavubu became political rivals and attempted to oust each other from power. The army, under Joseph Mobutu, intervened and took power. Lumumba sought refuge with United Nations forces at Leopoldville, but was later captured by the Congolese army at Stanleyville, and taken to Katanga, where he was mysteriously murdered in February 1961.

LUSUNGU EXPERIMENTAL STATION. An agricultural and sericultural experimental station established in 1925, directed by an agronomist specializing in sericulture, and employing about a hundred workers. The station cultivated about fifteen hectares of soya, tobacco, grapefruit, grains, black wattle, mulberries, jute, and a host of other agricultural plants. The station closed in 1927.

LWIGEMERA. *Umwami* Musinga's oldest son, who impressed the missionaries because they believed him to be of "excellent character and [was strongly attached] to Europeans."

LYGUS. A parasite that attacks coffee plants.

-M-

MAIZE. A crop grown both for domestic consumption and for sale.

MAKUZA, ANASTASE. Rwandan politician and member of PARMEHUTU. Mukuza, a native of Kinyamakara, Gikongoro, was educated at the Grand Séminaire and the Administration School of Kisantu. After completing his education, he worked in the colonial administration in 1955 and served as a member of the Conseil Superieur du Pays. In February 1960, he served as PARMEHUTU's representative at the Conseil Special Provisoire, and later in October served with the Conseil Provisoire. In the national government, he has served as minister of justice, representative from Kigali in 1961 and for Gikongoro in 1969, president of the National Assembly in 1964, minister of commerce, mines, and industry in 1965 and again in 1969, and minister of national education in 1967.

MALFEYT, JUSTIN-PRUDENT-FRANCOIS-MARIE (1862–1924). Belgian military commander, colonial civil servant, and vice governor-general of the Belgian Congo and governor of Ruanda-Urundi from 1916 to 1919. Malfeyt's military career began in 1883 and in 1891 he received a command at Tshoa in the Lower Congo, but because of illness was transferred to Boma. As the first Belgian royal high commissioner of the occupied territories after the defeat of the Germans, Malfeyt attempted to restore order to Rwanda and to signal cooperation with legitimate authorities. He restored Musinga to his throne and reinstituted the residency system used by the Germans. He appointed Major DeClerck, a veteran of twenty years in the Belgian Congo, to be the first Belgian Resident of Kigali.

MANDATE. Rwanda and Burundi were awarded to Belgium as a mandate of the League of Nations on May 30, 1919, by the Orts-Milner Convention. The terms of the mandate were confirmed by the Council of the League of Nations on July 20, 1922. The Belgian parliament formally accepted the mandate by the law of October 20, 1924. The territory of Rwanda and Burundi was united administratively with the Belgian Congo through a customs union. In 1946, the mandate became a United Nations Trustee Territory; Belgium continued to administer the territory.

MANIFESTE DES BAHUTU (BAHUTU MANIFESTO, 1957).

A political document and a statement of intent issued by the Committee of Nine on March 24, 1957. It was essentially the Hutu's response to the Mwami's High Council of Rwanda's Statement of Views. The signatories were M. Niyonzima, G. Kayibanda, C. Ndahoyo, I. Nzeyimana, C. Mulindahabi, G. Sentama, S. Munyambonera, J. Sibomana, and J. Habyarimana.

The manifesto attacked the whole concept of Belgian administration and maintained that the basic problem of the country was the conflict between Hutu and Hamite. It blamed the prevailing atmosphere and the *ubuhake* system for the lack of African initiative and the Hutu's lack of economic success. It objected to the assumption that the Tutsi were born to rule, and it maintained that the Tutsi political, economic, and social monopoly, which the Belgian administration had fostered, had led to a cultural monopoly. While the manifesto acknowledged that the Hutu was unskilled and poor, it warned that their condition would remain so under the prevailing system.

MANIOC. Its flour was exported to Belgium in the 1940s, where it was used to manufacture starch.

MANYURANE, MONSIGNOR BERNARD (1913–1961). Rwandan Catholic priest and the first bishop of Ruhengeri. Manyurane was a native of Rwaza, Ruhengeri. He was ordained a priest in 1940 and served at mission stations at Nemba and Rulindo. From 1956 to 1959, he studied canon law in Rome and was appointed the first bishop of Ruhengeri but died on May 8, 1961, before receiving episcopal confirmation.

MARZORATI, ALFRED-FREDERIC-GERARD (1881–1955). Lawyer, vice governor-general of the Belgian Congo and Governor of Ruanda-Urundi from 1920 to 1930, and professor at the Free University of Brussels. Marzorati was born in Bournai on September 28, 1881. He attended the

Free University of Brussels in 1899 and earned a doctorate of law five years later. He entered colonial service on February 19, 1912. He was royal commissioner at Bujumbura and became vice governor-general of the Belgian Congo and governor of the mandate territory from 1920 to 1930. Marzorati sought to extend coffee production and conducted several experiments with coffee growing in 1927, before the official coffee extension program in the 1930s. As judicial counsel for the colonial government at Brussels, he wrote legislation dealing with African labor, sanctioned the use of African *paysannats* to increase agricultural production, and advocated the temporary emigration of African labor to the industrial centers of Katanga. He believed that it was the duty of the Belgian government to sponsor the political, economic, and social development of Africans at all levels.

MASHIRA. The most important Hutu and most celebrated king from Nduga. Mashira was ruler of the *ababanda* (the Hutu royal dynasty or clan) and Bugara from the end of the fifteenth century to the beginning of the sixteenth century.

MATADI-LEOPOLDVILLE-STANLEYVILLE-ALBERT-VILLE-USUMBURA ROUTE. Merchandise originating from the western part of Belgian Africa often used this route. Matadi is an outlet to the Atlantic Ocean, situated eighty miles up the estuary of the Congo River on a narrow land corridor on the western side. It was also a transshipment point dependent on the Chemin de Fer de Matadi à Leopoldville (CFM) during the colonial era.

MAVRICAS LIMITED. A commercial transportation company operating internationally out of Kigoma on Lake Tanganyika. The company had two chartered liners, the *Itac,* which had a carrying capacity of 300 tons and flew the Belgian flag, and the *Good Adventure,* which had a carrying capacity of 40 tons and flew the British flag.

MAZIMPAKA, YUHI, UMWAMI OF RWANDA. Yuhi reigned from 1696 to 1720 and was responsible for territorial acquisitions in the central kingdom and the incorporation of some western territories.

MBONYUMUTWA, DOMINIQUE. Hutu who precipitated the uprising of November 1959. Mbonyumutwa was attacked by a gang of Tutsi youth on Sunday, November 1, 1959, in Gitarama. Although he escaped, rumors spread that he had been killed; local Hutu killed thousands of Tutsi and burned their homes in retaliation before calm was restored on November 14, 1959.

MEXICO COFFEE AGREEMENT (1957). At the international conference in Mexico, coffee producers decided to maintain an orderly flow of coffee to the consuming countries and to prescribe proportions of their exports. Latin American producers agreed to withhold a portion of their coffee supplies during the 1957–1958 period. The pact was successful during the first few months of operation. Coffee prices recovered from 53 cents in August and September 1957 to the 55–56-cents level in December 1957. But in late January and early February 1958, prices weakened again, partly in response to coffee expansion from 1950 to 1954 and increased production in Africa. A new coffee agreement in 1959 fixed the coffee quota for Rwanda and Burundi at 20,400 tons for the 1962–1963 growing season, and the price was fixed at 20 BF per kilo, or an increase of one franc over the price in 1959.

MIBAMBWE GISANURA, UMWAMI OF RWANDA. *See* GISANURA, MIBAMBWE.

MIBAMBWE MUTABAAZI, UMWAMI OF RWANDA. *See* MUTABAAZI, MIBAMBWE.

MIBAMBWE RUTARINDWA, UMWAMI OF RWANDA. *See* RUTARINDWA, MIBAMBWE.

MIBAMBWE SENTABYO, UMWAMI OF RWANDA. *See* SENTABYO, MIBAMBWE.

MIBIRIZI. A Catholic mission station, established in 1903, in the southwestern region of the country. The mission station planted the first coffee seedlings, which it distributed among the local African farmers.

MICOMBERO, MICHEL (1940–1983). Burundi military and political leader, prime minister in 1966, and president of the country from 1966 to 1976. Micombero ruthlessly crushed a revolt against his government by Hutu in 1972. Hundreds of thousands of Hutu were killed, including many of the educated Hutu elite, and many sought refuge in Rwanda and neighboring countries. Between 80,000 and 200,000 Hutu and Tutsi died in the disturbances, and about 100,000 Hutu sought refuge abroad, mainly in Tanzania. In November 1976, Micombero's army chief of staff, Jean-Baptist Bagaza, overthrew him in a nonviolent coup. Micombero died of a heart attack while in Somalia.

MINETAIN. *See* SOCIETE DES MINES D'ETAIN DU RUANDA-URUNDI (MINETAIN).

MINING. An important component of the Belgian colonial government's economic development policy. While the government was not directly involved in the exploitation of Rwanda's mineral resources (which included—in order of importance—tin, gold, silver, and tungsten), it rigorously controlled mining recruitment and contracts by companies and individual colonists. According to Ordonnance Loi of September 24, 1937, mining contracts had to be approved by the government. Permits were issued for two-year periods but could be renewed three times for two-year periods each time. Concessions were limited to 480,000 hectares. The permit gave the miner the right to prospect. Once he could prove that geological research had been conducted and ore was present, a ninety-nine-year lease could be obtained. Mining companies were required to pay the territorial administration a percentage of profits not to exceed a variable percentage of the company's assets.

MINISTRY OF COLONIES. An administrative department that was established in 1908 by the Belgian parliament. From its inception, the ministry stressed colonial solvency for all of Belgian Africa. It functioned as an advisory body to the king on colonial legislation and was part of the Council of Ministers in Belgium. The ministry served as the link between the Brussels government and the territories of Africa. It laid down the broad outlines of policy to be followed by the governor-general and other colonial administrators in the various Belgian African territories.

The minister had the predominant voice for regulating policy for Belgian Africa. He was responsible for the appointment and dismissal of administrative officials. The posts of governor-general, vice governor-general and deputy heads of services were made by *arrêté royal* upon the recommendation of the minister. All other appointments of European personnel were made by the minister.

MIRONKO. One of the major companies in the country, it manufactures plastics.

MIRRI FRERES. An engineering and construction company founded in 1963 and considered one of the major industrial companies in the country.

MISSION D'IMMIGRATION BANYARWANDA. A government agency responsible for settling Banyarwanda in the northern region of the Kivu from 1949 to 1951. Government agents were required to live in the areas where the inhabitants were settled. The personnel prepared the land, fixed boundaries, provided food, and constructed roads, dispensaries, and antierosion devices. Agents allotted each family a five-hectare plot and provided instruction on crop rotation.

Each family received a food allotment for the first six months and was exempt from colonial taxation, provincial taxes, and *corvée* for two years.

MOBUTU SESE SEKO (JOSEPH-DESIRE). Bengala politician, military leader, and president of the Republic of the Congo (now Zaire). Mobutu began his career as an enlisted man in the Force Publique after completing secondary school. After leaving the army, he worked as newspaper editor in Leopoldville, where he joined Patrice Lumumba's political party, the Mouvement National Congolais (MNC). Mobutu's rise to power occurred within the context of the disintegration of Belgian Africa and its movement toward independence.

When Lumumba came to power in 1960, Mobutu became his chief of staff in the new army with the rank of colonel. When the new government fragmented into two factions headed by Lumumba and Kasavubu, Mobutu staged a coup, suspended both civilian leaders, and formed his own commission of fifteen young college graduates to run the government in cooperation with the United Nations peacekeeping forces.

Mobutu finally took the reins of power in 1965, appointed himself president of the country, and suspended all provincial assemblies. Five years later he renamed the Congo "Zaire" and Africanized Belgian place-names throughout the country. He sought rapprochement with his neighbors, including Rwanda, and was reelected unopposed to seven-year terms as president beginning in 1970, and ruled the country without serious or sustained opposition.

MOKOTAS RESETTLEMENT PLAN. Begun in 1927, when the Belgian government proposed an elaborate plan to move Banyarwanda to the Kivu region in the Belgian Congo. A commission was created to study the feasibility of the plan to resettle families to Mokotas, located west of Baraka and Uvira, and the Mugila and Markungu mountains. The commission recommended that each family receive free cattle, and estimated that resettling 5,000 families would cost about 6.75 million BF, which did not include the cost of European personnel and the construction of access roads.

No action was taken on the recommendations until 1929, when a commercial research federation was created to assist and protect the Africans who would be transplanted. The immediate objective of the federation was to recruit Banyarwandan labor for European employers. The federation received approval from the Ministry for Colonies, but the project never got off the ground.

The plan resurfaced in 1935 with emigration fixed for the Niamitaba-Gishari, situated between lakes Sake and Mokotas, but the plan faltered because of a dispute between the government and CNKI. Two years later, a government agent was sent to Gishari to implement the program, and between 1937 and 1945 about 6,100 Banyarwanda were resettled in Gishari. A second phase occurred between 1945 and 1951, and included the areas in the northern Kivu district, such as Fizi, Lubero, Rutshuru, Masisi, and Kalehe. A Mission d'Immigration Banyarwanda was entrusted with the work, and over a three-year period (from 1949 to 1951) some 9,000 families were registered.

MOLE CRICKET. An insect that burrows beneath the surface and attacks the root system of coffee plants, thus affecting coffee yields. There was an attack of mole crickets during the 1933 planting season.

MORTEHAN, GEORGES. Resident of Rwanda from 1923 to 1929 and state inspector. In 1932, he was acting vice governor-general until the arrival of Eugene Jungers, who was appointed governor of the territory on June 30, 1932.

MOUVEMENT DEMOCRATIQUE REPUBLICAIN (MDR). The Democratic Republican Movement is a new party that was formed in March 1991. The party's formation was in response to political reforms taking place in the country and is in essence a reformation of the MDR-PARMEHUTU, one of the country's original parties. It was among the first of the new parties to complete registration formalities, and as of early August 1991, it had a membership of over 2,000.

One of its most influential members and key spokesman is Faustin Twagiramungu, the son-in-law of Rwanda's first president, Grégoire Kayibanda. According to Mr. Twagiramungu, MDR espouses democracy, the return of refugees, and an end to ethnic and regional quotas in the allocation of jobs and educational support. The party emphasizes the latter, since it is commonly believed that the party is strongly anti-Tutsi, and that its real intent is to unite southern Hutu against the northern Hutu who the MDR believe have benefited from the current president's regime.

By the end of 1991, the MDR had established a country-wide structure with some 240,000 followers, including seven of the delegates to the Conseil National pour le Développement (CND, Parliament). In mid-August 1992, the party was the most serious contender to the MRNDD. Much of its success is attributed to its association as the successor of Grégoire Kayibanda's PARMEHUTU. Because of its political base, MDR was succesful at the polls in September 1992. Its victory at the polls left the liberal faction in control of the party, but it was able to preserve its radical power base as well. Faustus Twagiramungu, who is perceived as a liberal, was elected president of the party, with Dimas Nsengiyaremye, the prime minister (also a liberal) becoming one of two vice-presidents. The chief radical, Emmanuel Gapyisi, retired, but his ally, Froudauld "Mandela" Karamira, was also appointed vice-president. Mr. Karamira is a staunch Kayibandist, and obtained his nickname, Mandela, after spending more than ten years as a political prisoner.

MOUVEMENT REVOLUTIONNAIRE NATIONAL POUR LE DEVELOPPEMENT (MRND)/MOUVEMENT REPUBLI-CAIN NATIONAL POUR LA DEMOCRATIE ET DEVE-

LOPPEMENT (MRNDD). The National Revolutionary Movement for Development was formed in July 1975 as the country's sole legal political party. Its creation commemorated the second anniversary of the Second Republic by President Habyarimana. The objective of the MRND, in which each Rwandan becomes a member at birth, is to unite and mobilize the population in economic, social, and cultural development, and to further cooperation between regions and ethnic groups. According to Habyarimana, the party's formation constituted the first step towards the civilianization of the government and, eventually, constitutional government.

The central committee of the party ideally includes representatives from all over the country, and the party is required to offer a choice of two candidates for each seat on the Conseil national pour le développement. Rwandans are supposed to be able to unionize; churches are supposed to have free reign to criticize the government in their publications. The party has been reorganized twice: once during the fifth MRND congress, which was held in December 1985 and again in 1991. The first reorganization included the creation of a school of ideology for party workers and salaried status for MRND officials. A year later, January 25, 1986 to be exact, the membership on the central committee was enlarged from twenty-one to twenty-five. The second reorganization in 1991 included a name change. The MRND changed its name to become the Mouvement Républicain National pour la Démocratie et Développement (MRNDD)—The National Republican Movement for Democracy and Development. The party had and still, under the new name and the movement toward democracy in mid-1991, continues to possess unlimited access to official media and state facilities. Its finances are also inextricably linked with that of the state. This fact has become a serious political issue in the new climate toward democratic rule with many opponents claiming that the governing party has an unfair advantage.

Opponents argue that President Habyarimana, the party's

founder and head, and party officials were and still are in-variably government officials and vice versa. They complain that the MRNDD possesses many vehicles, buildings, and other assets which were paid for by the government or the people. It also has a strong psychological grip on the population, and many opponents suggest that fear for career prospects may deter civil servants from joining other parties. Consequently, the MRNDD possesses an advantage that the other new political parties don't have.

MOUVEMENT SOCIAL MUHUTU (MSM). MSM was an all-Hutu political party, created at Kabgayi in June 1957 by Grégoire Kayibanda. Kayibanda eventually became the first president of the independent country in 1962. The party's platform supported social, economic, and moral development, as well as educational reform which would include broader inclusion of the Hutu and their increased participation in the political process. As a political party, MSM was weak and ineffectual, primarily because it failed to generate grassroots support in areas other than Gitarama and Kabgayi. MSM was later transformed into the Parti du Mouvement de l'Emancipation Hutu in 1959.

MRITHI. The famous 24-year-old, 400-pound silverback mountain gorilla and leader of a 12-member family since the late 1970s, it has become the latest casualty of the civil war in northern Rwanda. Mrithi, who made his film début in "Mountain Gorilla" and appears in "Gorillas in the Mist," was killed, when either government soldiers or members of the RPF stumbled upon his family while they were sleeping. His death occurred around 4 a.m. in the Parc des Volcans on May 21, 1992. The autopsy revealed that he was shot four times by light automatic assault weapons. Many believe that Mrithi's death was unintentional, because both sides in the conflict agreed not to harm the gorillas. But Mrithi's death shocked observers, who fear that the civil war will bring more deaths and loss to the gorilla sanctuary and habitat.

The RPF has already claimed that it has evidence that government forces killed the legendary gorilla, Titus, last year. Experts estimate that only 600 or so mountain gorillas remain in the wild, and they fear that Ukwacumi, the 12-year-old, silverback, male and possible successor to Mrithi, may be too young and inexperienced for leadership. Recent reports note that neither he nor the troupe has been seen in several weeks. It is possible that Ukwacumi might have stepped on a land mine, or become involved in a fight with another young silverback. If he does not return, his group may dissolve and the females will most likely find another male silverback.

MUDEYIDEYI. A Rwandan who hires out his labor to another Rwandan; he receives daily wages, food, and lodging.

MUGESERA. Natural lake in the southeastern region of the country.

MUKIGA (pl. BAKIGA). A man of the high country (of Rukiga in northern Rwanda), and akin to the Hutu, but according to one enthnographer, "not an ordinary one." According to the same source, a Mukiga "was considered to be a very strong black, quite muscular and industrious, but quite infantile and therefore, quite cruel with a simpleminded consciousness of good and evil." He was quite independent, a fierce warrior who was also a farmer. The Bakiga and the Rukiga region remained outside of Tutsi hegemony until the Belgians took control of the country. The Bakiga were able to resist Tutsi control successfully because of the nature of the environment—mountains and intractable marshes.

MUKOBANYA, KIGERI, UMWAMI OF RWANDA. Kigeri reigned from 1506 to 1528. He increased the ceremonial authority of the *ubwiiru* and the real powers of the monarchy by enhancing the legitimacy of royal authority when he assumed the title of *umwami*. He also incorporated the smaller

Tutsi states of the *abongera* and *abatsobe* clans from the western regions into the central kingdom.

MUKUNGWA-RWANDA HYDROELECTRIC POWER STA-TION. A donor-aid project that began construction in 1980 at an estimated cost of 30 million EUA. In 1983, the hydroelectric plant reduced Rwandan imports from Zaire's Ruzizi I plant from 55 GWH out of consumption of 63.8 GWH in 1981 to 10.9 GWH out of 83.9 GWH in 1984. An additional increase in consumption to 95 GWH was reported in 1986.

MULERA. A territorial unit in northern Rwanda that was brought into the kingdom of Rwanda in the 1920s. An area of tobacco production and the region where the most vigorous opposition to Tutsi control occurred. Kinship groups in this region (the Abagesera, the Abachuzi, and the Abasigi) put up strenuous resistance to Tutsi encroachment.

MULINDAHABI, CALLIOPE (1932–1971). Rwandan politician and member of the Committee of Nine and PARMEHUTU. Mulindahabi was a native of Rutarabana, Gitarama, attended the Petit Séminaire at Kabgayi, was secretary to the inspector of schools in 1946, and held the same position with the vicar of Kabgayi in 1956. As a member of the Committee of Nine, he helped to draft the Hutu Manifesto in 1957. He served as general secretary of PARMEHUTU in October 1959 and manager and later director of the TRAFIPRO cooperative. He was a member of the Conseil Provisoire in October 1960 and its national representative in 1961. He served as vice president and later president of the National Assembly. In October of 1961, he became minister of the national guard. He served as executive secretary of MDR from November 1965 to July 1967.

MULINDI TEA ESTATE. The Mulindi Tea Estate is situated in the north and is the largest tea plantation in the country. It produces about 60 percent of the country's tea export. Tea is the country's second largest foreign exchange earner after coffee. The Mulindi Estate is currently in the hands of the RPF, as are many other tea plantations. Since this area is the most fertile and supports most of the tea production in the country, the loss of income has seriously strained the government economically.

MUNYANGAJU, ALOYS. Rwandan politician and political activist, journal editor, and vice president of the Supreme Court. Munyangaju was born in Save, Butare. He attended the Grand Séminaire of Nyakibanda for three years, with studies in philosophy. He served as an agent for a commercial company in Bukavu from 1947 to 1957. In 1953, he served on the Shangugu Territorial Council and was mentor to Hutu activists living in Kinyaga. In 1956, he founded the journal *Soma,* which carried editorials about Tutsi abuses. Two years later, he became the editor of *Temps Nouveaux d'Afrique* at Bujumbura. He also contributed to the drafting of the Hutu Manifesto. In October 1960, he was vice president of APROSOMA and served as its representative in the Conseil Provisoire. Other political functions included administrative secretary in the Ministry of Foreign Relations, and the Butare national delegate to APROSOMA from 1961 to 1965. Later, he became the vice-president of the Supreme Court (and the constitutional court).

MUREGO, DONAT. Rwandan politician and vice-president of the Supreme Court. Murego was born in Muhororo, Ruhengeri, in 1936; he spent three years studying philosophy and one year in theology at the Grand Séminaire of Nyakibanda. He obtained a degree in political science and administration and became secretary-general in the Ministry of Interior. From 1965 to 1970, he was vice president of the Supreme Court. In 1980, he was implicated in the attempted coup led by ex-security chief Théoneste Lizinde. Murego was sentenced to ten years imprisonment. His case became a human rights issue because of pretrial irregularities. His supporters argued that his involvement in the case was at best tenuous, that he had served a year's pretrial detention in solitary confinement and complete darkness, and he reportedly became seriously ill as a result. He was also refused permission to have a lawyer or to see the prosecutor's evidence before being convicted.

MUSEVENI, YOWERI. President of Uganda and commander of the National Resistance Army (NRA). He was also the leader of the anti-Obote Patriotic Movement and the former Minister of Defense. Yoweri came to power on January 29, 1986, four days after his NRA took Kampala from government forces.

   Many Banyarwanda refugees living in Uganda had joined the NRA. As a reward for their services and assistance, Museveni as the new president offered blanket naturalization to them. Included in this category was John Kagame, the current leader of the RPF. Museveni's decision caused some opposition from the Ganda. Most recently, the Museveni and the Banyarwanda military connection has caused Uganda to be accused of complicity in the civil conflict between the RPF and Rwanda.

MUSHAO. A territory designation in the 1930s.

MUSINGA, YUHI V, UMWAMI OF RWANDA (1883–1944). One of three monarchs to reign during the German and Belgian colonial periods. Musinga was king from 1896 to 1931, and the last absolute monarch. He used the Germans to extend his authority from the central core of the kingdom. Viewed as an obstacle to progress, he was deposed by the Belgian administration. The Belgians perceived Musinga as a poor administrator and an individual who used passive resistance and hostility to keep them off balance. When he was deposed on November 14, 1931, the charges against him included moral turpitude. He was described as egotistical, oppressive, and opposed to all moral and social progress for his people. He opposed the economic development of the country, and did not concern himself with affairs of state. He did not attend meetings of the African tribunal, and he received his people with indifference and disdain.

MUSYETE. A Twa who achieved fame in the eighteenth century when he saved the queen mother from execution during a war of succession between two claimants to the throne. Musyete, who was to perform the execution, hid her from the enemy. When her son, Cyilima Rujugira, assumed the throne after defeating the contender, Musyete was ennobled. He became the ancestor of the *abasyete,* and his descendants were considered Tutsi.

MUTABAAZI, MIBAMBWE, UMWAMI OF RWANDA. Reigned from 1528 to 1552.

MUTARA RUDAHIGWA, UMWAMI OF RWANDA. *See* RUDAHIGWA, CHARLES-LEON-PIERRE.

MUTARA RWOGERA, UMWAMI OF RWANDA. *See* RWOGERA, MUTARA.

MUTARA SEEMUGESHI, UMWAMI OF RWANDA. *See* SEEMUGESHI, MUTARA.

MUVUNANYAMBO, CAPTAIN DONATE. Captain Donate Muvunanyambo is Hutu and a former army officer, who was imprisoned in the maximum security prison in Ruhengeri for nearly a decade. He was freed when RPF forces captured Ruhengeri on January 23, 1991 and released all political prisoners.

MUZUNGU. Muzungu is a Kinyarwanda designation for whites, Europeans, or non-Rwandans.

MWAMBUTSA II, UMWAMI OF BURUNDI. Mwambutsa

reigned from 1915 to 1966, serving under both German and Belgian colonial administrations. When the country gained its independence in 1962, he ruled as a constitutional monarch. He fled the country for Switzerland in October 1965 when the Hutu population attempted a coup. The coup failed, and his nineteen-year-old son, Charles Ndizeye, took the throne the following July as Ntare III. Mwambutsa protested from abroad but to no avail. His son was deposed later in the year by Michel Micombero, whom he had made prime minister. Micombero declared the country a republic.

MWAMI (UMWAMI). Term used for the legitimate and absolute ruler king of the country. He always came from the *abanyiginya* lineage, which had established the original kingdom. In traditional times, he was the sole property owner in the country; only he had the power to grant usufruct and to create large and small chieftaincies, all of which had titular heads. In exchange for land or usufruct rights, Africans had to perform certain prestations. He also had power over all the cattle in the country, and over sheep and goats, and he could claim actual possession at any time. He exercised this right more frequently over cattle than over land, and a contentious chief, who was considered to be dangerous to the king, might find himself dispossessed of all of his cattle. The confiscation of cattle was a constant threat which prevented Tutsi notables from becoming too independent.

The *umwami* could collect a tax on all occupied land, which could be considered a special kind of rent because in principle the leasing was of temporary duration and the occupation of the fields was of unspecified duration. The right to cultivate was revocable but only as a penalty or punishment. Once land was conferred, it became hereditary, The inheritor need only subordinate himself by pledging allegiance to either the king or chief.

During the Belgian colonial era, the *umwami*'s role was viewed as collaborative with European authorities. He was expected to make periodic visits throughout the kingdom and to make reports to the Resident at Kigali. He could exercise executive power through decrees rendered by proposals to the minister of colonies, who countersigned them.

MWAMI'S HIGH COUNCIL OF RWANDA (1957). During the movement for independence, the *umwami*'s faction, or council, presented the Statement of Views before the United Nations Visiting Trustee Council in February 1957. The statement dealt with four main areas: Belgium's failure to develop the country economically and the people politically; the failure of the educational system to train teachers and future leaders for the nation, or to create a national university; the absence of Africans in decision making for the country; and racism, particularly in the hiring practices of the administration. With respect to the last point, the statement noted that there were Africans who were better qualified and better educated than Europeans, but that they could not attain the lowest European level in the territorial administration. The statement also stressed the disparity in salaries between whites and blacks, but it praised the administration for what it had done for the Tutsi oligarchy and asked for its continued support.

-N-

NATIONAL COMMISSION ON AGRICULTURE (NCA). The National Commission on Agriculture (NCA) was established on March 23, 1990 by President Habyarimana. Its mission is to devise ways to increase agriculture production as a way of dealing with future famines.

NATIONAL ELECTIONS (1965). In the legislative elections, PARMEHUTU candidates were elected unopposed. The president (also a member of PARMEHUTU) was elected unopposed.

NATIONAL ELECTIONS (1969). The president and candidates

for the legislature, all from PARMEHUTU, the only political party in the country, were elected unopposed.

NATIONAL ELECTIONS (1981). A new political party, the Mouvement Révolutionnaire National pour le Développement, supplanted PARMEHUTU when Juvénal Habyarimana took power in 1973. The national legislature was abolished until the national elections of 1988. The elections returned the first freely elected legislature, the Conseil National de Développement.

NATIONAL PRICE COMMISSION. A government agency established in August 1974 under the price-control law of July 5, 1967. Its function is to establish prices and profit margins for all products, domestic and foreign, traded in the country, as well as to set charges for road transportation. The commission meets every six months to consider food prices.

NATIONAL RESISTANCE ARMY (NRA) OF UGANDA. The NRA was commanded by Yoweri Museveni, the former minister of defense and leader of the Uganda Patriotic Movement, who also served as Uganda's president. Museveni began the insurgency against the Milton Obote government in February 1981, and eventually came to power in 1986. His army provided sanctuary for many Banyarwanda who were refugees, persecuted by the Obote government since 1984. About a third of Museveni's forces of some 14,000 troops were Banyarwanda. It was this force of Banyarwanda that participated in the October 1, 1990, invasion of Rwanda.

NATIONAL SOLIDARITY TAX (APRIL 25, 1991). The National Solidarity Tax was passed on April 25, 1991 by the national government. It was designed to deal with inflation and a budget deficit of 23 billion RF ($178.6 million) caused by the October 1990 invasion. According to the provisions of the tax, all wage earners in the public and private sectors are required to pay 8 percent of their monthly net salary. The government hoped to earn about 800 million RF from this tax in the second half of 1991. In addition, the government froze salary increases for 1991, and a corresponding amount will be paid to the treasury by public and private companies. Parastatals will pay 5 percent and private companies 1 percent of their 1990 financial year turnover, which should give the treasury about 56 million RF and 657 million RF respectively.

NDABARASA, KIGERI, UMWAMI OF RWANDA. Kigeri reigned from 1768 to 1792. He conquered Ndorwa and Nubari, but he was unable to subdue Ndorwa completely. The latter was constantly in rebellion, in spite of the presence of the *umwami*'s royal compound in the region.

NDAHAYO, CLAVER. Rwandan politician, vice president of the Supreme Court, and member of the Committee of Nine. He served as a member of the Conseil Provisoire of the MDR/PARMEHUTU in 1960 as well as secretary of state for social affairs. He was counsel and then vice president of the Supreme Court from January 1961 to September 1963; from 1965 to 1969 he was general-secretary to President Kayibanda. In the latter part of 1969, he became national deputy of MDR for Gitarama and then deputy secretary.

NDAHINDURWA, JEAN BAPTISTE (KIGERI V), UMWAMI OF RWANDA. Kigeri V was the last reigning monarch for the country before the republic was declared in 1962. Jean-Baptiste was born in Kamembe in 1935 to Musinga. After his primary studies, he became a secretary in the colonial service at Butare and a *sous-chef* in 1959. He was designated the *umwami* after the mysterious death of his half-brother, King Mutara III Rudahigwa, in July 1959. Rudahigwa had been the *umwami* since 1931. Kigeri was proclaimed the new *umwami* by the *abiiru* clan. He was just twenty-four years old. His appointment to *umwami* signalled the formation of political parties in Rwanda and rebellion on the part of the Tutsi oligarchy and by the Hutu masses. He voluntarily left the country in May 1960 and was officially deposed on January 28, 1961. He currently lives in genteel poverty in a suburb of Nairobi and holds court for the exiled Banyar-wandan community each Wednesday morning in front of the Kenya Cinema.

NDAHIRO CYAAMATARE, UMWAMI OF RWANDA. *See* CYAAMATARE, NDAHIRO.

NDAHIRO RUYANGE, UMWAMI OF RWANDA. *See* RUYANGE, NDAHIRO.

NDOBA, UMWAMI OF RWANDA. Ndoba reigned from 1386 to 1410.

NDOORI, RUGANZU, UMWAMI OF RWANDA. Ruganzu reigned from 1600 to 1624 and was responsible for an early attempt to centralize the kingdom through religious and monarchal symbols and territorial incorporation. He created a new dynastic drum, established a new family of *abiiru* to care for it, commissioned dynastic poetry, and conquered and annexed formerly independent Hutu kingdoms.

NDORWA TAX REVOLT (1932). A tax revolt which lasted for several days and became the focus of a judicial inquiry in March 1932. It took place in the province of Mulera in the territory of Ruhengeri in February 1932, when a Tutsi tax collector, Kanabulenge, and some kinsmen sought to collect taxes and to take a census on the hill of Kinyababa. When asked to pay, the people of the hill claimed that most had already paid and those who had not could not afford to do so. The next morning, Kanabulenge apparently recognized some men who had not yet paid their taxes. He pursued them, a fight ensued, and a Hutu, Bigabo, was killed and eight suffered wounds, including one Tutsi. About forty combatants in all were involved. The conflict spread to a neighboring hill, Kilaro, in the province of Ndorwa, where a Tutsi chieftain and a raiding party burned Hutu huts and confiscated food and livestock because the inhabitants had also refused to pay their taxes.

NDUNGUTZE. Leader of a revolutionary movement in northern Rwanda. The rebellion, which culminated in 1912, sought to overthrow both Musinga and German rule, and was an expression of hostility toward askaris and Europeans as well as an indication of the antagonism that Hutu held against Tutsi notables. The regions in which this unrest was especially apparent was bordered by the great Twa swamp, Mruschoschi, lakes Bulera and Luhondo, the road between Kigali and Ruhengeri, and the Tschohoa-Basse. The rebel leader was killed by German troops on April 10, 1912, but this did not destroy resistance in the northern region.

NETWORK ZERO. Network Zero is a terrorist organization or death squad that has emerged in the country during the period of civil war and political instability. Network Zero is suppose to have connections with the ruling political elite or the MRNDD. It has been accused of the murder of a Catholic priest in November, 1992 and various opposition members. An international commission of enquiry, composed of nongovernmental organizations and human rights' groups arrived in Rwanda on January 7, 1993 to investigate.

NGABO. A military organization or regiment.

NGAGANO REVOLT (1923). The rebellion began near Cyangugu (now Shangugu) in 1923, where five of the rebel leaders were executed. Participants were Hutu.

NKORA PLANTERS COFFEE COOPERATIVE. A commercial coffee co-operative organized in 1956 in Kisenyi. The co-operative was equipped with a large depulping, washing, and drying installation.

NOUVELLES DU RWANDA. A periodical published by the Université Nationale du Rwanda.

NSANZIMANA, SYLVESTRE. Sylvestre Nsanzimana was the former deputy secretary general of the Organization of African Unity (OAU) and in 1991 was the minister of justice and a member of MRND. In this year of political reform and the movement toward representative government, Mr. Nsanzimana was appointed prime minister on October 10, 1991 by President Habyarimana and given the instructions to establish a transitional government with a new cabinet made up of representatives from six political parties. The transitional government would serve, pending new elections scheduled for December 1993. But his appointment was not accepted by the Committee of Consultation, a grouping made up of the MDR, PSD, and PL and opponents of MRND, the president's party, on the grounds that he was the president's man.

NSENGIYAREMYE, DISMAS. Dismas Nsengiyaremye is the prime minister of the coalition government. The latter emerged from talks between President Juvénal Habyarimana, Prime Minister Sylvestre Nsanzimana, who Mr. Nsengiyaremye replaces, and the twelve registered political parties. The meeting took place between February and March 1992.

The prime minister is a forty-seven-year-old, Belgian-trained veterinarian. He had, until his appointment, headed the Office of Valorisation des Produits d'Elevage au Mutara, a large ranching and settlement scheme in the northeastern region of the country. He is Hutu and comes from the central region. He has considerable and impressive credentials, including government service—having served as permanent secretary at the Ministry of Agriculture from 1984 to 1985. To his credit, it is said that he has not been accused of past abuse of office, so he has passed a significant hurdle.

NSORO SAMUKONDO, UMWAMI OF RWANDA. *See* SAMUKONDO, NSORO.

NTENDEZI-CYANGUGU ROAD. In 1981, the government received a loan from the ADF of $12 million of the $15 million needed for the construction of a thirty-two-kilometer stretch of the asphalted Butare-Cyangugu road between Ntendezi to Cyangugu.

NYABINGI. A religious movement involving primarily Hutu from northern and southwestern Rwanda (the areas of Byumba and northern Ruhengeri). Followers believed in the powers of Nyabingi (or Kiheko), a woman revered for her spiritual powers of protection in matters of health and fertility. She is represented on earth by *bagirwa,* or priests, who can communicate with her. They contact Nyabingi on behalf of those who seek her assistance or intervention. No formal ritual is associated with the worship of Nyabingi, except for a private séance with a Nyabingi priest who makes the personal appeal for assistance. The worship of Nyabingi in Rwanda has several traditions. One asserts that the religion entered Rwanda from the West prior to the 1900s. The other places the origin of the religion in another era and with the royal family in Ndorwa.

In the early 1920s, several thousand Hutu in the southwestern region followed a prophet of Nyabingi in attacking classrooms built by the missionaries and eagerly complied with his requests for gifts. The Belgians easily suppressed these demonstrations by arresting the prophet.

NYAMUHESHERA, KIGERI, UMWAMI OF RWANDA. Nyamuheshera reigned from 1648 to 1672. He conquered Kigali and extended the central kingdom northward to Lake Edward, eastward to Rusenyi, and westward to Kinyaga and portions of Ndorwa.

NYANZA. A territorial designation and the capital of the traditional government, which contained the official residence of the *umwami*. The territory is 3,451 square kilometers in area. The region's soil is quite poor, and the area was used primarily as pasture for the cattle herds of the *umwami*. In 1928, however, the Belgians began an intense agricultural-production campaign. The territory also contained the Nyanza School for the Sons of Chiefs, which had a six-year course of study, and trained secretaries and clerks for the administrative services and as mine recruiters and monitors. The school was closed in 1935.

NYUNDO MISSION. A Catholic mission at Bugoyi founded in 1901; it sponsored matmaking and had its own carpentry shop.

NZEYIMANA, ISIDORE. Rwandan politician and member of the Committee of Nine. Nzeyimana was born in Runyinya, Butare. He graduated from the Grand Séminaire and attended the Ecole d'Administration of Kisantu for four years. After completing the course of study, he became a civil servant in the Belgian colonial administration. He joined APRO-SOMA and was a member of its Conseil Spécial Provisoire in February 1960 and joined the Conseil Provisoire the following October. He served as secretary of state for education and president of the Supreme Court from January 1961 to September 1963. He was the national delegate for MDR/PAR-MEHUTU from 1965 to 1969 and then secretary-general in the Ministry of Posts, Telecommunications, and Transports.

-O-

OBOTE, OPOLLO MILTON. President of Uganda in 1966 after overthrowing the *kabaka*. He in turn was overthrown in January 1971 while away in Singapore by Idi Amin, but was elected president in 1980. He ruled Uganda until July 27,

1985, when he was ousted in a military coup led by
Brigadier General Basilio Okello. In 1969 Obote ordered the
registration of all Rwandan refugees in what was interpreted
as the first step towards their expulsion, but the takeover of
the government by Idi Amin in 1972 precluded the implementation of the expected action. In 1980 the Obote government disenfranchised Banyarwandans, and in October
teams of local officials, members of the youth wing of the
Uganda People's Congress (UPC), and special police attacked and destroyed Banyarwandan homes, forcing an estimated 100,000 to seek refuge in settlements in the southwestern region or to cross the border into Rwanda and
Tanzania. When the Obote government fell in 1985, some
31,000 Banyar-wanda refugees who had been forced to flee
in 1982 and 1983 into exile in Rwanda returned to Uganda
and reclaimed the land they had previously owned.

OCTOBER 1, 1990, INVASION. On October 1, 1990, the
Rwandese Patriotic Front (RPF) invaded Rwanda from
Uganda. The initial force of some 2,000 grew to about 7,000
fighters. Of this group, 4,000 had deserted from Uganda's
National Resistance Army (NRA). The remainder were civilians. This group, led by Major General Fred Rwigyema, in-
filtrated northern Rwanda at Kagitumba at about 10 a.m.
The few Rwandan government troops on the border were
unable to stop them. Consequently, the RPF was able to capture the tourist resort and barracks of Gabiro and the town of
Nykatare. But they were unable to hold these positions because the Rwandan army mounted an offensive, assisted by
Zairian troops and by French and Belgian military intervention and supplies. Government forces were also victorious at
Lyabega; they inflicted heavy casualties upon the RPF.
Majors Peter Bayingana and Chris Bunyenyezi were killed
in ambush along with scores of RPF troops.

By the end of October, the RPF having suffered heavy
losses reverted to guerrilla warfare by splitting up into

smaller groups. Heavy fighting was reported in November and December around Gatuna, Kaniga, and Ngarama. As the RPF became more successful, the Rwandan government began accusing Uganda of complicity in the invasion and with assisting RPF forces to strike against them from inside of Uganda. Even after receiving repeated assurances from President Museveni that Banyarwanda soldiers in the National Resistance Army (NRA) would never be allowed to attack Rwanda, the Rwandan government never wavered in its certainty of Ugandan complicity. Still the RPF, while capable of waging a long guerrilla campaign, with devastating effects on Rwanda, has not been able to seize power.

As the invasion progressed, the government proceeded to arrest suspected rebel sympathizers, mostly Tutsi, all over Rwanda. Some 5,000 people had been detained by the end of October 1990, although about half had been released by mid-November. But trials were announced in late December for 1,556 detainees for their roles in the "October War." While thirteen detainees were brought to court on January 3, 1991, only one was sentenced to death. Nine were sentenced to long prison terms. The most pressing concern from the government's vantage point is resolution of the conflict, primarily because the invasion has the potential for precipitating both an economic and political crisis in the country. The country is currently experiencing food shortages, chronic inflation and deficits, and a sharp decline in export earnings because of poor coffee prices.

Diplomatic efforts to resolve the conflict began almost immediately. On October 15, Wilfred Martens, Belgian Prime Minister, flew to East Africa. Two days later, peace talks commenced at Mwanza in Tanzania with Presidents Habyarimana, Museveni, and Mwinyi of Tanzania in attendance. They agreed upon a ceasefire for October 24, which could be monitored by neutral forces. They also called for a regional conference to resolve the refugee issue. President Habyarimana issued a statement from Paris on October 18 expressing a willingness to talk to any opposition group in or outside of Rwanda. Later that month, peace talks were held in Goma and Gbadolite with President Mobutu presiding.

None of these early efforts was fruitful. The ceasefire set for October 24 came and went, with both sides accusing the other of violations. As the RPF regained momentum under the leadership of Major Paul Kagame in November, President Habyarimana became less conciliatory, displaying an unwillingness to negotiate with "rebels," who occupied Rwandan territory. By the end of the year, the RPF, about 5,000 strong, had moved deep into Rwandan territory, south along the Tanzanian border and west along the Ugandan border.

OFFICE BELGE DU COMMERCE EXTERIEUR. The Belgian-based agency established a subsidiary branch in Bujumbura to foster the development of commercial exchange in commerce and trade, to find markets, and to keep local merchants and producers—Belgians and other Europeans—informed about the various export and import commodities.

OFFICE DE LA VALORISATION DE LA BANANERAIE RWANDAISE (OVIBAR). A private company that manufactures banana wine and other fruit drinks.

OFFICE DES CAFES INDIGENES DU RUANDA-URUNDI (OCIRU). A state regulatory agency established in 1945 and dissolved on December 31, 1963, when the economic union between Rwanda and Burundi was officially terminated. At that time, it became the Office des Cafés Indigènes du Rwanda. Its objectives were to provide technical assistance, implement standards in order to valorize coffee production, and maintain laboratories, markets, and depulping stations for the production of African coffee.

Its board of directors included three European functionaries, two African notables who represented the African planters, and two individuals chosen for their competence to represent mill owners, merchants, and exporters. It became a deliberating assembly the following year, and consisted of a president, the provisional commissioner of the territory, a provisional vice president, the director of the Service Provincial de l'Agronomie, the provincial chief of the Service of African Affairs, two members representing the African planters, and six private members with direct interest in the objectives of OCIRU. The African representatives and private individuals were nominated for two years by the governor-general upon recommendations of the governor of the territory from a list of four African representatives and about a dozen private candidates.

OCIRU also managed the Coffee Stabilization Fund, which was created on December 4, 1948, to protect the producer from the fluctuations in the international coffee market. After independence, Rwanda created its own Office des Cultures Industrielles du Rwanda (OCIR) in 1964. OCIR was assigned the mission of agricultural diversification, and has actively promoted increasing production in tobacco, cotton, pyrethrum, quinine, timber, and preeminently, tea. In 1978, it became the Office des Cafés (OCIR-*Café*) with the mission to develop coffee and other new agronomic industries and maintain the coffee stabilization fund.

OFFICE DES CITES AFRICAINES. The Bureau for African Housing was a state corporation that operated in both the Belgian Congo and the mandate territory (at Bujumbura). It was charged with constructing hygienic housing for Africans in accordance with the "modern principles of town planning." The bureau received working capital from a separate fund from the Belgian government, with no funds coming from the territorial extraordinary budget. Additional capital was provided by the proceeds from the sale or rental of the housing when completed. Among its plans was the creation of a self-contained community of 15,000 persons. Housing units would be constructed from permanent materials, and the cost of housing would vary from $600 for a bachelor's unit to $1,500 for a small four-bedroom apartment.

OFFICE DE VALORISATION AGRICOLE ET PASTORALE DU MUTARA (OVAPAM). The quasi-governmental organization for a rural settlement and ranching project designed by the World Bank in 1973 and under the jurisdiction of the Ministry of Agriculture. Mutara is a northern highlands area. The project's administrative office is located at Kigali.

OFFICE D'EXPLOITATION DES TRANSPORTS COLONI-AUX (OTRACO). A commercial company which monopolized colonial transportation of merchandise on Lake Kivu and the western half of the Congo basin. It operated the eighty-five-mile Chemin de Fer du Kivu, which ran from Uvira on Lake Tanganyika to Kamaniola.

OFFICE DU CAFE ARABICA. Originally the Kivu Coffee Agency, it was created in 1940. This state agency's activities were centered in four distinct fields. First, it sought to introduce better farming, harvesting, and processing methods. Second, it sought to form liaisons between scientific research bodies, such as INEAC, which developed the best varieties. Third, it sought to control the quality of the product and to make sure that standards were uniform. And last, it was responsible for the maintenance of processing installations and proper packing.

OFFICE DU COLONISATION. A state agency created by the Royal Decree of January 22, 1937, from the Ministry of Colonies. Under Article I, a mission was charged to study the feasibility of colonization in Belgian Africa from the vantage point of agriculture, industry, and commerce; to inform the candidates about the potential of the countries; to offer financial assistance to them; to implement legislation on immigration; to study and propose all suitable measures to promote the installation of *colons;* and to continue to monitor their activities. Article II pertained to the composition of a consultation (or executive) committee, in which members were nominated to a two-year term with an option for renewal by the Ministry of Colonies.

OFFICE DU PYRETHRE DU RWANDA (OPYRWA). A state agency established in 1978 as a distinct unit to promote the development of pyrethrum. The agency has recently been threatened with closure by the government because of problems with profitability within the industry.

OFFICE DU THE (OCIR-THE). A state agency that was originally part of OCIR but became separate in 1978, responsible for the development and marketing of tea. By 1984, the national tea office operated nine processing factories and accounted for about 80 percent of the national tea output. In March 1988, however, OCIR-THE suspended all projects not directly related to increasing production because of declining world prices.

OFFICE NATIONAL DE LA POPULATION (ONAPO). The National Office of Population was created in 1980 to promote demographic awareness by urging the people to conserve land resources through antierosion measures and to promote the use of contraceptive methods by placing emphasis on the wider spacing of pregnancies. The office notes that approximately 4 percent of women of childbearing age use contraception, and suggests that this figure may explain the very high fertility rate of 8.6 live births per woman.

OFFICE NATIONAL DES TRANSPORTS EN COMMUNE. A state agency responsible for the development of the national infrastructure.

OFFICE NATIONAL DU COMMERCE. A state agency established in the 1960s by President Grégoire Kayibanda to implement national planning. The office was abolished when General Juvénal Habyarimana assumed power in 1973.

OFFICE RWANDAIS DU TOURISME ET DES PARCS NATIONAUX (ORTPN). This national office was created in 1973 to encourage tourism in the country.

OFFICES DE COMMERCIALISATION. State agencies operating throughout Belgian Africa. They were created during World War II and reorganized in 1948. They played an important role in the modernization and exploitation of the European sectors of Belgian Africa. They regulated commerce, the treatment and exportation of crops, and arranged a number of industrial installations.

OFFICES DES PRODUITS AGRICOLES. State agencies established by the Belgian government to assist plantation owners in improving the quality of their production and to facilitate its sale. These were semiofficial organizations with special legal status.

OKELLO, BRIGADIER GENERAL TITO BASILIO. President of Uganda from 1985 to 1986. He assumed power when he ousted the former president, Milton Obote, in a military coup on July 27, 1985. Okello suspended the constitution, dissolved parliament, dismissed all ministers, and established a military commission as the highest authority in the country.

ORDONNANCE LOI. Legislative enactment passed by the parliament in Brussels and intended for the Belgian Congo. Also applicable in the rest of Belgian Africa after having been published by the governor-general.

ORDONNANCE LOI (REGULATION NO.) 1/47. An ordinance issued on March 7, 1947, and designed to regulate essential food crops in the African sector. The law prohibited the sale of certain crops—such as peas, maize, beans, wheat, and potatoes—by Africans, particularly in Kitega, Muramvya, Ngozi, and Bururi. Any infractions could bring imprisonment from one to seven days of penal servitude and a maximum fine of 200 BF.

ORDONNANCE LOI (REGULATION NO.) 37. A law designed to regulate the commercialization of coffee in the Africa sector. It was passed on August 21, 1925, and again as a royal decree on January 11, 1926. According to the law, African coffee could not be sold or purchased without the express permission of the governor of Ruanda-Urundi.

ORDONNANCE LOI (REGULATION NO.) 49. Of December 31, 1925, authorized the compulsory cultivation of nonseasonal crops by African farmers. The law also prohibited Tutsi chiefs and notables from denying land needed for cultivation by Hutu farmers, or preventing them from planting and harvesting the land.

ORDONNANCE LOI (REGULATION NO.) 52. Of November 7, 1924, required the Banyarwanda to plant and harvest export and food crops.

ORDONNANCE LOI (REGULATION NO.) 53 (AGRI). Of October 30, 1934, provided farmers with assistance in combating locust and cricket plagues.

ORDONNANCE LOI (REGULATION NO.) 70 (AIMO). Disease prevention and antierosion and pest-control legislation for drainage areas and irrigation ditches. The law was passed November 20, 1944, to empower the Resident to require each African individual or group occupying farmland or pastureland, to plant hedges and dig ditches, to maintain them, and to carry out other types of antierosion work in accordance with the instructions of the local African authorities. The Resident could require Africans to maintain any existing drainage and irrigation works on their own arable land or pasture and to take part in any community irrigation or drainage scheme. He could also require African communities to take part in campaigns to combat epiphytotic diseases and other plant enemies.

ORDONNANCE LOI (REGULATION NO.) 80 (AGRI). A law regulating the handling and storage of cottonseed and the destruction of seeds unfit for planting and of gin waste. The law was created on July 19, 1932.

ORDONNANCE LOI (REGULATION NO.) 64 (JUST). A law designed to restrict the movement of Africans in European areas. It was passed on September 24, 1931, and prohibited blacks from circulating between the hours of 9 p.m. and 5 a.m. The prohibition included European areas, and Ordonnance Loi 75 (JUST) of July 9, 1932, extended the prohibition to urban areas.

ORDANNANCE LOI (REGULATION NO.) 26 (AE). Of February 1, 1943, and Regulation No. 24 (AE) of January 25, 1946, created the government regulatory agency Commission des Devises et des Importations, which exercised control over all commercial imports. Its membership included the regional director of the Banque du Congo Belge and a delegate from the government. It operated out of Bujumbura and met on a weekly basis.

ORDONNANCE LOI (REGULATION NO.) 34 (AE). An ordinance from the governor-general's office on March 16, 1937. It was designed to establish standards of quality control and packaging requirements for the exportation of green coffee beans. According to Articles I and II, the following kinds of coffee could not be exported: unripe musty coffee; rotten beans with nauseating odor; beans containing more than 2 percent foreign materials; and beans having more than 10 percent black or partially black beans. Article III applied to the exportation of unripe coffees containing more than 6 percent broken beans, which could be exported if the package was labeled in capital letters at least five centimeters in height with the word "BRISURES" and if they were not covered by any of the categories in Articles I or II.

ORDONNANCE LOI (REGULATION NO.) 45 (AE). Law passed on June 21, 1947, establishing the minimum price paid to African coffee farmers.

ORDONNANCE LOI (REGULATION NO.) 90 (AE). Law regulating the marketing of green coffee from Rwanda and the rest of Belgian Africa. According to the ordinance of November 21, 1931, green coffee beans would be packaged in sacks of a particular dimension and labeled in large letters no less than five centimeters high with the name or mark of the planter, plantation, society, or the commercial expeditor of African coffee, and the name of the province; and the letters "IND" to indicate African coffee. The ordinance did not apply to coffees that were being reexported, and it became effective January 1, 1935.

ORDONNANCE LOI (REGULATION NO.) 41/35. Law regulating the purchase of coffee grown by African farmers. Under this ordinance of April 28, 1950, arabica coffee could only be purchased by those who had a purchasing license issued by the administration to those owning storage and processing facilities. The ordinance prohibited traders from buying coffee directly from African planters, but rather at specified markets supervised by administrative authorities. The law was designed to ensure that African planters offered good quality coffee and to permit supervision of the weight and price of coffee offered for sale by the producer.

ORDONNANCE LOI (REGULATION NO.) 22/408. Legislation regulating contract workers. The ordinance was passed on December 12, 1954, and established food rations and lodging allowances for wage laborers residing in extratribal centers.

ORGANISATION DE L'ASSISTANCE AUX COLONS. Organization providing financial assistance to future colons and coordinating assistance from the Institut National pour l'Etude Agronomique du Congo Belge.

ORGANISATION POUR L'AMENAGEMENT ET LE DEVELOPPEMENT DU BASSIN DE LA RIVIERE KAGERA. Initially a tripartite organization formed in 1978 by Rwanda, Burundi, and Tanzania to develop and manage the water, hydroelectric power, and mineral resources of the Kagera River basin. Uganda joined the group in 1980.

ORTS, PIERRE. Belgian foreign office official who represented Belgium in the Orts-Milner Convention in Paris in May 1919 regarding the disposition of the conquered territory in German East Africa.

ORTS-MILNER CONVENTION (1919). The convention encompassed several meetings between Pierre Orts, the Belgian envoy extraordinary and minister plenipotentiary, and Lord Milner, the British colonial secretary, in May 1919. The meetings were called when Belgium was informed without formal consultation through a Belgian news release that the Council of Four had decided on May 6 that the German colonies were to be administered as mandates by Great Britain, France, and Japan under League of Nations supervision. The Belgian government asked for a meeting to discuss the status of German East African possessions. The first meeting took place in Paris, and at its conclusion on May 12, Orts and Milner had agreed to modify the clause in the draft treaty concerning German East Africa to read "Great Britain and Belgium shall themselves determine the future administration of this colony and shall recommend its approval by the League of Nations."

After correspondence and several meetings between May 12 and May 15 a solution was proposed which included a Belgian Ruanda and Urundi and the exclusion of any British intervention with Portugal for the resolution of the problem of the lower Congo. The Belgian government, however, expressed its concern about the importance and priority of the Congo delta and access to the Atlantic Ocean. The Belgians proposed to exchange their conquered East African territory for the southern bank of the Congo River. Britain would receive the Belgian-occupied East African territory; Belgium would gain the Portuguese territory at the mouth of the Congo; Portugal would receive compensation from Britain in the southeast corner of German East Africa for losses to Belgium in the Portuguese Congo Province. The British would also pay Belgium a sum which would be used for development in the Belgian Congo and which would be dedicated to the Belgian military effort in East Africa.

Milner and Orts met on May 24 to discuss the Belgian proposal. Milner confirmed the arrangement that Belgium would retain Urundi and Ruanda, with the exception of the eastern part of Ruanda, which the British required for the Cape-to-Cairo railroad. He flatly refused the pecuniary compensation, but Orts insisted on it. On the issue of Portugal and the lower Congo, Milner informed Orts that the British government was prepared to offer Portugal territory in the south of German East Africa, but he doubted whether Portugal would accept it. Letters were exchanged on May 26 in which Ruanda and Urundi, compensation, and the Belgian proposal for territorial exchange with the Portuguese were discussed. On May 30, 1919, the Orts-Milner agreement was concluded. East Africa was partitioned between the British and the Belgian governments. Belgians were given control of Ruanda-Urundi. The issues of pecuniary compensation for Belgium and territorial exchange with Portugal were dropped.

OSTEND CONFERENCE (1961). Requested by the United

Nations General Assembly in December 1960 to discuss the future of Rwanda and Burundi on the eve of independence. A political conference was held at Ostend from January 7 to January 12, 1961. Participants at the conference discussed the date set for legislative elections. Some wanted to keep the original date set by the Belgian government and approved at the Kitega conference. Others agreed with the United Nations position to postpone the elections until the United Nations could provide adequate supervision. Participants also discussed a political union between Rwanda and Burundi. Most delegates thought that this issue should be decided between the governments themselves. The colloquium was scheduled to last for one week, but talks collapsed when Burundi's delegation refused to participate in a discussion of Rwanda's political future. The meetings were attended by United Nations observers.

-P-

PAGE, ALBERT (1883–1951). Catholic priest and member of the Missionnaires d'Afrique, or the White Fathers. Father Page served forty-two years as a priest in Rwanda. When he died on January 9, he had been father superior of the Nyundo mission since 1927. He arrived in Rwanda in December 1908, learned to speak Kinyarwanda quite well, and wrote many articles dealing with the social and cultural life of the country. He is known for his *Un royaume hamité au centre de l'Afrique* (1933).

PALIPEHUTU. Palipehutu is the principal Barundi Hutu opposition party. It members during a recent disturbance established camps inside the southern border of Rwanda with the sole purpose of carrying out raids against government forces in Burundi. The activities of Palipehutu during the early period of 1992 have caused strained relations between Burundi and Rwanda. Barundi authorities maintain that Rwandan officials have not done enough to stop these border incursions.

PALM TREES. Source of palm oil, which is produced primarily by Europeans. Palm oil production is centered in the Rumonge and Lake Nyanza regions.

PARC NATIONAL DE L'ALBERT/PARC NATIONAL DES VOLCANS. The national park, initially some 52,000 acres and located where the borders of northern Zaire (formerly the Belgian Congo), northern Rwanda, and southern Uganda converge, was created in stages beginning in 1910. In 1969, however, some 22,000 acres were removed from the park in Rwanda to make room for the cultivation of pyrethrum. Currently, the Zairian portion is called Parc des Virungas, the northern Rwandan area, Parc National des Volcans, and southern Uganda, the Kegezi Gorilla Sanctuary. The park is intended to serve as a sanctuary for the mountain gorillas and a conservation area for the Virunga volcano chain.

PARC NATIONAL DES VOLCANS. The Parc National des Volcans, which is located in northern Rwanda, was initially some 52,000 acres, but in 1969, 22,000 acres were removed from the park for the cultivation of pyrethrum. It is home to about 320 of the world's 600 or so mountain gorillas. In recent years, it has become a major tourist attraction and industry, providing some $68 million per year and second only to coffee as the largest source of foreign exchange for the country. When RPF forces established its guerrilla base near the park, conservationists feared that RPF troops or Rwandan armed forces would eventually shoot the gorillas or that these rare animals would contract human diseases. The recent shooting and death of Mrithi, a famous mountain gorilla, is evidence that their fears were not groundless. Both the government and RPF have expressed sympathy, but neither has ceased hostilities or has left the area. In fact, recent reports in 1993 note that government troops have been shelling suspected RPF sites in the park.

PARISH, LIEUTENANT FRANCIS RICHARD VON. German military officer. He and twenty-one askaris established themselves at Ischangi (Shangi) in Rwanda in 1902, where he had been nominated base commander (*chef de poste*). This was the main camp and the first German presence in the country. He remained for several months until designated to accompany Captain R. von Beringe and Dr. Engleland to Musinga's court at Nyanza. He traveled throughout the country, surveying Ndiza, Lake Luhondo, Gisenyi, Nyundo, Zaza, and Save, until he returned to Germany on medical leave in January 1903.

PARTI DEMOCRATIQUE CHRETIEN (PDC). The Parti Démocratique Chrétien (PDC)/Christian Democratic Party emerged in mid-1991 as a response to the movement toward democracy in the country. The party is led by Nayinzira Nepomuscen. Mr. Nepomuscen has close ties with the Catholic Church. On December 18, 1991, the PDC was one of seven opposition parties in attendance at a meeting called by President Habyarimana to discuss the composition of the coalition government for the transition to representative government, pending elections in December 1993. But the president's terms proved unacceptable to the MDR, PDS, PL, and the Parti Socialiste Rwandais (PSR), whose representative withdrew from the talks on the next day. Of the remaining four opposition parties, only the PDC could offer a substantial portfolio. In the cabinet that was formed on December 30, the PDC received only one cabinet appointment, the minister of commerce, industry, and crafts. This post was assumed by Caspard Ruhumuliza, a lawyer from Gitarama, who had been a permanent secretary and prefect of Kibuye.

PARTI DU MOUVEMENT DE L'EMANCIPATION DES BAHUTU (PARMEHUTU). The Hutu political party that was dominant in the country until 1973. It had formed in 1956, but did not publish its program until October 18, 1959, after the death of *umwami* Rudahigwa. The party condemned colonialism by the Tutsi oligarchy, but approved of a constitutional monarchy in which the *umwami* would have limited power or would serve as a figurehead. The party advocated universal suffrage, land reform, codification of traditional laws, and the democratization of education, and called for a referendum, supervised by the United Nations, on the issue of independence, which it did not expect for at least five to seven years.

PARTI ECOLOGISTE (PECO). The Parti Ecologiste (PECO) or the Ecologist Party is one of several opposition parties in the country that was formed in mid-1991 in response to a more tolerant atmosphere and a movement toward representative government. These new parties were sanctioned by the new constitution of June 1991. PECO attended the December 18 meeting, called by President Habyarimana, to form a coalition government which would rule the country until the elections of December 1993. After four of the larger and more substantial parties withdrew, PECO remained but was later declared ineligible because it lacked a substantial portfolio.

PARTI LIBERAL (PL). The Parti Libéral (PL) or the Liberal Party emerged in mid-1991 as a response to the movement toward democracy. The party is headed by Justin Mugenzi and is said to be the Tutsi party. The core of its support comes from businessmen. Its president is Justin Mugenzi, a Tutsi businessman, and its vice-president is Lanouald Ndasingwa, a Tutsi who was imprisoned after the RPF October invasion but was later released. The Liberal Party's secretary general, Agnea Ntambyariro, is a former central committee member of the MRND. Consequently, the party has considerable experience and political savvy. The PL attended the December 18 meeting, called by President Habyarimana to discuss the new coalition government. But the PL, along with the MDR, the PSD, and the Parti Socialiste Rwandais (PSR) withdrew from the meeting the following day. The major objection was the appointment of Mr. Nsanzimana as prime minister of the proposed transitional government.

PARTI POUR LA DEMOCRATIE ISLAMIQUE (PDI) The Parti pour la Démocratie Islamique (PDI) or the Islamic Democratic Party emerged during mid-1991, when the atmosphere in the country supported political diversity and when the new constitution signed in June 1991 sanctioned the formation of opposition parties. The PDI attended the December 18 meeting, called by President Habyarimana, to discuss the formation of a coalition government. After four of the stronger parties had withdrawn, the PDI was among the four that remained. However, it too was declared ineligible because it lacked a sufficient portfolio.

PARTI SOCIAL-DEMOCRATE (PSD). The Parti Social-Démocrate (PSD) or the Social Democrat Party, which emerged in mid-1991 as a response to the democratic movement in the country, is headed by two former ministers in President Habyarimana's government: Félicien Gatabazi and Frédéric Nzamurambaho, both from southern Rwanda. The PSD attended the December 18 meeting called by President Habyarimana as a member of the opposition. It withdrew the next day, because it objected to Mr. Nsanzimana's appointment as prime minister of the proposed transitional government. Politically, the PSD is a splinter from the MDR. It has its roots and support base in the south. The party opposes ethnic classification on identity cards and supports a more equal distribution of the country's wealth. Its membership contains some of the leading intellectuals in the country, and its president is a former minister of agriculture, Frédéric Nzamurambaho. Its secretary general and founder is Félicien Gatabazi, the former minister who held a number of portfolios in the national government during the 1970s and early 1980s. The PSD's vice president is presently the permanent secretary in the Ministry of Justice.

PARTI SOCIALISTE RWANDAIS (PSR). The Parti Socialiste Rwandais (PSR) or the Rwandan Socialist Party was also formed in response to the democratic movement. Its chief spokesman is George Hategekimana, who maintains that the party's primary concern is absentee landlords and their control of 30 percent of the country's arable land. The party supports land redistribution and bank loans for workers and peasants. PSR's representatives attended the December 18 meeting, called by President Habyarimana, to form a coalition government. The PSR withdrew the following day, protesting the appointment of Mr. Nsanzimana as prime minister of the proposed transitional government.

PARTY YOUTH WINGS. The party young wings are auxiliaries of the new political parties that emerged in 1991. They are sometimes referred to as militia, and it is believed by many observers that they have contributed to the political climate and instability in the country after August 1991. They have been accused of fighting among themselves and attacking one another's supporters. The MDR's wings are called Jeunesse Démocratique Républicain, the PL's Jeunesse Libéral, the PSD's *Bacobozi*, and the MRND's the *Interahamwe*. In February 1992, Radio Rwanda announced that six members of the Jeunesse Démocratique Républicain were arrested at a rally in Gisenyi for carrying pocket knives, scrap iron, screwdrivers, and catapults.

PAYS. The largest geopolitical subunit of the mandate and the trustee territory. The two *pays* were Urundi and Ruanda, divided into districts called *territoires* until 1960 when they became *arrondissements*. Each *pays* was ruled by an *umwami,* who was subject to Belgian veto.

PAYSANNAT. An essential component of the colonial and national governments' economic policy. The Belgian government established farming schemes in the 1950s to promote more efficient methods, raise production, and to increase the amount of arable land for export crops. Since the 1970s, the national government has used these farming communities, located in Kigali, Gitarama, and Butare, to increase the country's total coffee production.

PEANUTS. An important African food crop.

PEAS. An important African food crop.

PERRAUDIN, MONSIGNOR ANDRE. A Swiss Catholic priest in the Missionnaires d'Afrique, or the White Fathers. Perraudin was ordained in 1939 and served with various missions in Switzerland and Burundi before coming to Rwanda in 1950. He taught and later was rector at the Grand Séminaire of Nyakibanda. He became vicar apostolic at Kabgayi on December 19, 1955, and the archbishop of Kabgayi and Kigali and leader of the Catholic church in the country on November 10, 1959.

PETILLON, LEON-ANTONIN-MARIE. Belgian colonial civil servant, vice governor-general of the Belgian Congo and governor of Ruanda-Urundi from 1946 to 1952 and governor-general of the Belgian Congo from 1952 to 1958. Governor Petillon was born in Belgium on June 22, 1903. He studied law at Université Catholique de Louvain and entered government service in 1928. From 1928 to April 25, 1939, he was cabinet chief within the Ministry of Colonies under Baron Joseph Albert De Vleeschauwer. From 1939 to 1941, he served with the governor-general's office. He was nominated vice governor-general of the Belgian Congo and governor of the mandate territory of Ruanda-Urundi from 1946 to 1952, and became governor-general of the Belgian Congo from 1952 to 1958. After his governorship, he served as minister of colonies for six months. He was the father of Ruanda-Urundi's Ten-Year Plan (1951), and in 1959 he was appointed to a working group studying the political future of the Belgian Congo.

PETIT SEMINAIRE DE KABGAYI. Catholic mission school and seminary that was subsidized by the government as early as 1929. It taught African students from levels one through six.

PLAN DECENNAL, 1952–1961. The first of many economic and social development plans proposed by the Belgian colonial and later the Rwandan national government. They vary from five- to ten-year projections. This particular plan involved an expenditure of 3,670 million BF, or $73.4 million, for economic development, investment, scientific equipment, social and public services, and building construction and town planning; the Belgian government pledged advances of about 400 million BF annually. Additional financing was granted by the International Bank for Reconstruction and Development in the form of loans. Under the plan, gradual resettlement of about 40,000 families to the Belgian Congo was proposed. Between 1937 and 1947 about 25,000 inhabitants had been resettled in Gishari, near Lake Kivu.

Also proposed was an increase in social services and in the number of African agricultural assistants, from 26 to 118 before the end of 1959. The plan made provisions for the establishment of five vocational schools of agriculture and to increase the number of African monitors from 629 to 1,472 before 1959. The plan called for the creation of new artificial pasturage, which would increase the present grazing land by about 15 percent and would involve draining marshlands, clearing wooded savanna, and providing irrigation. It stressed the protection of forests rather than timber production: five new forest reserves, involving 3,750 hectares for the production of timber as well as firewood, were planned.

In terms of fisheries, the plan hoped to increase annual production of fish, an important source of animal protein, to 17,500 tons by 1959. A road program called for the improvement of 906 kilometers of existing roads and the construction of 515 kilometers of new roads. The plan estimated the cost would be about 1,000 million Belgian francs. It also proposed raising the number of European agricultural experts from 42 to 101, including 5 new school directors. The number of European veterinarians and assistants was to be increased from 26 to 49. In the public sector, the plan called for extensive construction of hospitals and dispensaries, child-care centers, an ambulance for every hospital, a medical laboratory at Butare, and a leprosarium and tuberculosis sanatorium, as well as professional schools for carpentry and metalworking. To implement this particular program, the plan called for the recruitment of 60 additional European medical personnel, including 40 doctors, and 2,244 African, personnel in categories of medical assistants, nurses, nurses' aides, midwife assistants, and orderlies. Four new schools were proposed to train medical support personnel, as were five schools for training agricultural assistants, monitors, and advertisers to encourage proper cultivation techniques. The role of the research institutes—such as INEAC and IRSAC—would be expanded to include research in nutrition, climate, geography, demography, language, history, psychology, and social anthropology to furnish solutions to problems of the land and of human behavior. The personnel for these institutes would be increased from 14 to 83 between 1950 and 1960.

Central to the plan was the European *colonat* in both agriculture and industry. The *colonat* would open new lands, provide capital, and develop industries and other resources that would generate foreign exchange. He would also serve an educational function as a role model for Africans in terms of sanitation and better work methods and habits. The administration offered between 50 and 200 hectares of land for the agricultural *colonat,* depending on the population density of the land under settlement. Industrial and mining *colonats* were given, according to the plan, "vast field of action." A budget deficit in 1956 resulted in considerable delay and the partial disorganization of the application of the Ten-Year Plan.

The Rwandan government has also published Plans Quinquennaux 1964–1968, 1965–1969, 1966–1970, 1972–1976, 1977–1981, 1982–1986, and 1986–91.

PLANTATIONS DU RUANDA-URUNDI (PLATURUNDI). A commercial agricultural export company with its home office in Brussels and an African branch at Kitega. In 1931, the company cultivated food crops, bred animals, and purchased, sold, and transported produce.

PLANTATIONS ET CAFEIERES DE KIGALI. Commercial coffee and agricultural company established in 1936 in Brussels. The company operated in Belgian Africa, cultivating, purchasing, and selling food crops. It also bred and sold livestock, and was active into the 1940s.

POLYGAMY TAX. A source of revenue for the colonial government and a tax on wealth. Created by an ordinance of December 24, 1924, it was initially directed against non-Africans (Muslims) until 1931 when the tax was extended to all Africans irrespective of nationality. A 1950 United Nations report noted that the tax was levied on 10 percent of the population.

PORTERAGE. The occupation of carriers or porters, who transported trade commodities from place to place. After 1930, it was no longer considered an important economic resource for the Banyarwanda. From 1931 to 1932, the number of porterage workers went from 151,978 daily to 23,267 daily.

PORT OF MATADI. A major colonial port facility in the Belgian Congo for the Atlantic Ocean trade.

PORT OF USUMBURA (now Bujumbura). A port on Lake Tanganyika. It was the principal port for the territory of Ruanda-Urundi, and 90 percent of all the products and merchandise of the territory passed through it. It was focal point for the Kigoma-Dar es Salaam route, the Dilolo-Lobito route, the Kigali-Kampala-Mombasa route, and the Albertville-Stanleyville-Matadi route. The port was administered by the Compagnie des Grands Lacs.

POSTIAUX, LOUIS-JOSEPH (1882–1948). Belgian colonial civil servant and vice governor-general of the Belgian Congo from 1926 to 1930. Postiaux was born in Antwerp on August 15, 1882. He was often described as a self-made man. Vice governor of the mandate territory, Postiaux found it necessary to advise his administrators to compromise with the notables after the devastating famine of 1927–1928. Consequently, administrative reforms were moderated, and he returned to an earlier policy of propping up the Tutsi notables' prestige and authority, as well as acknowledging the authority of *umwami* Musinga. He served on the Colonial Pension Commission in the 1930s, and as its vice president advocated protection for African professionals.

POSTULAT DES FRERES MONITEURS DE KABGAYE. An educational institution at Kabgayi that offered instruction and higher degrees for Africans in the 1920s.

POTATOES. Important crop in the African sector as early as 1916.

PREFECT. The individual responsible for administration of the prefecture, which replaced former *chefferies*.

PREFECTURES. Territorial and administrative units (similar to provinces) in present-day Rwanda. They came into existence in 1961 and are as follows:

	Area (sq. km.)	Population	Density (per sq.km.)
Butare	1,830	602,500	329.3
Byumba	4,987	521,351	104.5
Cyangugu	2,226	333,187	149.7
Gikongoro	2,192	370,596	169.1
Gisenyi	2,395	468,882	195.8
Gitarama	2,241	606,212	270.5
Kibungo	4,134	361,249	87.4
Kibuye	1,320	336,588	255.0
Kigali	3,251	698,442	214.8
Ruhengeri	1,762	531,927	301.9
Total	26,338	4,830,984	183.4

PREFERENTIAL TRADE AREA FOR EASTERN AND SOUTHERN AFRICA (PTA). PTA or the Preferential Trade Area for Eastern and Southern Africa is a regional and multilateral trade organization, comprising Angola, Burundi, the Comoros, Djibouti, Ethiopia, Kenya, Lesotho, Malawi, Mauritius, Mozambique, Namibia, Rwanda, Somalia, Sudan, Swaziland, Tanzania, Uganda, Zaire, Zambia, and Zimbabwe. It was established in 1981, and its administrative offices are housed in Lusaka. PTA attempts to improve commercial and economic cooperation among its members and to transform their structures and national economies. It promotes trade, the creation of institutional mechanisms, including monetary arrangements to facilitate trade, cooperation in agricultural development and improvement of transport links, attempts to equalize regional tariff rates, and concentrates on the development of technical and professional skills among its member states.

The Reserve Bank of Zimbabwe established a clearing house in 1984 for the transaction of goods and services within PTA. The Reserve Bank also enables member states to conduct multilateral trade in their own currencies. In July 1984, PTA introduced a system of tariff reductions that ranged from 10 percent to 70 percent for certain commodities. In 1987, it announced that an additional reduction of 10 percent would be made every two years for those very same commodities.

In 1986, a PTA Trade and Development Bank was established in Bujumbura, Burundi. In 1990, a Regional Investment Projects Forum, in conjunction with a program on monetary harmonization, a commodity futures market, and a stock exchange, was organized. In early 1992, member states made tentative plans to create a common market by 2000.

PRESTATIONS. Traditional Rwanda was basically a feudal society, where the king, or *umwami,* had absolute power and possessed all goods, land, and livestock. In recognition of certain great deeds, the *umwami* could distribute goods, land, and livestock among the Tutsi notables, who in turn redistributed these goods to lesser chiefs, who would then redistribute these same items to those at the bottom of the hierarchy. This distribution system was seen as a series of loan transactions, which were eminently precarious, since goods could be withdrawn at a moment's notice.

This cascade of transfers required reciprocal obligations that ranged from a long list of prestations in kind, such as honey, beer, peas, beans, sorghum, several kinds of mats and baskets, hoes, lances, and hides. Other traditional job obligations due to members of the oligarchy were *abarimyi,* or cultivator; *abungere,* or guardian of animals or cattle; *abakutsi,* or a servant charged with cleaning the kraals; *aba-kamkyi,* or an individual in charge of milking cows; *abateramyi,* or sentry; *abatetsi,* or cook; *inshoreke,* or a young woman employed in the service of the wife of a notable; *abakejuru,* or an old woman charged with keeping children; *abasuku,* or a nonclassified worker who draws water and does other kinds of domestic work; and *abashenyi,* or wood cutter.

Before the arrival of Europeans, prestations were levied in kind, and were distinct categories depending upon whether they were intended for land, social obligations, or work details: Tutsi notables always gave cows for land prestations and social obligations; Hutu provided utilitarian and luxury items which varied from one region to next (hoe, fiber bracelets, mats, honey, animal pelts), and for land they gave food products, such as peas, sorghum, and beans. For notables in the second rank in the hierarchy of authority, prestations were such that the great vassals (chiefs of the provinces or the chieftaincies) had to reside at court for fifteen days annually, and notables at lower ranks had to spend ten to twelve days with the notables at the provincial or chieftaincy level.

Maximum customary prestations were determined in the following ways: total number of worked days furnished to a district chief could not exceed one day per month for each subordinate; and the total prestations furnished to Tutsi notables and subchiefs for personal and communal labor could not exceed four days each month for each able-bodied adult male. These guidelines applied to everyone, and included initiatives taken by Tutsi notables and the European administration. Duties or types of work included construction of roads in the public interest, planting trees, provision of drainage, and maintenance of water crossings.

The burden of the system of prestations naturally fell to

the Hutu. In the administrative reforms of 1924 and 1928, the administration did not totally abolish all prestations for fear, according to one Belgian administrative official, of "provoking a total collapse of the social and political organization." The administration remarked that it was important to understand that customary prestations expressed the ultimate authority of the chiefs over their subjects and affirmed their power as administrators. Beginning in 1924, the government reduced prestations to forty-two days per year and abolished some traditional taxes. In the reforms of 1928, the government sought to reduce personal prestations gradually, and felt that those which served the interests of the collectivity were consistent with good administration, but it restricted personal prestations furnished to notables and subchiefs to no more than fifteen days per year, while those performed in the interest of the group would remain at forty-eight per year. Chiefs were warned that it was forbidden for them to have customary work prestations in the creation and maintenance of cash crops. Labor employed in these works had to be paid.

In 1933, the prestations in kind were abolished and replaced by a money payment to the Tutsi notables and subchiefs, payable annually and collected in lump sums with the annual head tax. An ordinance of December 15, 1933, fixed the rate of redemption of prestations in kind for the six territories. The rate was calculated from the local price of commodities at the end of the year, and the rate varied from 3.00 BF and 4.50 BF. However, food prestations that were required from all able-bodied adult males were reduced to three kilograms of peas or beans and six kilograms of sorghum each year. One-third of the contribution was to be given to the chief of the province and two-thirds to the subchief. Only *ubureetwa* was retained in its nonmonetary form, since it was an expression of the Hutu's obedience to a notable. In 1945 an optional redemption for all Africans without distinction for traditional prestations in work was put in force.

PREUD'HOMME, ANDRE. Belgian colonial civil servant and Resident of Rwanda from 1958 to 1960, the most crucial years for the mandate. Preud'homme was born in Wasmes in 1915, entered colonial services as a territorial administrator in 1937, fought as a volunteer during World War II, and when released from active duty held various colonial posts in the mandate territory after 1947.

PRINCE REGENT HOSPITAL FOR AFRICANS. One of the major hospitals for Africans in the trusteeship, constructed at Bujumbura in 1951. The hospital had facilities for 470 patients, two operating rooms, an x-ray plant, consulting rooms for specialists, and a laboratory. The hospital had a staff of nine European doctors and one dentist, and two African medical assistants. According to United Nations reports, the hospital treated 42,091 in-patients in 1953, and 75,246 patients were treated at the dispensary and some 1,520 maternity cases. Attached to the hospital was a school for male nurses.

PROGRAMME NATIONAL D'ACTIONS SOCIALES (PNAS). Programme National d'Actions Sociales (PNAS) or the National Program of Social Actions was presented to the donors' roundtable meeting in Kigali in October 1991. The proposed program is actually the third part of a more ambitious development project that includes the Public Investment Program (PIP) and an environmental component. The latter would cost about $115 million and would fund such projects as family planning, land reclamation, reforestation, and other projects with an environmental emphasis or impact. PNAS would concentrate on orphans, the handicapped, the elderly, widows, and potentially active persons who currently have little or no land and/or are jobless and living in urban centers. PNAS would cost between $119 million and $165 million and would provide between $43–$55 million in food aid to the indigent and about $32 million for a vast public works program for unemployed or the underemployed.

PROTANAG. *See* SOCIETE COLONIALE DES PRODUITS TANNANTS ET AGRICOLES (PROTANAG).

PROTESTANT MISSION AT IREMERA. The mission was located in Nyanza and offered primary and professional education for Africans during the late 1920s and early 1930s.

PROVINCIAL AND URBAN COUNCILS. In Belgian Africa, these councils assisted the governor of the province and some urban district commissioners in the administration of urban areas. Most of the councils were primarily consultative, except that the urban council had the authority to decide expenditures and to contract loans. African councils also included Europeans. Members could be elected or appointed. In Rwanda, the provincial council was called the Council of the Vice Governor-General.

PROVINCIAL CHIEFS. An administrative rank used by both traditional and colonial administrations. These notables could command labor and prestations from those they administered, and as members of the Belgian civil service they received salaries.

PUBLIC INVESTMENT PROGRAM (PIP). The Public Investment Program (PIP) was presented to the donors' roundtable meeting in Kigali in October 1991. It is designed to stimulate economic growth and involves donor support for some 441 development projects worth 250 billion RF. The funding for PIP would come from grants (about 56 percent), loans (some 33 percent), and from the national budget (about 11 percent). The government noted that 63 percent of the external financing had already been secured. In terms of allocation, some 22 percent of the investments would go to agriculture; 50 percent to infrastructure, mostly roads and energy; and 19 percent to "human resources."

PYRETHRUM. The cultivation of pyrethrum was introduced in

northern Kivu and in Rwanda by Belgian settlers around 1936 with seedlings gathered from Kenya. They conducted some initial trials in the Rwankeri concession, at an altitude of 2,150 meters. In 1943 the Belgian colonial authorities laid out 200-hectare plots in the Ruhengeri district in order to increase the supply of insecticide needed to combat coffee parasites, such as *antestiopsis, acraeceacerata,* and caterpillars, which also attack other indigenous crops. Between 1972 and 1975, Rwanda produced 8 percent of the world's pyrethrum. In 1978, the national government established the Rwandan Pyrethrum Office with headquarters at Ruhengeri. The new office acquired the building and equipment belonging to the United Nations Development Program project for pyrethrum expansion and extraction. The new agency also acquired the state-owned installation and plantations in the pyrethrum regions of Kinigi and Bonde. Presently, the United States imports most of Rwanda's pyrethrum; however, the market is quite soft, since production of the extract continues to decline.

-Q-

QUEEN MOTHER. The *umugabekasi,* who was a powerful figure in her own right at the *umwami*'s court. While she lived at court, she generally had her own lands, herds of cattle, and clients. The queen mother could come from any one of the four royal clans, including the *abega,* the *abakono,* or the *abanyiginya.*

-R-

RADIODIFFUSION DE LA REPUBLIQUE RWANDAISE. The state-controlled radio station, which broadcasts daily pro-

programs in Kinyarwanda, Swahili, French, and English to 250,000 radio receivers, according to 1986 estimates.

RASSEMBLEMENT DEMOCRATIQUE RWANDAISE (RA-DER). A moderate Tutsi political party formed on September 14, 1959, by chief Prosper Bwanakweri. It favored a constitutional monarchy, and it proposed to elect chiefs, subchiefs, judges, and all council members by universal suffrage. The party called for the equal distribution of land and title to all farmers, the codification of native law, and equal opportunity for education according to aptitude and merit rather than by wealth. It sanctioned autonomy by 1964 and independence by 1968. The party attracted Europeans as well as young Tutsi évolués, many of whom worked for the Belgian administration. Its seat was at Kigali. Once independence was achieved and PARMEHUTU achieved hegemony, members of RADER were purged. The principal leaders were either executed or forced into exile by 1964.

RASSEMBLEMENT TRAVAILLISTE POUR LA DEMOCRA-TIE (RTD). Rassemblement Travailliste pour la Démocratie (RTD) or the Democratic Labor Union emerged in response to the democratic movement in the country during the 1990s. The RTD is a splinter from the Parti Socialiste Rwandais. Its representatives attended the December 18, 1991, meeting, called by President Habyarimana, to discuss the formation of a coalition government. While four of the seven opposition parties withdrew from the discussion the following day, because they opposed the appointment of a prime minister for the proposed transition government, the RTD remained but was later declared ineligible. It had not announced its program or its membership, which was essential for accreditation.

RATION ALLOWANCE. An *ordannance loi* in October 1932 established the conversion of rations in kind to a cash payment that varied from seven to eleven Belgian francs per week.

RECHENBERG, BARON ALBRECHT VON (1892–1953). The governor-general of German East Africa from 1906 to 1912. He had been appointed to implement the colonial policy of the right-wing pressure groups in East Africa and in the Reichstag, who believed that white settlement, rather than peasant agriculture, ought to be pursued. However, von Rechenberg supported African agriculture. He administered German East Africa with a minimum of expense and force. He believed that the Maji Maji rebellion could have been avoided if beneficial economic policies for Africans had been in place. Consequently, he strongly supported indirect rule and indigenous agricultural production.

REFUGEES. The majority of Banyarwandan refugees, whether Tutsi, Hutu, or Hima, have lived in Uganda for more than thirty years; many have had voting rights in that country since 1980. They have not, however, lost the label of "foreigner" in the eyes of the Ganda. President Obote and his party fanned the flames of this hostility when he came into power. An estimated 200,000 Rwandans have refugee status in Tanzania, most of them having fled in the face of ethnic conflict in the early 1970s.

The United Nations High Commission for Refugees has attempted to resolve the refugee problem from the outset. But politics, civil conflict, and famine have clouded the issue and muted serious discussions. For example, in October 1982, Ugandan officials at Ankole moved Banyarwanda refugee camps on the Uganda-Tanzania border. Local chiefs and members of the Uganda People's Congress youth wing burned refugees' homes and stole their cattle, forcing many to flee into Rwanda for safety. In the talks that followed, the Ugandan government refused to acknowledge the seriousness of the problem, claiming that it had been exaggerated by United Nations officials and that their own operation in October had been designed to ensure better administration in the regions concerned.

In 1983, the Rwandan government accepted about 36,000 refugees, but only 6,000 were classified as official residents. The rest had crossed the border in 1990. UNHCR provided $4 million to assist the refugees in Rwanda in 1983; however, since July 1986 the Rwandan government has pursued a rather inconsistent policy, and has consistently maintained that demographic pressures make it difficult to allow Rwandan refugees in neighboring Tanzania, Uganda, and Zaire to return home. By late November, 1983, the UNHCR announced that the government had repatriated about 30,000 refugees from Uganda.

On April 10, 1990, 400 illegal refugees were expelled from Tanzania. About 150 returned to their original home; most were victims of the recent famine in the southern part of the country. In mid-May, about 5,000 refugees returned to Rwanda from Tanzania. The government sought international aid to assist with their resettlement. An estimated 18,000 Rwandans crossed the border into Tanzania between January 1986 and March 1990. Since the October war, the refugee problem has been exacerbated. Not only has the Banyarwandan refugee in exile continued to be a problem, but some 350,000 farmers and villagers south of the war zone and RPF-held territory within northern Rwanda have also been displaced by the fighting. Just recently, the Rwandan government has been forced to acknowledge that the issue of the refugee is one of its major problems and that it must be addressed in any future settlement with the RPF. International relief agencies describe the refugee situation and their camp sites inside Rwanda as second only to Somalia in terms of urgency.

REGIDESO. The principal electrical company in the country. Hydroelectric power is produced primarily by the Mururu and Nataruka dams.

RÉGIE MINIÈRE. The state mining company was established in 1990 with the mission to exploit the tin mines abandoned by SOMIRWA in 1985. Régie Minière, however, has not done well. In 1993, it reported company losses of some 50 million RF ($5 million) anuually, and that it may have to declare bankruptcy unless new prospecting is undertaken. The company's situation is extremely serious, and tin mining generally is in crisis. Most mining is now undertaken by small, informal outfits, but they have limited resources and equipment and are unable to dig very deeply. Therefore, they are less profitable.

REGIES. State monopolies where territorial chiefdoms, in cooperation with colonial technical authorities, established certain kinds of economic activity. These joint ventures occurred in areas lacking private initiative, and they sought to make available to the country resources useful to its development, such as the manufacture of bricks and tiles, pyrethrum, milk, lime, timber, beer, transportation for various goods, and to provide the chiefdom with certain materials at cost. The government's technical service was provided free of charge.

RELEVE, LA. A monthly French periodical founded in 1976 and published by the Office Rwandais d'Information. The periodical is devoted to politics, economics, and culture, and has a circulation of about 1,000.

RELIGION. The country supports a variety of religions. About 42 percent practice traditional beliefs. Catholicism, introduced in the early 1900s, is practiced by 57 percent of the population, or 2,764,000 people. Protestantism arrived on the heels of Catholicism. The Anglicans, about 120,000, were the first to arrive. Other Protestants number about 250,000, including a substantial number of Seventh-Day Adventists. There is also a small Islamic community.

RENKIN, JULES-LAURENT-JEAN-LOUIS (1862–1934). Belgian judge, member of the Belgian Chamber of Representatives, minister of colonies, and minister of state. He was considered a great Catholic parliamentarian, debater, and statesman. Before becoming the minister of colonies in 1908, Renkin had already distinguished himself in the political arena. In 1896, he became the senate representative from Brussels and was one of the founding members of the Christian Democratic Party, which challenged the old right and implemented social reforms, such as proportional representation. After World War I, he took charge of the Ministry of Railways in order to reorganize the country's transportation network.

RESIDENCY/RESIDENT OF RUANDA. A Belgian administrative subunit used during the mandate and trusteeship. The Resident had his seat at Kigali. He was charged with the relations with the African kings and policy directives, and was assisted by European deputies and assistants who represented him in the various administrative districts, as well as by specialized officers required for technical programs. Much of the colonial policy was executed at this level of the Belgian administration.

REVUE PEDAGOGIQUE. A periodical published by the Ministry of Primary and Secondary Education.

RICE. A food crop introduced in 1940.

ROBUSTA. Small quantities of robusta coffee are produced and exported.

ROSE WORM (VER ROSE). A parasite that attacks the cotton plant.

RUANDA-URUNDI. The official name given to the mandate territory (and the trusteeship of the United Nations in 1945), which was conferred on Belgium by the Allied Powers and the League of Nations after World War I. These two regions were formerly part of German East Africa. The port city of Usumbura (now Bujumbura), located in Urundi, was the seat of Belgian administration for the mandate and trusteeship. In 1961, the territory became Rwanda-Burundi.

RUBONA. A research station of about 3,000 acres that was created in 1927 and located at an altitude of 1,700 to 2,000 meters, between Nyanza and Butare. Some 750 acres have been placed under cultivation. Researchers are concerned with production and improvement of food crops and African cattle. The station also distributes drought-resistant hickory, giant maize, and sweet potato cuttings, and conducts research on African food crops, such as manioc and sweet potatoes, which were introduced into temperate regions of the country. Soil research is also conducted by the station.

RUDAHIGWA, CHARLES-LEON-PIERRE (MUTARA III, 1911–1959), UMWAMI OF RWANDA. The second of the three *umwami,* or kings, to rule the country during the colonial period. Rudahigwa reigned from 1931 to 1959. He was about twenty when he succeeded his father, Musinga, in 1931. He was Musinga's oldest son and the administration's candidate because he was, according to Father Classe and officials in the administration, "intelligent, educated, pro-European, and Catholic." Rudahigwa died mysteriously on July 25, 1959 in Bujumbura following an antibiotic injection. His death became part of the mythology associated with the movement for independence in the country. The Tutsi, who were members of the right wing, believed that he had been killed by the Belgians with Hutu complicity because he stood in the way of change. Progressive Hutu believed that Rudahigwa was killed by the Tutsi because he was developing progressive views and had moderated his stance in favor of sharing and extending the power base of society. Rudahigwa presided over the end of an era and sought to preserve tradition within the shadow of Belgian colonialism.

RUGANZU BWIMBA, UMWAMI OF RWANDA. *See* BWIMBA, RUGANZU.

RUGANZU NDOORI, UMWAMI OF RWANDA. *See* NDOORI, RUGANZU.

RUGO. Huts within enclosures (*ingo*) dispersed over the hills and situated in the middle of their fields in which the great Tutsi notables and most Banyarwanda live. One enters the enclosure through a narrow door or *umuryongo*. The enclosure often contains several huts, particularly if the owner is polygamous (spouses do not cohabit). Each of the huts, in the shape of a beehive and made of reeds and grass, is usually situated in a circular enclosure intersecting and communicating with the other enclosures in the compound. The enclosure contains granaries and a small hut devoted to the ancestral spirits. The circular fence is made of ficus hedges, and is at least six feet high. The open area can be used as a kraal for livestock, which is brought in at night, and the entrance way is blocked by trees and thorny branches.

In traditional times, each *rugo* was a highly independent social unit with little or no inclination to trespass on a neighboring unit. This kind of settlement did little to promote progress, change, or a sense of community. The current practice is to construct homes of brick.

RUGWE, CYILIMA, UMWAMI OF RWANDA. Cyilima reigned from 1482 to 1506 and was one of the earlier warrior kings. He occupied Kigali, conquered or assimilated the provinces of Buliza, Bumbogo, and Rukoma, and incorporated the *abiiru* into the royal hierarchy.

RUHENGERI. Presently one of the nine prefectures, or administrative units, of the country, as well as a principal town. It has an area of 1,762 square kilometers and a population (according to 1978 census) of 531,927, of which 16,025 live in the town of Ruhengeri. Considered as a marginal coffee- and tea-producing region, it functioned during the colonial period as an Asian commercial center and migrant transit point toward the Belgian Congo and northern Uganda. During the 1930s, the principal export of the territory was food, with most of it going to the Belgian Congo. Large quantities of food were also purchased by local merchants and by mining enterprises in Kigali.

RUJUGIRA, CYIRIMA, UMWAMI OF RWANDA. One of the five reformer-kings, he reigned from 1744 to 1768. His most important innovation was the creation of an army adminis- tration to control the frontier areas of Burundi, Gisaka, Ndorwa, and Bushi. Rujugira was responsible for expanding the empire southward to the Akanyaru River, which is the country's present boundary. He also commenced expansion to the northern, eastern, and western regions of the country. He frequently moved the royal capital as he attempted to ex- pand his hegemony over Tutsi colonizers, who were pushed northwest into Bugoyi, Bukonya, Budaha, and Rwankeri. The new system of army administration controlled areas in the northeast and in the southwest. He also instituted the practice of incorporating powerful lineages into the Court.

RUKEBA, FRANCOIS. Rwandan politician, refugee, and mem- ber of the *inyenzi,* or cockroaches. Rukeba was Kigali's na- tional representative to UNAR in 1961. He later became a po- litical refugee and the principal director of the *inyenzi* terrorists who invaded Rwanda in 1961 and again in 1962 and 1963.

RUSINGIZANDEKWE, OTTO. Rwandan teacher, civil servant, and politician. Rusingizandekwe was born in Kigarama, Ruhengeri. He was a teacher from 1937 to 1959, when he became a customs agent. In 1960, he became an interim chief and later in the year a member of the Conseil Provisoire of MDR/PARMEHUTU. Additional government offices included administrative secretary and minister in the Ministry of Foreign Relations, Ruhengeri's national representative in 1961, minister of public works and equipment in 1962, and minister of posts, telecommunications, and transports from 1965 to 1968.

RUTANGO. A region in Kigali and the administrative seat in Africa for SOMUKI, a cassiterite mining company.

RUTARINDWA, MIBAMBWE, UMWAMI OF RWANDA. Rutarindwa reigned from 1895 to 1896. He was the son of and successor to Kigeri Rwabugiri. Rutarindwa's reign was challenged by supporters of his half brother, Musinga, causing a civil war, and he was assassinated at Rucunshu.

RUTSINDINTWARANE, JEAN-NEP. Rwandan politician and president of UNAR, one of the early opposition parties, in 1959. He was also a member of the Conseil Spécial Provisoire in 1960. He was executed at Ruhengeri in 1963 because of his position in the opposition party and in retaliation for the attack by the *inyenzi*.

RUYANGE, NDAHIRO, UMWAMI OF RWANDA. Ndahiro was the first in chronological listing of the kings of Rwanda. His reign ended with his death in 1386, but little is known about his rule other than that he was a warrior-herdsman, credited with founding the kingdom. He also established his suzerainty over the Tutsi kinship groups on the central plateau.

RUZIZI II HYDROELECTRIC POWER STATION. A major donor project begun in 1981 on the Rwanda-Zaire border. The joint venture is a 40-million-watt hydroelectric power plant on the Ruzizi River, which forms their mutual frontier and links lakes Kivu and Tanganyika. It is intended to supply power to Burundi as well. Major funding sources include the European Economic Community, the African Development Bank, the OPEC Fund, the World Bank, and the French CCCE. The project will cost some 66 million ECU.

RWAAKA, KAREMEERA, UMWAMI OF RWANDA. Karemeera reigned from 1720 to 1744. It is reported that he abdicated because he suffered from *pian* (yaws), considered a shameful disease, in favor of Rujugira.

RWABUGIRI, KIGERI IV, UMWAMI OF RWANDA. Rwabugiri reigned from 1860 to 1895, during the last phase of expansion before the arrival of European colonialism, and he is considered the last of the great reformers. He is also referred to as the great warrior king, because he reorganized the army to provide conscripts for continuous warfare and expanded the kingdom to incorporate the previously independent Hutu states in the western region and territories in the east as well. He expanded the system of clientship to correspond with territorial acquisitions. He was also responsible for implementing new administrative institutions which altered the nature of the central court and enabled it to penetrate into the outlying areas from the central core of the kingdom. He destroyed the principle of hereditary succession and reduced the number of districts to twenty-one. Before his death, he had became an absolute monarch. He was the father of Musinga.

During his reign, he mounted military expeditions to Mpororo, Ijwi, Ndorwa, Mutara, and even into Burundi, as well as in the vicinity of Lake Edward, Butembo, Kigeai, Bunyabungo, Bushubi, and Nkore. He used terror and skillful manipulation of rivals to bring those notables who opposed him to their knees. Under his reign Tutsi notables expanded prestations to include *ubureetwa,* which conferred the right to requisition labor from cultivators under their authority. Rwabugiri also scattered *ibikingi* throughout the holdings of the more powerful notables to weaken their strength and to keep track of local developments. Rwabugiri received the first European explorer to visit the country, in 1894, and when he died his kingdom was engulfed in civil war between two of his sons—Mibambwe IV Rutarindwa and Yuhi V Musinga. The former was killed, and the latter reigned during the German and Belgian phases of Rwanda's colonial history.

RWANDA. A country in East Africa and part of the Great Rift Valley geological formation. It is bordered by the Akanyaru River and Burundi in the south, Tanzania in the east, Uganda in the north, and Lake Kivu and Zaire in the west. Its total area is 10,169 square miles, about the size of New Jersey. Its topography varies. The central region contains a plateau, precipitous slopes, and mountains with an average elevation of 7,500 feet. In the north, mountains, which separate the Nile Basin from the Congo Basin to the southwest, slope sharply down to Lake Kivu. This is a region of volcanoes, two of which are still active and are more than 14,000 feet high. East of the mountains the land declines gradually, dropping to about 4,500 feet in the Kagera Plains.

The country has three major rivers: the Kagera, which is the southernmost source of the Nile; the Nyawarongo, which is the torrential northern branch of the Kagera; and the Akanyaru, along a section of the border shared with Burundi.

The climate is of the tropical highland variety. The daily temperature range may exceed twenty-five° C while the annual range is about five° C. The altitude of the central plateau makes the climate pleasantly cool. The exceptions to this are the drier tropical lowlands in the Kagera River area and the Congo-Nile dividing range, where the nights are cold and the temperature frequently falls to the freezing point.

The amount of rainfall is quite irregular, but occurs from October to December and March through May. There are two dry seasons: the short season, in January and February; and the long season, lasting from June through September. Except for a remnant band of tropical forest along the western edge, Rwanda is savanna with some low, scrubby trees in the east. The main forest wedges are north and south of Lake Kivu; however, the country has the distinction of being the most eroded and deforested land in tropical Africa.

Permanent colonial occupation of Rwanda did not begin until 1899 with the creation of a military station at Bujumbura. In 1908, a German Resident was established at Kigali; German occupation was quite peaceful and lasted from 1908 to World War I. Rwanda became a Belgian mandated colony in 1916; until 1962 it was part of the Belgian mandate of Ruanda-Urundi. The territory was under the direction of the governor-general of the Belgian Congo, and was directed and managed by a vice governor-general who resided in Bujumbura, the capital. Rwanda was administered by a Resident, who had his own staff, as well as an assistant Resident. The country was divided into eight territories, administered by territorial administrators and staff and Tutsi notables.

The Rwandan economy is very weak, and depends heavily on foreign aid.

RWANDA-BURUNDI CONFLICT (1988). A renewal of ethnic tensions between Hutu and Tutsi within Burundi, and particularly in the northern provinces of Ngozi and Kirundo in August, led to the flight of an estimated 38,000 Hutu refugees into Rwanda. It was reported that casualties inside Burundi numbered more than 5,000. According to official reports, the incident began when Tutsi soldiers killed two Hutu in a private dispute at Ntega. The killings prompted a riot in which several hundred Tutsi were killed. A nationwide curfew followed and was not lifted until October 31.

RWANDA INDUSTRIAL PRODUCE BUREAU. The state bureau that replaced the joint Rwanda and Burundi Coffee Bureau in 1965. The agency organized and controlled agricultural exports, particularly coffee, and managed the Coffee Stabilization Fund, which supported the price paid to producers. The agency encouraged overall development of the agricultural sector through advice and technical training, and it purchased transport equipment and built storage facilities for the coffee crop.

RWANDA RUSHYA. The *Rwanda Rushya* is a new newspaper that is frequently critical of the government, and during the period of transition to democracy, beginning in 1991, the paper has become even more so. *Rwanda Rushya* accused the government of limiting freedom of expression and with interfering with the debates between the new political parties created during the year, and their political campaigns. The newspaper also reported MDR's charge that its members have been harassed by "delinquents" or the party youth wings connected with the government and MRND. According to its report, when MDR attempted to campaign in Ruhengeri in October 1991, party members were attacked. Its editor, Andre Kameya, according to RPF sources has received death threats from the army.

RWANDA-UGANDA BORDER CONFLICT (1976). A border dispute between Uganda and Kenya in April inadvertently caused the Rwandan economy to come to a standstill. The conflict began when Ugandan President Idi Amin imposed a blockade in a dispute with neighboring Kenya. Amin's ban on heavy vehicles from neighboring countries using Uganda's roads in 1977 added to rising petroleum prices, led to further hardship, and strengthened the Rwandan government's determination to find alternative outlets Consequently, coffee and other essential produce destined for the international market had to be flown out of the country by the national airline or by air cargo service.

RWANDA-UGANDA BORDER CONFLICT (1979). Because of the civil war and intense fighting within Uganda, the border with Rwanda was closed from February to May. Rwandan trade was again severely disrupted, and stockpiles of coffee and tea rose to unprecedented levels. There were serious shortages of petroleum and cement. Road transport on routes through Uganda was further disrupted by civil disorders in 1984 and 1985. In 1986, however, the governments of Rwanda and Uganda were able to come to an agreement to assure Rwanda's vital trade links through Uganda. In April 1986, a general cooperation agreement, covering security, trade, industry, transport, and communications, was concluded between the two countries. In August, the two countries agreed that trade was to be conducted on the basis of specific contracts between the two countries by individuals empowered to carry out specific activities.

RWANDA-UGANDA BORDER CONFLICT (1982). In October Rwanda closed its border with Uganda after an influx of 45,000 refugees, most of whom were Rwandan exiles fleeing Ugandan persecution. An additional 32,000 refugees collected in camps on the Ugandan side of the border. In March 1983 Rwanda agreed to resettle more than 30,000 refugees, but Ugandan persecution of ethnic Rwandans continued, and in December 1983 thousands crossed into Tanzania. In November 1985 it was reported that 30,000 ethnic Rwandan refugees had been repatriated to Uganda.

RWANDA-UGANDA COMMISSIONS. Established in the 1970s and 1980s to settle the Banyarwanda refugee problem.

RWANDAN-BELGIAN TECHNICAL AID AGREEMENT

(1966). The 1966 agreement was actually a renewal, extending the total Belgian aid to 180 million BF. The projects to be financed included agriculture and stockbreeding projects, the installation of a system of radio controls at Kigali airport, the construction of houses for civil servants, tourist facilities, and hospitals, as well as canceled hiring of 222 technical assistants, including 105 teachers and 16 agricultural experts.

RWANDAN-WEST GERMAN TECHNICAL AID AGREEMENT (1965). West Germany granted 5 million DM in the form of capital equipment and 2.8 million DM in the form of technical assistance.

RWANDESE ALLIANCE FOR NATIONAL UNITY. *See* RWANDESE PATRIOTIC FRONT.

RWANDESE PATRIOTIC FRONT (RPF). The Rwandan Patriotic Front (RPF) is a militant group of Rwandan refugees, primarily of Tutsi origin, living in Uganda. The RPF invaded Rwanda for Uganda on October 1, 1990. Initially, the front emerged from the Rwandese Alliance for National Unity in 1979 and operated clandestinely until 1983. In 1986, it began to operate openly and eventually changed its name to the RPF. Its "eight-point program" calls for national unity, democracy, the building of a self-sustaining economy, an end to misuse of public office, the establishment of social services, democratization of the security forces, a progressive foreign policy, and an end to "the system which generates refugees," which could be interpreted as the deposition of the Habyarimana regime in Rwanda and, at least, the sharing of power with any subsequent government that might emerge. It has a 26-member executive committee, composed of 11 Tutsi and 15 Hutu. Still, it is not a broadly based movement. Most of its participants are Tutsi refugees.

After its initial thrust into Rwanda, the RPF decided to abandon guerrilla warfare and to hold its ground. It has inflicted heavy losses on the Zairian troops sent to assist the Rwandan government, but the government in taking the offensive has inflicted heavy casualties at Lyabega on October 23. Majors Bayingana and Bunyenyezi were killed, along with many of their forces.

RWANDESE REFUGEES WELFARE FOUNDATION. The foundation was organized in 1979 in Uganda.

RWANDEX. A state agency that operated three depulping mills in the country in the 1970s to process coffee: at Kigali, Gisenyi (which treats coffee from the Lake Kivu region), and Ruhengeri.

RWAZA. A Catholic mission station established in 1903 in the northern province of Mulera. This particular station became significant in the 1920s for tobacco production. The mission opened a factory which made cigars sold throughout Rwanda. The production altered the standard of living of those Hutu farmers who were able to graft tobacco cultivation to their more traditional food-crop production. The White Fathers also introduced a flour mill and furniture workshop at the mission station, and they issued coffee plants to their catechists, who had begun growing cash crops on their outstation grounds.

RWIGYEMA, FRED. Fred Rwigyema was a Banyarwandan refugee, who became the first president of the Rwandan Patriotic Front (RPF) in 1989. Rwigyema was taken to Uganda from Rwanda as an infant during the Hutu uprising when some 130,000 Tutsi were expelled between 1959 and 1963. He fought against Idi Amin, Obote, and Okello and various other rebel groups after the National

Revolutionary Army brought Yoweri Museveni to power in Uganda in 1986. In Museveni's government he became deputy army commander and deputy minister of defense. He held the rank of major general in the Rwandan Patriotic Front. He led the October 1, 1990 invasion of Rwanda and may have been killed in battle or assassinated in a major internal power struggle with Major Peter Bayingana over tactics.

For those who accept the assassination theory it is rumored that Major Bayingana was in favor of an all-out push to Kigali, while Major General Rwigyema favored guerrilla warfare, to include harassing convoys and politicizing the peasantry. Allegedly, the two men quarrelled. There was a struggle and the major general was shot. He died instantly. Two weeks later, Major Peter Bayingana was killed in ambush by one of Rwigyema's henchmen or *kadogo*.

RWISIBO, JEAN BAPTISTE. Rwandan politician and member of Grégoire Kayibanda's administration and a very vocal critic of the traditional oligarchy. He served as minister of the interior and civil service in 1961. Rwisibo was born in Remera, Gitarama, in 1928. He attended the Petit Séminaire at Kabgayi and served in the Belgian administration from 1949 to 1959. In 1960, he became a member of the provisional council of MDR within PARMEHUTU. Besides his position in the interior ministry, he was minister of national education from 1961 to 1965 and the legislative representative for Gitarama from 1965 to 1969.

RWOGERA, MUTARA, UMWAMI OF RWANDA. Rwogera reigned from 1830 to 1860. He was concerned with centralizing his authority, particularly where new territorial acquisitions in the east were concerned. Consequently, *ubuhake* become regularized.

RYCKMANS (RIJCKMANS), PIERRE (1891–1959). A Belgian
colonial civil servant and the first civilian Resident of
Burundi, in 1924. He was governor-general of the Belgian
Congo from 1934 to 1946. He was also the general secretary
of the Colonial Union, professor at the Université Coloniale
de Belgique, and served as the president of UNAKI until his
nomination as governor-general of the Belgian Congo on
September 14, 1934. In 1950, he was appointed to the
Belgian Atomic Energy Commission.

Ryckmans was the principal apologist for the official policy of paternalism and a civilizing mission in Belgian
Africa. He supported African cultivation and the development of infrastructure to facilitate international trade. For
many years he pressured the colonial government at
Brussels to grant subsidies in support of African agricultural
development. With respect to European colonization, he believed that it could be beneficial provided it was well directed and thought out, and control was exercised from the
capital to protect the Africans' interests. His most controversial action was his support for African coffee cultivation,
which was opposed by European coffee planters in Belgian
Africa.

Ryckmans believed that a balance had to be maintained
between the interests of Africans and those of European settlers and entrepreneurs, but he also believed that Africans
had to be transformed into Europeans. He called for an
African policy that was flexible and patient, because he
thought that Africans would not be civilized in a day or a
generation. He saw the Belgian's role as that of a patient
gardener and not as a social engineer. Europeans had to become acquainted with African institutions; in economic affairs, Africans would serve as producers, while the
Europeans would provide the know-how and capital, princi-
pally in the industrial areas of Belgian Africa. Ryckmans
was the author of several books in which his basic colonial

philosophy is argued, including *Dominer pour servir* (1931) and *Barbara* (1947).

-S-

SAKANIA-ELIZABETHVILLE-ALBERTVILLE ROUTE. An important trade route during World War II, particularly for the exportation of coffee from Rwanda.

SAMEMBE, UMWAMI OF RWANDA. Samembe reigned from 1410 to 1434.

SAMUKONDO, NSORO, UMWAMI OF RWANDA. Samukondo reigned from 1434 to 1458.

SANDRART, GEORGES (1899–1951). An amateur ethnographer who in 1924 conducted research on the Tutsi, and helped combat the famine of 1929, which devastated eastern Rwanda. Sandrart was assistant Resident in 1933, and in 1937 he became professor of the *section supérieure* at the Group Scolaire, where he taught until 1940. He then served briefly as assistant Resident in Rwanda until March 1941, when he was appointed the Resident of Urundi at Kitega.

In 1944, he was asked by vice governor-general Jungers to leave his post in Urundi and come to Rwanda to coordinate the famine-relief effort. He was Resident of Rwanda in 1947 until he returned to Belgium in 1951. In Belgium, he worked as an assistant to Bagage at the Centre d'Information et de Documentation du Congo Belge et du Ruanda (CID) until his death several months later. In all, he had spent twenty-seven years in Rwanda and Burundi.

SAPHIRS DU RWANDA (SAPHDA). SAPHDA is a new company which prospects for sapphires. It was established in 1992.

SAVE. Catholic mission station established in 1900, located about twenty kilometers from Nyanza, where the king held Court and maintained a residence. *See also* ISSAVI.

SAVONNERIE DE KICUKIRO (SAKIRWA). A private company that manufactures soaps and washing powder.

SCHELE, F. R. VON. Governor of German East Africa from 1893 to 1895.

SCHNEE, DR. HEINRICH. The last governor of German East Africa, from 1912 to 1918. He pursued a policy of economic development and indirect administration.

SCHUMACHER, PETER. A German citizen and member of the Société des Missionaires d'Afrique, or White Fathers, who was born in the Rhineland. Father Schumacher arrived in Rwanda in 1907, where he remained for about twenty years working at various mission posts, such as Kabgayi, Save, and Nyundo. In 1928, he was permitted to devote all of his time to ethnographic studies, and at the age of sixty, obtained a doctorate from the University of Vienna. He returned to Rwanda after World War II to do linguistic work, and afterward retired to the home of the White Fathers at Gits, in East Flanders, where he died on August 26, 1957. He was known for his ethnographic studies of the Twa of the Kivu region, whom he identified as being true pygmies rather than a pygmoid variety.

SCIENTIFIC RESEARCH FUND. Designed to stimulate economic development in Belgian Africa.

SEBUNUNGULI, MONSIGNOR ADONIA. Rwandan Anglican bishop, born in Gahini, Kibungo, in 1922. He was ordained as a priest in 1955 and served in various parishes. He was elected assistant bishop in June 1965 and in the following year became the Anglican bishop of the new diocese of Rwanda on March 25, 1966.

SEKAMONYO, ABBE RAPHAEL. A Rwandan priest, ordained in 1942, the author of several pamphlets on Christian spirituality in Kinyarwanda. In 1956, he established the Famille Religieuse des Soeurs (or *abizeramariya* in Kinyarwanda), which consisted of sixty-seven teachers, twenty-seven novices, and about thirty postulates. They are divided into twelve communities, seven of which are located in the diocese of Butare, two in the archdiocese of Kabgayi, two in the archdiocese of Nyundo, and one in the archdiocese of Kibungo. The association's objective is to minister to needs of the sick, the needy, the homeless, the handicapped, the old, and distressed travelers.

SEMARASO. Or "Father of Blood." Leader of a revolt in late 1927 and early 1928 among the Hutu of Rukiga and Ndorwa against Belgian rule and Tutsi hegemony in the northern region of the country. The Hutu never knew his real name or his place of origin. They believed that he had come from the British territory to the north. In March 1928, he took a thousand or more followers and attacked several notables whom the Hutu had accused of abusing them. The Belgians and Tutsi mounted an offensive against him, but were unable to capture him before he escaped across the border into Uganda. He is remembered because he and his followers killed a dozen Tutsi notables, burned some forty or more residences, and stole a hundred cattle. In retaliation, the Tutsi killed several dozen people, jailed thirty or more, and destroyed the homes and harvests of a thousand Hutu. The rebellion was significant because it surprised the Belgians and resulted in military occupation of the region for three and a half years.

SEMUGESHI, MUTARA, UMWAMI OF RWANDA. Semugeshi reigned from 1624 to 1648 and is considered one of five reformer-kings. According to tradition, an *umwami* was never supposed to rule alone; his mother had to be enthroned with him. The *umwami* came from the *abanyiginya* lineage, which was responsible for the founding of the kingdom, and his mother came from another kinship group. Since each tended to support the interests of his or her paternal kin, the arrangement contained potential conflict between the two rulers. So Mutara Semugeshi decreed that the privilege of providing the queen mother would alternate among the four strongest royal kinship groups, including the *abega* and the *abakono*. He reformed the *abiiru* as well, by increasing their numbers and giving them authority to interpret the king's last will and testament or to name the king's successor. He decreed that the selection of royal names would follow a fixed cycle beginning with Mutara, followed by Kigeri, Mibambwe, and Yuhi. Names such as Nsoro, Ndahiro, and Ruganzu were abolished. Semugeshi also conquered Busanza, Bufundu, and Bungwe in Astrida territory.

SENTABYO, MIBAMBWE, UMWAMI OF RWANDA. Sentabyo reigned from 1792 to 1797. His short rule was plagued by calamity. First, when he assumed the throne he was challenged by his half brother, and then in 1797 he contracted smallpox and died. Before his death, however, he annexed the northern half of Bugesera.

SENTAMA, GODEFROID. Rwandan politician and member of the Committee of Nine. He was also national representative to MDR/PARMEHUTU from 1961 to 1969.

SERVICE DE L'AGRICULTURE. The Agricultural Service functioned in Rwanda as early as 1929. Its monitors visited African farmers to instruct them in the care of coffee plants. During the 1930s, it introduced the cultivation of pyrethrum in the higher altitudes in order to combat outbreaks of antestia, lygus, and volumnus, the last two of which entered Kivu territory in 1937. It was also charged with maintaining quality control for export crops, particularly coffee.

Much of its organizational structure was formed by 1938. It included departments devoted to agriculture, colonization, forestry, hunting, and fishing, as well as the department of *zootechnie* and epizootic diseases. A similar organizational structure existed at the provincial level. The *chef de province* had at his disposal agronomical engineers, veterinarians, and other specialists who supervised research, study, and publicity, as well as technical assistance to European and African operations.

The service was attached to the governor-general of Belgian Africa, was responsible for research and quality control, and was charged with providing technical service to the governor-general in matters of agronomy, colonization, forestry, hunting, and fishing, and conducted study missions, inspections, and control.

SERVICE DES AFFAIRES INDIGENES DE LA MAIN-D'OEUVRE (AIMO). AIMO, an agency within the Belgian administrative apparatus, was concerned with labor policy, social affairs, and the creation and operation of cooperatives in the African sector.

SERVIR. A bimonthly periodical published by the Frères de la Charité de Gand at the Groupe Scolaire from 1940 to 1966, and as a quarterly from 1966 to 1976. The review was directed primarily at students and graduates of the Groupe Scolaire, and during the colonial period it was referred to as *indatwa*. It contained articles on general subjects from a Christian perspective, as well as some articles about Rwanda.

SEVENTH-DAY ADVENTISTS. The Adventists established themselves at Gitwe in 1919, and by 1929 they had forty-seven schools with three European instructors and forty-seven monitors. Their school at Gitwe offered primary and professional education to approximately four hundred students of both sexes in a seven-year program of study. Monitors were also trained at the school.

In 1986, some members of the Adventists were arrested along with the *Abantu B'Mana* (Men of God) and the *Abarokore* (God's Elect) for refusing to perform community service, *umuganda*, and for failure to show respect for the national flag and to sing the national anthem. The trial took place in October at the state security court in Kigali, and the members of the three religious groups were given sentences ranging from twelve to fifteen years in prison. In April 1990, members of the Adventists received suspended prison sentences of two years for organizing unauthorized meetings.

SHANGUGU (formerly KAMEMBE; now CHANGUGU). A territory located near Costermansville and other European settlements which, during the 1930s, attracted over 30 percent of the territory's African labor force for European enterprises. The territory contained a thriving cattle market, and buyers came from central Rwanda and the Kivu to purchase cows. Cotton production prospered in the lower plains to the south (Bugarama), and the regions of higher altitude supported coffee cultivation. There was some mining activity at Nyongwe, which employed about a thousand African workers.

SHEBUJA. In the client-patron relationship, the *shebuja* was the lender with respect to cattle, and the prestationer was the *mugaragu*. In return for protection, the *shebuja* received prestations from his *mugaragu*, which included plowing fields for the lord, rebuilding and repairing his hut, and traveling with him on journeys. Failure by the *mugarugu* to fulfill his obligations would cause the *shebuja* to take his cattle back. The *shebuja* was also an administrative chief.

SHEEP. Presently an important source of income, but traditionally having no economic value. Sheepskin was appreciated for its softness and sold for a substantial sum, being used mostly as slings in which babies were carried.

SIBOMANA, MONSIGNOR JOSEPH. A Hutu Catholic priest and member of the Committee of Nine. Sibomana was born in Save, Butare, in 1915. He was ordained in 1940, served as vicar-general at Kabgayi in 1951 and father superior of the Petit Séminaire of Kabgayi in 1960. Following his consecration on December 3, 1961, he was appointed bishop of Ruhengeri on August 21, and the bishop of Kibungo in 1968.

SIMON, MAURICE (1892–1960). Assistant district commissioner in 1932 and 1933, assistant Resident and then Resident of Rwanda from 1933 to 1940. From 1940 to 1944, he was the assistant to Vice Governor-General Jungers. He was provincial commissioner in 1945 and in 1947.

SINDIKUBWABO, THEODORE. Rwandan politician and medical doctor. Sindikubwabo was born in Zivu, Butare. Before becoming a member of the Conseil Provisoire of APROSOMA in October 1960, he worked as a medical assistant in Butare. In 1961, he became the minister of technical affairs and later was minister of public works and mechanization from 1961 to 1962. He returned to his medical studies at the National University of Rwanda the following year and began to practice medicine in 1969. He became minister of public health in 1972.

SIRWA. A manufacturing company that produces paints and tiles.

SISAL. A commercial crop produced primarily by Europeans.

SLADDEN, GEORGES E. Belgian colonial agronomical engineer and director of the Agriculture Service in the 1950s.

SOCIETE ANONYME AGENCE BELGE DE L'EST AFRI-CAIN. A private Belgian transport company that operated concessions at Kigoma and Dar es Salaam.

SOCIETE ANONYME BELGE D'EXPLOITATION DE LA NAVIGATION AERIENNE (SABENA). Private Belgian air carrier, subsidized by the State as early as 1934. The company monopolized air transport of passengers and freight in Belgian Africa.

SOCIETE AUXILIAIRE AGRICOLE DU KIVU (SAAK). A private Belgian agricultural society in Rwanda during the 1930s. It had a branch in Kakondo.

SOCIETE BELGE DES MISSIONS PROTESTANTES. In 1926, the Belgian Protestant Missionary Society had three mission stations in the mandate territory: Kirinda, Lubengera, and Iremera. It competed with the Seventh-Day Adventists, the Church Missionary Society, and the Danish Baptist Mission, as well as with various Catholic orders.

SOCIETE CIM. *See* COMPAGNIE COMMERCIALE INDUS-TRIELLE ET MINIERE (SOCIETE CIM).

SOCIETE COLONIALE DES PRODUITS TANNANTS ET AGRICOLES (PROTANAG). A private company from Brussels established and managed by Crédit Agricole d'Afrique in 1927, with a branch office in Shangugu (Changugu). The society's first concession was some 7,000 hectares granted in 1927 for growing tannin-producing trees. The society also planted coffee trees and employed 1,500 African workers, including between 60 to 100 day laborers. In 1931, the society began producing shade trees and fertilizer, as well as tea production. It also modified its program to include a major concentration on coffee production. By 1933, the society had cultivated about 600 hectares in coffee, and it employed about 500 African workers.

PROTANAG allocated work by the piecework method, or by the type of job, and African workers were paid at a specific rate on a daily basis for ground clearing, woodcutting, surveying, planting, and general labor.

SOCIETE COMMERCIALE FINANCIERE ET AGRICOLE DU RUANDA (SOCOFINA). A Belgian company with home offices in Brussels and African offices in Kigali and in the Belgian Congo during the 1920s and 1930s. SOCOFINA had a warehouse at Butare with a large selection of food, wines and liqueurs, toilet objects, carpentry tools, sewing machines, and hardware. They also sold lion-skin, blankets, and milking soap (*savon de traite*) to Africans.

SOCIETE DE CREDIT AU COLONAT ET A L'INDUSTRIE. A lending agency established to promote in Belgian Africa (by way of long- and short-term credits) the establishment, improvement, transformation, and operation of agricultural, mining, handicraft, commercial, industrial, and professional undertakings of small and average size, whether managed by individuals or associations. Interest rates varied according to the kind of request—whether it was from a new or an established settler. Loans had to be repaid within five years; however, in 1955 the United Nations Trusteeship Council noted that the society had made fifteen loans to non-African settlers, amounting to 13.4 million BF, and that the society had planned to extend its credit facilities to Africans.

SOCIETE DES MINES D'ETAIN DU RUANDA-URUNDI (MINETAIN). A private Belgian mining company created in Brussels in 1930. Its African branch was located in Kigali, and the company had exclusive prospecting rights for ninety years over 2.1 million hectares and mining rights over 43,000 hectares. It mined cassiterite in Kisenyi and gold in Riumba, Astrida, and Muhinga. The company found major cassiterite and gold deposits in 1933, when MINETAIN had a staff of 12 Europeans and 500 African workers. By

1935, Africans employed with the company numbered 4,050, with 37 percent employed permanently.

SOCIETE DES MINES DU RWANDA (SOMIRWA). A government-controlled Rwandan-Belgian company that has mined cassiterite since its creation in 1873. When it was established, it had capital assets of 898 million RF. The company also mined tantalite, tungsten, and beryl, and it smelted its own tin. The Rwandan government held a 49 percent share, and GEOMINES, a Belgian company, held 51 percent interest. It employed between eight thousand and nine thousand people, and it dealt with tens of thousands of individuals and small cooperatives around the country who produced and sent in their ore. About 28 percent of the cassiterite produced came from these contributors, most of whom are located in Gatumba and Rutsiro. In 1986 the company went into bankruptcy after the insolvency of its major Belgian shareholder. Its insolvency coincided with the collapse of the world tin market, but its problems began in 1983 when it opened its own tin foundry. The construction proved an immense drain on company liquidity, and there were the added costs of transporting the tin to Mombasa and the accumulation of huge tin stocks. The minister of industry, mining, and artisan production considered forming cooperatives under the umbrella of a national Coopérative de Promotion de l'Industrie Minérale Artisanale (COPIMAR) in lieu of attempting to find fresh capital for the defunct company.

SOCIETE DES MISSIONNAIRES D'AFRIQUE (THE ORDER OF THE WHITE FATHERS). The order was founded in 1874 by the French cardinal Lavigerie to work exclusively in Africa. The cardinal believed that Christianity would be widely accepted in a country only when it was adopted by the chiefs and the ruling classes. Lavigerie instructed his missionaries to give the ruling class as much latitude as possible with respect to church teachings and with such issues as monogamy.

The society ventured into Rwanda and Burundi as early as 1879. Its initial efforts were slow and painful. In 1881, a group of White Fathers were massacred by a minor chief, but the order was able to establish its first mission in 1900. By 1904 they were considered an alternative power source in the politics of the kingdom. The missionaries were often asked to mediate conflicts and settlement disputes with contending groups in the country. They also initiated innovations in agriculture. They were the first to introduce and experiment in their mission stations with wheat, barley, potatoes, rye, to plant vegetables, coffee, eucalyptus, and to raise pigs. All of these innovations were later incorporated into the African productive sector during the colonial period. The society also fought to abolish the slave trade and to establish mission schools at all of their stations to teach reading, writing, arithmetic, and catechism.

SOCIETE DES PLANTATIONS DU TANGANYIKA (PLA-TANGA). A commercial society that began coffee cultivation in Rwanda in 1929. It established nurseries and organized an export agency to oversee the sorting and classification of coffee. It also acquired a coffee-treatment mill. The costs for services were shared by those with an interest in the enterprises. By 1931, the society had a large number of palm tree nurseries and was planning to work in collaboration with the Banyarwanda in palm oil production.

SOCIETE D'ETUDES ET DE PLANTATIONS AU RUANDA-URUNDI. A private commercial company located in Kigali. It had coffee nurseries, and it distributed coffee trees to Africans.

SOCIETE GENERALE D'EXPORTATION VAN SANTEN ET VANDEN BROECK (GENEX). An Antwerp company with African branches in Bujumbura, Ruhengeri, and Kigali. In 1932, the management of the African office was carried on by ESTAF, a French company with its main office in the

Belgian Congo. ESTAF sold food, alcoholic beverages, clothing, and toiletries for Europeans and items of hardware and trade for Africans. GENEX purchased cattle, goats, and hides from Africans. It maintained its own coffee nurseries and collaborated with the Belgian administration in the implementation of the coffee cultivation campaign in the African sector within Ruhengeri.

SOCIETE INDUSTRIELLE ET AGRICOLE DU RUANDA-URUNDI. A private commercial society that worked closely with African farmers in the 1930s. The company assisted the administration with the propaganda campaign to increase the production of coffee in the African sector. The company also operated a dairy in Butare.

SOCIETE MINIERE AU RUANDA-URUNDI. A Brussels-based company established in 1938 with a branch office at Bujumbura. The company had mining concessions in the mandate territory during the 1940s.

SOCIETE MINIERE DE LA KAGERA-RUANDA. A private mining company with an office in Africa located at Gatsibu. The company originated in Brussels and it operated in Belgian Africa during the 1920s and 1930s.

SOCIETE MINIERE DU MUHINGA ET DE KIGALI (SO-MUKI). A private mining company established at Antwerp in 1933. It was a subsidiary of Compagnie du Kivu and exploited tin and gold mines in its concessions in Rwanda and Burundi. In Rwanda, the company operated in Rutango in the territory of Kigali, but it had concessions in Muhinga and Myarwanu as well. The company mined gold and cassiterite, and it had a reputation for abusive recruiting practices. In 1935, the company employed 23 Europeans, including 3 mining engineers, a doctor, and about 4,000 African workers, of whom 79.5 percent were employed as day laborers. By 1938, the company had sixteen gold and cassiterite mines with a total area of 14,010 hectares. Its work force had increased to include 43 Europeans and 5,144 African workers.

SOCIETE NATIONALE D'ASSURANCES DU RWANDA (SONARWA). One of two insurance companies in the country. SONARWA was established in 1975 with capital of 500 million RF.

SOCIETE NATIONALE DE TRANSPORTS AERIENS DU RWANDA (SONATAR). The national airline of the country; it was established in 1975 to operate domestic passenger and cargo service and international cargo flights to Bujumbura, Goma, Entebbe, Tanzania, Kenya, and destinations in Europe.

SOCIETE RWANDAISE D'ASSURANCES (SORAS). The second of two insurance companies in the country. It was founded in 1984 and has capital of some 150 million RF.

SOCIETE RWANDAISE POUR LA PRODUCTION ET LA COMMERCIALISATION DU THE (SORWATHE). A state agency established in 1978 and concerned with the production and sale of tea.

SOCIETE TABARUDI. *See* LE SYNDICAT DES TABACS DU RUANDA-URUNDI ET DU CONGO BELGE.

SOCIGAZ. Socigaz is Zairian-Rwandan company that was created in 1991 to exploit the methane gas in Lake Kivu, partly for the benefit of the cement factories at Mashyuzu in Rwanda and for Katana in Zaire.

SODEN, J. F. VON. Governor of German East Africa from 1891 to 1893.

SOEURS BLANCHES. The order of Soeurs Missionnaires de

Notre-Dame d'Afrique was formed in 1869 in Algiers to assist the White Fathers. The first postulates were eight women from Brittany, France. In Rwanda, the White Sisters also taught at the Group Scolaire and operated a school for girls at Save.

SORGHUM. A Rwandan staple crop. In 1950, 157,500 tons were produced, and some 134,000 hectares were devoted to its cultivation.

SOURCE, LA. A periodical established in 1971 by the Christian Community of the National University of Rwanda (Communauté Chrétienne de l'Université Nationale du Rwanda) at Butare, led by the Conseil Pastoral, which includes both Catholics and Protestants, and in 1975 became the Fédération des Confessions Chrétiennes. *La Source* has a circulation of about 300, and contains general articles dealing with the problems of African Christians, some student poetry in Kinyarwanda and French, and such student issues as the cost of courses and their availability, the examination system, relationships among students, academic statistics, sports, and conferences.

SOUS-CHEF. An administrative rank in both traditional and colonial times. A Tutsi notable could command labor from those he administered, and he implemented the policy from Belgian administrators, as well as from traditional authorities.

STABILIZATION FUND. Created December 4, 1948, by Regulation No. 53/421, designed to protect producers from fluctuation in the international commodities markets. The fund was managed by OCIRU, which could appropriate, with the approval of the governor-general, sums for the maintenance of the purchasing price of African coffee. The proceeds of the tax levied on every kilogram of cleaned coffee exported were paid into this fund.

In 1947, the fund contained over 25 million BF. The fund was used in the event of a major slump on the world coffee market, preventing African producers from obtaining a sufficiently remunerative price. The United Nations Visiting Mission noted in 1957 that the fund contained 400 million BF, and that part of it was presently invested in Congolese loans.

STANLEYVILLE (now Kisangani)-PANTHEIRVILLE ROUTE. Part of the international route toward the Atlantic from the interior of Belgian Africa. This stretch is seventy-eight miles.

STATEMENT OF VIEWS (MISE AU POINT). This 1957 document was prepared by the High Council of Rwanda, composed primarily of Tutsi notables, and presented to the Belgian authorities. It was essentially a list of demands designed to prepare them for eventual independence and self-rule. First, it urged that Banyarwanda be trained for self-government immediately. Second, it demanded the expansion of secondary education, and the development of university education to train an elite who would eventually be "proficient technically" to participate directly in State affairs. Third, it urged the Belgian government to consider reforms in administrative and civil services. Finally, noting the council's lack of real power and its advisory status, the statement called for the establishment of frank collaboration between indigenous political institutions and corresponding organizations of the Belgian government.

The statement noticed a lack of economic development and social policy, and suggested that federation with the Belgian Congo be given serious consideration and encouraged the Belgians to stimulate industrialization and foreign capital investment in the mandate. It also sanctioned an end to color prejudice.

STATION EXPERIMENTALE D'AGRICULTURE ET DE SERICICULTURE. This particular agricultural experimental station was established at Lusunyu in 1925 and was directed by a European-trained agronomist. The station cultivated soya, tobacco, grapefruit, various grains, black wattle, and jute, but failed to make silkworm production workable. It employed about a hundred Africans and volunteers. The station was closed in 1927, and its operations were transferred to Rubona, located between Nyanza and Butare and considered more centralized.

STOCKBREEDING. A major economic activity performed by the Banyarwanda. Africans breed both cattle and smaller livestock. Most of the stockbreeders are Tutsi, but there are presently a large number of Hutu who own cattle. The breeding of goats is considerable and is almost exclusively in the hands of the Hutu, for whom it is a source of real income. A small number of goats are owned by the Twa.

Sheepbreeding is practiced on a much smaller scale, and the breeding of pigs is practiced chiefly in the districts of Butare, Ruhengeri, and Nyanza. European *colons* and missionaries also engaged in stockbreeding, but only to supply milk, butter, pork, and poultry to the people of the towns and to produce manure for farming.

STRUCTURAL ADJUSTMENT PROGRAM (SAP). The Structural Adjustment Program (SAP), backed by the World Bank and IMF and implemented because of the declining coffee earnings and increasing petroleum prices brought on by the Gulf crisis and the civil war has caused the Rwandan government to devalue the Rwandan franc, to review its customs policy, import duties, and its tax structure. According to the program, all duties on exports other than coffee should be eliminated in order to stimulate economic diversification and to reduce Rwanda's dependency on coffee production. The program is designed to stimulate a more liberal policy for import licensing fees. Under SAP, importers would pay an additional duty of 5 percent of the value of the imports, and the minimum customs duty would be increased from 5 percent to 10 percent.

Generally, the reform program has two key policy objectives: increased efficiency, especially in agriculture and in energy and transportation policies; and cost savings and efficiency gains in the public sector, primarily education and health. The government hopes that by the end of 1993 real Gross Domestic Product (GDP) growth would increase by 4 percent and the rate of inflation would decrease to 5 percent; balance of payments deficit, not including transfers, would be reduced to 10 percent of GDP; and that external reserves would be raised to the equivalent of three months' imports.

For its part, the government has reduced ministerial salaries by 5 percent, allocated 30 percent of foreign exchange to pay a commission of 5 percent. This commission is designed to limit demand. In terms of public finances, the government has undertaken to reduce arrears in payment of foreign debt, to make parastatals more profitable, and to broaden the tax base and to improve tax administration.

To improve the quality of coffee, the government intends to use electronic sorting and more effective spraying with insecticides. Tea and food production are to be boosted by greater use of fertilizers. The government is presently experimenting with a scheme to produce lime locally. In the mining sector, the government plans to privatize the only foundry in the country, currently operating at 30 percent capacity, and to boost output by handling tin from Tanzania and Zaire.

Besides the World Bank and the IMF, several other countries, including Belgium, France, and Austria have offered financial assistance. Belgium has pledged $34 million for general aid programs and $14.2 million for balance of payments support. It has also increased its military aid to $1.4 million. France has pledged $14 million towards Rwanda's balance of payments. Austria's pledge of $10 million in April 1991 also was directed toward the balance-of-payment problem. On September 9, 1991, an EC delegate in Kigali also announced that the EC would provide 5.6 million RF or $46 million toward the support of the country's SAP. Also the European Investment bank has extended credit with soft terms worth 6 million ECU or $7.7 million to support the private sector of the economy. The United States has pledged $25 million to support SAP as well. By the end of 1991, a total of $170 million from all sources was pledged to support SAP. In 1992, the Japanese government provided a grant of $3.5 million to be used to support the importation of drugs, cars, and iron and steel.

SULFO RWANDA. An Asian-controlled company that manufactures soap, confectioneries, and cosmetics.

SWEET POTATOES. A major African food crop. Production in 1948 was approximately 950,500 tons, with some 170,000 hectares devoted to cultivation.

SYNDICAT DES TABACS DU RUANDA-URUNDI ET DU CONGO BELGE, LE (TABARUNDI). A private Belgian company with two concessions in Belgian Africa in the 1930s: one in Ruhengeri and one in Kisenyi. The company cultivated, harvested, and manufactured tobacco. It supplied African planters with young plants and purchased their harvests for its cigarette factory in Bujumbura. In 1933, the syndicate cancelled its lease in Ruhengeri, terminated cultivation, and limited itself to buying tobacco from African planters.

SYNDICAT D'ETUDES DU TRAVAIL INDIGENE. A company that recruited African laborers in the Kivu region.

-T-

TANTALOCOLUMBITE. Small quantities are mined in the country.

TEMPORARY EXPERT COMMISSIONS. An administrative category that was established when the need arose. In 1928, for example, a Native Labor Committee was created to draw up a scheme for restriction of the grant of concessions to those whose demand for labor could be met locally; and in 1934, a Special Commission was appointed to study and report on measures for increasing trade between Belgium and the Belgian Congo.

TEMPS NOUVEAUX D'AFRIQUE. A weekly news magazine of general information that replaced *L'Ami* in 1955. It was published out of Bujumbura.

TERRITORIAL SERVICE. Responsible for the control and regulation of commerce in the African sector. It ensures that African vendors receive proper payment for products sold for exports. The agency also receives regular market reports of the prevailing prices paid by exporters at Bujumbura. On the basis of these reports the service can calculate the price that should be paid to the African, after allowing for the cost of transportation and the normal remuneration of the trader collecting the produce. The administration also sets a minimum buying price for coffee in parchment based on the prices prevailing on the New York coffee market.

THE GOVERNMENT PROJECT AND DEMOCRATIC INITIATIVES IN RWANDA/PROJET DE GOUVERNANCE ET INITIATIVES DEMOCRATIQUES. "The Government Project and Democratic Initiatives in Rwanda" is a joint United States and Rwandan governments initiative, in which the United States has allocated $9 million in aid funding to strengthen democratic structures and to increase popular participation in anticipation of democratic elections. The election, scheduled for 1993 but postponed because of the civil conflict, is estimated to cost about $4.7 million. The United Nations, Belgium, France, Switzerland, Germany as well as the United States have pledged financial assistance and observers.

The project would also facilitate the process of democratization at the national and local levels. In the former, it would provide training in the United States for members of the Conseil National pour le Développement (CND), furnish technical and material assistance to the National Assembly, and support the creation of a national association of burgomasters. At the local level, the project would help to create a nonprofit organization, the Centre pour l'Action civile et des Initiatives démocratiques, which would act as a forum for discussion, a funding agency for civic action programs, and a training center. To assist a free and independent press, the Project will support the newly created Centre pour une Presse libre et indépendante. The project recognizes that a highly professional staff of journalists can keep the Rwandan public better informed.

TIBBAUT, BARON. A Belgian who supported the European planter's interests in Belgian Africa. He was president of the Chambre des Représentants de Belgique and of the Association Belge d'Agriculture Tropicale et Subtropicale. In the annual meeting of the association on January 24, 1930, the baron argued that unreasonable demands and heavy financial charges that the colonial government requested in many of the concessions placed an unfair burden on industrial enterprise.

TILAPIA. A fish introduced into lakes Mohasi, Bulera, Kivu, and Mugesera from lakes in Uganda and the Belgian Congo in 1936. Its introduction was designed to provide an additional source of protein and to change the eating habits of Banyarwanda, who found eating fish distasteful. Many of the fish found in the lakes of the country were neither abundant nor edible. The fish is sold primarily to foreigners.

TILKENS, AUGUSTE-CONSTANT. A member of the Belgian colonial civil service. He was born on October 1, 1869, and entered colonial service on February 12, 1916. He became governor-general of Belgian Africa on December 27, 1927. He served until 1934.

TOBACCO. The crop was cultivated in Kisenyi and Mulera, and in 1929 the annual harvest was estimated at two hundred tons, which was used in the domestic market.

TOMBEUR, CHARLES-HENRI-MARIE-ERNEST (BARON TOMBEUR DE TABORA, 1867–1947). Vice governor-general of the Belgian Congo and Lieutenant General of the Belgian army. The baron's military career began at the age of sixteen, when he joined the Ninth troop division. At age twenty, he was admitted to military school. He saw service in the Congo Free State in 1902 and served as state inspector in the province of Katanga in 1912. During World War I, he commanded Belgian forces on the eastern frontier of the Belgian Congo in the vicinity of lakes Tanganyika and Kivu. During the April offensive in 1916 against the Germans in Rwanda, his forces entered the country from Tabora. He was nominated the vice governor-general of the Belgian Congo in 1917 and served until July 1920.

TRAIT D'UNION. A church affairs bulletin founded in 1942 by the vicar apostolic of Rwanda and published, either in type setting or by stencil, about ten times a year. The bulletin notes the arrival and departures, nominations, promotions, ordinations, studies, anniversaries, health and well-being, and deaths of Catholic church officials and officials of the lay brotherhoods and religious congregations. It also contains information about the organization and activities of ecclesiastic authorities, such as declarations, decisions, pastoral letters, circulars, visitations by the bishop, conferences, news from the various schools and missions, social activities, movement of Catholic authorities, statistical information about the Church congregations, and the distribution of Catholic newsletters. It discusses the relationship between Church and civil authorities, and notes any declaration from civil authorities related to the functioning of the Church.

TRAVAIL, FIDELITE, PROGRES (TRAFIPRO). A private

commercial cooperative that operates nationally under Swiss sponsorship, staffing, and financing since 1962. TRAFIPRO was originally established by the Catholic church in the territory of Nyanza in 1957. It has five branches: Rwaza, Byimana, Zaza, Kabgayi, and Nyanza. Its overall goal is to develop commercial enterprises that will provide service to consumers. Vital imports are brought in and sold throughout the country at minimum markup. Officials from the cooperative travel throughout the country to encourage the development of cash crops, which are in turn purchased and exported by the cooperative. During the harvest season, agents from the cooperative make sure that farmers are paid the official price for their produce by buying in competition with private agents. The cooperative has established its own commercial stores, transportation network, repair facilities, and administrative staff. Its headquarters is in Gitarama, and its membership is over 70,000.

TRIBUNAUX DE CHEFFERIE. One of two classes of African courts in the territory. The second was *tribunaux régionaux*. These courts were supervised by local administrative officials, who attended court, advised the judge, and reviewed any sentence on appeal at his own initiative. They could also void any sentence which was contrary to public morals.

TRIBUTE. The aim and function of the traditional administrative structure were fiscal, in that the country had to provide the ruler with consumption goods. Consequently tribute collecting was methodically organized into seventy to ninety districts, and was performed at harvest time. Tribute in labor was also required annually.

TSHYANGUGU. A port of call on Lake Kivu, where commodities destined for international trade and the Atlantic Ocean were transported to Costermansville, and then by wagon or truck to Tanganyika where they were shipped on to Albertville.

TUTSI. The singular and plural forms are *Abatutsi* and *Batutsi*, respectively. The Tutsi are an ethnic group related to the Hima, which made up the ruling classes in almost all inter-lacustrine kingdoms in east and northeast Africa. According to oral tradition, the Hima came from the Kitara kingdom, but physical anthropology suggests Ethiopia as a possible origin. The Tutsi arrived in Rwanda before the fourteenth century and settled in the eastern region. Their infiltration into Rwanda was initially peaceful, and over time they became the ruling class in the country through assimilation and warfare.

During colonial rule, both the Germans and the Belgians saw the Tutsi as natural rulers because, as colonial officials believed, "they possessed superior intelligence and leadership abilities." However, Belgian authorities also believed that their mentality had to be changed in that "they had to become more humane and more concerned with serving the interest of the people" in order to become capable and efficient civil servants. Tutsi reign came to an end in 1962 when the country gained independence and the Hutu achieved hegemony. The Tutsi comprises 13.7 percent of the total population of the country.

TWA. The singular and plural forms are *Abatwa* and *Batwa* respectively. The Twa are perhaps the oldest inhabitants of the country, and some authorities have argued that they were the first to enter Rwanda from Bwisha. They are interbred pygmies and were initially hunters and gatherers and pottery makers. Before independence in 1962, they could be found in the western part of the country in high proportions. They were considered good dancers and poets, and they were retained by the Royal Court to perform at important occasions, such as the marriage festival. Because of their impish wit, they were court jesters. But those who did not reside in heavily forested areas were frequently used as field hands. However, their integration into society has always been very difficult, because they were considered pariahs who lived outside of the society. After independence, they have gradually become agriculturalists. They currently represent 1.32 percent of the total population.

-U-

UBUCURABWENGE. Genealogical poetry that symbolized the importance of kingship.

UBUHAKE. A form of cattle clientship or lease, in which a powerful person, or patron, provided protection for a weaker individual, who could be either a peasant or a noble herder. *Ubuhake* comes from *guhakwa*, a verb meaning to pay one's respect to a superior in his Court. It denoted the relationship that existed between a person called *garagu*, or client, and another called the *shebuja*, or lord. A grant of a cow infeudated the arrangement. In return for protection, the *umugaragu*, or client, had to build the *shebuja*'s residence, cut lumber for him, serve as his messenger, and accompany him when he was in trouble and when he became old. The duties performed depended upon the rank of the individual. If he were a notable, he could delegate others to perform the actual duties for him.

Beginning in 1945, the administration attempted to suppress the *ubuhake* contract but with very little success; by 1951, with goals assigned in the Ten-Year Plan to meet pressures of land and population, it became apparent that the institution had to be abolished. An additional rationale was that its abolition would assure the reduction of the excess cattle population. *Ubuhake* was abolished in April 1954 by *umwami* Mutara Rudahigwa on the advice of the Belgian Resident, in a three-stage process. The first year required the consent of both parties; in the second year, unilateral dissolution of the contract was permitted; and in the third year, all other contracts had to be terminated.

UBUREETWA. A traditional institution that was symbolic of chiefly power and associated with clientship within the Rwandan sociopolitical and economic structures. Chiefs used the institution to requisition unpaid labor from the peasantry in return for the use of land. They could also pass this privilege on to their clients.

The Belgians were ambivalent about the traditional institution, and it took decades to dismantle it. The first attempt occurred in 1924, when they ordered that in the future Hutu were to do two days labor out of seven, instead of two days out of five. In 1927, the Belgian administration issued another edict limiting *ubureetwa* service for each Hutu adult male to one day per seven-day week. *Ubureetwa* service was further reduced in 1933, when the Belgian administration limited service to thirteen days per year for each adult male, or three days for the provincial chief and ten days for the local hill chief. It was not abolished officially until 1949.

UBUTEGA (pl. *AMATEGA*). An anklet made of raffia fibers from the forest lianas and woven into highly distinctive patterns. It was also an important item of trade in nineteenth-century Rwanda, being both an item of fashion and a form of currency. The anklet was imported from the region of Buhavu and was highly prized as an item of apparel by Rwandan women. They were worn on the leg and covered the calf from the ankle to the knee. A woman would wear several hundred to be considered well dressed.

UBWIIRU. The ritual and sacred, esoteric code of the traditional Court.

UGANDA-RWANDA CONFLICT (1976). The conflict began in 1976, when Idi Amin, the president of Uganda, accused Kenya of holding up more than 300 petroleum tankers for Uganda and permitting only one tanker per day to cross the border. He also accused Kenya of confiscating goods passing through his country on their way to the neighboring states of Burundi, Rwanda, Sudan, and Zaire. In July, the Ugandan government seized thirty or more oil tankers destined for Rwanda, Zaire, and the Sudan in retaliation against Kenya. The seizure brought industry to a halt in Rwanda. Both governments met at Kabale Park in western Uganda later in the year to discuss mutual problems. They signed an agreement to end smuggling over their common borders; the Ugandan government agreed to inspect and then seal vehicles transporting goods in and out of Rwanda; and they discussed the problems of guest workers in Uganda.

UGANDA-RWANDA CONFLICT (1986). Uganda's civil war resulted in the closing of the border between the two countries, and the government had to rely upon weekly flights of Air Rwanda to Mwanza in Tanzania and to Goma in eastern Zaire. The first enabled truck operators destined for Rwanda to route their vehicle to Mwanza from the improvised road through Tanzania and the second facilitated the trip by air to western Africa via Kinshasa.

UMUCANCURO (pl. *ABACANCURO*). A term used to denote an extremely poverty-stricken peasant who works for someone else and over time may become a permanent contract laborer in a foreign land. *Umucancuro*, a traditional and colonial designation, is still used today.

UMUGANDA. *Umuganda* or a system of rural development based on voluntary community or public works that the population performs one day a week was introduced by the Habyarimana government of February 4, 1974. The system is designed to promote food self-sufficiency and the development of social services and infrastructure. The community is called upon to construct terracing in order to improve soil fertility and to develop marshlands. Volunteers build schools, health centers, water supply and purification systems, and roads. *Umuganda* was reorganized in 1990, because of recent famine. The new orientation is directed towards terracing projects, fertilizing fields, and reclaiming marshlands.

UMUGANURA. The annual festival of the first fruits of the harvest that ensured the richness of the country. It was performed by the *umwami* and was an integral part of his ritual responsibilities. The festival was abolished by the Belgian administration in 1924, because they associated the ritual aspect of the festival with sorcery.

UMUGARAGU (pl. ABAGARAGU). The client, or less powerful individual, in the client-patron relationship in the Rwandan feudal system.

UMUHINZA. A divine Hutu king recognized in areas occupied by autonomous Hutu kingdoms. It comes from the word *guhinga*, meaning "to cultivate." The *muhinza* was therefore an agriculturalist par excellence, and he governed a race of cultivators. He could also be called the *umwami*. This political office within Hutu states coexisted with neighboring Tutsi kingdoms in the period before Tutsi consolidation and hegemony. These Hutu principalities were located in the southwest, west, and north. Hutu and Tutsi states coexisted peacefully and carried on trade involving the exchange of cattle for agricultural products.

UMUHORO. A kind of billhook and the primary agricultural implement besides the hoe (*isuka*) used for cultivation.

UMUKARAANI (pl. ABAKARAANI). Chiefs or subchiefs during the colonial period who began their careers as clerks.

UMULYANGO. The members of a major lineage segment in northern Rwanda and the patrilineage of the Hutu. Its members were very active in the communal elections of 1960; it remains the dominant form of political organization in the northern part of the country.

UMUNYUBUTAKA (pl. ABANYABUTAKA). Officials named by the traditional Royal Court to control the distribution of arable land and to collect a return on its use.

UMUSOZI. The hill. It designates the place where Rwandans live and have access to land. In colonial and traditional times it was both a geographical feature and a sociopolitical unit. As a geographical feature it corresponds to the original county. As a sociopolitical unit, it was the smallest traditional administrative unit in the kingdom, and it was commanded by the hill chief. On each hill there were usually several neighborhoods. In each, one of the family heads was chosen as its head by the hill chief. He was called *umukoresha*.

UMUZUNGU (pl. ABAZUNGU). *Umuzungu* is a Kinyarwanda designation for a white, European, or non-Rwandan.

UMWAMI. *See* MWAMI (UMWAMI).

UMWIIRU. *See* ABIIRU (sing. UMWIIRU).

UNION AGRICOLE DES REGIONS DU KIVU (UNAKI). A major pressure group formed to protect the interests of European planters in Belgian Africa. The union was strongly opposed to coffee cultivation in Rwanda by African farmers, and it opposed the administration's policy of *zone de protection*, which was to be discussed in the Conseil Colonial in October 1932, without guarantees in return for their capital investments. The Conseil Colonial cancelled the policy of *zone de protection* in 1934. The union continued to be critical of the African coffee farmers in Belgian Africa; its major complaints concerned maintenance and the quality of coffee.

UNION DU PEUPLE RWANDAIS (UPR). Union du peuple rwandais (UPR) or the Rwandan People's Union is a new political party established on November 9, 1990 by Silas

Mayjambere, the former president of Rwanda's chamber of commerce. Mr. Mayjambere is currently living in exile in Belgium, and his is the first political party to come into existence prior to President Habyarimana's announcement of political reform and tolerance on November 13, 1990. The president urged all Rwandans interested in forming political parties to do so. He remarked that by June 15, 1991 there would be a referendum on the "national political charter" or the rules by which parties would operate. He also urged exiles such as Mr. Mayjambere to return home and to present their ideas within the national forum.

UNION MINIERE DU HAUT-KATANGA (UMHK). This large copper-mining company was created in 1906 and became the basis for colonial industrialization in the Belgian Congo. The company was also the major labor recruiter in the mandate as early as 1925. It recruited labor until 1929. When the company resumed recruitment in 1948, it recruited selectively. About 500 Africans from the mandate were recruited annually after a short training period. It permitted newlyweds to bring their wives and paid wages higher than those in the mandate. A labor recruiter visited the mandate on a bimonthly basis, and usually spent three weeks to a month recruiting labor, operating out of Butare and Ruhengeri. In the 1920s, the company assumed responsibility for the construction of new roads; refurbished others in Butare, Gitega, and Nyanza in order to facilitate recruiting in Gatsibu and Ruhengeri; and built shelters to house recruits at the camps at Usumbura, Butare, and Nyanza.

UNION NATIONALE RWANDAISE (UNAR). A militantly pro-monarchal and anti-Belgian party that was established on September 3, 1959, with François Rukeba, a Hutu, as chairman. The union had organized informally as early as 1952, and membership included members of the Tutsi oligarchy and the nouveau riche among the Hutu. It took a nationalist stance, and advocated immediate autonomy from

Belgian rule and independence by 1962. It condemned ethnicity and racial hatred, and it appealed to all Banyarwanda to preserve national traditions and pride.

During the troubles in 1961 and 1963, when both militant Tutsi and Hutu monarchists fled Rwanda as refugees to surrounding countries, UNAR militants among the refugees organized themselves into guerrilla bands. They called themselves *inyenzi* ("cockroaches") as they attacked Rwanda from Uganda, Tanzania, Burundi, and Zaire. They targeted Hutu officials, but the end result of their attacks was that Hutu in Rwanda lashed out at Tutsi residents.

In February and March 1962, the *inyenzi* attacked Biyumba from Uganda, killing a number of Hutu officials, including three policemen and two civil servants. In revenge, Hutu massacred several thousand Tutsi. Additional massacres occurred on December 21, 1963, when the *inyenzi* attacked from Burundi. The Hutu in retaliation killed an estimated 10,000 Tutsi.

UNITED NATIONS RESOLUTION NO. 1579. Issued December 20, 1960, after the Gitarama coup of 1959. It called upon Belgium to delay legislative elections until there was more of a spirit of "peace and harmony." It asked the administration to grant a general and unconditional amnesty in order to allow all the political leaders exiled or imprisoned to participate in "normal and democratic political activities." A three-member commission was to be created to observe and assist in the elections.

UNITED NATIONS RESOLUTION NO. 1580. This United Nations resolution was issued on December 20, 1960, after the Gitarama coup of 1959, when the *umwami* had left the country for Belgium. The resolution called for his return as the legitimate head of the country, until such time as his future could be decided by referendum.

UNITED NATIONS TRUSTEESHIP AGREEMENT (1946).

The agreement on December 20, 1946, approved the mandate status of Rwanda and Burundi to Belgium by the United Nations General Assembly. The basis for this action is found in Chapters XI through XIII of the United Nations Charter pertaining to the declaration regarding non-self-governing territories, the trusteeship system, and the Trusteeship Council.

The three chapters discuss the well-being of all inhabitants, the establishment of international peace, and the right of the granting authority to submit a questionnaire to the administrative authority for answers to political, economic, social, and educational matters within their territories. It should be noted that Articles 73b and 76b of the charter emphasize progressive self-government, political aspirations, development of free political institutions, and the freely expressed wishes of the people under trusteeship. The agreement required a system of elementary education, access to advanced education, and professional instruction (Article 2), and Article 6 required participation of the inhabitants in representative organizations.

UNITED NATIONS TRUSTEESHIP VISITING MISSION (1948). The visiting mission severely criticized Belgian efforts to advance the African population politically within the territory and administratively within the Belgian colonial civil service. The mission was also critical of Belgian reliance upon missionary schools and its lack of progress in promoting public school education, as well as the total absence of higher education. In fact, the delegate from the Philippines noted that not one student had been sent to Belgium for higher education. The mission was also concerned about the subservient status of the Hutu masses.

UNITED NATIONS TRUSTEESHIP VISITING MISSION (1951). The United Nations mission considered the Ten-Year Plan to be of great importance for the future of the territory. The mission congratulated the Belgian administration for its efforts at comprehensive and long-range planning. It believed that the plan had concrete proposals for the solution of the cattle problem, as well as plans to establish indigenous agricultural communities as a means of encouraging village life. It expressed the hope that the plan would involve Banyarwanda through provisions of self-help and in the implementation of development projects.

The United Nations criticized the administration's lack of effort in integrating indigenous political organizations and general services common to both countries. it thought that public health, education, finance, labor, and public works of Rwanda and Burundi could be integrated. To the mission, integration was essential, since it believed that Rwanda and Burundi had a common future as a single country. It urged the administration to take immediate steps to establish procedures and institutions which would bring about regular collaboration between the indigenous authorities on matters of common concern. The mission recommended a central legislative body and believed that the Council of the Vice Government-General of Ruanda-Urundi could be utilized for this purpose. It urged the administration to increase the number of African members on the council.

UNITED NATIONS TRUSTEESHIP VISITING MISSION (1954). The mission considered it regrettable that a lower priority had been given to political development. While it accepted the administration's response that its emphasis on economic, social, and cultural development was designed to promote political progress, and that these were necessary foundations and prerequisites of the political process, it nonetheless urged the Belgian administration to give serious attention to increasing political education of the people by granting them "increasing doses of political power and responsibility." It proposed that chiefs become popularly elected representatives of the people. It warned that failure to formulate a concrete program of political education and progress implied a failure to recognize the growing forces of nationalism in Africa. The administration's oversight indicated that it envisaged a prolonged period of tutelage covering three or four generations. Its own prognosis was that self-government could be accomplished in one generation.

UNITED NATIONS TRUSTEESHIP VISITING MISSION (1957). The mission noted that Belgium's annual report to the General Assembly for 1955 provided a brief account of its efforts to accomplish and implement political participation. The showpiece was the Council of the Vice Government-General of Ruanda-Urundi, established in 1947. The report noted that the *umwami* had been admitted to the Council in 1949, and it was opened to other Africans later on. The report also mentioned judicial reorganization and the reform of the political structure in 1952, the establishment of lists for the electoral college, the general election in 1956, and the establishment of the General Council in 1957.

The mission remarked that Rwanda had reached an important stage in its political development, and that it was capable of assimilating more far-reaching reforms in its transition from feudalism to democracy. The mission hoped that this transition would occur with a minimum of tension, friction, and difficulties. It expressed concern about the ability of the Banyarwanda to express opinions without fear of retaliation. Private communications to the mission were often anonymous for fear of prosecution or persecution by the administration.

The mission discussed the most recent development—the Manifesto of the Bahutu and the Statement of Views. It asked the administration whether the Hutu manifesto reflected a broad social and political consciousness. The administration believed that it did not. In its review of the Statement of Views, which expressed the concerns of the Tutsi oligarchy and made little reference to the Hutu, the mission noted that the High Council had no Hutu representation. It urged the administration to accelerate its efforts to emancipate the Hutu and to involve them in the administration of the country. It also said that it was not optimistic about rapprochement between the races. In fact, it believed that the problem would grow worse. Salvation or a possible solution would come only if the younger generations had forums in which they could come together.

It discussed the progress of the Decree of July 14, 1952, between 1953 and 1957. The decree established four types of councils: subchiefdom council, chiefdom councils, district councils, and high councils of the states. The decree outlined the electoral process and the composition of each of the councils. The administration was extremely concerned about the lack of representation in the election by peers, but it commended the administration on the number of Hutu participating in the electoral college at the level of the subchiefdom council. It expressed some concern that the general structure of the Decree of July 14, 1952, did not reflect proportional representation of the ethnic groups.

UNITED NATIONS TRUSTEESHIP VISITING MISSION (1960). The United Nations mission noted that the political reforms announced by the Belgian government in November 1959 had already been superseded by events, especially the ethnic rioting and murder that had occurred at Gitarama. It noted that the incident had almost plunged the country into civil war. It urged national reconciliation and hoped that the Belgian administration would encourage dialogue, possibly a roundtable conference in Brussels, similar to the one held in January 1960 for the Belgian Congo. It believed that this conference could deal with the whole territory of Ruanda-Urundi and would provide a forum to discuss self-government and independence. The Belgian government agreed and told the United Nations that this conference would take place in August 1960.

The mission recommended that the communal elections, scheduled to take place in June and July, be postponed until after the August conference, and urged that the national elections, scheduled for early 1961, be supervised by the United Nations and be conducted by universal suffrage. It called for the formation of a national assembly and urged the Belgians to be ready to discuss the question of independence at the 1961 session of the General Assembly.

UNITED STATES FINANCIAL ASSISTANCE AGREEMENT (1964). Under the agreement the United States would provide fifteen scholarships for Rwandan students and would lend $600,000 for development projects.

UNIVERSITE COLONIAL. The colonial university located at Antwerp was responsible for educating the colonial civil service. The university curriculum extended over a period of four years, with military service spent between the second and third years. The course of training was given by the faculty of political science. Competitive examinations were given at the end of the first year, after which only the number of students for which there were vacancies in the colonial service were allowed to continue with the administrative course.

UNIVERSITE NATIONAL DU RWANDA (UNR). The National University of Rwanda was established by a Canadian Catholic order in the 1960s at Butare. A second branch was opened in Ruhengeri in the northern part of the country in the 1980s.

UNIVERSITE OFFICIAL DU CONGO BELGE ET DU RUANDA-URUNDI. The Official University of the Belgian Congo and Ruanda-Urundi was created by decree on October 26, 1955. It was located at Elizabethville; it catered to the needs of the colony and the mandate territory. Its administrative offices were located in Brussels.

URUHARO. "Friendship," or the feudal client relationship between a poor peasant and a stronger, richer peasant. To consolidate the arrangement, the poor peasant asked for a hoe, and the resulting relationship was expressed in terms of friendship. Once the hoe was received, the poor peasant was required to work in the fields of his "friend" for two days out of a week until the hoe became a stump (*ifuni*).

URUNANA. A religious newspaper published three times a year by the Grand Séminaire de Nyakibanda at Butare. The paper was founded in 1967.

URUNDI. The Swahili name for Burundi, meaning "land of the Rundi people." The name was used by the Germans when they ruled Burundi from 1894 to 1916. It formed one of the districts of German East Africa until the League of Nations awarded it to Belgium as part of the dual mandated territory of Ruanda-Urundi in 1919. The Belgians continued to use "Urundi" as the official name of half of the mandate (it became a trusteeship in 1946 under the United Nations) territory until 1961, when independence was granted and the Kirundi form was adopted.

Urundi shares its southern border with Rwanda, and relations between the two states have not been friendly since precolonial times. Both were traditional kingdoms ruled by an *umwami*, but in Rwanda the kingdom was more centralized. Each of the kingdoms contain the same ethnic groups: Tutsi, Hutu, and Twa. The Tutsi notables dominated the sociopolitical and economic structures in both kingdoms. However, the kingdom of Urundi was founded about the mid-seventeenth century by Tutsi immigrants from the western Tanzania Ha states. Its first monarch, Ntare Rushatsi, established his capital in the center of the country. His successor gradually expanded the kingdom outward. The greatest period of expansion occurred during the reign of Ntare II Rugaamba, who extended the country's borders beyond their present locations. Unlike Rwanda, the Rundi state was never highly centralized, and during the nineteenth century, the kingdom was plagued by civil war and disputes between the ruling monarch and his territorial chiefs. These rivalries continued during the colonial period.

Under both German (from the 1890s to 1916) and Belgian colonial rule (to 1961), Urundi complained that Rwanda was given more than its share and was favored by the colonial administrators. When the Hutu in Rwanda overturned Tutsi domination in 1959 and established an independent state, tensions between the two countries became more intense. Armed conflict almost developed in 1964, when Tutsi refugees attacked Rwanda from bases in Burundi. Relations remained strained until the overthrow of President Kayibanda of Rwanda in 1973. The slaughter of Hutu in Burundi in 1972, 1973, and again in 1988 has affected ethnic relations in Rwanda, where the Hutu attacked Tutsi in reprisal.

Burundi achieved its independence in 1961 with Louis Rwagasore, the son of the reigning king Mwambutsa II, serving as the country's prime minister. Rwagasore was assassinated, and civil war ensued between Tutsi and Hutu. In 1962, peace was restored and the country became independent as a constitutional monarchy under King Mwambutsa II. After an abortive coup in 1965, however, Mwambutsa II fled the country to Europe. His son, Charles Ndizeye, usurped the throne and was installed as Ntare III the following year, but his government lasted only a few months. Michel Micombero, the country's defense minister, staged a coup, deposed the king, and established a republic with himself as president.

USUMBURA (now Bujumbura). The Swahili name for Bujumbura. Usumbura became Bujumbura in 1962 when the city was incorporated fully into Burundi after the nation was declared independent. It was a major trading center and was considered the southernmost entry-exit point in Rwanda. The major exports from Rwanda (coffee, cotton, cassiterite, and hides) were transported from here to either Matadi or Dar es Salaam. The easterly route had the initial advantage in terms of cost; of the two routes (Usumbura-Kigoma-Dar es Salaam and the Usumbura-Costermansville-Stanleyville-Matadi), the unit cost per ton per mile was 2,173.5 BF and 2,939/3,567 BF, respectively. However, the easterly route included an additional tax levied at the Suez Canal of some 300 to 400 BF per ton. The Usumbura to Dar es Salaam route is 210 kilometers by lake transport and 1,245 kilometers by rail, and the Usumbura to Albertville route is 1,170 kilometers by lake and river transport and 2,065 kilometers by rail. Other trade routings from Usumbura include Dilolo to Lobito, Kigali-Port Kagera-Mombasa, and the Kigali-Kampala-Mombasa.

USUMBURA-ASTRIDA (BUTARE-KIGALI) ROUTE. This stretch of road, from northeastern Burundi to the central plateau region of Rwanda, is 265 kilometers.

USUMBURA-BUKAVU ROUTE. This stretch of road, from Burundi to Zaire, is 130 kilometers.

-V-

VICARIAT APOSTOLIQUE DU KIVOU. In 1919, the Apostolic Vicariate of the Kivu included the Catholic mission of Rwanda, Burundi, and Buha.

VICARIAT APOSTOLIQUE DU RUANDA. In 1922, Monsignor Leon Classe was director of the Apostolic Vicariate of Rwanda, which included twelve Catholic missions. In 1952, this vicariate was divided into two apostolic parishes: Kabgayi and Nyundo.

VICE GOVERNOR-GENERAL. An administrative office that came into being after 1914. In 1925, the mandate territory was organized as a vice government-general, which meant that the head of the administration in the territory had the same limited powers of legislation in local matters as were exercised by the governor-general for the rest of Belgian Africa. Measures that applied to the Belgian Congo did not operate in the mandate unless specifically applied by the governor-general. The Belgian vice governor-generals of Ruanda-Urundi were as follows:

> Justin-Prudent-François-Marie Malfeyt (1916–1919)
> Alfred-Frédéric-Gérard Marzorati (1920–1930)
> Charles-Henri-Joseph Voisin (1930–1932)
> Eugène-Jacques-Pierre-Louis Jungers (1932–1946)
> Léon-Antonin-Marie Pétillon (1946–1952)
> Alfred-Maria-Josephus-Ghislencus Claeys-Boúúaert (1952–1955)
> Jean-Paul Harroy (1955–1962) and Resident-General as of 1961

VIRUNGA. A highland region in the northern part of the country, dominated by a chain of volcanoes, the Virunga, whose highest peak is Karisimbi (4,519 meters).

VOISIN, CHARLES-HENRI-JOSEPH (1887–1942). A Belgian colonial civil servant. Voisin was born at Flobecq on October 29, 1887. He was trained in the law and had a judgeship. He entered colonial service in 1910, and became vice governor-general of the Belgian Congo and Governor of the territory on November 9, 1926. He sponsored the first coffee campaign in Rwanda, as well as the idea that coffee cultivation should be an exclusively African enterprise. He discouraged European settlement as well as its encroachment in the coffee and tobacco industries. The governor believed that the population in the territory was much too high in areas where soils were not fertile enough to support additional European settlement. Voisin advocated a policy in which Africans and Europeans would form a collaboration. They were not to be competitors, especially in marginal areas or densely populated environments. In spite of some initial defeats and disappointments due to lack of technical personnel, his initial trials were satisfactory.

He believed that African colonial agriculture could ensure the stability of the mandate's economy and finances. In the preamble of the 1930 Annual Report to the League of Nations, he enunciated the following program: the regrouping of traditional chiefdoms to facilitate better administrative control; the improvement of agriculture to include concentration on coffee production; the improvement of livestock; reforestation and mineral prospecting; and the construction of roads. His immediate task, however, was dealing with the consequences of the famine of 1928 and 1929.

The development program that he instituted formed the basis for agricultural development in the mandate. It called for swamp drainage to provide new land, the development of seasonal crops (such as a new resistant strain of manioc), a reduction in the number of cattle, and erosion prevention. He sought to develop markets in order to provide Africans with currency and to increase their purchasing power. Market development required the development of extensive road networks. Governor Voisin also encouraged the granting of mining concessions as a means of gaining valuable foreign exchange. He died at Tournai on November 20, 1942.

-W-

WASSAWA, LIEUTENANT COLONEL ADAM. Lt. Colonel Adam Wassawa was second-in-command of the Rwandan Patriotic Front (RPF), which invaded Rwanda from Uganda on October 1, 1990. A Tutsi with a Kiganda name, Wassawa was a member of Uganda's president Yoweri K. Museveni's armed forces. He was killed in a car crash in Uganda in July 1991, where he was going for clandestine medical care.

WATSHURUZI. A peddler who travels around the countryside purchasing products from Africans, which he then resells to retail merchants in the urban centers.

WIGNY, PIERRE-LOUIS-JEAN-JOSEPH. Belgian lawyer, member of parliament, and minister of colonies in the 1940s. He visited Rwanda and Burundi in 1949.

WILMIN, H. A Belgian colonial civil servant who was district commissioner in Rwanda from February to April 1929. He served as Resident of Rwanda from September to December 1929. In 1931, he became the Resident of Burundi.

WINTGENS, CAPTAIN MAX. A German citizen and Resident of Ruanda from December 1913 to May 1916, replacing Dr. Richard Kandt. During the war, he commanded several German units at Kigali and transformed the African police force into a competent military force as well. He also levied the first tax in the country in 1914, on Rwandans who lived near the European centers of Kigali, Gisenyi, and Cyangugu. Wintgens sought to stimulate the economy, and believed that taxes would draw more currency into the country, which would eventually force Banyarwanda to exchange their products for money. Modern exchange would then stimulate productive enterprises. He also advocated the construction of a rail line, which was never built.

WISSMANN, H. VON. Governor of German East Africa from 1895 to 1896.

WORKERS COOPERATIVE OF SOMUKI. This workers cooperative was organized in 1953 in the territory of Kigali.

WORKING GROUP TO STUDY POLITICAL PROBLEMS (1958). The decade of the 1950s was a time of extreme political stress for all segments of Rwandan society. In December 1958, at the encouragement of the United

Nations, the Belgian government appointed a Working Group to study the political problems in Rwanda and Burundi. In April 1959, the Working Group arrived in Rwanda and received delegations representing all political points of view from the two countries. They presented their findings in September, but the Belgian government did not publish them until November. The Working Group's report sanctioned a political commission, appointed and approved by the Mwami's Grand Council of Rwanda, to oversee elections in the country. In preparation for self-government, the Working Group also sanctioned the creation of mayors and councils at the communal level, which would be chosen by universal male suffrage. These officials would in turn choose territorial council members.

The Mwami's Grand Council would be composed of a delegate from each commune, and the council at the communal level would be responsible for legislation, supervising the communes, and tending to indigenous affairs.

-X-Y-Z-

YAMS. Basic African food crop.

YUHI GAHIMA, UMWAMI OF RWANDA. *See* GAHIMA, YUHI.

YUHI MAZIMPAKA, UMWAMI OF RWANDA. *See* MAZIMPAKA, YUHI.

YUHI MUSINGA, UMWAMI OF RWANDA. *See* MUSINGA, YUHI.

ZAIRE. In geographic terms, it is located at the continent's center, and it encompasses the entire Congo River basin, including a great variety of topography. Its soils are suitable for agriculture and contains a vast range of rich resources, such as cobalt, copper, and diamonds. The river is perhaps its greatest asset, since it is the potential source of 13 percent of the world's hydroelectric power. The country also links Africa from west to east, and eastern Zaire has been influenced by forces from East Africa, primarily Swahili, Arab, and Nyamwezi traders. Formerly the Belgian Congo, with which Rwanda and Burundi were integrated administratively by the Belgians in 1925, the territory became independent on June 30, 1960, becoming the Democratic Republic of the Congo. Its current president, Marshal Mobutu Sese Seko, seized power in 1965, ousting Joseph Kasavubu in a military coup. He banned party politics, and in 1971 established the Second Republic as a one-party state. The name of the state was changed to Zaire in 1971.

ZAIRE-NIL CRETE. A highland area in the northern part of the country.

ZAZA MISSION. A Catholic mission station at Gisaka in the Kibungu territory that was established by the White Fathers in 1900.

ZAZU. Territory in the eastern region.

ZEEHANDELAER SYSTEM. A plan devised to organize and regulate African labor within the *zone de protection* and in the Kivu. It was based on a daily or piecework allotment, with a daily or weekly salary schedule, rather than a labor-recruitment contract for longer periods of time. It was generally believed that the piecework system was more efficient and achieved greater yields with fewer workers; it was less expensive than the contract system; and it incurred less government intervention. Opponents believed that the Zeehandelaer system was subject to abuse on account of the need to use African chiefs as intermediaries or recruiters.

Others described it as a "floating labor force" which was not reliable and did not guarantee workers' presence on the job.

ZONE DE PROTECTION. A Belgian policy that began to take shape in 1928. It envisioned a partnership between private enterprise and African labor in order to ensure prosperity and the development of economic production in the mandate. The administration designated protective zones, not to exceed 70,000 hectares or a period of ten years, in order to give enterprises the necessary security for industrial undertakings. In the area of agricultural production, the government would provide lots of 500 hectares with ninety-nine-year leases to companies to plant crops and raise livestock. These zones were to act as model farms, and the Africans in the zones were to be sources of labor for agricultural and industrial enterprises.

The policy was discussed in the Conseil Colonial during the 1930s. The major objection to the policy came from the League of Nations at Geneva and the Union Agricole des Régions du Kivu. The league was concerned about the utilization of African labor within the zones, while the union was concerned with protecting the interests of its planters, the issue of free trade, and guarantees for capital investment.

The plan put before the Conseil Colonial called for the creation of zones of industrial and commercial activity, and stipulated that each zone would be reserved for the development of a single crop or industry. To avoid competition, the zones would be spaced accordingly. The companies within the zone would be licensed at a fee of 10,000 BF to purchase produce from Africans, provided it also constructed a processing mill or had put up sufficient capital to ensure that one would be built. It was this provision that generated the most opposition from the Union Agricole des Régions du Kivu, because it believed that the provision discriminated against those planters who did not have sufficient capital to construction a permanent mill or pay for a license. Nor did it provide protection for those agricultural companies then operating in the territory.

A compromise was reached in 1934, when the Conseil Colonial withdrew the decree to create officially, the *zones de protection* and loosened the requirements for granting a purchasing license.

BIBLIOGRAPHY

The following bibliography is divided into six categories: books and dissertations, articles and papers, United Nations documents, resource materials from the National University of Rwanda at Butare, and bibliographical citations from the Royal Library and archival materials from the African Archives in Brussels, Belgium. All the materials cited, including those from the individual repositories in Rwanda and Belgium (the single exception being the archival materials), are also available from the Library of Congress and most large research libraries with African Studies sections. The materials listed here represent only a fraction of the resources available for Rwanda. There are numerous materials for the humanities, the social sciences other than history, the applied sciences, economics, agriculture, and rural development. The majority of the available materials is in French; however, the availability of English-language materials is increasing, and in recent years the Rwandan government has also encouraged the publication of materials in Kinyarwanda.

With respect to bibliographies, most are outdated. Only a few of the highly specialized ones that deal with the press, law, and religion, respectively, have been listed here: Jean Berlage's *Répertoire de la presse du Congo belge, 1884–1954, et du Ruanda-Urundi, 1920–1954;* Filip Reyntjens's *Essai de bibliographie juridique du Rwanda;* and Gilles-Marius Dion's *Bibliographie rwandaise.* Theodore Heyse has also published bibliographies dealing with medicine, journalism, transportation systems, geology, education, language, economy, agriculture, and land tenure. Most of his works were published in the late 1940s and early 1950s. Only his *Bibliographie du Congo et du Ruanda-Urundi (1939–1949)* has been listed; the rest are quite common and can be found in most bibliographic data programs. Recently Marcel d'Hertefelt, with Danielle de Lame, has published a two-volume bibliography dealing with Rwandan society, culture and history. The set, over 1,800 pages, contains annotations on various kinds of bibliographic format from monographs, to articles from journals, to dissertations, to press releases. It is the most comprehensive bibliography available and encompasses printed materials from 1863 to 1987.

For primary source materials, the guide and catalog of Madeleine van Grieken-Taverniers of the African Archives in Brussels and Father Lamey of the Archives of the Generalate of the White Fathers in Rome should be consulted. Full bibliographical citations are listed below. Archival materials on microfilm and ephemera within the United States are available at the Consortium for Africa Microfilm Project (CAMP) in Chicago, Illinois, and the Congo Manuscript Collection at the Michigan State University Library in East Lansing. All of the above contain reports, correspondence, and documentation, including news releases and biographical sketches of personnel of the German and Belgian colonial periods in Rwanda. Bibliographical citations of statistical and census data and development plans are available in the union list compiled by Victoria K. Evalds.

No comprehensive history of Rwanda is currently available, but there are a variety of works that cover specific aspects of the country's history. For information about traditional society prior to European control, the following should be read: Jean Hiernaux's *Cultures préhistoriques de l'âge des métaux au Ruanda-Urundi et au Kivu (Congo belge). Partie II. Suivi de deux sites archéologiques à briques en territoire de Walikali (Kivu);* Jacques Nenquin's *Contributions to the Study of the Prehistoric Cultures of Ruanda and Burundi;* Louis de Lacger's *Ruanda;* Luc de Heusch's *La Rwanda et la civilisation interlacustre;* Marcel d'Hertefelt's *Les anciens royaumes de la zone interlacustre méridionale* and *Les clans du Rwanda ancien. Eléments d'ethnosociologie et d'ethnohistoire;* and R. Bourgeois's *Banyarwanda et Barundi.* For the African point of view, see Alexis Kagame's *Les milices du Rwanda precolonial* and his two-volume history, *Un abrégé de l'ethno-histoire du Rwanda* and *Un abrégé de l'histoire du Rwanda de 1853 à 1972;* the works of Ferdinand Nahimana, R. Nizuregero, and Bashizi Cirhagarhula in *La civilisation ancienne des Peuples des Grands Lacs.*

There are a number of dissertations and monographs dealing with the colonial period of the mandate. For works about the country's political history, see René Lemarchand's *Rwanda and Burundi;* Helen Codere's "The Biography of an African Society"; Alison Desforge's "Defeat Is the Only Bad News"; René Bourgeois's *Témoignage,* M. Catherine Newbury's *The Cohesion of Oppression: Clientship and Ethnicity in Rwanda, 1860 to 1960;* and Jean-Paul Harroy's *Rwanda: de la féodalité à la démocratie, 1955–1962.* Ian Linden's *Church and Revolution in Rwanda* and Paul Rutayisire's *La Christianisation du Rwanda (1900–1945),* describe missionary activities in Rwanda. For economic descriptions and analysis, see Learthen Dorsey's "The Rwandan Colonial Economy, 1916–1941" and Fred E. Wagnor's "Nation Building in Africa."

In-depth analyses of the national period and economic development of Rwanda in monographic form or in dissertation could not be located; however, the London Economist Unit's quarterly country reports and annual supplements provide current political, social, and economic information about the country. The *African Research Bulletin* and daily newspapers, such as the *Christian Science Monitor,* are also excellent sources for current information about Rwanda.

BOOKS, PERIODICALS, AND DISSERTATIONS

Adolph Frederick, duke of Mecklenburg-Schwerin. *In the Heart of Africa.* London and New York: Cassell, 1910.

Africa: Review 1986. Essex: World of Information, 1986.

Africa South of the Sahara, 17th edition. London: Europa Publications, 1987.

———, 18th edition. London: Europa Publications, 1988.

———, 20th edition. London: Europa Publications, 1991.

——— 21st edition. London: Europa Publications, 1992.

Amselle, Jean-Loup, and Elikia M'bokolo, eds. *Au coeur de l'ethnie: Ethnies, tribalisme et état en Afrique.* Paris: Editions la Découverte, 1985.

Anstey, Roger. *King Leopold's Legacy: The Congo Under Belgian Rule, 1908–1960.* London and New York: Oxford University Press, 1966.

Bayton, W. H., R. E. Downs, Yolande Jemai, and S. E. Ross-Larson. *A Report on Assistance to a National Maternal and Child Health and Family Planning Program in Rwanda.* Washington, 1981.

Belgian Congo and Ruanda-Urundi Information and Public Relations Office. *Ruanda-Urundi: Economy I.* Brussels, 1960.

———. *Ruanda-Urundi: Geography and History.* Brussels, 1960.

Berger, Elena L. *Labour, Race, and Colonial Rule: the Copperbelt from 1924 to Independence.* Oxford: Clarendon Press, 1974.

Berlage, Jean. *Répertoire de la presse du Congo belge, 1884–1954, et du Ruanda-Urundi, 1920–1954.* Brussels: Commission Belge de Bibliographie, 1955.

Bindseil, Reinhart. *Ruanda und Deutschland seit den tagen Richard Kandts/Le Rwanda et l'Allemagne depuis le temps de Richard Kandt.* Berlin: D. Reimer, 1988.

Bourgeois, René. *Témoignage*. Tervuren: Musée Royal de l'Afrique Centrale, 1982.

Dak, O. *A Geographical Analysis of the Distribution of Migrants in Uganda*. Occasional Paper No. 11. Kampala: Makerere University College, Department of Geography, 1968.

DesForge, Alison L. "Defeat Is the Only Bad News: Rwanda Under Musinga, 1896–1931." Ph.D. diss., Yale University, 1972.

Dion, Gilles-Marius. *Bibliographie rwandaise*. Kigali: Dialogue, 1984.

Dorsey, Learthen. "The Rwandan Colonial Economy, 1916–1941." Ph.D. diss., Michigan State University, 1983.

Elkan, Walter. *The Economic Development of Uganda*. London and Nairobi: Oxford University Press, 1961.

—— *Migrants and Proletarians: Urban Labour in the Economic Development of Uganda*. London: Oxford University Press for the East African Institute of Social Research, 1960.

Encyclopedia of the Third World, 4th edition. New York: Facts on File, Inc., 1992.

Evalds, Victoria. *Union List of African Censuses, Development Plans and Statistical Abstracts*. New York: Hans Zell Publishers, 1985.

Fetter, Bruce. "The Colonial Tie in the Making of Elisabethville." Ph.D. diss., University of Wisconsin, 1968.

————. *The Creation of Elisabethville, 1910–1940*. Stanford, Calif.: Hoover Institute Press, 1976.

Fossey, Dian. *Gorillas in the Mist.* Boston: Houghton Mifflin Company, 1983.

Goris, Jan-Albert. *Belgium.* Berkeley: University of California Press, 1946.

Gravel, Pierre B. "A Play for Power: Description of a Community in Eastern Rwanda." Ph.D. diss., University of Michigan, 1962.

————. *Remera: A Community in Eastern Ruanda.* The Hague: Mouton, 1968.

Grieken-Taverniers, Madeleine van. *La colonisation belge en Afrique centrale: Guide des archives africaines du Ministère des affaires africaines, 1885–1962.* Brussels: Ministère des Affaires Etrangères, du Commerce Extérieur et de la Coopération au Développement, [1981]. A 14-page supplement to this guide was published in [1984].

Hailey, Lord. *An African Survey: A Study of Problems Arising in Africa South of the Sahara.* London: Oxford University Press, 1938.

Hayes, Harold T. P. *The Dark Romance of Dian Fossey.* New York: Simon and Schuster/Touchstone, 1990.

Helmreich, Jonathan E. *Belgium and Europe: A Study in Small Power Diplomacy.* The Hague and Paris: Mouton, 1976.

Henige, David P. *Colonial Governors from the Fifteenth Century to the Present.* Madison: University of Wisconsin Press, 1970.

Heremans, Rogers. *Introduction à l'histoire du Rwanda.* Kigali: Editions Rwandaises, 1973.

Hertefelt, Marcel d'. *Les anciens royaumes de la zone interlacustre méridionale.* London: International African Institute, 1962.

————. *Les clans du Rwanda ancien: Eléments d'ethnosociologie et d'ethnohistoire.* Tervuren: Musée Royal de l'Afrique Centrale, 1971.

Hertefelt, Marcel d', and André Coupez. *La royauté sacree de l'ancien Rwanda.* Tervuren: Musée Royal d'Afrique Centrale, 1964.

————, and Danielle de Lame. *Société culture et histoire du Rwanda: Encyclopédie bibliographique, 1863–1980/87. Tome I: A-L.* Tervuren: Musée Royal de l'Afrique Centrale, 1987.

————. *Société culture et histoire du Rwanda: Encyclopédie bibliographique, 1863–1980/87. Tome II: M-Z, Index.* Tervuren: Musée Royal de l'Afrique Centrale, 1987.

Heusch, Luc de. *Le Rwanda et la civilisation interlacustre.* Brussels: Université Libre de Bruxelles, Institut de Sociologie, 1966.

Heyse, Theodore. *Bibliographie du Congo belge et du Ruanda-Urundi (1939–1949).* Brussels: G. van Campenhout, 1950.

Hiernaux, Jean. *Cultures préhistoriques de l'âge des métaux au Ruanda-Urundi et au Kivu (Congo belge). Partie II. Suivi de deux sites archaéologiques à briques en territoire de Walikali (Kivu).* Brussels, 1960.

Higginson, John E. "The Making of an African Working

Class: The Union Minière du Haut-Katanga and the African Mine Workers, 1907–1945." Volumes I and II. Ph.D. diss., University of Michigan, 1979.

Kagame, Alexis. *Les milices du Rwanda précolonial.* Brussels: Académie royal des Sciences d'Outre-Mer, 1963.

Kerken, Georges van der. *La crise économique en Afrique belge.* Brussels: E. Bruylant, 1931.

Kimble, George H. T. *Tropical Africa. Volume II. Society and Polity.* Garden City, N.Y.: Doubleday, 1962.

Lacger, Louis de. *Ruanda. II. Le Ruanda-Urundi moderne.* Namur: Grands Lacs, 1959.

Lamey, R. *Catalogue I. Annexes des archives de la Maison Généralice des Pères Blancs.* Rome, April 25, 1970.

Lemarchand, René. *Rwanda and Burundi.* London: Pall Mall Press, 1970.

————. *The World Bank in Rwanda.* Bloomington: Indiana University Press, 1982.

Leubuscher, Charlotte. *Tanganyika Territory: A Study of Economic Policy Under Mandate.* London: Oxford University Press for the Royal Institute of International Affairs, 1944.

Linden, Ian, with Jane Linden. *Church and Revolution in Rwanda.* New York: Manchester University Press/ Africana Publishing Company, 1977.

Lipschutz, Mark R., and R. Kent Rasmussen. *Dictionary of African Historical Biography.* Chicago: Aldine Publishing Company, 1978.

————. *Dictionary of African Historical Biography,* 2nd edition. Berkeley: University of California Press, 1986.

Louis, William Roger. *Ruanda-Urundi, 1884–1919.* Oxford: Clarendon Press, 1963.

Maquet, Jacques J. *The Premise of Inequality in Ruanda.* London and New York: Oxford University, International African Institute, 1961.

Martelli, George. *Leopold to Lumumba: A History of the Belgian Congo.* London: Chapman and Hall, 1962.

Meeus, Adrien de. *History of the Belgians.* New York: Frederick A. Praeger, 1962.

Michiels, A., and N. Laude. *Notre Colonie: Congo belge et Ruanda-Urundi. Géographie et Notice Historique.* Brussels: Edition Universelle, 1949.

Nenquin, Jacques A. E. *Contribution to the Study of the Prehistoric Cultures of Rwanda and Burundi.* Tervuren: Musée Royal de l'Afrique Centrale, 1976.

Newbury, M. Catherine. *The Cohesion of Oppression: Clientship and Ethnicity in Rwanda, 1860–1960.* New York: Columbia University Press, 1988.

Prioul, Christian, and Pierre Sirven. *Atlas du Rwanda.* Paris: Ministère de la Coopération, 1981.

Reed, Harry A. "Cotton-Growing in Central Nyanza Province, Kenya, 1901–1939: An Appraisal of African Reactions to Imposed Government Policy." Ph.D. diss., Michigan State University, 1975.

Reyntjens, Filip. *Essai de bibliographie juridique du*

Rwanda. Butare: Université Nationale du Rwanda, Faculté de Droit, 1978.

Rutayisire, Paul. La Christianisation du Rwanda (1900–1945). Fribourg: Editions Universitaires Fribourg, 1987.

Sullivan, Jo. Africa, 3rd edition. Guilford, Conn.: Dushkin Publishing Group, 1989.

Ungar, Sanford. Africa: The People and Politics of an Emerging Continent, 3rd edition. New York: Simon and Schuster/Touchstone, 1989.

United States Committee for Refugees. Exile from Rwanda: Background to an Invasion. Issue Paper. Washington, February 1991.

Vail, David Jeremiah. "The Public Sector as Stimulus of Innovation Adoption in African Smallholder Agriculture: A Case Study in Teso District, Uganda." Ph.D. diss., Yale University, 1971.

Vali, Jamal. "The Role of Cotton and Coffee in Uganda's Economic Development." Ph.D. diss., Stanford University, 1976.

Wagnor, Fred E. "Nation Building in Africa: A Description and Analysis of the Development of Rwanda." Ph.D. diss., American University, 1968.

Weinstein, Warren. Historical Dictionary of Burundi. Metuchen, N.J.: Scarecrow Press, 1976.

World Bank. Agricultural Sector Review. Rwanda Report 1377-RW. Regional Project Department, East Africa Regional Office. June 30, 1977.

Wrigley, C. C. Crops and Wealth in Uganda: A Short Agrarian History. Kampala: East African Institute of Social Research, 1959.

Yearbook of International Organizations, 1992/1993. New York: Union of International Associations and Saur, 1992.

ARTICLES AND PAPERS

African Research Bulletin (various issues in volumes 6 through 13 [1976] and volume 1 [1977]).

Bart, François. "Le Café dans l'Agriculture rwandaise: L'exemple de Kidahire (Runyinya)," Les Cahiers d'Outre-Mer XXXIII, 132 (October-December 1980), pp. 301–317.

Bessel, J. M. "Nyabingi," Uganda Journal VI (1938–1939), pp. 73–86.

Biographie coloniale belge I (1948), pp. 281–282, 420–423, 719–720, and 939–946 (Goetzen, Dardenne, and Moulaert).

Biographie coloniale belge III (1952), pp. 504–518 and 588–592 (Lavigerie and Malfeyt).

Biographie coloniale belge IV (1956), pp. 515–518 and 748–753 (LePlae and Renkin).

Biographie coloniale belge V (1958), pp. 146–158, 428–446, 563–566, 625–629, and 870–873 (Classe, Hirth, Loupias, Musinga, and Voisin).

Biographie belge d'outre-mer VI (1968), pp. 34, 115–121, 421–422, 516–517, 539–547, 695–704, 768–772, 803–806, 831–833, and 1022–1025 (Barthélémy, Brard, Goubau, Hurel, Jasper, Marzorati, Rudahigwa, Pages, Postiaux, and Tombeur).

Botte, Roger. "Rwanda and Burundi, 1889–1930: Chronology of a Slow Assassination, Part I," *International Journal of African Historical Studies* XVIII, 1 (1985), pp. 53–91.

———. "Rwanda and Burundi, 1889–1930: Chronology of a Slow Assassination, Part 2," *International Journal of African Historical Studies* XVIII, 2 (1985), pp. 289–314.

Chrétien, Jean-Pierre. "Des sédentaires devenus migrants: Les motifs des départs des Burundais et des Rwandais vers l'Uganda (1920–1960)," *Culture et Développement* X, 1 (1978), pp. 71–101.

Cirhagarhula, Bashizi. "Mythe hamite, formations étatiques et acculturation interlacustres." In Colloque de Bujumbura (4–10 September 1979). *La civilisation ancienne des peuples des Grands Lacs.* Paris: Editions Karthala; Bujumbura: Centre de Civilisation Burundaise, 1981. Pp. 218–243.

Department of State. Office of Central African Affairs. (AFIC). Telecopier Transmittal. "Project de gouvernance et initiatives démocratiques." Washington, D.C., May 25, 1993. 6pp.

Economist Intelligence Unit. *The Quarterly Review of the Congo Republic, Rwanda and Burundi/Zaire, Rwanda, Burundi.* London, various issues from 1964 to 1993, including the annual supplements.

Gildea, Ray Y., Jr., and Alice Taylor. "Rwanda and Burundi," *Focus* XIII, 6 (February 1963), pp. 1–6.

Hance, William A., and Irene S. van Dongen. "Matadi: Focus of Belgian African Transport," *Annals of the Association of American Geographers* XLVIII, 1 (March 1958), pp. 41–72.

Hategekimana, Grégoire. "Alexis Kagame (15 mai 1912–2 decembre 1981)," *Revue Trimestrielle Ugurezi Ubuhanga N'Umuco/Education, Science and Culture* 1 (January-March 1982), pp. 143–163.

Heimo, Marcel C. "Réflexion sur les conditions et les perspectives du développement économique au Rwanda," *Genève-Afrique* VII, 1 (1968), pp. 7–29.

International Development Association. *The Economy of Rwanda.* Washington, July 2, 1968.

Jewsiewicki, Bogumil. "Le colonat agricole Européen au Congo belge, 1910–1960: Questions politiques et economiques," *Journal of African History* XX, 4 (1970), pp. 559–571.

———. "Notes sur l'histoire socio-économique du Congo," *Etudes d'Histoire Africaine* III (1972), pp. 209–241.

———. "Zaire Enters the World System: Its Colonial Incorporation as the Belgian Congo, 1885–1960." In Guy Gran and Galen Hull, eds., *Zaire: The Political Economy of Underdevelopment.* New York: Praeger, 1979. Pp. 29–53.

Kagabo, Jose, and Vincent Mudandagizi. "Complainte des gens de l'argile: Les Twa du Rwanda," *Cahiers d'Etudes Africaines* XIV, 1 (1974), pp. 75–87.

Kagame, Alexis. "Le code ésotérique de la Dynastie du Ruanda," *Zaire* IV (1947), pp. 363–386.

Lemarchand, René. "Power and Stratification in Rwanda: a Reconsideration," *Cahiers d'etudes Africaines* VI (1966), pp. 592–610.

LePlae, Edmund. "Les Plantations de Café au Congo belge: Leur histoire (1881–1935), leur importance," *Institut Royal Colonial Belge,* mémoires 8, III (1936), pp. 1–248.

Leurquin, Phillipe. "La vie économique du Paysan ruanda, l'exemple de Karama, Nyaruguru," *Zaire* II (January 1959), pp. 41–67.

Lugan, Bernard, and Antoine Nyagahene. "Les activités commerciales du sud Kivu au XIXe siècle à travers l'exemple de Kinyaga (Rwanda)," *Cahiers d'Outre-Mer* XXXVI, 141 (1983), pp. 19–48.

Maquet, Jacques J. "Rwanda Castes." In Arthur Tuden and Leonard Platnicov, eds., *Social Stratification in Africa.* New York: Free Press, 1973. Pp. 93–124.

Masolo, D. A. "Alexis Kagame (1912–1981) and 'La Philosophie bantu-rwandaise de l'être,'" *Africa* (Rome) XXXVIII, 3 (September 1983), pp. 449–454.

Meschi, Lydia. "Evolution des structures foncières au Rwanda: La cas d'un lignage hutu," *Cahiers d'Etudes Africaines* XIV, 1 (1974), pp. 39–51.

Molitor, G. "Campagnes de propagande pour l'Introduction et le développement de la Culture du Caféier Arabica chez l'indigène du Ruanda-Urundi," *Journées d'Agronomie Colonial* (Louvain, 1937), pp. 238–249.

Nahimana, Ferdinand. "Expansion du pouvoir central des rois abanyiginya au Rwanda septentrional: Mythes et realites," *Revue Trimestrielle Uburezi Ubuhanga N'Umuco/Education, Science and Culture* 3 (July-September 1982), pp. 44–85.

———. "Les principautés hutu du Rwanda septentrional." In Colloque de Bujumbura (4–10 September 1979). *La civilisation ancienne des peuples des Grands Lacs.* Paris: Editions Karthala; Bujumbura: Centre de Civilisation Burundaise, 1981. Pp. 115–137.

Newbury, David S. "Lake Kivu Regional Trade in the Nineteenth Century," *Journal des Africanistes* L, 2 (1980), pp. 6–30.

Newbury, M. Catherine. "Ubureetwa and Thangata: Comparative Colonial Perspectives." In Colloque de Bujumbura (4–10 September 1979). *La civilisation ancienne des peuples des Grands Lacs.* Paris: Editions Karthala; Bujumbura: Centre de Civilisation Burundaise, 1981. Pp. 138–147.

Nkulikiyimfura, J. Nepomuscene. "Problèmes de chronologie en histoire précoloniale du Rwanda," *Revue Trimestrielle Uburez Ubuhanga N'Umuco/Education, Science and Culture* 9 (January-March 1984), pp. 141–148.

Phillips, J. E. T. "The Nyabingi: An Anti-European Secret Society in Africa," *Congo* I (1928), pp. 310–321.

Pottier, Johan P. "The Politics of Famine Prevention: Ecology, Regional Production and Food Complementarity in Western Rwanda," *African Affairs* LXXXV, 339 (April 1986), pp. 207–237.

Powesland, P. S. "History of Migration in Uganda." In Audrey I. Richards, ed., *Economic Development and Tribal Change: A Study of Immigrant Labour in Buganda.* Cambridge: W. Heffer and Sons for the East African Institute of Social Research, 1954. Pp. 17–51.

"Le programme économique dans le Ruanda-Urundi," *Congo* I (June 1921), pp. 253–269.

"La Rapport sur l'Administration belge au Ruanda-Urundi pendant l'année 1923," *Congo* I (January-May 1924), pp. 747–757.

"La Rapport sur l'Administration belge au Ruanda-Urundi pendant l'année 1934," *Congo* II (June-December 1935), pp. 765–778.

Rennie, J. K. "The Precolonial Kingdom of Rwanda: A Reinterpretation, *Transafrican Journal of History* II, 2 (1972), pp. 11–54.

Reyntjens, Filip. "Les élections rwandaises du 26 décembre 1983: considérations juridiques et politiques," *Le Mois en Afrique* XX, 223–224 (August-September 1984), pp. 18–28.

Richards, A. I. "The Travel Routes of the Travellers." In Audrey I. Richards, ed., *Economic Development and Tribal Change: A Study of Immigrant Labour in Buganda.* Cambridge: W. Heffer and Sons for the East African Institute of Social Research, 1954. Pp. 52–76.

Rwabukumba, Joseph, and Vincent Mudandagizi. "Les formes historiques de la dépendance personnelle dans l'état rwandais," *Cahiers d'Études Africaines* XIV, 1 (1974), pp. 6–25.

Ryckmans, Pierre. "Le problème politique au Ruanda-Urundi," *Congo* I, 3 (March 1925), pp. 407–413.

Sladden, George E., and L. Michel. "Methodes de Commercialisation du Café arabica produit par les Indigènes du Ruanda-Urundi," *Numero spécial du Bulletin Agricole du Congo Belge* XLIII (1952), pp. 63–84.

"Territoires sous Mandat," *Congo* I (January-May 1937), pp. 184–191.

"Territoires sous Mandat," *Congo* I (January-May 1938), pp. 223–230.

"Territoires sous Mandat," *Congo* I (January-May 1939), pp. 99–106.

United States Committee for Refugees. *Human Rights in Uganda: The Reasons for Refugees.* Washington, August 1985.

———. *Refugees in Uganda and Rwanda: The Banyarwanda Tragedy.* Brief Issues. New York, April 12, 1983.

United States Government. Department of State. Foreign Economic Trends (FET) Report. Rwanda. American Embassy, Kigali. January 1978.

———. Foreign Economic Trends (FET) Report. Rwanda. American Embassy, Kigali. September 12, 1986.

van Tichelin, H. E. "Problèmes du Développement économique du Ruanda-Urundi," *Zaire* II (May 1957), pp. 451–474.

Vellut, Jean Luc. "Rural Poverty in Western Shaba, c. 1890–

1930." In Robin Palmer and Neil Parson, eds., *The Roots of Rural Poverty in Central and South Africa.* Berkeley and Los Angeles: University of California Press, 1977. Pp. 294–316.

Vidal, Claudine. "Economie de la société féodale rwandaise," *Cahiers d'Etudes Africaines* XIV, 1 (1974), pp. 52–74.

———. "Le Rwanda des anthropologues; ou, Le Fétichisme de la vache," *Cahiers d'Etudes Africaines* IX, 3 (1969), pp. 384–401.

Weinstein, Warren. "Ruanda-Urundi (Rwanda-Burundi)." In Gregory Henderson, Richard Ned Lebow, and John G. Stoessinger, eds., *Divided Nations in a Divided World.* New York: David McKay, 1974. Pp. 341–377.

Winter, Roger P., and Thomas Brennan. *Human Rights in Uganda: A Season of Hope for Its Refugees and Displaced Persons.* Issue Brief. Washington: United States Committee for Refugees, May 1986.

LEAGUE OF NATIONS AND UNITED NATIONS

Permanent Mandates Commission, 7th Session, New York, 1925.

Permanent Mandates Commission, 16th Session, New York, 1929.

Permanent Mandates Commission, Minutes and Reports, 18th Session, New York, 1938.

Trusteeship Council. *Trusteeship Agreement for the Territory of Ruanda-Urundi.* Lake Success, N.Y., 1946.

United Nations Trusteeship Council. Study of Population, Land Utilization and Land System in Ruanda-Urundi, prepared by the Secretariat to the Committee on Rural Economic Development of the Trust Territories, 26 March 1957. T/AC.36/L.60.

United Nations Visiting Mission to Trust Territories in East Africa, 1949. Report on Ruanda-Urundi. Trusteeship Council, 4th Session, Supplement No. 2, 1950.

————, 1951. Report on the Trust Territory of Ruanda-Urundi. Trusteeship Council, 11th Session, Supplement No. 2, 1952.

————, 1954. Report on Ruanda-Urundi. Trusteeship Council, 15th Session, Supplement No. 2, 1955.

————, 1957. Report on Ruanda-Urundi. Trusteeship Council, 21st Session, Supplement No. 3, 1958.

————, 1960. Report on Ruanda-Urundi. Trusteeship Council Official Records, 26th Session, Supplement No. 3, 1960.

CONSORTIUM FOR AFRICA MICROFILM PROJECT
(CAMP), CHICAGO, ILLINOIS

MF 1552. Rwanda. Miscellaneous Correspondence, 1916–1919. Notice sur le Ruanda—1916.

Film No. 34, Reels 1 and 2. J. M. Derscheid Collection. Territoire du Ruanda-Urundi. Résidence du Ruanda:

Territoire d'Astrida. Rapport de Sortie de Charge. September 23, 1933.

Territoire de Biumba. Rapport de Sortie de Charge, de l'Administrateur territorial, A. J. F. Stevens, du territoire de Biumba. October 12, 1933.

Film No. 34, Reel 3. J. M. Derscheid Collection. Territoire de Ruanda-Urundi. Résidence du Ruanda:

Territoire de Nyanza. Rapport établi en reponse au questionnaire adressé en 1929, par M. le Gouverneur du Ruanda-Urundi à l'Administrateur du territoire d'Astrida.

MF 1552. Rwanda. Miscellaneous Archival Material, 1925–1941:

Rapport annuel [n.d.]. Développement moral et social des indigènes. 3è Partie: Protection du Travail. Chapitre III: Instruction publique et d'établissements d'enseignement [n.d.].

NATIONAL UNIVERSITY OF RWANDA,
BUTARE, RWANDA

Adriaenssens, J. *Le système foncier du Rwanda*. Butare: Université Nationale du Rwanda, 1967 (photocopy).

Codere, Helen. "The Biography of an African Society: Rwanda—Based on Forty-eight Rwandan Autobiographies," *Institut National de Recherche Scientifique,* Publication no. 12 (1973).

Delepierre, G. "Les régions agricoles du Rwanda." *Institut des Sciences Agronomique du Rwanda* (ISAR) 13 (1974).

Historique et chronologie du Ruanda. [Kabgayi], 1956.

Kagame, Alexis. *Un abrégé de l'ethno-histoire du Rwanda,*

tome premier. Butare: Editions Universitaires du Rwanda, 1972.

———. *Un abrégé de l'histoire du Rwanda de 1853 à 1972,* tome deuxième. Butare: Editions Universitaires du Rwanda, 1975.

———. *Yuhi Musinga: Un Regne mouvemente.* Unpublished manuscript.

Leroy, Pierre. *Législation du Ruanda-Urundi.* Usumbura [Bujumbura], 1949.

Murego, Donat. *La révolution rwandaise, 1959–1962: Essai d'interprétation.* Louvain: Publications de l'Institut des Sciences Politiques et Sociales, 1975.

Nduwayezu, Augustin. "Le café au Rwanda." Université de Dakar, Faculté des Lettres et Sciences Humaines, Département de Géographie, 1974.

Paternostre de la Mairieu, Baudouin. *Le Rwanda: Son effort de développement, antecédents historiques et con-quêtes de la révolution rwandaise.* Brussels: Editions A. DeBoeck, 1972.

Reisdorff, I. *Enquêtes foncières au Ruanda.* 1952. (stencil copy).

Ruzindana, Emmanuel. "L'évolution du commerce au Rwanda du dernier quart du XIXème siècle à 1950." Mémoire de licence, Louvain, 1974 (stencil copy).

Twagirayezu, Ephrem. "Le café arabica et le développement économique du Rwanda et du Burundi." Université Lovanium de Leopoldville, Faculté des Sciences Politique, Sociales et Economiques, 1964 (stencil copy).

ROYAL LIBRARY, BRUSSELS, BELGIUM

Agriculture et Elevage au Congo Belge et dans le Colonies Tropicales et Subtropicales:

"Agriculture indigène: grandes lignes du programme agricole du Gouvernement," neuvième année, 5 (May 1935), pp. 72–73.

"Déclarations de M. le Gouverneur Général Ryckmans," neuvième année, 12 (December 1935), pp. 184–185.

De Ryckman de Betz, J. "La mise en valeur du Ruanda-Urundi," quatrième année, 4 (February 22, 1930), pp. 52–53.

———. La mise en valeur du Ruanda-Urundi," quatrième année, 8 (April 19, 1930), pp. 121–123, 125.

"Les Plantations de Café du Ruanda-Urundi," troisième annee, 6 (March 23, 1929), pp. 88–89.

"La politique du cafe dans les territoires sous mandat," neuvième année, 8 (August 1935), pp. 123–124.

"Les Zones de Protection du Café en Ruanda-Urundi," septième année, 6 (May 1933), p. 66.

Annuaire official du Ministère des Colonies (de Belgique). Brussels: A. Lesigne, 1921–1959.

Arianoff, A. d' *Histoire des Bagesera: Souverains du Gisaku.* Brussels: IRCB, Tome XXIV, fasc. 3, 1952.

Arnoux, A. *Les pères blancs aux sources du Nil (Ruanda).* Namur: Collection Lavigerie, 1947.

"L'avenir de nos coopératives," *L'Ami* 116 (August 1954), pp. 291–294.

Becquet, A. "Moyens mis en oeuvre et les résultats obtenus dans la lutte contre la famine au Ruanda," *Journées d'Agronomie Coloniale* (June 23–24, 1933), pp. 39–42.

Belgian Congo and Ruanda-Urundi Coffee Growers' Union. *Coffee in the Belgian Congo and Ruanda-Urundi.* Brussels, 1958.

Bourgeois, R. *Banyarwanda et Barundi. L'évolution du contrat de bail à cheptel au Ruanda-Urundi.* Brussels: ARSG, 1958.

Bulletin officiel du Ruanda-Urundi 24–25 (1947–1948), pp. 68–428.

"Le Congo et le Ruanda-Urundi," *Réalités Africaines* 33 (1958), pp. 55–353.

DeVuyst, P., and R. Paquay. "La fumure minérale du caféier d'arabie au Rwanda et Burundi," *L'Institut National pour l'Etude Agronomique du Congo* 73 (1964), pp. 1–43.

Dubois, E. "La politique économique coloniale, 1932–1934," *Bulletin l'Institut des Sciences Economiques,* sixième année, 2 (February 1935), pp. 129–143.

Dufays, Felix. *Pages d'epogée africaine.* Ixelles: Weverbergh, 1928.

Gourou, Pierre. *La Densité de la Population au Ruanda: Esquisse d'une Etude Géographique.* Brussels: [Institut

Royal Colonial Belge, Section des Sciences Naturelles et Médicales, mémoire, tome XXI, fasc. 6], 1952.

Gouvernement belge, Ministère des Colonies:

L'agriculture au Congo belge et au Ruanda-Urundi de 1948 à 1952. Brussels, 1954.

Major Declerk. "Rapport d'ensemble sur la situation de la Résidence du Ruanda et sur l'activité de l'Administration" [n.d.].

Rapport sur l'Administration belge des territoires occupés de l'Est Africain Allemand. Brussels: Imprimerie E. Guyst, 1921.

Rapport sur l'Administration belge du Ruanda et de l'Urundi, 1921–1923. Brussels: Goemaere, 1922– 1924.

Rapport presenté par le Gouvernement Belge au Conseil de la Société des Nations au Sujet de l'Administration du Ruanda-Urundi pendant l'Année 1924. Genève: Société des Nations, 1925.

Chambre des Représentants, Session de 1923–1924. *Rapport sur l'Administration Belge du Ruanda-Urundi presenté aux Chambres.* Brussels: F. Van Gompel, Imprimeur-Editeur, 1924.

Rapport presenté par le Gouvernement Belge au Conseil de la Société des Nations au Sujet de l'Administration du Ruanda-Urundi pendant l'Année 1925–1926. Brussels: F. Van Gompel, Imprimeur-Editeur, 1926–1927.

Rapport presenté par le Gouvernement Belge au

Conseil de la Société des Nations au Sujet de l'Administration du Ruanda-Urundi pendant l'Année 1927–1932. Brussels: Etablissements Emile Bruylant, 1928–1933.

Rapport presenté par le Gouvernement Belge au Conseil de la Société des Nations au Sujet de l'Administration du Ruanda-Urundi pendant l'Année 1933. Brussels: Imprimerie E. Guyot, 1934.

Rapport presenté par le Gouvernement Belge au Conseil de la Société des Nations au Sujet de l'Administration du Ruanda-Urundi pendant l'Année 1934–1946. Brussels: Etablissements Généraux d'Imprimerie, 1935–1948.

Rapport soumis par le Gouvernement Belge à l'Assemblée Générale des Nations Unies au Sujet de l'Administration du Ruanda-Urundi pendant l'Année 1947–1949. Brussels: Etablissements Généraux d'Imprimerie, 1948–1950.

Rapport soumis par le Gouvernement Belge à l'Assemblée Générale des Nations Unies au Sujet de l'Administration du Ruanda-Urundi pendant l'Année 1951. Brussels: Etablissements Généraux d'Imprimerie, 1952.

Rapport soumis par le Gouvernement Belge à l'Assemblée Générale des Nations Unies au Sujet de l'Administration du Ruanda-Urundi pendant l'Année 1952. Brussels: Etablissements Généraux d'Imprimerie, 1953.

Rapport soumis par le Gouvernement Belge à l'Assemblée Générale des Nations Unies au Sujet de l'Administration du Ruanda-Urundi pendant l'Année 1953. Brussels: Etablissements Généraux d'Imprimerie, 1954.

Rapport soumis par le Gouvernement Belge à l'Assemblée Générale des Nations Unies au Sujet de l'Administration du Ruanda-Urundi pendant l'Année 1954. Brussels: Imprimerie F. R. van Muysewinkel, 1955.

Rapport soumis par le Gouvernement Belge à l'Assemblée Générale des Nations Unies au Sujet de l'Administration du Ruanda-Urundi pendant l'Année 1955. Brussels: Imprimerie F. R. van Muysewinkel, 1956.

Rapport soumis par le Gouvernement Belge à l'Assemblée Générale des Nations Unies au Sujet de l'Administration du Ruanda-Urundi pendant l'Année 1956. Brussels: Imprimerie F. R. van Muysewinkel, 1957.

Rapport soumis par le Gouvernement Belge à l'Assemblée Générale des Nations Unies au Sujet de l'Administration du Ruanda-Urundi pendant l'Année, 1957. Brussels: Imprimerie F. R. van Muysewinkel, 1958.

Rapport soumis par le Gouvernement Belge à l'Assemblée Générale des Nations Unies au Sujet de l'Administration du Ruanda-Urundi pendant l'Année 1958. Brussels: Imprimerie Clarence Denis, 1959.

Rapport soumis par le Gouvernement Belge à l'Assemblée Générale des Nations Unies au Sujet de l'Administration du Ruanda-Urundi pendant l'Année

1959. Brussels: Imprimerie F. R. van Muysewinkel, 1960.

Rapport soumis par le Gouvernement Belge à l'Assemblée Générale des Nations Unies au Sujet de l'Administration du Ruanda-Urundi pendant l'Année, 1960. Brussels: Imprimerie F. R. van Muysewinkel, 1961.

Service des Territoires des Colonies. Dossier AE/11, No. 1847, portefeuille 3288X. [n.d.].

Harroy, Jean-Paul. *Rwanda: De la féodalité à la démocratie, 1955–1962*. Brussels: Hayez, 1984.

———, J. Lebrun, V. G. Philemotte, Y. Biche, R. Laurent, J. J. Symoens, and H. Guillaume. *Le Ruanda-Urundi: Ses ressources naturelles, ses populations*. Brussels: Les Naturalistes Belges, 1956.

Kagame, Alexis. *Le Codes des Institutions politiques du Rwanda Précolonial*. Brussels: Editions du Marais, 1952.

Lefebrve, Jacques. *Structures économiques du Congo Belge et du Ruanda-Urundi*. Brussels: Editions de Treurenberg, 1955.

Leurquin, Philippe. "Les limites physiques de le production de Subsistence," *Bulletin de l'Institut de Recherche Economiques et Sociales* (Université de Louvain), XXIII, 2 (1957), pp. 48–66.

Molitor, G. "L'Introduction et le Développement de la Culture du Caféier Arabica chez les Indigènes du Ruanda-Urundi," *Le Matériel Colonial* ASBL, 27ème Année, 6 (March 1937), pp. 154–180.

"Nos chefs, la carrière du gouverneur général E. Jungers," *L'Ami* 26 (February 1947), p. 26.

Pages, Albert. "Un Royaume Hamité au centre de l'Afrique," *IRCM* (Brussels), I (1933), pp. 195–232.

Ryckmans, Pierre. "Une Page d'Histoire Coloniale: l'Occupation Allemande dans l'Urundi," *IRCB* (Brussels), XXIX (1953), pp. 1–20.

———. *La Politique Coloniale.* Brussels: Les Editions Rex, 1934.

"Tribal Traditions Hinder Progress in Ruanda-Urundi," *Bulletin Nations Unies* XVI, 7 (April 1954), pp. 267–269.

van Bilsen, A. A. J. *Vers l'indépendance du Congo et du Ruanda-Urundi: Réflections sur les devoirs et l'avenir de la Belgique en Afrique centrale.* Kraainens: Chez l'auteur, 1958.

van Overschelde, A. *Un audacieux pacifique Monseigneur Léon-Paul Classe apôtre du Ruanda.* Namur: Collection Lavigerie, 1948.

Vansina, Jan. *L'évolution du royaume Rwanda des Origines à 1900.* Brussels: Académie Royale des Sciences d'Outre-Mer, 1962.

AFRICAN ARCHIVES, BRUSSELS, BELGIUM

Carton AGRI (106), Dossier 47 FEDECAME Accord de Mexico, 1957, 4ème Direction Général, Agriculture, Forêts, Elevage, Colonisation, 1ère Direction à FEDE-

CAME. Crédit accordés en faveur de la production du Café. [n.d.].

Carton AGRI (107), Dossier 49, Du Café, Correspondances et documentations concernent la Conférence Internationale du café à Rio et le signature de la Convention Café. Address by Mr. Andres Uribe representing the Pan American Coffee Bureau. To Pacific Coast Coffee Association Convention, Pebble Beach, California. May 20, 1958.

Dossier 50. Du Café, 1ère Session de la Commission préparatoire de l'Organisation Internationale du Café, Rio de Janeiro, 1958. International Bank for Reconstruction and Development. The Coffee Problem. April 8, 1958. Prepared by Dragoslav Avramovic, economic staff. Report No. EC-61a.

ABOUT THE AUTHOR

Learthen Dorsey (B.S., Pennsylvania State University; M.A. and Ph.D., Michigan State University) is Assistant Professor of History at the University of Nebraska, Lincoln. He has served as Director of the Sahel Documentation Center at Michigan State University, East Lansing, and has taught at Clemson University, Clemson, South Carolina. Professor Dorsey's *Historical Dictionary of Rwanda* stems in part from archival and field research in Belgium and Rwanda. His Ph.D. thesis, *The Rwandan Colonial Economy, 1916–1941*, is currently being revised for publication.